FREUD on WOMEN

By Elisabeth Young-Bruehl

Mind and the Body Politic
Anna Freud: A Biography
Vigil
Hannah Arendt: For Love of the World
Freedom & Karl Jasper's Philosophy

FREUD

ON

WOMEN

A READER

~~~~~~~~~~~~~~~~

Edited and with an Introduction by
Elisabeth Young-Bruehl

W·W·Norton & Company
New York · London

The text of this book is composed in Electra, with display type set
in Baker Signet. Composition by PennSet, Inc. Manufacturing by
The Murray Printing Company. Book design by Charlotte Staub.
First Edition

Library of Congress Cataloging-in-Publication Data

Freud, Sigmund, 1856–1939.
    [Selections. English. 1990]
    Freud on women : a reader / edited and with an introduction
by Elisabeth Young-Bruehl.—1st ed.
        p.   cm.
    Includes index.
        1. Freud, Sigmund, 1856–1939—Views on women.   2.
Women and psychoanalysis.   3. Women—Psychology.   4. Sex
(Psychology)
    I. Young-Bruehl, Elisabeth.   II. Title.
    BF175.F77513   1990
    155.3'33—dc20   89-35686

ISBN 0-393-02822-4

W. W. Norton & Company, Inc.
500 Fifth Avenue, New York, N.Y. 10110
W. W. Norton & Company Ltd.
37 Great Russell Street, London WC1B 3NU
    1   2   3   4   5   6   7   8   9   0

Acknowledgments

Excerpt from *Sigmund Freud and Lou Andreas-Salomé Letters* by Ernst Pfeiffer, English translation copyright © 1972 by Sigmund Freud Copyrights and Ernst Pfeiffer, reprinted by permission of Harcourt Brace Jovanovich, Inc. (p. 213)

Letter to Carl Mueller-Braunschweig, from the collection of Dr. Edith Weigert, translated by Dr. Helm Stierlin, published in *Psychiatry: Journal for the Study of Interpersonal Processes* (vol. 34, August 1971, p. 329) (pp. 340–41)

Selections on pages 51–52 from *The Standard Edition of the Complete Psychological Works of Sigmund Freud* translated and edited by James Strachey are excerpted by permission of Sigmund Freud Copyrights Ltd., The Institute of Psycho-Analysis and The Hogarth Press.

Selections on pages 50–68 are reprinted by permission of the publishers from *The Complete Letters of Sigmund Freud to Wilhelm Fliess, 1887–1904*, Jeffrey Moussaieff Masson, translator and editor, Cambridge, Mass.: The Belknap Press of Harvard University Press, Coypright © 1985 and under the Bern Convention Sigmund Freud Copyrights Ltd., Copyright © 1985 J. M. Masson for translation and editorial matter. All rights reserved.

Selections on pages 70, 90, 146, 154, 167, 183, 191, 196, 205, 216, 242, 267, 272, 285, 294, 301, 305, 316, and 322 are excerpted by permission of the publishers, Basic Books, Inc.

Selections on pages 275, 319, 342, and 363 are excerpted by permission of the publishers, W. W. Norton & Company, Inc.

Contents

A Note on the Texts

All of the Freud texts in this anthology are based upon the monumental twenty-four volumes of translations and indexes prepared primarily by James Strachey: *The Standard Edition of The Complete Psychological Works of Sigmund Freud*, issued by Hogarth Press and The Institute of Psycho-Analysis in London between 1953 and 1974. The longer texts have been abridged, however, and many notes have been eliminated from even the shorter pieces, in order that *Freud on Women* could be one uncomplicated, manageable volume. Abridgments in the texts are indicated with asterisks (* * *), but both Freud's and Strachey's notes have sometimes been cut without indication. For scholarly purposes, therefore, not this anthology but only *The Standard Edition* should be quoted. References made in my Introduction or my notes to Freud texts not included in this anthology but available in *The Standard Edition* will be indicated with volume and page number (e.g., 22:213.) Strachey's English spellings of technical terms have been retained in his translations, while my texts employ American spellings. My notes to the texts are set within braces, while those presented in brackets are by Strachey. The sources for quotations from Freud's letters and from letters to Freud will be noted in my comments, but there is also a guide to these correspondences in the Annotated Bibliography at the back of this volume.

Preface

A s a title for an anthology of Sigmund Freud's main statements on female psychology, *Freud on Women* will strike many as all too apt. They will feel that it could also grace a cartoon: Psychoanalytic Imperialism, in the person of Freud, standing on top of a vanquished motherland, the "dark continent" (as he once put it) of Female Psychology. Others will feel that only *Freud on Fin De Siècle Women* or perhaps *Freud and Women: Products of Patriarchy* would accurately signal the cultural limitations of both Freud's views and his subjects' lives. Some readers will argue that there should be equal time for *Women on Freud*.

Ever since he made his first major theoretical statements about female sexuality and psychology, Freud's views have been the focus of intense debates—both within psychoanalysis and without. Initially, Freud's critics protested his claim that there is such a thing as "infantile sexuality" and refused to believe that women could suffer from frustrations of sexual desire, since they were not supposed to have any. After the First World War, the debate from without was headed up by feminists who objected to what they perceived as a denigration of women in psychoanalytic theory; this feminist quarrel with Freud has gone on to the present day, aided by work within psychoanalysis, largely by female analysts.

Freud himself also responded to the first decade of debates with three important essays in which he encouraged further inquiry by admitting that he thought of his own formulations as tentative and in need of review. He asked his friend Marie Bonaparte his famous question, "What do women want?" at this time. After the end of the Second World War, while psychoanalysts added little to the views advanced by Freud and his contemporary critics, the debate from without grew toward a crescendo of hostility in the early 1970s. In the late 1970s, just as the psychoanalytic community finally began responding to feminist critiques, there was also a turn toward reconsideration among feminists. But the lines of battle had become so many and so crisscrossed during the whole long controversy that it has not been easy to reconsider the terrain; indeed, after so many decades, it is not even easy to see the original *casus belli* clearly.

I hope that this anthology will encourage current and new generations of debaters, and discourage the circulation of simplistic versions of what Freud supposedly said about women. It has often been assumed that Freud's views were merely a reflection of his patriarchal or misogynistic prejudices, but this assumption, I think, completely neglects both his changing clinical practice and his struggle for verifiability and internal coherence in his science. The texts assembled here are arranged chronologically to emphasize the evolution of Freud's views, which the Introduction will present in three main periods: before the text that was and is fundamental, the 1905 *Three Essays on the Theory of Sexuality*; from 1905 to 1924, when Freud made many alterations in his general theory and also repeatedly revised the *Three Essays* to reflect his explorations; and after 1924, when Freud stopped revising the *Three Essays* and wrote a series of separate essays on female sexuality. The Introduction and my brief commentaries throughout the volume will also key the evolution of Freud's views on women to the shifts in his clinical practice and in his theories.

By providing selections of his work that show these broader theoretical and therapeutic contexts, I hope to make it clear that Freud was consistently concerned with a characteristic women and men share, and which was obvious to him in clinical settings: bisexuality. As Freud noted in his *Three Essays on the Theory of Sexuality*, "without taking bisexuality into account, I think it would scarcely be possible to arrive at an understanding of the sexual manifestations that are actually to be observed in men and women." At the end of my Introduction, I will try to show what happened to this governing concept and also to chart the main types of criticism that emerged in response to it and to Freud's evolving female psychology in general. An Annotated Bibliography will indicate how the criticisms of Freud's contemporaries were reiterated after his death in 1939.

FREUD on WOMEN

Introduction

1. HYSTERIA: QUESTIONS OF CAUSE

Freud's first contribution to female psychology was a quarrel with medical and psychiatric orthodoxy in Vienna about the causes of hysteria in women and men. From this quarrel came both a cure for hysteria, a disease long considered specific to women and incurable, and a theoretical foundation for a therapy with much wider applications—psychoanalysis.

The name "hysteria," the thirty-two-year-old neurologist wrote in 1888, comes from the ancient word *hysteria*, "womb," and is a "precipitate of the prejudice, overcome only in our own days, which links neuroses with diseases of the female sexual apparatus" (1:41). The renowned French neurologist Jean Martin Charcot, with whom Freud studied for a year in Paris, had finally surmounted this prejudice and directed clinical attention at hysterics rather than persecuting them as witches or heaping moral opprobrium on them as malingerers. Charcot's superb descriptive work had both defined hysteria as a distinct psychological disease with a hereditary base, and also distinguished it from neurasthenia, a general condition of nervous debilitation arising from nonpsychological current causes. Charcot's work made it a much easier matter for doctors to diagnose the "petite hysterie" of people with medically unexplainable nervous coughs, painful breathing, migraines, muteness, depressed unsociability, and forced, somewhat artificial boredom with life. The more dangerous hysterical symptoms—horribly contorted facial muscles, paralyzed limbs, painful vaginal spasms, tics, and fainting spells—that kept thousands of people wretchedly confined in hospitals like Charcot's Salpêtrière were better understood, but still incurable.

Charcot, Freud noted, was someone who "can find no rest till he has correctly described and classified some phenomenon with which he is concerned, but . . . he can sleep quite soundly without having arrived at the physiological explanation of that phenomenon" (1:13). In his own restless search for hysteria's mechanisms, Freud was spurred by the remarkable—though temporary—cures another French neurologist, Hyppolite Bernheim, had achieved with hypnotic techniques, and compelled by the fact that he thought of himself as mildly hysterical (1:259). What he slowly discovered was a psychological explanation: hysterics, he said, suffer from reminiscences.

As he treated patients with neurological techniques like electrical stimulation or hydropathy and with hypnosis, Freud catalogued differences in male and female sexual dysfunction and abnormality, and he made comparisons of neurasthenia and hysteria in men and women. Many of his conclusions were first set out in lengthy letters and draft manuscripts for his chief audience, Wilhelm Fliess, a Berlin ear, nose, and throat specialist with a vivid and often quite strange scientific imagination. Excerpts from Freud's remarkable letters are presented here with commentary. In them, it is obvious how crucial Fliess was as a supporter and collaborator during the years when Freud was struggling to verify what he called "the sexual thesis," the claim that neurasthenia and hysteria are disturbances of sexuality, the first from a current cause and the second from an earlier sexual experience the memory of which has been repressed or forced—and kept—out of consciousness.

Freud was impressed by how seldom young women were neurasthenic before their marriages or in the early years of their marriages. He suggested in 1892 that "neurasthenia in women is a direct consequence of neurasthenia in men," and then he realized that it is frequently the practice of coitus interruptus which induces neurasthenia in both women and men (1:177–84). In neurasthenia sexual desire or libido, Freud thought, invariably got "dammed up." Hysteria, too, he speculated, was not so much a hereditary disease as a conflict between desire—often desire of which the desirer was not conscious—and defense against the desire. In neurasthenics, the blockage could be due to lack of sexual opportunity, masturbation, contraceptive practices, or fear of disease; in hysterics, a past traumatic experience, specifically sexual and usually quickly repressed and dissociated from other memories, was involved. Desire dammed up seeks a substitute outlet in symptoms, and for hysterics the symptoms constituted their entire sexual lives. Freud looked at hysterical symptoms as though they were hieroglyphs needing decoding, archeological clues to lost cultures—to the unconscious mind, the domain of repressed desires and experiences.

The work Freud coauthored with his older Viennese colleague Josef Breuer, *Studies on Hysteria* (1895), presented the novel therapeutic technique they had developed, along with a version of the "dammed up libido" theory mild enough to satisfy Breuer, who was very apprehensive about Freud's shocking "sexual thesis." When a hysteric (with or without hypnosis) was able to talk about the traumatic event underlying his or her symptoms, the symptoms disappeared. The trauma was "abreacted" or deprived of its active force in this therapeutic process, which Freud eventually came to distinguish from hypnosis. In the nonhypnotic "talking cure" Freud advocated and called "psychoanalysis," patients "free associated" and discovered their own pasts as the repression upon their memories lifted, rather than receiving suggestions from a hypnotist. Hypnotic cures, Freud discovered, lasted only as long as the patients felt they were satisfying the hypnotist (and see 7:150, n. 1).

The social conditions of the predominantly female patients, however, remained the same no matter what the therapy. Freud and Breuer stressed how often a monotonous married life, without adequate intellectual engagement, contributed to their patients' tendencies to fantasize; and how being unhappily single and materially dependent produced overwhelming sexual needs (see the the case of Miss Lucy R. in *Studies on Hysteria*, 2:106–25). They were very well aware that differences in both constitution and upbringing between girls and boys greatly influenced their attitudes toward sexual experience: "The tendency toward fending off what is sexual is intensified by the fact that in a young unmarried woman sensual excitation has an admixture of anxiety, of fear of what is coming, what is unknown and half-suspected, whereas in normal and healthy young men it is unmixed aggressive instinct" (2:246). Many hysterias, Breuer noted, share with neurasthenia "their origin in the marriage bed" because intercourse is frequently "not an erotic seduction but a violation," and because "perverse demands made by the husband, unnatural practices, etc." are so common (2:246). But Freud argued that hysterias also invariably have a "presexual" root (2:133), by which he then meant a root before marriage, in puberty. This was obviously the case with a peasant girl named Katharina, who told Freud much more freely than "the prudish ladies of my city practice" how her father had forced his way into her bed when she was fourteen. That even earlier childhood experiences were also involved was a hypothesis Freud advanced in 1896, after his collaboration with Breuer came to an end and his quarrel with the Viennese establishment had left him with only Fliess for intellectual company.

Freud was operating with the assumption that specific types of sexual experiences were conducive to specific types of neuroses (or to what he called the "choice of neurosis"). His claim that the hysteric's experiences were always "of a passive nature" combined with his (unexamined) assumptions about "the natural sexual passivity of women" to explain why women are more inclined to hysteria than men (1:228). To his conclusion that such passive (usually seductive) experiences were "premature" (1:220) for young women, Freud added the observation that their fathers had played a great role in the early lives of his female hysterical patients. He was sure that idealized fathers determined his patient's "high standards in love, their humility toward their lover, or their being unable to marry because their ideals are unfulfilled" (1:243). But in 1897 Freud was unsure whether there was always a "father as the originator of neurosis" (1:253) in the quite different sense that female hysterics were the victims of childhood seduction or abuse specifically by their fathers.

While he was trying to answer this question by reconstructing the childhoods of his patients and developing a technique, "self-analysis," for exploring his own childhood, Freud also observed his six children and their friends and considered the hysterical children he had treated earlier in Berlin outpatient clinics (on an 1886 internship) and in the Vienna Kassowitz Institute for Children's Diseases (from 1887 to 1896). He became more convinced that memories from childhood—not just puberty—lay in the background of adult hysterias, and all his evidence pointed toward the crucial importance for women and men of precisely when their childhood traumatic experiences had taken place.

In his correspondence with Fliess, Freud drew up a table of

childhood stages, suggesting that the "primal experience" conducive to hysteria dated from before the age of four. Then, in a very important letter that is quoted below, he formulated a theory of "erotogenic zones"—the mouth, the anus, and the genitals—exciting to children at different stages of their development (1:229, 268; below, p. 57). Satisfaction and dissatisfactions connected to oral experiences (nursing, or later sucking) were, he concluded, particularly important in the psychic histories of hysterics. In all psychoneuroses, the role of infantile masturbation was, he thought, very large. But what the theory of erotogenic zones most importantly implied was that in the etiology of the psychoneuroses, spontaneous childhood sexual activities and autoerotic pleasures were involved—not only passive or seductive experiences initiated by adults.

The letters to Fliess show clearly that, while he was writing his monumental work *The Interpretation of Dreams* between 1897 and 1899, Freud also became increasingly aware of the part childhood fantasies play in generating hysterical symptoms. He felt that children as young as six months could witness things, particularly the "primal scene" of parental intercourse, that would later be woven into their fantasies and dreams (1:244, 247). His hysterical female patients, especially, tended to mingle up in their fantasies childhood identifications with people of "low morals," often "worthless women" connected sexually with their fathers or brothers, and to develop habits of self-reproach and guilt. It is tragic that "the action of the head of the family in stooping to a servant-girl is atoned for his daughter's self-abasement" (1:249).

At this time, Freud was exploring with Fliess the hypothesis that the process of repression in hysteria is "sexualized" in the sense that it is directed at the sexual images and memories opposite to the anatomical sex, so that women repress representations they feel are "masculine." But Freud's observations did not lend support to this view. "It is to be suspected that the essentially repressed element is always what is feminine. This is essentially confirmed by the fact that women as well as men admit more easily to experiences with women than with men" (1:251). Men essentially repress "the paederastic element" (the feminine element in themselves) just as women repress their memories of passive, feminine desires, not their "homosexual" desires.

Freud's formulation reflected Fliess's great interest in bisexuality, but not Fliess's conjecture about the sexualization of repression. Freud later gave up his own first conjecture—that the feminine in everyone is repressed—and argued against any form of sexualization of repression (below pp. 236–37), but it is important to note that he initially connected repression with the feminine. What this meant was that in his female patients, who admitted more easily to experiences with women than with men, what was most obvious to Freud was their unrepressed "masculinity." He had earlier even briefly considered, as a letter to Fliess quoted below (p. 63) indicates, the hypothesis that all libido or desire is masculine and "male" homosexuality directed at the father is the primitive form of sexual longing in both women and men. What struck him so forcefully was the ubiquity among female children and adult hysterics of clitoral masturbation, which he considered "masculine" because he thought of the clitoris as the female's homologue of the masculine genital (and then-current embryology reinforced his idea that the clitoris is an undeveloped penis).

Eventually, Freud gave up his speculation about primordial masculine homosexuality in both sexes and about sexualization of repression, but he remained puzzled by the complexities of an active "masculinity" in the girl's tie to her father. The rudiments of what came to be known as the Oedipus complex had appeared to Freud in 1897, as he noted in a long, self-revelatory letter to Fliess (p. 54). By analyzing his own dreams and memories and considering children's fantasies, Freud began to interpret identifications with, and rivalrous death wishes against, parents: "Hostile impulses against parents (a wish that they should die) are also an integral constituent of neuroses. . . . It seems as though this death-wish is directed in sons against their father and in daughters against their mother" (1:255). In its earliest form, Freud's theory of the Oedipus complex assumed opposite-sex love and same-sex rivalry in both boys and girls. In *The Interpretation of Dreams* Freud stated this conclusion (4:257) with a certainty that it took him years to overcome: " . . . a girl's first affection is for her father and a boy's first childish desires are for his mother." But the girl's affection for her father still seemed to him very problematic because of the "masculine" masturbatory activity involved in it.

As he added these new elements to his causal theory of the neuroses, Freud kept considering his "seduction hypothesis." But he slowly and with much vacillation abandoned it. He did not, of course, claim that seductions do not take place or that they are rare, as some recent commentators have tried to argue. Rather, he became convinced that all children are sexual from birth, through the oral, anal, and genital stages, and that all children feel love for parents of the oposite sex; seduction, which was not universal, had to be seen against this universal background. Moreover, the seduction theory had failed to effect therapeutic "abreactions" in all the hysterics Freud treated, and many patients left his care before he could even effect relief of their symptoms. Freud began to suspect that he had been suggesting the idea of father-daughter seduction to his patients, thus repeating the problem of suggestion that had years before led him to abandon hypnosis as a technique.

Theoretically, the seduction hypothesis also could not account for the layering and reworking of fantasies and symptoms Freud constantly encountered. A single source of illness seemed more and more unlikely, particularly as Freud learned of cases in which seduction had not given rise to later illness. So he focused on the role of "the wish fulfillment of the repressing thought" in dreams, in fantasies, and in symptoms. When he abandoned the idea that behind every hysteria lay a literal seduction, he could see conflicts among fantasies—and symptoms. There is no single type of mental content—like "the feminine"—repressed by everyone. In general, he concluded that single causes for mental activities and structures are not to be found: "in a word, over-determination is the rule" (7:60).

As an example, in 1899 he sketched the case of a woman whose hysterical attacks fulfilled both her wish to be pregnant and her wish to lose her beauty and not be sexually attractive—equally strong but contradictory wishes (1:278). Specifically, and crucially, the broadening of his causal theory allowed Freud to begin to reconsider the bisexuality so apparent in his female patients' fantasies: he became convinced that their bisexuality had to involve some kind of "masculinity" preceeding their love for their fathers or their sexual experiences with males (possibly including their fathers). He also became convinced that there is no such thing as an inborn or primordial femininity uncompounded with masculinity.

Later, between about 1905 and 1908, when Freud was again preoccupied with fantasies, he recapitulated his conclusions that no hysterical symptom corresponds to a single unconscious fantasy; that all are compromises between opposite impulses—one sexual and one repressing; and that modes of oral, anal, and genital satisfaction in infantile life are recreated and disguised in symptoms. In a 1908 essay "Hysterical Phantasies and Their Relationship to Bisexuality," he added the further formula that often, if not always, "hysterical symptoms are the expression on the one hand of a masculine unconscious sexual phantasy, and on the other hand a feminine one. . . . In psycho-analytic treatment it is very important to be prepared for a symptom's having a bisexual meaning. We need not then be surprised or misled if a symptom seems to persist undiminished although we have already resolved one of its sexual meanings; for it is still being maintained by the— perhaps unsuspected—one belonging to the opposite sex" (p. 152). This theory of bisexuality marked the beginning of a more complicated notion of the Oedipus complex as composed, for both females and males, of loves for *both* the same-sex and the opposite-sex parent. The idea that a girl might love her mother before she turned to her father came to Freud very slowly.

The only full-scale case study of a hysteric that Freud ever wrote, which was prepared in 1901 but not published until 1905, explores the two loves reflected in his patient's dreams and symptoms. The patient called "Dora" has two "objects" (to use Freud's term for mental representations of loved ones or loved things): her father and her father's mistress (not a servant girl of "low morals," but nonetheless a mistress). In Dora's analysis, however, the less accessible love of the father's mistress and its connection to Dora's mother was barely touched upon (7:60), for Dora—like many earlier hysterical patients—left the treatment after only a few months. Freud had often complained to Fliess that his patients fled after the first remission of thier symptoms, but with this case it became clear to him why they fled. A treatment can relieve existing symptoms and stop formation of new symptoms without halting the "productive powers of the neurosis," which goes right on creating a special type of mental structure to which he gave the name "transference." Impulses and fantasies made conscious in the analysis do not lose their power, they are reproduced as transferences, "re-editions or facsimiles" in which important famale and male figures from childhood are replaced by the person of the analyst. The patient had not escaped from her Oedipal desires, she had refocused them.

Freud understood that Dora's loves had been replayed in her transference to him, and that the treatment should have included exploration of the transference, expecially of the female or maternal transference, which was hardest for him to detect. As he noted in a letter to Fliess (p. 66), the issue of Dora's bisexuality was ready "for detailed treatment . . . on another occasion." At the time, Freud proposed to write a book called *Human Bisexuality*, but what he wrote instead was *Three Essays on the Theory of Sexuality*.

In general, after the Dora case study Freud seems to have retreated from his tendency not only to influence his patients by suggestion, but to inflict his interpretations on them and even to insist on their compliance—that is, to behave toward women like Dora with a therapeutic-scientific version of Victorian patriarchal preemption. It is obvious in the study that he felt a great deal of sympathy for Dora's manipulative father and her married suitor, but not much for Dora herself. Later, when Freud had assimilated the results of his own self-analysis—as he noted to Fliess, "in my life, as you know, woman has never replaced the comrade, the friend" (p. 67)—and in the process gotten over his tie to his comrade Fliess, there was an abatement in his tendency to tolerate behavior in males that made him impatient in females, to employ a psychologically rooted but culturally sanctioned double standard. He also became willing to accept females as colleagues, even comrades, in the growing psychoanalytic movement. Similary, his 1920 case study of a female homosexual is very different in tone from the Dora case. Freud gave the name "countertransference" to the presumptions and unconscious fantasies a psychoanalyst brings to the treatment.

The case of Dora gave Freud the chance to show his theory of dream interpretation in action while he was presenting his causal theory of hysteria. He had not only two dense, vivid dreams to analyze, but a story rich in the scenes and experiences he considered characteristic of hysteria (without involving a childhood seduction). The eighteen-year-old Dora had a childhood memory of blissful oral satisfaction in thumb-sucking; childhood neurotic symptoms (dyspnea or painful breathing at the age of eight); memories of sexual enlightenment by means of books belonging to her father's mistress; an erotic encounter at age sixteen with her father's friend Herr K., to which she reacted with further neurotic symptoms; and a homosexual love-object not initially accessible to consciousness. Freud's preliminary ideas about the "Oedipus complex" as the centerpiece of the psychoneuroses crystallized as he worked through this material, but he only felt sure of them when he had tested them in nonpathological domains. In *The Psychopathology of Everyday Life* (1901) and *Jokes and Their Relation to the Unconscious* (1905), Freud extended his science by showing that everyday actions like slips of the tongue or pen and witty stories share mechanisms with neurotic symptoms (as well as with dreams and fantasies). Then he was ready for a treatise that systematically combined his psychopathology with a theory of normalilty or normal development.

Three Essays on the Theory of Sexuality (1905) was, like *The Interpretation of Dreams*, organized to reflect a journey of discovery: from psychopathology to normality, from specific types of perversion and neurosis to the elements of "sexual constitution" shared by all people. The journey presented in *Three Essays* was also Freud's first public statement of why he felt that no monocausal theory of neurosis—such as the seduction theory—would ever be adequate: "To look for the aetiology of the neuroses exclusively in heredity or in the constitution would be just as one-sided as to attribute that aetiology solely to the accidental influences brought to bear upon sexuality in the course of the subject's life—whereas better insight shows that the essence of these illnesses lies solely in a disturbance of the organism's sexual processes" (7:279). In the neuroses, the causes are always plural; the result, however, is always, no matter how nonsexual in appearance, fundamentally a "disturbance of the organism's sexual processes."

2. "Normal" Femininity and Bisexuality

At the turn of the century, most of Freud's medical readers— like many today—would have considered "psychoneurotic" and "perverse" to be overlapping terms: all perverse persons were considered psychoneurotic, and many psychoneurotics were known to be perverse. So, from its opening pages, Freud's *Three Essays on the Theory of Sexuality* was shocking, for he began by explaining why he considered the psychoneuroses to be "the negative of the perversions," that is, of those choices of love objects or love acts generally considered abnormal. A perverse person expresses in fantasies or behavior his or her abnormal love-choices and love-acts; a psychoneurotic represses these and replaces them with symptoms. A person who chooses a love object considered abnormal—say, a homosexual—is not a psychoneurotic for that reason; he or she may be "quite sound in other respects" (7:148). (In Freud's one full case study of a homosexual, the eighteen-year-old female patient is said (p. 246 and 250 below) to be "not in any way ill," quite remarkably "without one hysterical symptom," and unusual only for having taken "the path that is banned by society.") By contrast, psychoneurotics have fallen in love without knowing it, their love having been repressed, and the whole of their lives is usually affected by the symptoms with which they replace the love.

These distinctions, hard enough to accept, required that Freud's readers also be willing to accept that (1) people's physical (or anatomical) characteristics, (2) their mental characteristics or attitudes, (3) their male or female object choices, and (4) their preferences in sexual aims or types of practices could be combined in a very great number of variations. Contrasts like the one between "heterosexual" and "homosexual," if made in the usual way—by noting opposite-sex or same-sex object choice alone—appeared to Freud by 1905 as simplified to the point of meaninglessness. His own fourfold scheme was radically complex; only on the matter of mental sexual characteristics was it conventional. For example, Freud thought of shyness, modesty, and need for instruction or assistance (7:144) as typically and exclusively female mental qualities, impossible for men to possess. Women, on the other hand, could assume male mental characteristics—and this possibility of "character inversion" was one thing that distinguished women from men (7:142). With the exception of this kind of conventionality about mental characteristics, however, Freud's fourfold scheme was so novel that few of his readers would even have noticed the conventional ground that he shared with them.

Freud opened his treatise with his barrage of distinctions in order to do two things at once: he tried to persuade his fin de siècle readers to suspend their immediate equation of perversity (particularly homosexuality) with degeneracy or insanity so that he could argue for the even more shocking idea that "perverse" love-choices and love-acts lie in the early history of each and every person. He was setting down a train of thought that led to a revolutionary goal: the idea that perversity is normal for children (and for peoples in the childhood of the human race—either "primitive" societies or ancients like the Greeks) and is overcome only by a process of restriction or narrowing of possibilities. The price of mature sexuality for individuals is *limitation*; and only those who can pay this price by redirecting their sexual energies into other activities, like cultural projects, rather than simply repressing them can avoid the inevitable modern unhappiness— the discontent of civilization. (This general view, and the analogy between individual and social development, is advanced in popular prose in " 'Civilized' Sexual Morality and Modern Nervous Illness," pp. 166–81 below.)

Sexual normality is, Freud argued, a complicated and culturally prescriptive notion. Similarly, sexual abnormality—however defined—is a notion much more frequently to be found in thunderous sermons than in scientific discussions. In his attitude toward sexual abnormality, Freud was certainly a man of his milieu and times, but he was most unusual in his effort at scientific impartiality (7:50):

> We must learn to speak without indignation of what we call the sexual perversions—instances in which the sexual function has extended its limits in respect either to the part of the body concerned or to the sexual object chosen. The uncertainty in regard to the boundaries of what is to be called normal sexual life, when we take different races and different epochs into account, should itself be enough to cool the zealot's ardour. We surely ought not to forget that the perversion which is the most repellent to us, the sensual love of a man for a man, was not only tolerated by a people so far our superiors in cultivation as were the Greeks, but was actually entrusted by them with important social functions. The sexual life of each one of us extends to a slight degree—now in this direction, now in that—beyond the narrow lines imposed as the standard of normality.

Freud insisted that it is completely "inappropriate to use the word perversion as a term of reproach" (7:160). Specifically: "Psychoanalytic research is most decidedly opposed to any attempt at separating off homosexuals from the rest of mankind as a group of special character" (7:145). This dictum unfortunately had little effect on subsequent psychoanalytic research and none at all on psychiatric classifications, which (in America) labeled homosexuality as a disease until the 1970s, when they were revised for reasons quite other than the authority of Freud.

When we are infants, Freud argued, our sexual desire or libido is neither focused on a particular type of sexual object (a person or a part of a person's body) nor aimed at a particular type of sexual activity. The sexual instinct is "initially independent of its object" (7:148), and children are of a sexually undifferentiated disposition. Starting at about the end of the second year of life, the sexual instinct begins to become tied to objects. A sexual "efflorescence" of several years' duration is followed after about the fifth year by a calmer period of "latency" (when children become more educable and are, traditionally, enrolled in school). There is second efflorescence in puberty. When the first efflorescence, with all its genital excitement and clear choices of love objects (7:189, 199), recedes in latency, most of it and of the sexual activity that preceded it sink behind a curtain of "infantile amnesia." This amnesia, which was still strong in most of Freud's scientific contemporaries, who denied the very existence of infantile sexuality, makes it difficult to reconstruct the activities and feelings of the first two or three years of life.

Before latency, infants and toddlers engage in diverse activities as they respond to the stimuli or sensations arising in their bodies, to which Freud gave the collective title "instincts." (The German word *Triebe* clearly indicates the stimuli themselves, and not habits of responding to stimuli as the English word "instincts" often does.) In early infancy, there is often a period of genital masturbation or general touching of sensitive areas—ears, breasts. After weaning, children replace the pleasure of their nursing with another oral pleasure, like thumb-sucking, which is autoerotic, that is, involves the infant's own body parts as objects and sources of pleasure. (Freud reiterated his earlier observations on orality and hysteria by noting: "Many of my women patients who suffer from disturbances of eating, globus hystericus, constriction of the throat and vomiting, have indulged energetically in sucking during their childhood," 7:182.) Toddlers in what is popularly known as "the terrible twos" assert themselves actively through the agency of their musculature, exhausting their caretakers with their incessant mobility and "instinct for mastery" (7:198, 202). Passive sexual aims, focused on the anus, also draw surrounding people into action. Children who "hold back their stool till its accumulation brings about violent muscular contractions, and, as it passes through the anus, is able to produce powerful stimulation of the mucous membrane," please or displease their caretakers with their compliance or lack of compliance with toilet training (7:186, 198).

In addition to the instinctual-drive sensations arising in the oral and anal zones and the musculature, infants have "component instincts" that appear independently of these zones and involve other people from the start: these are scopophilia (love of looking), exhibitionism (love of being looked at), and cruelty, in an active form (sadism) and a passive form (masochism).

Gradually, in normal people, these early-appearing component instincts (and another that emerges between the ages of three and five, the instinct for knowledge or research) are integrated under the dominance of genital sexuality. Freud assumed that before this integration, and while the oral and anal zones still command a great deal of a child's activity, there are no essential differences between the sexes—though in later life the significance of the sexual activities as remembered or unconsciously active may be different for women and men, as is the case with orality for female hysterics. The main reason for assuming that childhood sexuality is the same for girls and boys is that they both actively seek pleasure in the oral, anal, and genital erotogenic zones. "Auto-erotic" meant for Freud active pleasure-seeking, not pleasure-receiving, even when the aim of the pleasure-seeking activity, like anal retention, was passive.

In his late work, Freud revised his ideas about the sexes before the period of genital dominance (or, to use later terms, during the pregenital or pre-Oedipal period) and about how the developments of the sexes diverge, but for the moment it is important to consider his view in the *Three Essays* (in all the editions up to 1924). Freud claimed that girls and boys alike are led by their instinct for knowledge first to the riddle of where babies come from, and later to the question of the distinction between the sexes (pp. 121–22). For boys, he said, the existence of two sexes is not problematic because boys simply assume—even in the face of visual evidence to the contrary—that everyone has a penis. That is, they deny that women have genitals of a different kind. By contrast: "Little girls do not resort to denial of this kind when they see that boys' genitals are formed differently than their own. They are ready to recognize them immediately and are overcome by envy for the penis—an envy culminating in the wish, which is so important in its consequences, to be boys themselves" (p. 122). Both boys and girls, as they undertake their "sexual re-searches," fail to discover "the fertilizing role of semen and the existence of the female sexual orifice," and the frustration they then feel over the riddle of where babies come from leads to "a renunciation which not infrequently leaves behind it a permanent injury to the instinct for knowledge" (p. 123). (Another presentation of these ideas can be found in the 1908 essay "On the Sexual Theories of Children.")

Freud's distinction—later so controversial—between little boys who deny anatomical difference and then struggle for realism and little girls who start out as realists and then turn into deniers was drawn initially only in the context of his "instinct for knowledge" discussion. He gave no phase-developmental explanation of why boys and girls should react so differently except in a parenthetical remark indicating that boys have to struggle for realism because of their "castration complex" (7:195), by which he meant all the conscious and unconscious fears boys have about losing their genital. In 1924, Freud did address this issue of sexual difference by taking a phase-developmental approach. He added to the *Three Essays* the conclusion he had reached in "The Infantile Genital Organization," a 1923 essay (pp. 267–73), which also reflects Freud's approval of a 1920 paper by his colleague Karl Abraham, "Manifestations of the Female Castration Complex." Freud argued that there is a third phase of pregential or pre-Oedipal development after the two phases called oral and anal. The third phase:

> presents a sexual object and some degree of convergence of sexual impulses upon that object; but it is differentiated from the final organization of sexual maturity in one essential respect. For it knows only one kind of genital: the male one. For that reason I have named it the 'phallic' stage of organization.

Freud also made one other adjustment in the theory of the genital phase. Reconsidering the "instinct for knowledge" at this stage, he noted (in 1920): "We are justified in speaking of a castration complex in women as well. Both male and female children form a theory that women no less than men originally had a penis, but that they have lost it by castration."

Despite these additions, however, key questions are passed over: Why do girls envy the penis? How should their phase development at the time be described? (Freud considered the phallic and genital phases largely in terms of masturbatory activity, making no distinctions between girls and boys except to note in passing that he thought girls frequently give up active masturbation for "a process in the nature of a nocturnal emission" (p. 118). by which it seems he meant "spontaneous discharges" of clitoral excitement (p. 137).) Is it simply fear of castration that produces denial in boys and (according to the 1920 theory) girls? This is the phase in which love objects are chosen—do those choices effect the "castration complex" in girls and boys?

Freud's text is uncharacteristically vague and cursory over the topic of penis envy and the castration complex—the topic that becomes central in his approach to female sexuality. But the next section of the *Three Essays*, "The Transformations of Puberty," reverts to the topic because it deals extensively with how the two sexes diverge psychologically as their primary and secondary sexual organs and characteristics mature. Both girls and boys choose new sexual objects (which usually echo their earlier Oedipal choices); both subordinate all erotogenic zones to the genital zone; and both tend toward a new sexual aim or sexual act, which allies to itself all the component instincts. But the aims are quite different.

The pubertal male's sexual aim is discharge of his sexual excitation and his semen. It is important to note that the aim is not reproduction, though discharge does of course serve reproduction; Freud was not, as all sorts of puritans have understood well, a proponent of the idea that the sexual instinctual drive aims directly at reproduction. What the female's sexual aim is Freud does not at first say. He simply notes, cryptically, that her development "enters upon a kind of involution" while the male's proceeds straightforwardly. That the male's aim or sexual act is Freud's main concern is obvious from his masculine point of view in describing "the sexual act" (p. 130):

> The penultimate stage of that act is once again appropriate stimulation of an erotogenic zone (the genital zone itself, in the glans penis) by the appropriate object (the mucous membrane of the vagina) . . . . [The] last pleasure is the highest in intensity . . . brought about entirely by discharge.

This passage is followed by several pages on sexual excitation and release—all focused on males. Then Freud took up the female story and offered a discussion that has been a second focus of intense controversy.

The male child's external genital erotogenetic zone consists of the penis, Freud notes, leaving the scrotum out of consideration because children seem uninterested in it, and the female's consists of her clitoris: the two organs have in common their autoerotic or "active" masturbatory pleasure-seeking functions. This claim to functional similarity had always led Freud to another claim— and not by ordinary standards a very logical one. As he had said again and again in the letters to Fliess, because female childhood sexuality is "active," it is "of a wholly masculine character" (p. 135). Similarly, the excitability of the female's leading erotogenic zone, the clitoris, is "a piece of masculine sexuality" (p. 137). Despite a long footnote (p. 136) added in 1915 to distinguish various usages of the terms "masculine" and "feminine," the claims remain obscure and confusing.

When Freud explains that "libido is invariably and necessarily of a masculine nature, whether it occurs in men or in women . . . ," he means primarily that libido is always active. But, even if we accept that there is no such thing as passive libido or instinct, because any search for passive aims or acts that involve pleasure-receiving or retaining objects in the body is an active search, that is no reason for equating the one active instinct with masculinity. In Freud's own systematic understanding, it would have been more consistent to say that libido, which in all people vacillates between male and female objects, and between active and passive aims, is itself bisexual or organized for bisexuality. Occasionally he did express himself in this way, as in his rejection of the "sexualization of repression" mentioned above: ". . . we can only see that both in male and female individuals masculine as well as feminine instinctual impulses are found, and that each can equally well undergo repression and so become unconscious" (p. 239).

Freud never did call the libido bisexual, however, because he felt that no satisfactory way to link the concept of bisexuality (in relation to objects and aims) to the psychoanalytic theory of the instincts had been found. The matter of the theoretical missing link was made quite complex, as we will see, by the number of forms the instinct theory itself took between 1915 and 1925. But, even though Freud never did retract his equation of active libido and masculinity, it is important to realize that he viewed the equation as a shorthand, a piece of conventionality that was a serviceable first word rather than a scientific last word. His position was most clearly articulated in the 1932 lecture entitled "Femininity" (p. 359):

> Sexual life is dominated by the polarity of masculine-feminine; thus the notion suggests itself of considering the relation of the libido to this antithesis. It would not be surprising if it were to turn out that each sexuality had its own special libido appropriated to it, so that one sort of libido would pursue the aims of a masculine sexual life and another sort those of a feminine one. But nothing of the kind is true. There is only one libido, which serves both the masculine and the feminine sexual functions. *To it itself we cannot assign any sex; if, following the conventional equation of activity and masculinity, we are inclined to describe it as masculine, we must not forget that it also covers trends with a passive aim.* Nevertheless, the juxtaposition 'feminine libido' is without any justification. Furthermore, it is our impression that more constraint has been applied to the libido when it is pressed into the service of the feminine function, and that—to speak teleologically—Naure takes less careful account of its [that function's] demands than in the case of masculinity. And the reason for this may lie—thinking once again teleologically—in the fact that the accomplishment of the aim of biology has been entrusted to the aggressiveness of men and has been made to some extent independent of women's consent. {italics added}

This masculine aggressiveness is not, as Freud often indicated, a matter of sexual pursuit—as animal and human females often take on the pursuit function. He thought in terms of active sexual penetration in intercourse and the assumed relative activity of the spermatozoan in relation to the ovum. But the relation of these biological functions to human psychology is not obvious, as Freud was well aware. In the 1938 *An Outline of Psychoanalysis* he reiterated that no individual is limited to the modes of reaction of a single sex: "For distinguishing between male and female mental life we make use of what is obviously an inadequate empirical and conventional equation: we call everything that is strong and active male, and everything that is weak and passive female. {But} this fact of psychological bisexuality, too, embarrasses all our enquiries into the subject {of male and female characteristics} and makes them harder to describe."

This last late passage points to the main motive in Freud's equation of libido and active masculinity: it explained female bisexuality. As the bisexuality in both sexes became more and more obvious to Freud clinically—he wanted to write a treatise on bisexuality, as we noted, when he finished the Dora case—he found that he could explain it in males but not in females. In males bisexuality emerges with the castration complex: male children start out loving their mother, but the threat of castration deters them, and in response to it they either identify with their father (and later love a substitute for their mother) or identify with their "castrated" mother (and love their mother by being like her while they imagine themselves loved by their father), or identify in both ways. But, if the little girl loves her father from the start (as Freud thought in his early work) how does she ever come to love a female object? Freud's answer was that she does not start off loving her father. Rather, she starts off with a "masculine" active libido, so that when she discovers the anatomical difference she is reluctant to give up her accustomed mode. To a greater or lesser extent, she enviously identifies with males and loves in the "masculine" manner; and, to a greater or lesser extent, she admits her "castration" and turns toward her father. Hence her bisexuality. The theory, of course, became much simpler when Freud stressed in his late statements on female sexuality that the girl starts off actively loving her mother like a boy. Penis envy then became the main vehicle for explaining why she would ever give her mother up and turn to a male, her father: she does so propelled by her hatred for her mother, who brought her into this world so ill equipped. But even at this later stage in his theorizing, Freud kept the idea of masculine libido for both the sexes—for both the little infant mother-lovers.

In addition to the main thought that female bisexuality is explained by the equation of masculinity and libido, however, a number of subsidiary thought-streams meet in the equation, and these helped secure its place in Freud's work. One stream came from an old problem: why are so many women hysterical? Freud considered women less endowed with libido by nature or constitutionally. In various essays he speaks of women as possessing "a weaker sexual instinct" (9:192) and in the passage quoted above from "Femininity" he indicates that nature made the libido in females more amorphous or polymorphous than in males, in whom "a greater amount of activity is ordinarily characteristic" (pp. 357–58). Clinically, Freud's view allowed him to explain why men, being more active, incline more frequently to the perversions, in which their component sexual instincts can be expressed, while women incline more to hysteria or other psychoneuroses, in which they have symptoms rather than sexual activity. Second, Freud felt that the sexual instinct in females is more easily repressed—more liable to become, so to speak, inactive. Terming the sexual instinct "masculine" also contributed to making comprehensible (Freud thought) the postulated "involution" in female sexuality at puberty. "Puberty, which brings about so great an accession of libido in boys, is marked in girls by a fresh wave of *repression*," in which it is precisely clitoral sexuality that is affected. "What is overtaken by repression is a piece of masculine sexuality. . . ." This repression turns girls toward femininity, toward the passive act or aim of receiving the penis in the vagina, and consequently toward becoming pregnant.

To speak more concretely: girls have to repress their sexuality since, in obedience to social conventions, they must wait some five years after the onset of puberty to be sexually active, which means to renew their clitoral excitability and also to experience vaginal sensations and stimulation. Young men have the conventional outlets (including prostitutes) and masturbatory activity that are, in Freud's view, consonant with their eventual mature "active" sexual role. He assumes that female sexuality must be discussed in the context of the anesthesia (lack of clitoral and vaginal sensitivity) that repression of masturbation and lack of sexual intercourse during adolescence produces in females (p. 137):

> When at last the sexual act is permitted and the clitoris itself becomes excited, it still retains a function: the task, namely, of transmitting the excitation to the adjacent female sexual parts {labia and vagina}. . . . Before this transference can be effected, a certain interval of time must often elapse, during which the young woman is anesthetic. This anesthesia may become permanent if the clitoral zone refuses to abandon its excitability, an event for which the way is prepared precisely by an extensive activity of that zone in childhood. . . .

This is Freud's view of why masturbation can be harmful: it habituates females to clitoral stimulation and contributes to later frigidity, which means fixation on clitoral (phallic) sensation rather than development of the vaginal (genital) sensitivity he considered characteristic of mature sexuality. As he put the matter succinctly in the 1908 essay called " 'Civilized' Sexual Morality and Modern Nervous Illness" (p. 179), women who have preserved their virginity by resorting to perverse practices and masturbation "show themselves anaesthetic to normal intercourse in marriage."

It should be noted that Freud did not, in these texts or elsewhere, distinguish between clitoral and vaginal *orgasms* or say that the two organs are unconnected; he understood that clitoral stimulation is involved in vaginal excitation even after the vagina becomes the leading erotogenic zone. But this insight of his makes all the more puzzling his belief that women experience vaginal excitation primarily in intercourse or upon being penetrated; he might have concluded that clitoral masturbation is the great initiator, or that intercourse confirms what women can know before it by masturbating—that the vagina is a very pleasurable site. Freud does not seem to have considered this possibility, and over the issue of the age when sensations arise spontaneously in the vagina, when it becomes erotogenic, he remained convinced that the answer was puberty.

In the late 1920s, Freud's colleagues began to report evidence of earlier vaginal sensations, but Freud himself remained conservative: "It is true that there are a few isolated reports of early vaginal sensations as well, but it could not be easy to distinguish these from sensations in the anus or vestibulum {vaginal canal}; in any case they cannot play a great part. We are entitled to keep our view that in the phallic phase of girls the clitoris is the leading erotogenic zone" (p. 347). About what Freud once, in an early paper (3:133), called "menstrual excitation" and about what menstruation means in the lives of young females, he did not comment (except to note the common "horror of blood" in "On the Sexual Theories of Children" (p. 162) and "The Taboo of Virginity" (p. 204).)

The *Three Essays* discussion of puberty concludes with another passage relating the repression of "masculine" masturbation to hysteria and the other psychoneuroses:

> When erotogenic susceptibility to stimulation has been successfully transferred by a woman from the clitoris to the vaginal orifice, it implies that she has adopted a new leading zone for the purpose of her later sexual activity. . . . The fact that women change their

leading erotic zone in this way, together with the wave of repression at puberty, which, as it were, puts aside their childish masculinity, are the chief determinants of the greater proneness of woman to neurosis and especially hysteria.

It is as though the female's libido suddenly in puberty loses activity—becomes virtually inactive under a wave of repression. This diminution of bisexuality or demasculinization (to speak in Freud's manner) is "related to the essence of femininity" (7:221). The male, who does not have a "masculine" and a "feminine" genital zone, who does not change zones, does not repress his femininity in a comparable way: he represses it without giving up a sexual pleasure like masturbation, and he does so in the throes of his childhood "castration complex" rather than in puberty. In Freud's view, the power of masculinity when it is repressed with such difficulty in females was much stronger than that of repressed femininity in males, and thus women's bisexuality in adulthood was much more obvious in psychoneuroses and symptoms in which the repressed masculinity struggles for expression. (This is another way of explaining why males incline more frequently to the perversions, in which their femininity is acted out, and females to the psychoneuroses.)

In the third of the *Three Essays*, it is obvious that Freud's presentation of masculine sexuality at puberty is from the point of view of normality, even though he is aware of the frequency of male impotence under conditions of 'civilized' sexual morality. His presentation of female sexuality, on the other hand, is from the point of view of neurosis—or of a form of hysteria he considers so common as to be typical, that is, genital anesthesia or frigidity. But the "brake upon sexuality" in females that Freud posited was not biological or constitutional. Indeed, the wave of repression in female puberty runs counter to Freud's biological theory of two libidinal "effloresences" in both sexes, one in the Oedipal period, one at puberty. Those adults responsible for controlling young females have understood well that their task was to counter biology, as Freud notes:

> It is clear that education is far from underestimating the task of suppressing a girl's sensuality till her marriage, for it makes use of the most drastic measures. Not only does it forbid sexual intercourse and set a high premium on the preservation of female chastity, but

> it also protects the young woman from temptation as she grows up, by keeping her ignorant of all the facts of the part she is to play and by not tolerating any impulse of love in her which cannot lead to marriage. . . .

When she does marry, a girl is "still attached to her parents, whose authority has brought about the suppression of her sexuality; and in her physical behavior she shows herself frigid. . . ." (p. 176)

There is no further discussion in Freud's *Three Essays* of this crucial wave of pubertal repression. He does note (as in the 1908 essay just cited; see pp. 166–81 below) that some girls at puberty retreat from sexual life by concealing their libido "behind an affection which they can express without self-reproaches, by holding fast throughout their lives to their infantile fondness, revived at puberty, for their parents or brothers and sisters" (p. 142). In girls, the two currents of love Freud had designated "affectionate" and "sensual," the former originating in childhood loves, the latter in pubertal loves, are little separated. Further, he specifies that the sexual activity of girls is "particularly subject to the watchful guardianship of their mothers," which may contribute an element of hostility toward their own sex. But all of these remarks simply confirm that the wave of repression in puberty is not biological but is rather a matter of social organization and conventions.

In these remarks, Freud shows himself very sympathetic to the distortions in female sexuality produced by forms of social life based upon oppression of women. He also implicitly offers an explanation of why severe hysterias of the sort he saw so often are relatively rare now in communities where girls are more free sexually, where sex education is more available, and where active living and public roles for women are encouraged. That the symptom complexes Freud called "disturbances of eating" and we call "eating disorders" are still very common—even epidemic in some communities—does signal, however, that problems traceable to the oral stage are no less prevalent in contexts less restrictive for later developmental stages.

At the time when he was concentrating his attention on hysteria, Freud was not as alert as he later became to the period called "pre-Oedipal" and to early mother-daughter bonds. On the other hand, Freud's followers, much more concerned with the pre-Oedipal period, question whether the hysterical symptoms

Freud saw so commonly, like genital anesthesia, are as crucial for understanding femininity under more liberal social conditions. Is there any need to stress the difference between clitoral and vaginal sexuality—between "masculine" and "feminine" sexuality—unless anesthesia is apparent? Similarly, if there were no social stigma attached to masturbation could this not prevent the "dammed up libido" condition of neurasthenia and hysteria in women (and of the psychoneuroses in general, for both sexes)?

Freud indicated quite clearly in the passage from " 'Civilized' Sexual Morality and the Modern Neuroses" already cited, and again in the 1912 discussion on masturbation also anthologized here, that he thought lifting social bans on female sexuality in puberty to allow "unrestricted satisfaction" of sexual urges *would not* eliminate "pathogenic effects" arising from the sexual instincts themselves or from their manifestation in masturbation. His chief reason for this conclusion as it applies to masturbation is stated in the " 'Civilized' Sexual Morality" essay: "In the fantasies that accompany {masturbatory} satisfaction the sexual object is raised to a degree of excellence which is not easily found again in reality." Unrestrained—unrepressed—masturbatory activity would leave its own traces or psychic habits: no real person would be likely to satisfy someone raised, as it were, on masturbation. Similarly, people become guilt-ridden not over masturbation itself—whether socially stigmatized or not—but over an incestuous "fantasy, which, although unconscious, lies at its root" (17:95). However, Freud noted in one of his last essays, the 1938 *An Outline of Psychoanalysis* (23:190), that no empirical study had been made of the effects on boys or girls of life in "civilizations which do not suppress masturbation in children."

About the possible effects of deregulating sexual intercourse during puberty, Freud did not comment directly, but he did write in the essay entitled "The Taboo of Virginity" (p. 209) that a woman's incestuous fantasies will influence her attitude toward her first male sexual partner no matter what the timing or conditions of her defloration. Such studies as exist of the careful empirical and cross-cultural sort Freud hoped for have shown his assessment of the harmfulness of masturbation to be exaggerated and his sense of inevitability over the "wave of repression" in female puberty to be time-bound.

3. Revisions: Narcissism and Masochism

The claims Freud made in the *Three Essays* about sexual differentiation first in the phallic phase and then at puberty were magnets for later debates. So, too, were the two larger claims that (1) libido is masculine, which seemed to make feminine sexuality a derivative of masculine sexuality rather than something existing independently; and that (2) individuals and human societies, like microcosm and macrocosm, evolve toward limitations of their sexual aims (and specifically toward the heterosexual monogamy discussed in " 'Civilized' Sexual Morality and Modern Nervous Illness"). We will return to these four fronts of debate. But first we need to note Freud's own later revisions of his first systematic treatise on the theory of sexuality.

Between 1905, when the first edition of the *Three Essays* was published, and 1924, when Freud revised and supplemented the text for the last time, his theory of sexuality was consolidated, but not fundamentally changed. He concentrated in specific essays on facets of the theory, and three of these short pieces are anthologized here: "On Transformations of Instinct as Exemplified in Anal Erotism" (1917), "The Infantile Genital Organization" (1923), and "The Dissolution of the Oedipus Complex" (1924). The first essay was indebted to a 1916 work by Freud's colleague Lou Andreas-Salomé, who was famous as a writer and a *femme savante* when she began to study psychoanalysis in 1912, and the essay is particularly important for what it has to say about how women overcome their penis envy through an unconscious equation of penis and baby, through coming to desire a "penis-child" from their fathers. This is Freud's explanation of how girls put their clitoral "masculine sexuality" behind them and prepare to accept a masculine sexual partner. It is also his explanation of how reproduction or making a baby comes, in a derivative fashion, to be an aim of the sexual instinct. He does not assume that females are born with a desire to reproduce or preserve the species. Rather, just as women acquire this desire in consequence of their disappointment and the diminution of their overt bisexuality, so they later feel their babies (particularly sons) to be compensations.

In the paper called "The Dissolution of the Oedipus Complex," Freud began to reconsider his theory that a boy's love of his mother and a girl's of her father develop analogously. But this reconsideration did not advance very far until it was spurred by the consequences of a profound upheaval in Freud's thought. Paradoxically, it was just while the theory of sexuality was consolidating that the foundation on which it sat—the instinct theory—began to shift. First, Freud abandoned his long-held assumption that we humans are, like the animals, moved by "love and hunger," that is, that we have sexual instincts aimed at sexual discharge and resulting in species preservation and ego instincts aimed at self-preservation. Particularly as he collaborated just before the First World War with his Swiss colleague Carl Jung, who was examining closely the processes of the psychoses, Freud realized that a fuller description of the sexual instinct's aims was needed. For his female psychology, this realization was as important as the next and final shift in his instinct theory, toward what is known as the "dual instinct theory." In that final instinct theory, articulated after the First World War in *Beyond the Pleasure Principle* (1921), Freud distinguished the sexual instinct in all its forms and aims, Eros, from "the death instinct."

The first step in Freud's revision of his instinct theory was made in the 1914 essay "On Narcissism: An Introduction." Two forms of the sexual instinct are distinguished: sexual instinct aimed at the ego and sexual instinct aimed at representations of people in the world, narcissism and object-love. Freud explains that the distinction grew out of his effort to add a theory of psychotic (paranoid and schizophrenic) retreat from the world and pathological self-love to his theory of the neuroses (hysteria, obsessional neurosis, phobias). After the Dora case, his full case studies of both neuroses and psychoses had focused only on male patients. In 1909 he published both an important case study of a boy with a phobia ("Little Hans") and an intricate report on an obsessional ("The Rat Man"); in 1918 he published his lengthiest case study, of a young Russian ("The Wolf Man") who was first phobic and then (between the ages of four and ten) obsessional. His 1911 study of a journal written by a paranoid man named Schreber was a vehicle for preliminary formulations about the psychoses. Throughout this period Freud made remarks on female sexuality, continuing the lines of thought laid down in the *Three Essays*; but the paradigmatic female illness, hysteria, with frigidity as its most ubiquitous symptom, receded into the background of his work. What came forward instead is apparent in "On Narcissism."

The narcissism concept allowed Freud to enrich his description of a child's pregenital sexuality: by showing how the autoeroticism of the oral, anal, and phallic stages becomes narcissistic, Freud could indicate that the infant not only finds pleasure in its body and body parts, but loves them—and this narcissistic love continues on even when the child comes to love of others (so-called object love). First love is not, as Freud had originally thought, objectless—parts of the child's own body and gratifying parts of other's bodies (like the mother's breast) are its objects. Sometimes the child's narcissism continues to the point of determining that the later objects loved shall be like itself. That is, in some people the "primary narcissism" common to everyone plays a predominating role in later object-love. Such people do not eventually transfer their narcissistic love of themselves onto other people, and thereby idealize or overvalue other people; rather, they continue to love narcissistically and seek other people who help sustain their narcissistic love. In general, these descriptions of love types were extensions of the investigation of mental sexual characteristics Freud had launched in the *Three Essays*—they both enriched and fortified his conventional notions of male and female attitudes.

For males, the narcissism concept gave a new dimension to the phallic phase and the boy's conviction that all people have penises. The boy's overevaluation of the phallus is narcissistic: to give up his certainty that all people have penises—to experience "castration threat"—is to experience the limits of self-love. In puberty, boys typically transfer their self-love to the girls they love—they worship, they see no faults. Similarly, the narcissism concept gave new dimensions to Freud's descriptions of both the Oedipal and puberty periods in females. Another way to say "penis envy" is to say "narcissistic wound." That is, girls feel their lack of a penis as a blow to their self-love, for they feel that they lack not only the superior equipment for masturbation but also the sadistic and exhibitionistic pleasures that the penis affords, pleasures of mastery (for example, standing to urinate) and of commanding admiration. With the narcissism concept, Freud could give an answer to the question of why girls find the penis so enviable.

A variation on this answer will, of course, do for why boys—and girls—find their fathers' penises so enviable: they are bigger, more visible and thus admirable, more powerful sexually and for producing long arches of urination, and so forth. Similarly, when

Freud discussed the boy's envy for the female womb (and sometimes breasts), or for the female ability to have babies, an envy
obvious in the "Little Hans" case, he stressed the boy's feeling of
lack, his wounded narcissism. (The degree of phallus worship and
womb mystery in a child's social environment usually affects the
way his or her envy is constructed—but Freud construed this as
more a matter of phylogenetic heritage than actual present en-
vironmental influence.)

In puberty, along with the maturation of their sexual organs,
girls feel "an intensification of the original narcissism." Their self-
love compensates them (12:89) for the "wave of repression" flowing from the social restrictions put on their possibilities for object
love. They do not breach the social rules by seeking out love
objects; their desire is for being loved. Given this interplay of
anatomical and social factors, boys and girls end up comple-
menting each other in the manner of the Beauty and the self-
sacrificing Beast characters so common in nineteenth-century
novels. The young men typically give up their own narcissism
and love narcissistic coquettes. Young women, loving predominantly themselves, are brought to a semblance of object love by
their lovers' overvaluing adoration. Such narcissistic women,
when they marry and have children, can achieve object love—
finally—by loving their chidren as parts of themselves. (In general,
parental love for children carries in it the story of the parents'
own narcissism and the fate it has undergone; see 12:91.) Other
girls, who love more according to the "masculine type" of overvaluation, often look for a man who fulfills their earlier narcissistic
self-image of masculine virtue and beauty—that is, they love the
man they would like to have been themselves.

As delineations of pure types, Freud's descriptions are certainly
astute. They may very well reflect his own understanding of himself as a young man adoringly courting his wife, and they certainly
do reflect the ideas he stimulated in his new friend Lou Andreas-
Salomé, who later wrote a remarkable paper on narcissism. That
pure types of the sort Freud sketched hardly ever exist in fact, he
knew quite well, and he also noted that his association of object
love with males and narcissistic love with females was limited:
". . . these differences are not universal" (14:88). There are persistently narcissistic males, too, and these only achieve a semblance of object love with the help of self-sacrificing and
overvaluing lovers, female or male. But Freud does not call such

male narcissists "feminine," while he does say that overvaluing females love according to the "masculine type." This asymmetry echoes the idea from the *Three Essays* that women can assume mental sexual characteristics of the masculine type while men cannot have the feminine type—even if their chosen object is male and their chosen love aim is "passive" or homosexual. Loving is active in Freud's scheme (and thus associated with the masculine), while being loved, the narcissistic desire, is passive (and thus associated with the feminine).

The one full-scale case study of a female that Freud wrote after the *Three Essays*, "The Psychogenesis of a Case of Homosexuality in a Woman" (1920), both depended upon his new insights about narcissism and offered a revision. The eighteen-year-old homosexual patient loved according to the "masculine type" a woman whom she overvalued. The patient also found in the beloved older woman's lithe figure her own masculine ideal, which was modeled on the patient's older brother, the boy she would have liked to be. Her love object, that is, was characteristically bisexual, although the homosexual element in her love predominated. While Freud was tracking these complexities in a summary statement at the end of the case, he revised his long-held idea that males cannot have female mental sexual characteristics. This was an important—though completely unheralded—step in the direction of the realization that males not only love their mothers but identify with them, sometimes to the degree of becoming female in their sexual attitudes (even if their love objects are female or heterosexual). As we will see shortly, this revision and the topic of infantile identifications emerged clearly three years later as Freud wrote *The Ego and the Id*.

But the case of the female homosexual is also very important in Freud's oeuvre for containing his first indication that a woman's original attachment to her mother plays a crucial role in her later sexual aims, her object choices, and her mental sexual characteristics. The patient, grievously disappointed in her father's love and jealous of her mother for taking the place she wanted, for becoming pregnant with the father's child, repudiated men; but at that point she also turned toward her mother—and this turn needed further explanation. Freud was not able to offer the explanation until 1925, however, for its prerequisites were both the second revision of the instinct theory and the theory of identifications in *The Ego and the Id*. These prerequisites were met as

Freud took into account the cases and the conclusions he had presented in a complex exploratory essay, " 'A Child Is Being Beaten,' " (1919).

Freud wrote this clinical essay just after the First World War, when the small bands of psychoanalysts in Vienna, Berlin, and Budapest were trying to reestablish their professional societies, their practices, and their research after a period of deprivations and horror. Much of their effort went into study of "war neurotics," while the young people attracted to the movement extended psychoanalysis to work with children—particularly with children left homeless and orphaned by the war and children who had become delinquents in the upheaval. Freud's youngest daughter Anna Freud, an elementary school teacher who became one of the founders of child analysis, underwent a training analysis with him between 1918 and 1922, and her case was one of the ones on which Freud based " 'A Child Is Being Beaten.' "

The four female patients presented in this essay (only one of whom was a hysteric) had in common a recurrent fantasy with three variant forms. They fantasized that a father figure beat a child, then that he beat the female fantasizer herself, and finally that he beat either the fantasizer in a male guise or a group of male children. Freud suggested that the multiform fantasy of being beaten was a fantasy of being loved which had been reworked until it became acceptable to the fantasizer's conscience (to which Freud would soon give the title "superego"). Assuming a male guise in the fantasy also served the females' purpose of avoiding interpsychic censorship of incestuous desires for the father. (Here Freud emphasized that a variation of female bisexuality is asexuality or asceticism—refusing to love any object as a means of avoiding incestuous love of the father.)

Although the male patients Freud studied did not have to change sex in their fantasies, they too were avoiding incest guilt. They changed their beater into a female, in order to disguise their desire for their father's love, a homosexual desire in which they themselves were "feminine." Against Freud's expectation, the beating fantasy took a different form in males than in females, and this difference prompted his reconsideration of the theory that male and female children develop their Oedipal loves in mirror image. But for both sexes it was the case that masochistically enjoyed love—being beaten—was guiltless love.

Freud suggested that a beating fantasy is the "essence of masochism" (19:189) because it is the crucial mechanism by which a pleasurable but guilt-inducing love is converted into a painful but pleasurably guilt-free love. The importance of guilt in these fantasies led Freud directly to his formulation that a particular agency of the psyche, to which he gave the name "superego," forbids incestuous desires. This step was key to his 1923 text *The Ego and the Id*, in which he announced the so-called "structural theory" of superego, ego, and id. Here he indicated that the ego has to mediate between the desires of the id—the realm of the instincts—and the censorious commands of the superego, which represent parental and societal norms as they are internalized and at least partially unconscious in the psyche.

By 1924, when Freud returned to the topic of masochism in "The Economic Problem of Masochism," he was working with both the "structural theory" and the "dual instinct theory." The fact that such a great deal of recent theoretical innovation was presumed in "The Economic Problem of Masochism" made the essay very difficult for Freud's contemporaries to understand, and its role in Freud's evolving view of female psychology was not easy to appreciate—and still is not. The matter was made particularly complex by the further fact that many psychoanalysts found Freud's dual instinct theory unacceptable and rejected the "death instinct" hypothesis. Within feminist criticism of Freud's views of female psychology, the death instinct theory is hardly ever even mentioned, so the theory of masochism built upon it is frequently misinterpreted.

Freud's formulation of the death instinct in 1920 had been designed to explain how it can be that people persist in fantasies (like beating fantasies) and actions that go against the pursuit of pleasure ("the pleasure principle") that seems so obviously to govern the sexual instinct in all its forms. What is going on when people—repetitively, even compulsively—hurt themselves or arrange to have themselves hurt, in fantasy or in fact? Freud posited a kind of masochism more fundamental than the kind he had called a component instinct in the *Three Essays* and than the guilt-relieving kind he had studied in " 'A Child Is Being Beaten.' " There is, he argued, a "primal masochism" or "erotogenic masochism" in all people. Eros (narcissism and object love) and the death instinct (aimed at detachment, quietude, repose) are originally fused in each person, and the death instinct leaves its trace in the libido even after the better part of it is projected outward as acts of aggression, acts of mastery, or will to power. The remaining trace of the death instinct then accompanies the libido and takes different forms in the libido's different stages; it is the basis for pleasure in pain, and it is (we can infer) strongest in people whose means for being aggressive in their earliest years were interfered with. We can make this abstract postulation concrete by noting that children who are, for example, kept from free movement, from messy play, from expressions of anger—as children of both abusive and depressive parents often are—are likely to be well supplied with "primary masochism." When their wild aggressiveness and bursts of rage are simply quashed, rather than modified through their established libidinal ties, such children do not develop the ability to control their aggression. Rather they turn it against themselves, where it becomes bound up with the libido and with feelings of pleasure. Freud connects this theory directly to women in his 1932 lecture "Femininity" (p. 345): "the suppression of women's aggressiveness which is prescribed for them constitutionally and imposed on them socially favors the development of powerful masochistic impulses. . . ."

In this new scheme, the masochism Freud had studied in " 'A Child Is Being Beaten' " is a derivative masochism produced when instinctual excitation, converted into aggression and projected outward, is turned back on the projector to rejoin whatever degree of unprojected "primal masochism" exists. Aggression is turned inward after painful experiences or threats of pain in the world, and these experiences or threats are reflected in the fantasies of derivative masochism at each of the oral, anal, and phallic libidinal stages. A child imagines being eaten, being beaten (particularly being spanked on the buttocks), and, in the phallic stage, being castrated.

A particular type of derivative or secondary masochism, called "feminine masochism," takes its name from the content of the painful phallic-stage fantasies that give pleasure—fantasies of being castrated, being copulated with, giving birth—because these are associated with being female. As he considers cases, all of them male, not female, Freud alludes to the male beating fantasies he had studied earlier, where males were being beaten (that is, loved) by their homosexual object, their father. This is a typical male masochistic fantasy, in which being loved as a "female" involves pain, specifically involves being castrated. Freud does not, curiously, enough, offer an example of a female masochist's fantasies in his essay.

This omission can be remedied by recalling the females in " 'A Child Is Being Beaten,' " who imagined themselves as males. It seems that Freud meant that these masochistic women, like masochistic men, fantasized themselves as castrated or as being castrated, being turned into females. In the process, their fantasies regressively assumed prephallic, or anal content—being beaten on the buttocks—and they gave up their pleasure in clitoral ("masculine") masturbation. The precondition for the masochistic fantasy in these cases, then, was a denial of anatomical femininity or the continued longing for a penis that Freud called the "masculinity complex." But other varieties of female masochistic fantasies, such as rape fantasies, obviously exist and could be coordinated to Freud's discussion. At any rate, there is nothing in the discussion Freud does offer that supports the claim that women or female activities are naturally or intrinsically masochistic—a common misconstrual of Freud's meaning.

Another type of derivative or secondary masochism, called "moral masochism," is masochism relieved of the kind of sexual content necessary to "feminine masochism"—it is masochism desexualized. Moral masochists take their pleasure in being tormented by ideas or in being exquisitely sensitive to moral standards. Fate or God punishes moral masochists, and the humiliation they feel can come to substitute in their lives for sexual activity (as often happens, for exmaple, with religious cult members).

The very density of formulation in Freud's masochism essay— the first one he wrote after he had undergone major oral surgery for cancer in the fall of 1923—made his ideas hard to grasp. Their elusiveness helped foster the notion that Freud thought female anatomy implied a masochistic destiny, even though he had carefully indicated that feminine masochism is common in both men and women. As noted, the essay does not have an answer to the question: Is there a specifically female version of "feminine masochism"? But a line of thought about the significance for the female of her "castration complex" (the sum of her conscious and unconscious attitudes toward castration) does run from this paper through to the major statement on pre-Oedipal female mother-love that Freud offered in 1925.

When Freud took a new look at female development prior to

the Oedipal period, he was drawing together his questions about the differences between female and male beating fantasies and his sense, expressed in the case study of the female homosexual, that the early mother-daughter bond is crucial in female homosexuality. He was probably also influenced by the fact that his female patient population was changing. After the First World War, he analyzed women, including his daughter, who were set on intellectual careers or on training to be psychoanalysts. These were not hysterics. Most came for what are known as "character analyses," not for relief from debilitating psychoneuroses, and most were, in Freud's terms, examples of the feminine "masculinity complex." Their bisexuality, so sustaining to their creativity and formative to their characters, may well partly explain why Freud's analysand trainees were not critical of his female psychology—the criticism came from outside his circle, and outside the reach of the transferences he received.

Types of character and libidinal types (see the 1931 essay of that title anthologized here) were of great interest to Freud in this period, as they were to the psychoanalytic critics of his views of women. Urged on by Ernest Jones, Karen Horney and Melanie Klein began to make their dissent known in the mid-1920s. Freud responded to his critics in each of the three essays he dedicated specifically to female psychology after he stopped revising the *Three Essays* in 1924.

4. FEMALE DEVELOPMENT IN THE PRE-OEDIPAL PERIOD

As we have noted, before his new look Freud had assumed that prior to the phallic phase, which is contemporaneous with the onset of the Oedipus complex (19:174), girls and boys have parallel developments. They diverge only when girls discover the difference between female and male genitals, give up their "masculine" clitoral masturbation, and love their fathers. Boys, meanwhile, fearing castration from their fathers and threatened in their narcissism, repress the Oedipus complex (their mother-love) and emerge from it with a superego made up largely of identifications with their parents, especially their father-rivals. Freud had summarized his views about the less dramatic, and therefore more obscure, female course of development in his 1924 paper "The

Dissolution of the Oedipus Complex": "The girl's Oedipus complex is much simpler than that of the small bearer of the penis; in my experience, it seldom goes beyond the taking of her mother's place and the adopting of a feminine attitude toward her father. Renunciation of the penis is not tolerated by the girl without some attempt at compensation. She slips—along the line of a symbolic equation, one might say—from the penis to a baby. . . ." Her superego is less overbearing and strict, because she does not have to respond with repression to a paternal injunction against incest with the mother. That is, the (paternal) threat of castration that is so decisive to a boy is not part of the story of the already "castrated" girl.

Freud's reconsideration of his generalizations was announced in his 1925 paper "Some Psychical Consequences of the Anatomical Distinction between the Sexes," where he candidly admitted that psychoanalytic investigation had typically focused on males and then been extrapolated to females by noting variations from the male model that would explain the different ultimate destinies of the two sexes. What was chiefly at issue was whether females, like males, have a true phallic stage. Karen Horney of Berlin had recently argued that a girl's penis envy does not mark a true developmental stage and is not determinative of her character unless or until it is reinforced while she defends herself against her Oedipal father-love. Horney postulated "secondary penis envy" (see 21:243) as a defensive superstructure. From Freud's point of view this looked like a denial of the bisexuality he took as clinically obvious in females. If Horney was right, primary penis envy would not have the power Freud attributed to it: the power to precipitate the girl's turn toward her father (or from her bisexuality to femininity with a repression of her masculinity).

Freud thought that Horney's view implied a rejection of bisexuality because, as he noted in a letter to Carl Mueller-Braunschweig (pp. 340–41 below), he thought that it would logically lead her to postulate a primordial femininity, an inborn disposition to take male love objects, to love heterosexually and (as Horney actually did argue) to aim at reproduction. In his essay, Freud countered Horney's "secondary penis envy" claim, chided those (unnamed) analysts who declare that "they have never found a sign of the existence of the castration complex" in women (19:254), and indicated that he himself had *underestimated* (not overestimated) the consequences of the female "masculinity complex" for the development of female character and mental sexual characteristics. His catalogue of consequences was even more formidable than the very influential one Karl Abraham had drawn up in 1920.

Among the consequences Freud notes are the female's sense (stemming from the "narcissistic wound") that all women are inferior beings; her jealousy as a translation of penis envy into characterological terms; and her hostility toward her mother, who "sent her into the world so insufficiently equipped" (12:254). Freud also admits that he had understated a "wave of repression" common in the little girl's phallic phase—like a forerunner of the one in puberty. This wave is directed specifically at masturbation of the clitoris, which the girl has so recently discovered to be inferior in comparison to a boy's penis. The little girl renounces masturbation out of her narcissistic humiliation. This repression, too, prepares the way for her turn to her father—it is, like the repression in puberty, a repudiation of the "masculine sexuality" of the clitoris and an accession of femininity.

The girl who does not repress her clitoral masturbation—or does so unsuccessfully—and continues to hope for a penis is marked by her "masculinity complex" in every phase of her life, and may tend toward a homosexual object choice. To put the same matter another way: her bisexuality remains so strong (or so balanced) that it is difficult for femininity to emerge in puberty. (As noted, we may also infer on the basis of " 'A Child Is Being Beaten' " that if a girl renounces—rather than represses—masturbation by substituting a beating fantasy for the masturbatory pleasure, she may be an example of "feminine masochism.")

With this 1925 paper, Freud went even further in the direction of "anatomy is destiny" than he had before. The girl's phallic phase is not just a period of realistic discovery followed by envy; it is a period of repression. And once again repression is the key to leaving behind bisexuality and assuming a feminine attitude. The girl's Oedipus complex is not simpler than the boy's. Repression in response to paternal castration threat brings the boy's Oedipus complex to an end, but the female Oedipus complex *commences* with very severe repression of phallic or clitoral sexuality. To put the same idea another way: her Oedipus complex is not, in distinction from the boy's, dissolved or broken apart under the impact of repression commanded by a rigidifying superego; rather, it is set firmly in place by ego repression, which instigates the unconscious equation of desire for a penis with desire for a baby (19:256). Women often do not overcome the Oedipus complex at all.

Freud reviewed these conclusions in his 1931 paper "Female Sexuality," but he did so in a different context: a look at how the girl's development toward femininity and the father-love of the Oedipus complex can be inhibited by her pre-Oedipal first love, her love for her mother. By this point in his work, Freud had completely abandoned his early certainty that the girl's first love is her father. In his late work, the importance of the mother for both girls and boys is everywhere emphasized, if often said to be mysterious in girls, where it usually lies hidden behind intense father-love. The interplay of the little girl's loves is obscure, but the consequence is not: "Bisexuality . . . comes to the fore much more clearly in women than in men" (21:227). Freud had always been of this opinion, but in his early work he held it because he thought women had such difficulty repressing their masculinity, while in his later work he added the idea that they had trouble repressing their powerful first love for their mothers.

This first love of girls (and boys), Freud suggested, might be more thoroughly uncovered in analysis by female analysts, who could be the recipients of mother-transference more easily. In his 1931 paper, he acknowledges work by two of his training analysands, the Dutch physician Jeanne Lampl-de Groot and a Pole trained in Vienna, Helene Deutsch, as he had earlier acknowledged important work on the pre-Oedipal period by another trainee, Ruth Mack Brunswick, an American. He was also drawing on child analytic work done by his daughter and a group of her colleagues at the Vienna Training Institute. He may also have reflected back on his own early descriptions of hysteria, where he had noted the connection between disturbances of the oral phase and eating problems. Indeed, it is one of the puzzles in Freud's development that he, who had so clearly observed and emphasized the oral eroticism of hysterics, was so slow to think concretely of that orality as originating with love at the maternal breast.

The pre-Oedipal period is, Freud summarized, more important for women than for men because a girl must negotiate a turning away from the very person, her mother, who has been the center of her existence, the supplier of her needs. As noted, this first tie makes her later bisexuality even more comprehensible than it was when Freud was stressing only the girl's achieved love for her father. The attitude a girl has toward her mother, which is often characterized by a volatile mix of love and hate (ambivalence) from the moment when weaning introduces disappointment in the mother, has a profound effect on her later life and on her later object-choices. (Her lover or husband may inherit that childhood attitude, as Freud had remarked of heterosexual women in "The Taboo of Virginity" and implied about the female homosexual in his case study.) The three lines of development most typical for women—revulsion from sexuality, continued entanglement in "the masculinity complex," and progress toward the "normal" feminine or positive form of the Oedipus complex—are directly influenced by the type of the initial mother-love. Similarly, the girl's pre-Oedipal mother-love as well as her love of her mother during the Oedipal period (which Freud called her "negative Oedipus complex") are marked by a mix of passivity and activity in each phase. Especially important to a girl are her passive experiences of being suckled and of having her anal and genital areas washed, experiences to which she often responds with activity—biting, washing a doll, and so forth. Freud added a final turn to his old story of how influential seduction fantasies are in a child's development by noting that a little girl's enjoyment of having her genitals washed and touched by her mother or her nurse can be reworked: when she turns toward her father, she fantasizes that her father has seduced her. Phallic phase activity—masturbation—with the mother as its fantasy object is also common: like a boy, a girl wishes to have a baby with her mother. The inevitable frustration of this wish adds its weight to the repression of masturbation that usually accompanies the girl's turn to her father. This "heterosexual" turn is, in sum, the product of multiple losses, disappointments, and humiliations.

During the last year of his life, in the London refuge he and his family found after their flight from Nazi-occupied Vienna, Freud was still mulling over the riddles of sexual differentiation, the stories of castration anxiety in males and penis envy in females. He wrote Sections III and VII of *An Outline of Psychoanalysis*, which give a succinct and clear indication of the view that had crystallized out of nearly half a century of clinical practice and theorizing. The female's envy of masculinity or "repudiation of femininity," he maintained in a similar 1937 summary in *Analysis*

Terminable and Interminable (23:252), is the "bedrock"—he even says the *biological* bedrock—of the riddle of her sexuality.

4. FOCUSES OF CRITICISM

Although many specific dimensions of Freud's very complex and many-times revised presentation of female psychology have been criticized, it is no exaggeration to say that behind every specific criticism looms one large objection. Freud, so this objection goes, viewed femininity as failed masculinity. His claim that the libido is not just active but masculine has correlatives in every facet of his theory. Females start out like males and then—disappointed in their mother-love, humiliated over their lack of a penis, self-deprived of their masturbatory pleasure—take a fall into femininity. A girl who finds she cannot be a man settles for being a mother with a "penis-child." A male, by contrast, must renounce his mother but need never give up loving a woman, fears for his genitals but does not despise them, and has no pubertal shift to make from one erotogenic zone to another, from clitoral to vaginal sexuality.

This general criticism has been highlighted by feminists for two quite different purposes. And between the extremes of these two purposes lie the whole range of feminist responses to Freud. On the one hand, the fact that psychoanalytic theory is obviously not an equal-opportunity theory has meant for some that it should be rejected or radically cleansed of its bias against women. On the other hand, the psychoanalytic portrait of the female as a failed male has been accepted as the deepest analysis available of the effects of patriarchy (or the nuclear family as the carrier of patriarchy) on men's attitudes toward women and women's attitudes toward themselves. Here it is not the view that is objected to, but the reality which the view reflects, the reality that must be addressed by any truly radical social reform. In the last decade, proponents of the second approach have been more and more influential. Previously, hostility prevailed in many variant forms, more or less rejectionist, more or less tied to developments within professional psychoanalysis.

Within psychoanalysis, debates over the phallocentrism or androcentrism of Freud's general view have framed specific debates, although his key reason for equating masculinity and libido—the need to explain female bisexuality—has not been acknowledged or dealt with by would-be revisionists. Like the feminist critics, many of the pscyhoanalytic critics charge Freud with presenting femininity as failed masculinity when, as I have tried to show, what he actually argued was that femininity is a development from—a limitation of—bisexuality, just as masculinity is a development from bisexuality. The two developments take two different forms, Freud concluded, and bisexuality remains more obvious—clinically and observationally—in women.

Karen Horney and later Ernest Jones focused critical attention on the girl's phallic stage and her penis envy, but their underlying purpose was to assert some form of primordial femininity, a femininity not derived from masculinity by limitation or negation—a true psychosexual difference. Freud, as was noted above, took this as an attack on his theory of female bisexuality. While her dissent from Freud's general view was growing more and more pronounced, Horney made further efforts to redress the imbalance she saw in it—an imbalance she charged to male narcissism. She suggested that psychoanalysis had underestimated how much males envy females what is uniquely female and tied to primordial, not derivative, feminine desires: pregnancy, childbirth, and nursing. Margaret Mead similarly called the attention of anthropologists to "womb envy" in cross-cultural studies of birth rituals. Horney and others also insisted that a girl has vaginal sensations in childhood (not just in puberty) and that she is not, thus, as monolithic in her ideas about genitals as Freud thought. As was also noted above, Freud did not deny the possibility of early vaginal sensations, but he insisted, in reply, that they did not influence the girl's estimation of the penis.

In more recent psychoanalytic studies, the questions raised by Horney and Jones have been re-posed and addressed with child analytic—rather than adult analytic—research. At Anna Freud's London clinic, extensive use of analytic data yielded a distinction between the girl's "phallic-narcissistic phase" and a succeeding phallic phase that is part of the Oedipal configuration. This distinction deemphasizes or even eliminates the girl's "negative Oedipal" relation to her mother: girls do not usually, these researchers argue, actively desire their mothers and want to have a baby with them like a little boy. Pre-Oedipally, both boys and girls relate to their mothers not as little men but as little narcissists—looking, wanting to be looked at, focusing on themselves and trying to draw adult attention to themselves. Penis envy can be quite transitory in this scheme (as in Karen Horney's earliest view). Other recent contributions place even less emphasis on instinctual-drive development and bring to the fore issues of identity formation. Girls and boys are said to have a "core gender identity" based on their primary identification with the mother (in girls) or disidentification from her (in boys). A related theory attributes the motive for penis envy to the girl's struggle in separating from her mother— something that, it seems to the girl, comes more easily to "the little bearer of the penis."

In general, Freud's tendency to take penis envy as crucially determinative and universal has met with various views in which it is acknowledged but relativized and discussed in terms of pregenital mother-bonds. It is not surprising, therefore, from Freud's own point of view, that with the diminished emphasis on penis envy has come an increased emphasis on how tightly tied to their mothers girls are, and how often they remain so. For him, penis envy was the means of separation, the means of repudiating the mother and turning eventually toward heterosexuality; repressing penis envy was equivalent to leaving bisexuality for femininity. In more recent psychoanalytic work, the question Freud thought key—What turns the girl toward her father?—is not much posed, and by the followers of the child analyst Melanie Klein it is not posed at all. The Kleinians argue that infants are innately endowed with knowledge of both male and female sexual parts and functions and develop from the start in the medium of these "object relations" and the very severe anxieties they involve. Problems of the pre-Oedipal or pregenital period take up the better part of the current psychoanalytic agenda, and that historical development is also related, within the realm of female psychology, to critique of Freud's universal penis-envy theory.

Out of the original debate over the phallic phase and penis envy grew another debate, which also is still current. Here the opponents of the Freudian view also insisted on relativizing the universal penis-envy theory, but for different reasons than their child-analytic counterparts. These analysts stressed the effects of socialization (including tolerance or intolerance for masturbation) and culturally transmitted estimation of the phallus. In America, where Karen Horney emigrated in 1933, a school of psychoanalysis known generally as "Cultural Psychoanalysis," sometimes as "Neo-Freudian Psychoanalysis," took the later view, which Clara Thompson summarized thus: "So, the attitude called penis envy is similar to the attitude of any unprivileged group toward those in power." This more sociologically oriented Freudianism has been very influential on feminists committed to future family structures in which women and men will live and parent their children in greater equality.

The female phallic stage was the main focus of debate within psychoanalytic circles until Helen Deutsch offered her two-volume work, *The Psychology of Women*, in 1944–45. Deutsch reiterated in terms even stronger than Freud's the importance of the female's transition in puberty from clitoral to vaginal sexuality, and she also tended to link vaginal sexuality and giving birth to feminine masochism—a link completely unacceptable to a majority of Freud's followers and not (as we noted above) implied by Freud himself. The physiological connection between the clitoris and the vagina Freud had noted disappeared in Deutsch's formulation, and she insisted that only vaginal sensations arising passively in response to a penis constitute normal mature sexuality. She also insisted, in distinction from Freud, that for a female only sexual pleasure culminating in reproduction is truly satisfying.

The most influential reply to this ultra-Freudian view came from empirical sex researchers like Masters and Johnson, who tried to demonstrate that orgasms produced by different means are not distinguishable on a physiological basis (although, they indicated, they vary with psychological factors). They claimed that the vagina is intensely active in different forms of sexual engagement, and this conclusion was seconded by the many research projects demonstrating both that female libido is hardly less—and may even be more—strong than male and that women are far more orgasmic than had been dreamt in Freudian psychology.

Deutsch's emphasis on motherhood (and not orgasm per se) as a primordial female desire did align her work with that of primordial-femininity proponents like Horney, however, and other psychoanalysts, like Erik Erikson, have continued this train of thought by arguing that a female's "inner space" genitalia orient her passively toward nurturing in the private world of children, family, and interpersonal relationships. (Erikson did alter his views somewhat, however, when feminist critics pointed out to him that

he was lending theoretical support to an unprogressive stereotype.)
More recent child analytic researchers have suggested that girls
show wishes for babies before the phallic phase and that they may
also make attachments to their fathers before that phase—that is,
before their castration complex supposedly turns them toward the
father. In general, this trend of psychoanalytic research, even
though it often very questionably underplays bisexuality, has been
important because it has focused attention on specifically female
biological and psychological issues—like the onset of menstruation and fear of vaginal penetration or internal harm, which Freud
really ignored as factors in puberty and adolescence.

In the 1960s, another strand of debate was added. Freud had
assumed that civilization evolves slowly toward sexual control in
the form of conventions determining female virginity before marriage, fidelity in marriage, and opposition to "perverse" practices.
His own attitude toward this evolutionary movement was liberally
reformist, but certainly neither optimistic nor revolutionary. Research in the late 1930s by Alfred Kinsey in America had indicated, however, that sexual control was not as great a success as
its proponents like to believe and that many more people than
was commonly thought engaged in premarital, extramarital, and
"perverse" sex. Kinsey's conclusions were hotly debated until the
1960s, when it was obvious to both Kinsey's defenders and his
detractors that social reality in much of America was openly in
accord with Dr. Kinsey. (Since then, discussion of Kinsey has
focused on his methods and whether his surveys were set up in
a sexist manner.) The history of sexuality is now an area of very
great scholarly activity, and no resolution seems in sight to the
question whether " 'civilized' sexual morality" as Freud described
it in 1908 is over the long term waxing or waning; whether it was
or is inevitable or aberrational, specific to certain religious, ethnic,
and racial groups or general in developed societies, peculiar to
patriarchal societies or not.

Similarly, sociopolitical thinkers differ drastically over whether
" 'civilized' sexual morality" is something to be accepted with
stoic resignation and sublimation or something to be revolution-
ized behind the banners of women's liberation, gay liberation,
the sex education movement, organizations for contraceptive and
abortion rights, and so forth. The heritage of Freud was viewed
by his immediate followers—many of them socialists in the 1920s
and 1930s—as progressive and revolutionary. Since then, psy-

choanalysis has been a house of as many sociopolitical mansions as any other mental health specialty. However, the wing of it that has remained determinedly progressive is psychoanalytic child guidance, and it is in child analytic work that the commitment of the first generations of analysts to therapy for people of all means, all social strata, has been most consistently maintained. Perhaps nowhere more clearly than in an urban child-study center can one imagine what it was like for Freud to discover, behind the mysterious somatic symptoms of hysteria, Oedipal and pre-Oedipal desires. For in such centers the three current frontiers in psychoanalytic work are all represented, all involving focuses on pre-Oedipal development that will have consequences for female psychology. There are analysts who are taking into account ongoing neurophysiological and genetic research and working to extend Freud's theory and therapy to borderline, autistic, and psychotic patients, including victims of seduction and abuse; and, on the other hand there are analysts working to extend their science to the full range of normal—not pathological—development. But in child-study centers there is, in addition, research designed to differentiate childhood pathologies from adult ones. Freud started with the psychiatric classifications of his day, offered revisions, and went on in search of causes. His heirs in child analysis have pointed out that many of the pathologies observable in children do not accord with psychiatric classifications developed for adults or with Freud's own descriptions of infantile neuroses. Another search for adequate description and for causes is under way.

About female psychology specifically, there is no current consensus within psychoanalysis. There is a great deal of ferment, and a healthy attention to feminist critiques—many of them currently from France—posed in both psychoanalytic and nonpsychoanalytic terms. This is a moment in which Freud's urge to generalization—his urge to speak of "femininity" and "normal femininity," to speak in the abstract singular and in the normative—stands thwarted. His idea that the story of civilization can be read off in the miniature of an individual psyche has disappeared under a good volley of questions: Which civilization is Civilization? By what standards of progress, evolution? At what cost of ignored diversity? The current answer to his question "What does a woman want?" is a fragmentation of it: "What have various psychological types/social groups/historical eras of women wanted and how can we tell their wants from what has been wanted for them? What do their stories mean for now? In what languages of theory and practice—in and outside of psychoanalysis—shall women answer their questions about themselves?" Freud's views on female psychology remain the uniquely important and influential touchstone in the current discussion, but the advice he delivered when he was seventy-six, at the end of his 1932 lecture entitled "Femininity," has grown more appropriate with each decade since:

> That is all I have to say to you about femininity. It is certainly incomplete and fragmentary and does not always sound friendly . . . If you want to know more about femininity, enquire of your own experiences of life, or turn to the poets, or wait until science can give you deeper and more coherent information.

Chronology of Freud's Life and Work

1856   Freud born (May 6) in Freiberg, Moravia, oldest child of Amalie and Jacob Freud, who soon relocate in Vienna.

1873   Finishes Gymnasium and enters University of Vienna; works from 1876–1882 in Brucke's physiology laboratory.

1882–86   Engagement and marriage to Martha Bernays; employment at General Hospital in Vienna, including a study year (1885) in Paris with Jean Martin Charcot.

1886–95   Birth of first five Freud children (Mathilde, Martin, Oliver, Ernst, Sophie); friendship (starting in 1887) with Wilhelm Fliess grows deeper; papers on diseases of the nervous system, motor paralyses, hypnotism, hysteria, obsessions and phobias, anxiety neurosis.

1895   Birth of sixth child, Anna; *Studies on Hysteria* published with Josef Breuer.

1900   Publication of *The Interpretation of Dreams*; writing of "Dora" case (published in 1905); beginning of end of Fliess friendship.

1905   *Three Essays on the Theory of Sexuality.*

1908   "Hysterical Phantasies and Their Relation to Bisexuality," "On the Sexual Theories of Children," " 'Civilized' Sexual Morality and Modern Nervous Illness"; Freud's publications and newly reorganized Vienna Psychoanalytic Society attract important adherents—Karl Abraham, Ernest Jones, Sandor Ferenczi, Max

Eitingon, then Carl Jung—and first international psychoanalytic congress is convened.

1909   "Analysis of a Phobia in a Five-Year-Old Boy" (Hans); trip to America for lectures, a sign of growing reputation.

1912–13 Contributions to a discussion on masturbation; Lou Andreas-Salomé hears Freud's lectures; disagreements with Jung lead toward a final break in 1913.

1914   First War World War begins, two of Freud's sons in German Army; decline in patients leaves more time for writing; "On Narcissism: An Introduction."

1917   "On Transformations of Instinct as Exemplified by Anal Erotism."

1918   End of First World War; psychoanalytic training patients, including Anna Freud; "The Taboo of Virginity," an outgrowth of *Totem and Taboo* (1912).

1919   " 'A Child is Being Beaten.' "

1920   "The Psychogenesis of a Case of Female Homosexuality"; *Beyond the Pleasure Principle* presents "dual instinct theory"; death of Freud's daughter Sophie.

1923   *The Ego and the Id* and "The Infantile Genital Organization"; Freud's cancer diagnosed.

1924   "The Economic Problem of Masochism" and "The Dissolution of the Oedipus Complex."

1925   "Some Psychical Consequences of the Anatomical Distinction between the Sexes"; beginning of theoretical debates with Melanie Klein, Karen Horney, Ernest Jones; death of Karl Abraham.

1930   *Civilization and Its Discontents.*

1931   "Libidinal Types" and "Female Sexuality."

1932   "Femininity" delivered, one of New Introductory Lectures (1933).

1933   Hitler comes to power in Germany, German psychoanalysts begin to emigrate; death of Sandor Ferenczi.

1938   Freud and family members then remaining in Vienna flee to England; work on never-completed *An Outline of Psychoanalysis* in London.

1939   Death soon after outbreak of Second World War (September 23).

Excerpts from Freud's Letters to Fliess

D r. Wilhelm Fliess, an ear, nose, and throat specialist from Berlin, attended Sigmund Freud's lectures during a study period in Vienna. Afterward, in 1887, the two men began to correspond. Their friendship grew through their frequent letters and their periodic meetings ("congresses"); they began to exchange not just their unorthodox and challenging scientific ideas but confidences about their family lives, healths, practices, careers, and—in Freud's case—self-analysis.

Only Freud's letters have survived, and his life and work are very vivid in them. In the first letters, about 1887 to 1895, he is obsessed with his "sexual thesis" about the principal cause of the psychoneuroses, which he had been unable to argue in Studies on Hysteria, partly because he was not ready and partly because his collaborator Josef Breuer was unconvinced. Then, as Freud got caught up in analyzing his own dreams, he turned his attention almost entirely to the manuscript that became The Interpretation of Dreams (1900). When this book was published, and greeted with indifference or incomprehension by almost everyone but Fliess, Freud returned to the "sexual thesis," hoping to succeed on the basis of his dream theory and the general psychology that supported it.

He had not, until then, been able to complete a psychoanalytic treatment; he had relieved many people of their symptoms, but without the "sexual thesis" and the technique it finally implied, he always fell short. A patient called "Dora," who came for treatment in this last period, is discussed in the letters to Fliess as one of the first cases where sure insight fianlly came, even though the analysis was broken off. (Selections from Freud's study of this case are presented below, pp. 69–88.

While Freud was struggling—and his letters make palpable the inten-

sity of his struggle as well as the hardships of isolation and economic precariousness it brought him—Fliess was building an intricate theoretical structure. One key element of this strange, baroque edifice was the postulate that there are correspondences between regions of the nose and genital regions. Fliess thought hysterical genital anesthesia might be curable, for example, with nasal surgery. Another key element was a theory of bisexuality involving periodicities: each person had a twenty-eight-day female cycle and a twenty-three-day male cycle manifest in both physiological and psychological ways. (On the basis of these cycles, Fliess hoped to be able to discover a truly effective and safe means of contraception.) Among Fliess's experiments were a series trying to link pronounced bisexuality with left-handedness, on the assumption that everyone is ambidextrous but most people—the right-handed ones—repress their left-handedness as they repress the characteristics of the sex opposite to their anatomical one. In vast medical and mathematical detail, Fliess labored to expand both the correspondence theory and the periodicity theory into cosmological theories. He was in search of general laws of nature, not just of human nature, Freud's domain.

The following excerpts from Freud's letters were selected to show the two elements of his work that became most important for his female psychology. First, Freud comes to appreciate Fliess's ideas about the importance of bisexuality while he rejects his colleague's narrow definition of what is repressed in favor of a much more elaborate scheme of "erotogenic zones" with pleasures and excitements that undergo repression. This scheme is connected to a distinction between masculine and feminine types of sexual development. Second, he confirms his emphasis on sexuality while he rejects "the seduction theory," a version of sexual theory that posited an actual childhood experience of seduction as the precipitating cause of the psychoneuroses.

In 1895, Fliess received from Freud case reports, preliminary formulations, and statements of bafflement (October 16, 1895):

※ ※ ※ I am still all mixed up. I am almost certain that I have solved the riddles of hysteria and obsessional neurosis with the formulas of infantile sexual shock and sexual pleasure, and I am equally certain that both neuroses are, *in general*, curable—not just individual symptoms but the neurotic disposition itself. This gives me a kind of faint joy—for having lived some forty years not quite in vain—and yet no genuine satisfaction because the psychological gap in the new knowledge claims my entire interest.

Four days later (October 20, 1895), Freud wrote ecstatically that his bafflement had evaporated:

* * * Now listen to this. During an industrious night last week, when I was suffering from that degree of pain which brings about the optimal condition for my mental activities, the barriers suddenly lifted, the veils dropped, and everything became transparent—from the details of the neuroses to the determinants of consciousness. Everything seemed to fall into place, the cogs meshed, I had the impression that the thing now really was a machine that shortly would function on its own. The three systems of n[eurones]; the free and bound states of Qn [quantity]; the primary and secondary process; the main tendency and the compromise tendency of the nervous system; the two biological rules of attention and defense; the characteristics of quality, reality, and thought; the state of the psychosexual group; the sexual determination of repression; finally, the factors determining consciousness, as a function of preception—all that was correct and still is today! Naturally, I can scarcely manage to contain my delight.

If I had only waited two weeks longer before reporting to you, everything would have turned out so much clearer. Yet it was only in attempting to report it to you that the whole matter became obvious to me. So it could not have been done any other way.

Through 1896 and 1897, the year after his father's death. Freud went up and down with breakthroughs and theoretical collapses. He took himself as a case—and he did not break off his analysis (August 14, 1897):

* * * This time you are losing nothing at all [by not hearing] my tales. Things are fermenting in me; I have finished nothing; am very satisfied with the psychology, tormented by grave doubts about my theory of the neuroses, too lazy to think, and have not succeeded here in diminishing the agitation in my head and feelings; this can happen only in Italy.

After having become very cheerful here, I am now enjoying a period of bad humor. The chief patient I am preoccupied with is myself. My little hysteria, though greatly accentuated by my work, has resolved itself a bit further. The rest is still at a standstill. That is what my mood primarily depends on. The analysis is more difficult than any other. It is, in fact, what paralyzes my psychic strength for describing and communicating what I have won so far. Still, I believe it must be done and is a necessary intermediate stage in my work.

Fliess received the news that the "seduction theory" of causality in the psychoneuroses did not hold universally, and Freud's reasons for abandoning it and appreciating the importance of fantasies (September 21, 1897):

* * * I was ready to give up two things: the complete resolution of a neurosis and the certain knowledge of its etiology in childhood. Now I have no idea of where I stand because I have not succeeded in gaining a theoretical understanding of repression and its interplay of forces. It seems once again arguable that only later experiences give the impetus to fantasies, which [then] hark back to childhood, and with this the factor of a hereditary disposition regains a sphere of influence from which I had made it my task to dislodge it—in the interest of illuminating neurosis.

If I were depressed, confused, exhausted, such doubts would surely have to be interpreted as signs of weakness. Since I am in an opposite state, I must recognize them as the result of honest and vigorous intellectual work and must be proud that after going so deep I am still capable of such criticism. Can it be that this doubt merely represents an episode in the advance toward further insight?

It is strange, too, that no feeling of shame appeared—for which, after all, there could well be occasion. Of course I shall not tell it in Dan, nor speak of it in Askelon, in the land of the Philistines, but in your eyes and my own, I have more the feeling of a victory than a defeat (which is surely not right).

The key turn came shortly after this announcement about the seduction theory, as Freud was examining some scenes from his early childhood that had risen up in his memory. His mother was able to confirm some of the memories about his nurse and about herself, and Freud felt convinced enough by the experience to venture "a single idea of general value." In this letter (October 15, 1897), what came to be known as "the Oedipus complex" is sketched for the first time, and is set next to the theoretical issue that later proved so important for Freud's female psychology—the role of "the feminine" in repression. But, it is important to note, the Oedipus complex is here discussed only for males (although Freud speaks of its universality).

My self-analysis is in fact the most essential thing I have at present and promises to become of the greatest value to me if it reaches its end. In the middle of it, it suddenly ceased for three days, during which I had the feeling of being tied up inside (which patients complain of so much), and I was really disconsolate until I found that these same three days (twenty-eight days ago) were the bearers of identical somatic phenomena. Actually only two bad days with a remission in between. From this one should draw the conclusion that the female period is not conducive to work. Punctually on the fourth day, it started again. Naturally, the pause also had another determinant—the resistance to something surprisingly new. Since then I have been once again intensely preoccupied [with it], mentally fresh, though afflicted with all sorts of minor disturbances that come from the content of the analysis.

My practice, uncannily, still leaves me a great deal of free time. The whole thing is all the more valuable for my purposes, since I have succeeded in finding a few real points of reference for the story. I asked my mother whether she still remembered the nurse. "Of course," she said, "an elderly person, very clever, she was always carrying you off to some church; when you returned home you preached and told us all about God Almighty. During my confinement with Anna (two and a half years younger), it was discovered that she was a thief, and all the shiny new kreuzers and zehners and all the toys that had been given to you were found in her possession. Your brother Philipp himself fetched the policeman; she then was given ten months in prison." Now look at how this confirms the conclusions of my dream interpretation. It was easy for me to explain the only possible mistake. I wrote to you that she induced me to steal zehners and give them to her. In truth, the dream meant that she stole them herself. For the dream picture was a memory of my taking money from the mother of a doctor—that is, wrongfully. The correct interpretation is: I = she, and the mother of the doctor equals my mother. So far was I from knowing she was a thief that I made a wrong interpretation.

I also inquired about the doctor we had had in Freiberg because one dream concentrated a good deal of resentment on him. In the analysis of the dream figure behind which he was concealed, I also thought of a Professor von Kraus, my history teacher in high school. He did not seem to fit in at all, because my relationship with him was indifferent or even comfortable. My mother then told me that the doctor in my childhood had only one eye, and of all my teachers Professor Kraus was the only one with the same defect! The conclusive force of these coincidences might be weakened by the objection that on some occasion in my later childhood, I had heard that the nurse was a thief and then apparently had forgotten it until it finally emerged in the dream. I myself believe that that is so. But I have another, entirely irrefutable and amusing proof. I said to myself that if the old woman disappeared from my life so suddenly, it must be possible to demonstrate the impression this made on me. Where is it then? Thereupon a scene occurred to me which in the course of twenty-five years has occasionally emerged in my conscious memory without my understanding it. My mother was nowhere to be found; I was crying in despair. My brother Philipp (twenty years older than I) unlocked a wardrobe [*Kasten*] for me, and when I did not find my mother inside it either, I cried even more until, slender and beautiful, she came in through the door. What can this mean? Why did my brother unlock the wardrobe for me, knowing that my mother was not in it and that thereby he could not calm me down? Now I suddenly understand it. I had asked him to do it. When I missed my mother, I was afraid she had vanished from me, just as the old woman had a short time before. So I must have heard that the old woman had been locked up and therefore must have believed that my mother had been locked up too—or rather, had been "boxed up" [*eingekastelt*]—for my brother Philipp, who is now sixty-three years old, to this very day is still fond of using such puns. The fact that I turned to him in particular proves that I was well aware of his share in the disappearance of the nurse.

Since then I have got much further, but have not yet reached my real point of rest. It is so difficult and would carry us so far afield to communicate what I have not yet finished that I hope you will excuse me from it and content yourself with the knowledge of those elements that are certain. If the analysis fulfills what I expect of it, I shall work on it systematically and then put it before you. So far I have found nothing completely new, [just] all the complications to which I have become accustomed. It is by no means easy. Being totally honest with oneself is a good exercise. A single idea of general value dawned on me. I have found, in my own case too, [the phenomenon of] being in love with my mother and jealous of my father, and I now consider it a universal event in early childhood, even if not so early as in children who have been made hysterical. (Similar to the invention of parentage [family romance] in paranoia—heroes, founders of religion). If this is so, we can understand the gripping power of *Oedipus Rex*, in spite of all the objections that reason raises against the presupposition of fate; and we can understand why the later "drama of fate" was bound to fail so miserably. Our feelings rise against any arbitrary individual compulsion, such as is presupposed in *Die Ahnfrau* and the like; but the Greek legend seizes upon a compulsion which everyone recognizes because he senses its existence within himself. Everyone in the audience was once a budding Oedipus in fantasy and each recoils in horror from the dream fulfillment here transplanted into reality, with the full quantity of repression which separates his infantile state from his present one.

Fleetingly the thought passed through my head that the same thing might be at the bottom of *Hamlet* as well. I am not thinking of Shakespeare's conscious intention, but believe, rather, that a real event stimulated the poet in his representation, in that his unconscious understood the unconscious of his hero. How does Hamlet the hysteric justify his words, "Thus conscience does make cowards of us all?" How does he explain his irresolution in avenging his father by the murder of his uncle—the same man who sends his courtiers to their death without a scruple and who is positively precipitate in murdering Laertes? How better than through the torment he suffers from the obscure memory that he himself had contemplated the same deed against his father out of passion for his mother, and—"use every man after his desert, and who should 'scape whipping?' " His conscience is his unconscious sense of guilt. And is not his sexual alienation in his conversation with Ophelia typically hysterical? And his rejection of the instinct that seeks to beget children? And, finally, his transferral of the deed from his own father to Ophelia's? And does he not in the end, in the same marvelous way as my hysterical patients, bring down punishment on himself by suffering the same fate as his father of being poisoned by the same rival?

I have kept my interest focused so exclusively on the analysis that I have not yet even attempted to try out, instead of my hypothesis that in every instance repression starts from the feminine aspect and is directed against the male one, the opposite hypothesis proposed by you. I shall, however, tackle it sometime.

Unfortunately, I barely participate in your work and progress. In this one respect I am better off than you are. What I can tell you about mental frontiers [*Seelenende*] of this world finds in you an understanding critic, and what you can tell me about its celestial frontiers [*Sternenende*] evokes only unproductive amazement in me.

The problem of repression continued to occupy Freud, and he was soon able to send Fliess some notes that foreshadowed the theory of "erotogenic zones" and the reflections on female puberty that he advanced later in the Three Essays on the Theory of Sexuality *(November 14, 1897).*

* * * A few weeks ago came my wish that repression might be replaced by my knowledge of the essential thing lying behind it; and that is what I am concerned with now. I have often had a suspicion that something organic plays a part in repression; I was able once before to tell you that it was a question of the abandonment of former sexual zones, and I was able to add that I had been pleased at coming across a similar idea in Moll. (Privately I concede priority in the idea to no one; in my case the notion was linked to the changed part played by sensations of smell: upright walking, nose raised from the ground, at the same time a number of formerly interesting sensations attached to the earth becoming repulsive—by a process still unknown to me.) (He turns up his nose = he regards himself as something particularly noble.) Now, the zones which no longer produce a release of sexuality in normal and matue human beings must be the regions of the anus and of the mouth and throat. This is to be understood in two ways: first, that seeing and imagining these zones no longer produce an exciting effect, and second, that the internal sensations arising from them make no contribution to the libido, the way the sexual organs proper do. In animals these sexual zones continue in force in both respects; if this persists in human beings too, perversion results. We must assume that in infancy the release of sexuality is not yet so much localized as it is later, so that the zones which are later abandoned (and perhaps the whole surface of the body as well) also instigate something that is analogous to the later release of sexuality. The extinction of these initial sexual zones would have a counterpart in the atrophy of certain internal organs in the course of development. A release of sexuality (as

you know, I have in mind a kind of secretion which is rightly felt
as the internal state of the libido) comes about, then, not only
(1) through a peripheral stimulus upon the sexual organs, or
(2) through the internal excitations arising from those organs, but
also (3) from ideas—that is, from memory traces—therefore also
by the path of deferred action. (You are already familiar with this
line of thought. If a child's genitals have been irritated by someone, years afterward the memory of this will produce by deferred
action a release of sexuality far stronger than at the time, because
the decisive apparatus and the quota of secretion have increased
in the meantime.) Thus, there exists a nonneurotic deferred action
occurring normally, and this generates compulsion. (Our other
memories operate ordinarily only because they have operated as
experiences.) Deferred action of this kind occurs also in connection with a memory of excitations of the abandoned sexual zones.
The outcome, however, is not a release of libido but of an unpleasure, an internal sensation analogous to disgust in the case
of an object.

To put it crudely, the memory actually stinks just as in the
present the object stinks; and in the same manner as we turn away
our sense organ (the head and nose) in disgust, the preconscious
and the sense of consciousness turn away from the memory. This
is *repression*.

What, now, does normal repression furnish us with? Something
which, free, can lead to anxiety; if psychically bound, to rejection—that is to say, the affective basis for a multitude of intellectual processes of development, such as morality, shame, and
the like. Thus the whole of this arises at the expense of extinct
(virtual) sexuality. From this we can see that, with the successive
thrusts in development, the child is overlaid with piety, shame,
and such things, and how the nonoccurrence of this extinction
of the sexual zones can produce moral insanity as a developmental
inhibition. These thrusts of development probably have a different
chronological arrangement in the male and female sexes. (Disgust
appears earlier in little girls than in boys.) But the main distinction
between the sexes emerges at the time of puberty, when girls are
seized by a *non*neurotic *sexual* repugnance and males by libido.
For at that period a further sexual zone is (wholly or in part)
extinguished in females which persists in males. I am thinking of
the male genital zone, the region of the clitoris, in which during
childhood sexual sensitivity is shown to be concentrated in girls

as well. Hence the flood of shame which the female shows at that period—until the new, vaginal zone is awakened, spontaneously or by reflex action. Hence, too, perhaps the anesthesia of women, the part played by masturbation in children predisposed to hysteria, and the discontinuance of masturbation if hysteria results.

And now for the neuroses! Experiences in childhood which merely affect the genitals never produce neurosis in males (or masculine females), but only a compulsion to masturbate and libido. But since as a rule experiences in childhood have also affected the two other sexual zones, the possiblity remains open for males, too, that libido awakening through deferred action may lead to repression and to neurosis. Insofar as memory has lighted upon an experience connected with the genitals, what it produces by deferred action is libido. Insofar as it has lighted upon an experience connected with the anus, mouth, and so on, it produces deferred *internal disgust*, and the final outcome is consequently that a quota of libido is not able, as is ordinarily the case, to force its way through to action or to translation into psychic terms, but is obliged to proceed in a *regressive* direction (as happens in dreams). Libido and disgust would seem to be associatively linked. We owe it to the former that the memory cannot lead to general unpleasure and the like, but that it finds a psychic use; and we owe it to the latter that this use furnishes nothing but symptoms instead of aim-directed ideas. The psychological side of this would not be hard to grasp; the organic factor in it is whether abandonment of the sexual zones takes place according to the masculine or feminine type of development or whether it takes place at all.

It is probable, then, that the choice of neurosis—the decision whether hysteria or obsessional neurosis or paranoia emerges—depends on the nature of the thrust (that is to say, its chronological placing) which enables repression to occur; that is, which transforms a source of internal pleasure into one of the internal disgust.

This is where I have got to so far—with all the inherent obscurities. I have resolved, then, henceforth to regard as separate factors what causes libido and what causes anxiety. I have also given up the idea of explaining libido as the masculine factor and repression as the feminine one. These are, in any case, important decisions. The obscurity lies mainly in the nature of the change by which the internal sensation of need becomes the sensation of disgust. I need not draw your attention to other obscure points.

The main value of the synthesis lies in its linking the neurotic process and the normal one. There is now a crying need, therefore, for a prompt elucidation of common neurasthenic anxiety.

My self-analysis remains interrupted. I have realized why I can analyze myself only with the help of knowledge obtained objectively (like an outsider). True self-analysis is impossible; otherwise there would be no [neurotic] illness. Since I am still contending with some kind of puzzle in my patients, this is bound to hold me up in my self-analysis as well.

After a late December, 1897 "congress" in Breslau, Freud made an effort to blend into his thinking Fliess's latest speculations about bisexuality (January 4, 1898):

It is of great interest to me that you are so affected by my still negative attitude to your interpretation of left-handedness. I shall try to be objective, for I know how difficult it is.

To me, it seems to be as follows: I literally embraced your stress on bisexuality and consider this idea of yours to be the most significant one for my subject since that of "defense." If I had a disinclination on personal grounds, because I am in part neurotic myself, this disinclination would certainly have been directed toward bisexuality, which, after all, we hold responsible for the inclination to repression. It seems to me that I object only to the permeation of bisexuality and bilaterality that you demand. Initially, I did not take any stand on this idea because I still felt too remote from the subject. On the second afternoon in Breslau I felt as though I had been hit on the head as a result of the nasal reaction; otherwise I should no doubt have been able to turn the doubt I felt into an objection; or, rather, been able to seize upon it [the idea] when you yourself said that each of the two halves probably contains both kinds of sex organs. But where, then, is the femininity, for instance, of the left half of a man if it carries a testicle (and the corresponding lower male/female sexual organs) just like the right one? Your postulate that for all results male and female must unite is already satisfied, after all, in one half!

I had the impression, furthermore, that you considered me to be partially left-handed; if so, you would tell me, since there is nothing in this bit of self-knowledge that might hurt me. It is your doing if you do not know every intimate detail about me; you have surely known me long enough. Well, then, I am not aware of any preference for the left hand, either at present or in my childhood; rather I could say that years ago I had two left hands. There is only one thing I would have you consider: I do not know whether it is always obvious to other people which is their own right and left and where right and left are in others. In my case (in earlier years) it was rather a matter of having to think which was my right; no organic feeling told me. I used to test this by quickly making a few writing movements with my right hand. As far as other people are concerned, I must to this day work out their position and so on. Perhaps this fits in with your theory; perhaps it is connected with the fact that I have an infamously low capability for visualizing spatial relationships, which made the study of geometry and all subjects derived from it impossible for me.

This is how it appears to me. But I know very well, indeed, that it nevertheless may be otherwise, and that the aversion to your conception of left-handedness I have so far felt may rest on unconscious motives. If they are hysterical, they certainly have nothing to do with the subject matter, but merely latch onto a catchword; for example, that I have been up to something that one can only do with the left hand. In that case the explanation will turn up some day, God knows when.

The terrific enthusiasm Freud felt for Fliess's bisexuality thesis—minus the left-handedness part—was submerged during most of 1898 while Freud worked feverishly on his "dream book." His reports to Fliess are often very sketchy, but it is clear that he continued to hope that he would arrive at a solution for hysteria (or for the psychoneuroses in general) by means of the dream book and its conclusions (January 3, 1899):

In the first place, a small bit of my self-analysis has forced its way through and confirmed that fantasies are products of later periods and are projected back from what was then the present into earliest childhood; the manner in which this occurs also emerged—once again by a verbal link.

To the question "What happened in earliest childhood?" the answer is, "Nothing, but the germ of sexual impulse existed." The thing would be easy and a pleasure to tell you, but writing it out would take half a sheet so [I shall keep it] for our congress at Easter, together with other elucidations of the story of my early years.

In the second place, I have grasped the meaning of a new psychic element which I conceive to be of general significance and a preliminary stage of symptoms (even before fantasy).

January 4. I got tired yesterday, and today I cannot go on writing along the lines I intended because the thing is growing. There is something to it. It is dawning. In the next few days there certainly will be some additions to it. I shall write you then, when it has become transparent. I want to reveal to you only that the dream schema is capable of the most general application, that the key to hysteria as well really lies in dreams. I now also understand why in spite of all my efforts I have not yet finished the dream [book]. If I wait a little longer, I shall be to present the psychic process in dreams in such a way that it also includes the process in the formation of hysterical symptoms. So let us wait.

This line of thought about dreams and hysteria continued to be productive through the spring (February 19, 1899):

My last generalization has held good and seems inclined to grow to an unpredictable extent. Not only dreams are wish fulfillments, so are hysterical attacks. This is true of hysterical symptoms, but probably applies to every product of neurosis, for I recognized it long ago in acute delusional insanity. Reality—wish fulfillment—it is from these opposites that our mental life springs. I believe I now know what determines the distinction between symptoms that make their way into waking life and dreams. It is enough for the dream to be the wish fulfillment of the repressed thought, for dreams are kept at a distance from reality. But the symptom, set in the midst of life, must be something else besides: it must also be the wish fulfillment of the repressing thought. A symptom arises where the repressed and the repressing thought can come together in the fulfillment of a wish. The symptom is the wish fulfillment of the repressing thought, for example, in the form of a punishment; self-punishment is the final substitute for self-gratification, which comes from masturbation.

This key opens many doors. Do you know, for instance, why X.Y. suffers from hysterical vomiting? Because in fantasy she is pregnant, because she is so insatiable that she cannot bear being deprived of having a baby by her last fantasy lover as well. But she also allows herself to vomit, because then she will be starved and emaciated, will lose her beauty and no longer be attractive to anyone. Thus the meaning of the symptom is a contradictory pair of wish fulfillments.

When The Interpretation of Dreams *was almost finished, Freud felt very pleased with it, and with the paths he expected would lead from it to the psychoneuroses—in theory and in his practice. But the connection between his own work and Fliess's remained unexplored, although Freud saw it daily in his therapeutic work (August 1, 1899):*

The farther the work of the past year recedes, the more satisfied I become. But bisexuality! You are certainly right about it. I am accustoming myself to regarding every sexual act as a process in which four individuals are involved. We have a lot to discuss on this topic.

Not much came of Freud's effort to turn his attention back from the dream book to his studies on hysteria or to the bisexuality thesis, but occasionally an idea leapt up and was sent off to Fliess before Freud even had time to weigh it—or reject it, as he did this one (October 17, 1899):

What would you say if masturbation were to reduce itself to homosexuality, and the latter, that is, male homosexuality (in both sexes) were the primitive form of sexual longing? (The first sexual aim, analogous to the infantile one—a wish that does not extend beyond the inner world.) If, moreover, libido and anxiety both were male?

This short letter reveals where Freud had been going with his obscurely expressed suspicion (see January 3, 1899, above) that there is a "preliminary stage of symptoms (even before fantasy)." He was after "the primitive form of sexual longing." But shortly he had a better conception of it and a new name—"autoerotism" (December 9, 1899).

* * * I may recently have succeeded in gaining a first glimpse of something new. The problem confronting me is that of the "choice of neurosis." When does a person become hysterical instead of paranoid? In my first crude attempt, made at a time when I was still trying to take the citadel by force, I thought it depended on the age at which the sexual trauma occurred—the person's age at the time of the experience. That I gave up long ago; but then I was left without a clue until a few days ago, when I saw a connection with the sexual theory.

The lowest of the sexual strata is autoerotism, which dispenses with any psychosexual aim and seeks only locally gratifying sensations. It is then succeeded by alloerotism (homo- or heteroerotism), but certainly continues to exist as an undercurrent. Hysteria (and its variant, obsessional neurosis) is alloerotic, since its main path is identification with the loved one. Paranoia again dissolves the identification, reestablishes all the loved ones of childhood who have been abandoned (compare the discussion of exhibitionistic dreams), and dissolves the ego itself into extraneous persons. So I have come to regard paranoia as a forward surge of the autoerotic current, as a return to a former state. The perversion formation corresponding to it would be the so-called idiopathic insanity. The special relations between autoerotism and the original "ego" would throw a clear light on the nature of this neurosis. At this point the thread breaks off again.

Two of my patients have almost simultaneously come up with [self-]reproaches following the nursing and death of their parents and have shown me that my dreams about this were typical. The reproach is in every instance bound to attach itself to revenge, spiteful glee, taking satisfaction in the ill person's excretory difficulties (urine and stools). Truly a neglected corner of psychic life.

In the late winter of 1900, as Freud began to realize that The Interpretation of Dreams *was not going to be heralded as the pioneering work he knew it to be—indeed, that it was not even going to get very many respectful reviews—Freud entered into a period of resignation, a letdown that was also a much needed rest (February 1, 1900):*

* * * Perhaps hard times are ahead, both for me and for my practice. On the whole, I have noticed that you usually overestimate me greatly. The motivation for this error, though, disarms any reproach. For I am actually not at all a man of science, not an observer, not an experimenter, not a thinker. I am by temperament nothing but a conquistador—an adventurer, if you want it translated—with all the curiosity, daring, and tenacity characteristic of a man of this sort. Such people are customarily esteemed only if they have been successful, have really discovered something; otherwise they are dropped by the wayside. And that is not altogether unjust. At the present time, however, luck has left me; I no longer discover anything worthwhile.

The scanty, uncomprehending reviews, Freud told Fliess, mattered little to him; he was only worried by how Fliess seemed to be retreating, not sharing his own research or involving Freud in his projects, for which Freud still professed such admiration. He wrote to Fliess at the time of his forty-fourth birthday, full of brooding, alleviated only by hopes for the future of his six children (May 17, 1900):

Many thanks for such cordial words! They are so flattering that I might almost believe part of them—if I were in your company. However, I see things a little differently. I would have no objection to the fact of splendid isolation if it were not carried too far and did not come between you and me as well. On the whole—except for one weak point, my fear of poverty—I have too much sense to complain and at present I feel too well to do so; I know what I have and I know, in view of the statistics of human misery, how little one is entitled to. But no one can replace for me the relationship with the friend which a special—possibly feminine—side demands, and inner voices to which I am accustomed to listen suggest a much more modest estimate of my work than that which you proclaim. When your book is published, none of us will be able to pass judgment on its truth, which, as with all great new achievements, is reserved for posterity. The beauty of its conception, though, the originality of its ideas, its simple coherence, and the assurance of the author will create an impression that will give you the first compensation for your arduous wrestling with the demon. It is different with me. No critic (not even the stupid Löwenfeld, the Burckhard of neuropathology) can see more clearly than I the disparity arising from the problems and the answers to them; and it will be a fitting punishment for me that none of the unexplored regions of psychic life in which I have been the first mortal to set foot will ever bear my name or obey my laws. When it appeared that my breath would fail me in the wrestling match, I asked the angel to desist; and that is what he has done since then. But I did not turn out to be the stronger, although since then I have been limping noticeably. Yes, I really am forty-four now, an old, somewhat shabby Jew, as you will see for yourself in the summer or fall. My family nevertheless wanted to celebrate the day. My own best consolation is that I have not deprived them of all future achievements. They can have their experiences and conquests, to the extent that may be in their power. I have left them a foothold for a start, but am not leading them to the peak from which they could climb no farther.

By the beginning of the new year, however, Freud could report that he was halfway through The Psychopathology of Everyday Life *and that he had written a case study, under the little "Dreams and Hysteria"— the case of Dora—in which the linkage between his dream book and "the sexual thesis" was preliminarily set down. He told Fliess (January 25, 1901): "It is the subtlest thing I have written so far, and will put people off more than usual." And then he described it further (January 30, 1901):*

"Dreams and Hysteria," if possible, should not disappoint you. The main thing in it is again psychology, the utilization of dreams, and a few peculiarities of unconscious thought processes. There are only glimpses of the organic [elements], that is, the erotogenic zones and bisexuality. But bisexuality is mentioned and specifically recognized once and for all, and the ground is prepared for detailed treatment of it on another occasion. It is a hysteria with tussis nervosa and aphonia, which can be traced back to the character of the child's sucking, and the principal issue in the conflicting thought processes is the contrast between an inclination toward men and an inclination toward women.

The bisexuality issue continued to attract Freud's attention, and he even took up Fliess's left-handedness speculations by experimenting with the few patients who came to his consulting room. As he told Fliess (February 15, 1901): "I have also introduced testing for left-handedness—with the dynamometer {for testing hand strength} and threading needles {for dexterity}."

But this was the last sign of real intellectual collaboration between the two friends, and they drew apart as well on personal grounds. Freud complained to Fliess that Fliess had rendered judgments on people in their circle—Frau Fliess's sister was married to one of Freud's pediatrician friends—that were unsympathetic and unnecessarily sharp, and said that he suspected Fliess's wife of trying to put distance into their friendship. To Fliess's opinion that Josef Breuer was a man who needed a male friend, but only one at a time, Freud replied (August 7, 1901):

As to Breuer, you are certainly quite right about *the* brother, but I do not share your contempt for friendship between men, probably because I am to a high degree party to it. In my life, as you know, woman has never replaced the comrade, the friend. If Breuer's male inclination were not so odd, so timid, so contradictory—like everything else in his mental and emotional makeup—it would provide a nice example of the accomplishments into which the androphilic current in men can be sublimated.

Having gotten this off his chest, Freud turned around a paragraph later and acknowledged once more his androphilic debt to Fliess, along with the hope—a piece of unrequited love—that they would once again collaborate scientifically:

And now, the main thing! As far as I can see, my next work will be called "Human Bisexuality." It will go to the root of the problem and say the last word it may be granted me to say—the last and the most profound. For the time being I have only one thing for it: the chief insight which for a long time now has built itself upon the idea that repression, my core problem, is possible only through reaction between two sexual currents. I shall need about six months to put the material together and hope to find that it is now possible to carry out the work. But then I must have a long and serious discussion with you. The idea itself is yours. You remember my telling you years ago, when you were still a nose specialist and surgeon, that the solution lay in sexuality. Several years later you corrected me, saying that it lay in bisexuality—and I see that you are right. So perhaps I must borrow even more from you; perhaps my sense of honesty will force me to ask you to coauthor the work with me; thereby the anatomical-biological part would gain in scope, the part which, if I did it alone, would be meager. I would concentrate on the psychic aspect of bisexuality and the explanation of the neurotic. That, then, is the next project for the immediate future, which I hope will quite properly unite us again in scientific matters as well.

The book to be called "Human Bisexuality" never came into being—although the later Three Essays on the Theory of Sexuality *fulfilled its purpose. Fliess jumped to the conclusion that Freud was intending to usurp the bisexuality idea, and Freud had to reassure him (September*

19, 1901) that this was not the case, that he only wanted to deal with the psychological, not the biological, dimensions of bisexuality. The correspondence between the two men, after this misunderstanding, dwindled away, and all that was left was a footnote Freud wrote for his Psychopathology of Everyday Life *(6:143–44) as an illustration of the mechanisms of forgetting:*

One day in the summer of 1901 I remarked to a friend with whom I used at that time to have a lively exchange of scientific ideas: "These problems of the neuroses are only to be solved if we base ourselves wholly and completely on the assumption of the original bisexuality of the individual." To which he replied: "That's what I told you two and a half years ago at Br[eslau] when we went for that evening walk. But you wouldn't hear of it then." It is painful to be requested in this way to surrender one's originality. I could not recall any such conversation or this pronouncement of my friend's. One of us must have been mistaken, and on the *"cui prodest?"* principle it must have been myself. Indeed, in the course of the next week I remembered the whole incident, which was just as my friend had tried to recall it to me; I even recollected the answer I had given him at the time: "I've not accepted that yet; I'm not inclined to go into that question." But since then I have grown a little more tolerant when, in reading medical literature, I come across one of the few ideas with which my name can be associated, and find that my name has not been mentioned.

Selections from "Fragment of an Analysis of a Case of Hysteria"

A bout a year after the first edition of The Interpretation of Dreams appeared, Freud analyzed for three months the bright, attractive eighteen-year-old hysteric whom he called "Dora" in "Fragment of an Analysis of a Case of Hysteria," a text he completed in January, 1901. Dora's treatment had involved two elaborate dream interpretations and Freud was eager to offer them as illustrations of his major work. But the case also gave him an opportunity to return, with new clinical experience—and with the insights he had expressed to Fliess (above, p. 59) about bisexuality and stages of childhood sexual development—to topics he had considered in Studies on Hysteria (1895).

In his "Prefatory Remarks" (not included here), Freud links his case study with his earlier work on hysteria, explains the reservations about patient confidentiality that kept him from publishing the study for nearly five years, notes the ways in which the case was incomplete, and comments on how psychoanalytic technique has evolved. On this last count, he observes that the psychoanalyst must not try to cure a hysteric's symptoms one by one—such cures do not go very deep and do not last. Rather, the patient's story-telling or free associations should be followed, even though this means that information about any given symptom will come forth "piecemeal, woven into various contexts, and distributed over widely separate periods of time" (7:12). The analyst must listen not just to what the patient tells, but to what she does not tell—the "blanks" in her memory, called amnesias; what she can only tell in a confused or uncertain way; what she tells in her mistakes or diverting elaborations, called paramnesias. Restoration of the patient's memory is as much a goal of treatment as relief of symptoms.

The passages presented here from "The Clinical Picture" and "Postscript," parts 2 and 5 of Freud's case study, focus on Dora's symptoms

*and how their formations became visible to Freud as she told her story
and entered into the analytic transference relationship. Freud paid careful
attention to all the details of her "human and social circumstances" so
that he could correlate these to "the somatic data and the symptoms of
the disorder" (7:18). His theoretical goal was to be able to explore Dora's
symptoms in all their complexity of physiological and particularly psychological determination; he wanted to be able to say why she had one
symptom and not another, when the symptom first arose, whether it
changed over time, and so forth.*

*To understand the sections presented here, a brief summary of Dora's
"human and social circumstances" is necessary—although these circumstances were so intricate that Freud himself needed over a hundred dense
pages to map them. Dora was brought to Freud for treatment by her
father, whom she adored, after he found a suicide note she had written.
Since her eighth year she had had neurotic symptoms: first chronic
dyspnea (painful breathing), later migraine, tussis nervosa (nervous
coughing), aphonia (loss of voice), gastric pains. Her later symptoms
appeared after she became involved in a troubling love drama: she was
being courted by a friend of her father's, called Herr K. in Freud's study.
Herr K.'s wife, Frau K. was Dora's father's mistress. An episode in which
Herr K. pressed his suit had been traumatic for Dora, especially because
her father refused to believe her version of the events—a stolen embrace
and kiss—when Herr K. denied it. Her father also denied his affair with
Frau K., who had been Dora's own confidante and older friend before
Dora became aware of the affair. Dora herself felt that she was being—
in effect—offered up by her father to Herr K. in exchange for the cuck-
old's silence about his wife's affair.*

*In the passages presented here, Freud shows a good deal of sympathy
for how girls and women, caught in intolerable domestic situations, resort
to the only weapon they are familiar with—illnesses. But he also assumes
that Dora could not possibly have found Herr K.'s advances anything
but exciting. As we pick up the text, Freud has just connected Dora's
aphonia to her excitement over Herr K.'s embrace, and noted how her
symptoms fluctuated with Herr K.'s comings and goings on business
trips.*

⌇⌇⌇⌇⌇

* * * Am I now going on to assert that in every instance in which
there are periodical attacks of aphonia we are to diagnose the
existence of a loved person who is at times away from the patient?
Nothing could be further from my intention. The determination
of Dora's symptoms is far too specific for it to be possible to expect

a frequent recurrence of the same accidental aetiology. But, if so, what is the value of our elucidation of the aphonia in the present case? Have we not merely allowed ourselves to become the victims of a *jeu d'esprit?* I think not. In this connection we must recall the question which has so often been raised, whether the symptoms of hysteria are of psychical or of somatic origin, or whether, if the former is granted, they are necessarily *all* of them psychically determined. Like so many other questions to which we find investigators returning again and again without success, this question is not adequately framed. The alternatives stated in it do not cover the real essence of the matter. As far as I can see, every hysterical symptom involves the participation of *both* sides. It cannot occur without the presence of a certain degree of *somatic compliance* offered by some normal or pathological process in or connected with one of the bodily organs. And it cannot occur more than once—and the capacity for repeating itself is one of the characteristics of a hysterical symptom—unless it has a psychical significance, a *meaning.* The hysterical symptom does not carry this meaning with it, but the meaning is lent to it, soldered to it, as it were; and in every instance the meaning can be a different one, according to the nature of the suppressed thoughts which are struggling for expression. However, there are a number of factors at work which tend to make less arbitrary the relations between the unconscious thoughts and the somatic processes that are at their disposal as a means of expression, and which tend to make those relations approximate to a few typical forms. For therapeutic purposes the most important determinants are those given by the fortuitous psychical material; the clearing-up of the symptoms is achieved by looking for their psychical significance. When everything that can be got rid of by psycho-analysis has been cleared away, we are in a position to form all kinds of conjectures, which probably meet the facts, as regards the somatic basis of the symptoms—a basis which is as a rule constitutional and organic. Thus in Dora's case we shall not content ourselves with a psycho-analytic interpretation of her attacks of coughing and aphonia; but we shall also indicate the organic factor which was the source of the 'somatic compliance' that enabled her to express her love for a man who was periodically absent. And if the connection between the symptomatic expression and the unconscious mental content should strike us as being in this case a clever *tour de force,* we shall be relieved to hear that it succeeds in creating the same impression in every other case and in every other instance.

I am prepared to be told at this point that there is no very great advantage in having been taught by psycho-analysis that the clue to the problem of hysteria is to be found not in 'a peculiar instability of the molecules of the nerves' or in a liability to 'hypnoid states'—but in a 'somatic compliance'. But in reply to the objection I may remark that this new view has not only to some extent pushed the problem further back, but has also to some extent diminished it. We have no longer to deal with the *whole* problem, but only with the portion of it involving that particular characteristic of hysteria *which differentiates it* from other psychoneuroses. The mental events in all psychoneuroses proceed for a considerable distance along the same lines before any question arises of the 'somatic compliance' which may afford the unconscious mental processes a physical outlet. When this factor is not forthcoming, something other than a hysterical symptom will arise out of the total situation; yet it will still be something of an allied nature, a phobia, perhaps, or an obsession—in short, a psychical symptom.

A *motive* for being ill is sharply to be distinguished as a concept from a *liability* to being ill—from the material out of which symptoms are formed. The motives have no share in the formation of symptoms, and indeed are not present at the beginning of the illness. They only appear secondarily to it; but it is not until they have appeared that the disease is fully constituted.[1] Their presence

---

1. [*Footnote added* 1923:] This is not quite right. The statement that the motives of illness are not present at the beginning of the illness, but only appear secondarily to it, cannot be maintained. In the very next paragraph motives for being ill are mentioned which were in existence before the outbreak of illness, and were partly responsible for that outbreak. I subsequently found a better way of meeting the facts, by introducing a distinction between the *primary* advantage derived from the illness and the *secondary* one. The motive for being ill is, of course, invariably the gaining of some advantage. What follows in the later sentences of this paragraph applies to the secondary gain. But in every neurotic illness a primary gain has also to be recognized. In the first place, falling ill involves a saving of psychical effort; it emerges as being economically the most convenient solution where there is a mental conflict (we speak of a 'flight into illness'), even though in most cases the ineffectiveness of such an escape becomes manifest at a later stage. This element in the primary gain may be described as the *internal* or psychological one, and it is, so to say, a constant one. But beyond this, external factors (such as in the instance given

can be reckoned upon in every case in which there is real suffering and which is of fairly long standing. A symptom comes into the patient's mental life at first as an unwelcome guest; it has everything against it; and that is why it may vanish so easily, apparently of its own accord, under the influence of time. To begin with there is no use to which it can be put in the domestic economy of the mind; but very often it succeeds in finding one secondarily. Some psychical current or other finds it convenient to make use of it, and in that way the symptom manages to obtain a *secondary function* and remains, as it were, anchored fast in the patient's mental life. And so it happens that any one who tries to make him well is to his astonishment brought up against a powerful resistance, which teaches him that the patient's intention of getting rid of his complaint is not so entirely and completely serious as it seemed. * * *

The motives for being ill often begin to be active even in childhood. A little girl in her greed for love does not enjoy having to share the affection of her parents with her brothers and sisters; and she notices that the whole of their affection is lavished on her once more whenever she arouses their anxiety by falling ill. She has now discovered a means of enticing out her parents' love, and will make use of that means as soon as she has the necessary psychical material at her disposal for producing an illness. When such a child has grown up to be a woman she may find all the demands she used to make in her childhood countered owing to her marriage with an inconsiderate husband, who may subjugate her will, mercilessly exploit her capacity for work, and lavish neither his affection nor his money upon her. In that case ill-health will be her one weapon for maintaining her position. It will procure her the care she longs for; it will force her husband to make pecuniary sacrifices for her and to show her consideration, as he would never have done while she was well; and it will compel him to treat her with solicitude if she recovers, for otherwise a relapse will threaten. Her state of ill-health will have every appearance of being objective and involuntary—the very doctor who treats her will bear witness to the fact; and for that

---

[in the following paragraphs in the text] of the situation of a woman subjugated by her husband) may contribute motives for falling ill; and these will constitute the *external* element in the primary gain.

reason she will not need to feel any conscious self-reproaches at making such successful use of a means which she had found effective in her years of childhood.

And yet illnesses of this kind *are* the result of intention. They are as a rule levelled at a particular person, and consequently vanish with that person's departure. The crudest and most commonplace views on the character of hysterical disorders—such as are to be heard from uneducated relatives or nurses—are in a certain sense right. It is true that the paralysed and bedridden woman would spring to her feet if a fire were to break out in her room, and that the spoiled wife would forget all her sufferings if her child were to fall dangerously ill or if some catastrophe were to threaten the family circumstances. People who speak of the patients in this way are right except upon a single point: they overlook the psychological distinction between what is conscious and what is unconscious. This may be permissible where children are concerned, but with adults it is no longer possible. That is why all these asseverations that it is 'only a question of willing' and all the encouragements and abuse that are addressed to the patient are of no avail. An attempt must first be made by the roundabout methods of analysis to convince the patient herself of the existence in her of an intention to be ill.

It is in combating the motives of illness that the weak point in every kind of therapeutic treatment of hysteria lies. This is quite generally true, and it applies equally to psycho-analysis. Destiny has an easier time of it in this respect: it need not concern itself either with the patient's constitution or with his pathogenic material; it has only to take away a motive for being ill, and the patient is temporarily or perhaps even permanently freed from his illness. How many fewer miraculous cures and spontaneous disappearances of symptoms should we physicians have to register in cases of hysteria, if we were more often given a sight of the human interests which the patient keeps hidden from us! In one case, some stated period of time has elapsed; in a second, consideration for some other person has ceased to operate; in a third, the situation has been fundamentally changed by some external event—and the whole disorder, which up till then had shown the greatest obstinacy, vanishes at a single blow, apparently of its own accord, but really because it has been deprived of its most powerful motive, one of the uses to which it has been put in the patient's life.

Motives that support the patient in being ill are probably to be found in all fully developed cases. But there are some in which the motives are purely internal—such as desire for self-punishment, that is, penitence and remorse. It will be found much easier to solve the therapeutic problem in such cases than in those in which the illness is related to the attainment of some external aim.[2] In Dora's case that aim was clearly to touch her father's heart and to detach him from Frau K.

None of her father's actions seemed to have embittered her so much as his readiness to consider the scene by the lake as a product of her imagination. She was almost beside herself at the idea of its being supposed that she had merely fancied something on that occasion. For a long time I was in perplexity as to what the self-reproach could be which lay behind her passionate repudiation of this explanation of the episode. It was justifiable to suspect that there was something concealed, for a reproach which misses the mark gives no lasting offence. On the other hand, I came to the conclusion that Dora's story must correspond to the facts in every respect. No sooner had she grasped Herr K.'s intention than, without letting him finish what he had to say, she had given him a slap in the face and hurried away. Her behaviour must have seemed as incomprehensible to the man after she had left him as to us, for he must long before have gathered from innumerable small signs that he was secure of the girl's affections. * * *

As she kept on repeating her complaints against her father with a wearisome monotony, and as at the same time her cough continued, I was led to think that this symptom might have some meaning in connection with her father. And apart from this, the explanation of the symptom which I had hitherto obtained was far from fulfilling the requirements which I am accustomed to make of such explanations. According to a rule which I had found confirmed over and over again by experience, though I had not yet ventured to erect it into a general principle, a symptom signifies the representation—the realization—of a phantasy with a sexual content, that is to say, it signifies a sexual situation. It would be better to say that at least *one* of the meanings of a symptom is the

2. [Later, however, Freud took a very different view of the therapeutic difficulties in cases of *unconscious* desire for self-punishment. See, e.g., Chapter V of *The Ego and the Id* (1923*b*).]

representation of a sexual phantasy, but that no such limitation
is imposed upon the content of its other meanings. Any one who
takes up psycho-analytic work will quickly discover that a symptom
has more than one meaning and serves to represent several unconscious mental processes simultaneously. And I should like to
add that in my estimation a single unconscious mental process
or phantasy will scarcely ever suffice for the production of a
symptom.

An opportunity very soon occurred for interpreting Dora's nervous cough in this way by means of an imagined sexual situation.
She had once again been insisting that Frau K. only loved her
father because he was *'ein vermögender Mann'* ['a man of means'].
Certain details of the way in which she expressed herself (which
I pass over here, like most other purely technical parts of the
analysis) led me to see that behind this phrase its opposite lay
concealed, namely, that her father was *'ein unvermögender Mann'*
['a man without means']. This could only be meant in a sexual
sense—that her father, as a man, was without means, was impotent.[3] Dora confirmed this interpretation from her conscious
knowledge; whereupon I pointed out the contradiction she was
involved in if on the one hand she continued to insist that her
father's relation with Frau K. was a common love-affair, and on
the other hand maintained that her father was impotent, or in
other words incapable of carrying on an affair of such a kind. Her
answer showed that she had no need to admit the contradiction.
She knew very well, she said, that there was more than one way
of obtaining sexual gratification. (The source of this piece of
knowledge, however, was once more untraceable.) I questioned
her further, whether she referred to the use of organs other than
the genitals for the purpose of sexual intercourse, and she replied
in the affirmative. I could then go on to say that in that case she
must be thinking of precisely those parts of the body which in
her case were in a state of irritation,—the throat and the oral
cavity. To be sure, she would not hear of going so far as this in
recognizing her own thoughts; and indeed, if the occurrence of
the symptom was to be made possible at all, it was essential that
she should not be completely clear on the subject. But the conclusion was inevitable that with her spasmodic cough, which, as

3. ['*Unvermögend*' means literally 'unable', and is commonly used in the sense
of both 'not rich' and 'impotent'.]

is usual, was referred for its exciting stimulus to a tickling in her throat, she pictured to herself a scene of sexual gratification *per os*[4] between the two people whose love-affair occupied her mind so incessantly. A very short time after she had tacitly accepted this explanation her cough vanished—which fitted in very well with my view; but I do not wish to lay too much stress upon this development, since her cough had so often before disappeared spontaneously. * * *

The less repellent of the so-called sexual perversions are very widely diffused among the whole population, as every one knows except medical writers upon the subject. Or, I should rather say, they know it too; only they take care to forget it at the moment when they take up their pens to write about it. So it is not to be wondered at that this hysterical girl of nearly nineteen, who had heard of the occurrence of such a method of sexual intercourse (sucking at the male organ), should have developed an unconscious phantasy of this sort and should have given it expression by an irritation in her throat and by coughing. Nor would it have been very extraordinary if she had arrived at such a phantasy even without having had any enlightenment from external sources—an occurrence which I have quite certainly observed in other patients. For in her case a noteworthy fact afforded the necessary somatic prerequisite for this independent creation of a phantasy which would coincide with the practices of perverts. She remembered very well that in her childhood she had been a thumb-sucker. Her father, too, recollected breaking her of the habit after it had persisted into her fourth or fifth year. Dora herself had a clear picture of a scene from her early childhood in which she was sitting on the floor in a corner sucking her left thumb and at the same time tugging with her right hand at the lobe of her brother's ear as he sat quietly beside her. Here we have an instance of the complete form of self-gratification by sucking, as it has also been described to me by other patients, who had subsequently become anaesthetic and hysterical.

One of these patients gave me a piece of information which sheds a clear light on the origin of this curious habit. This young woman had never broken herself of the habit of sucking. She

4. {"By mouth," i.e., *fellatio*, penis-sucking.}

retained a memory of her childhood, dating back, according to
her, to the first half of her second year, in which she saw herself
sucking at her nurse's breast and at the same time pulling rhythmically at the lobe of her nurse's ear. No one will feel inclined to
dispute, I think, that the mucous membrane of the lips and mouth
is to be regarded as a primary 'erotogenic zone',[5] since it preserves
this earlier significance in the act of kissing, which is looked upon
as normal. An intense activity of this erotogenic zone at an early
age thus determines the subsequent presence of a somatic compliance on the part of the tract of mucous membrane which begins
at the lips. Thus, at a time when the sexual object proper, that
is, the male organ, has already become known, circumstances
may arise which once more increase the excitation of the oral
zone, whose erotogenic character has, as we have seen, been
retained. It then needs very little creative power to substitute the
sexual object of the moment (the penis) for the original object
(the nipple) or for the finger which does duty for it, and to place
the current sexual object in the situation in which gratification
was originally obtained. So we see that this excessively repulsive
and perverted phantasy of sucking at a penis has the most innocent
origin. It is a new version of what may be described as a prehistoric impression of sucking at the mother's or nurse's breast—
an impression which has usually been revived by contact with
children who are being nursed. In most instances a cow's udder
has aptly played the part of an image intermediate between a
nipple and a penis.

The interpretation we have just been discussing of Dora's throat
symptoms may also give rise to a further remark. It may be asked
how this sexual situation imagined by her can be compatible with
our other explanation of the symptoms. That explanation, it will
be remembered, was to the effect that the coming and going of
the symptoms reflected the presence and absence of the man she
was in love with, and, as regards his wife's behaviour, expressed
the following thought: 'If *I* were his wife, I should love him in
quite a different way; I should be ill (from longing, let us say)
when he was away, and well (from joy) when he was home again.'

5. [Cf. Section 5 of the first of Freud's *Three Essays* (1905).]

To this objection I must reply that my experience in the clearing-up of hysterical symptoms has shown that it is not necessary for the various meanings of a symptom to be compatible with one another, that is, to fit together into a connected whole. It is enough that the unity should be constituted by the subject-matter which has given rise to all the various phantasies. In the present case, moreover, compatibility even of the first kind is not out of the question. One of the two meanings is related more to the cough, and the other to the aphonia and the periodicity of the disorder. A closer analysis would probably have disclosed a far greater number of mental elements in relation to the details of the illness.

We have already learnt that it quite regularly happens that a single symptom corresponds to several meanings *simultaneously*. We may now add that it can express several meanings *in succession*. In the course of years a symptom can change its meaning or its chief meaning, or the leading role can pass from one meaning to another. It is as though there were a conservative trait in the character of neuroses which ensures that a symptom that has once been formed shall if possible be retained, even though the unconscious thought to which it gave expression has lost its meaning. Moreover, there is no difficulty in explaining this tendency towards the retention of a symptom upon a mechanical basis. The production of a symptom of this kind is so difficult, the translation of a purely psychical excitation into physical terms—the process which I have called 'conversion'—depends on the concurrence of so many favourable conditions, the somatic compliance necessary for conversion is so seldom forthcoming, that an impulsion towards the discharge of an unconscious excitation will so far as possible make use of any channel for discharge which may already be in existence. It appears to be far more difficult to create a fresh conversion than to form paths of association between a new thought which is in need of discharge and the old one which is no longer in need of it. The current flows along these paths from the new source of excitation to the old point of discharge—pouring into the symptom, in the words of the Gospel, like new wine into an old bottle. These remarks would make it seem that the somatic side of a hysterical symptom is the more stable of the two and the harder to replace, while the psychical side is a variable element for which a substitute can more easily be found. Yet we should not try to infer anything from this comparison as regards the relative importance of the two elements. From the point of view of mental therapeutics the mental side must always be the more significant.

Dora's incessant repetition of the same thoughts about her father's relations with Frau K. made it possible to derive still further important material from the analysis.

A train of thought such as this may be described as excessively intense, or better *reinforced*, or 'supervalent' [*'überwertig'*] * * * It shows its pathological character in spite of its apparently reasonable content, by the single peculiarity that no amount of conscious and voluntary effort of thought on the patient's part is able to dissipate or remove it. A normal train of thought, however intense it may be, can eventually be disposed of. Dora felt quite rightly that her thoughts about her father required to be judged in a special way. 'I think of nothing else', she complained again and again. 'I know my brother says we children have no right to criticize this behaviour of Father's. He declares that we ought not to trouble ourselves about it, and ought even to be glad, perhaps, that he has found a woman he can love, since Mother understands him so little. I can quite see that, and I should like to think the same as my brother, but I can't. I can't forgive him for it.'[6]

Now what is one to do in the face of a supervalent thought like this, after one has heard what its conscious grounds are and listened to the ineffectual protests made against it? Reflection will suggest that *this excessively intense train of thought must owe its reinforcement to the unconscious.* It cannot be resolved by any effort of thought, either because it itself reaches with its root down into unconscious, repressed material, or because another unconscious thought lies concealed behind it. In the latter case, the concealed thought is usually the direct contrary of the supervalent one. Contrary thoughts are always closely connected with each other and are often paired off in such a way that *the one thought is excessively intensely conscious while its counterpart is repressed and unconscious.* This relation between the two thoughts is an effect on the process of repression. For repression is often achieved by means of an excessive reinforcement of the thought contrary

6. A supervalent thought of this kind is often the only symptom, beyond deep depression, of a pathological condition which is usually described as 'melancholia', but which can be cleared up by psycho-analysis like a hysteria.

to the one which is to be repressed. This process I call *reactive reinforcement*, and the thought which asserts itself with excessive intensity in consciousness and (in the same way as a prejudice) cannot be removed I call a *reactive thought*. The two thoughts then act towards each other much like the two needles of an astatic galvanometer. The reactive thought keeps the objectionable one under repression by means of a certain surplus of intensity; but for that reason it itself is 'damped' and proof against conscious efforts of thought. So that the way to deprive the excessively intense thought of its reinforcement is by bringing its repressed contrary into consciousness.

We must also be prepared to meet with instances in which the supervalence of a thought is due not to the presence of one only of these two causes but to a concurrence of both of them. Other complications, too, may arise, but they can easily be fitted into the general scheme. * * *

I must now turn to consider a further complication to which I should certainly give no space if I were a man of letters engaged upon the creation of a mental state like this for a short story, instead of being a medical man engaged upon its dissection. The element to which I must now allude can only serve to obscure and efface the outlines of the fine poetic conflict which we have been able to ascribe to Dora. This element would rightly fall a sacrifice to the censorship of a writer, for he, after all, simplifies and abstracts when he appears in the character of a psychologist. But in the world of reality, which I am trying to depict here, a complication of motives, an accumulation and conjunction of mental activies—in a word, overdetermination—is the rule. For behind Dora's supervalent train of thought which was concerned with her father's relations with Frau K. there lay concealed a feeling of jealousy which had that lady as its *object*—a feeling, that is, which could only be based upon an affection on Dora's part for one of her own sex. It has long been known and often been pointed out that at the age of puberty boys and girls show clear signs, even in normal cases, of the existence of an affection for people of their own sex. A romantic and sentimental friendship with one of her school-friends, accompanied by vows, kisses, promises of eternal correspondence, and all the sensibility of jealousy, is the common precursor of a girl's first serious passion for a man. Thenceforward, in favourable circumstances, the homo-

sexual current of feeling often runs completely dry. But if a girl
is not happy in her love for a man, the current is often set flowing
again by the libido in later years and is increased up to a greater
or lesser degree of intensity. If this much can be established without difficulty of healthy persons, and if we take into account what
has already been said about the fuller development in neurotics
of the normal germs of perversion, we shall expect to find in these
latter too a fairly strong homosexual predisposition. It must, indeed, be so; for I have never yet come through a single psycho-
analysis of a man or a woman without having to take into account
a very considerable current of homosexuality. When, in a hysterical woman or girl, the sexual libido which is directed towards
men has been energetically suppressed, it will regularly be found
that the libido which is directed towards women has become
vicariously reinforced and even to some extent conscious.

I shall not in this place go any further into this important
subject, which is especially indispensable to an understanding of
hysteria in men, because Dora's analysis came to an end before
it could throw any light on this side of her mental life. But I
should like to recall the governess, whom I have already mentioned, and with whom Dora had at first enjoyed the closest
interchange of thought, until she discovered that she was being
admired and fondly treated not for her own sake but for her father's;
whereupon she had obliged the governess to leave. She used also
to dwell with noticeable frequency and a peculiar emphasis on
the story of another estrangement which appeared inexplicable
even to herself. She had always been on particularly good terms
with the younger of her two cousins—the girl who had later on
become engaged—and had shared all sorts of secrets with her.
When, for the first time after Dora had broken off her stay by
the lake, her father was going back to B——, she had naturally
refused to go with him. This cousin had then been asked to travel
with him instead, and she had accepted the invitation. From the
time forward Dora had felt a coldness towards her, and she herself
was surprised to find how indifferent she had become, although,
as she admitted, she had very little ground for complaint against
her. These instances of sensitiveness led me to inquire what her
relations with Frau K. had been up till the time of the breach. I
then found that the young woman and the scarcely grown girl
had lived for years on a footing of the closest intimacy. When
Dora stayed with the K.'s she used to share a bedroom with Frau

K., and the husband used to be quartered elsewhere. She had been the wife's confidante and adviser in all the difficulties of her married life. There was nothing they had not talked about. Medea had been quite content that Creusa should make friends with her two children; and she certainly did nothing to interfere with the relations between the girl and the children's father.[7] How Dora managed to fall in love with the man about whom her beloved friend had so many bad things to say is an interesting psychological problem. We shall not be far from solving it when we realize that thoughts in the unconscious live very comfortably side by side, and even contraries get on together without disputes—a state of things which persists often enough even in the conscious.

When Dora talked about Frau K., she used to praise her 'adorable white body' in accents more appropriate to a lover than to a defeated rival. Another time she told me, more in sorrow than in anger, that she was convinced the presents her father had brought her had been chosen by Frau K., for she recognized her taste. Another time, again, she pointed out that, evidently through the agency of Frau K., she had been given a present of some jewellery which was exactly like some that she had seen in Frau K.'s possession and had wished for aloud at the time. Indeed, I can say in general that I never heard her speak a harsh or angry word against the lady, although from the point of view of her supervalent thought she should have regarded her as the prime author of her misfortunes. She seemed to behave inconsequently; but her apparent inconsequence was precisely the manifestation of a complicating current of feeling. For how had this woman to whom Dora was so enthusiastically devoted behaved to her? After Dora had brought forward her accusation against Herr K., and her father had written to him and had asked for an explanation, Herr K. had replied in the first instance by protesting sentiments of the highest esteem for her and by proposing that he should come to the manufacturing town to clear up every misunderstanding. A few weeks later, when her father spoke to him at B——, there was no longer any question of esteem. On the contrary, Herr K. spoke of her with disparagement, and produced as his

7. {Medea, in Euripides' play of the same name, tolerates her husband's mistress Creusa but becomes enraged when he decides to marry the girl. She wreaks a terrible revenge on Jason by murdering not only Creusa but her own two sons, Jason's heirs.}

trump card the reflection that no girl who read such books and was interested in such things could have any title to a man's respect. Frau K., therefore, had betrayed her and had calumniated her; for it had only been with her that she had read Mantegazza and discussed forbidden topics. It was a repetition of what had happened with the governess: Frau K. had not loved her for her own sake but on account of her father. Frau K. had sacrificed her without a moment's hesitation so that her relations with her father might not be disturbed. This mortification touched her, perhaps, more nearly and had a greater pathogenic effect than the other one, which she tried to use as a screen for it,—the fact that she had been sacrificed by her father. Did not the obstinacy with which she retained the particular amnesia concerning the sources of her forbidden knowledge point directly to the great emotional importance for her of the accusation against her upon that score, and consequently to her betrayal by her friend?

I believe, therefore, that I am not mistaken in supposing that Dora's supervalent train of thought, which was concerned with her father's relations with Frau K., was designed not only for the purpose of suppressing her love for Herr K., which had once been conscious, but also to conceal her love for Frau K., which was in a deeper sense unconscious. The supervalent train of thought was directly contrary to the latter current of feeling. She told herself incessantly that her father had sacrificed her to this woman, and made noisy demonstrations to show that she grudged her the possession of her father; and in this way she concealed from herself the contrary fact, which was that she grudged her father Frau K.'s love, and had not forgiven the woman she loved for the disillusionment she had been caused by her betrayal. The jealous emotions of a woman were linked in the unconscious with a jealousy such as might have been felt by a man. These masculine or, more properly speaking, *gynaecophilic* currents of feeling are to be regarded as typical of the unconscious erotic life of hysterical girls.

In Freud's full text, "The Clinical Picture," from which the selections above came, was succeeded by two long sections in which Dora's dreams are analyzed. Many details are added to the case, and the technique of dream interpretation is both presented in operation and discussed. The full text then concludes with a "Postscript," one portion of which follows. This is Freud's first major discussion of "transference" as a factor in the therapeutic process of psychoanalysis.

* * * I must go back a little, in order to make the matter intelligible. It may be safely said that during psycho-analytic treatment the formation of new symptoms is invariably stopped. But the productive powers of the neurosis are by no means extinguished; they are occupied in the creation of a special class of mental structures, for the most part unconscious, to which the name of *'transferences'* may be given.

What are transferences? They are new editions or facsimiles of the impulses and phantasies which are aroused and made conscious during the progress of the analysis; but they have this peculiarity, which is characteristic for their species, that they replace some earlier person by the person of the physician. To put it another way: a whole series of psychological experiences are revived, not as belonging to the past, but as applying to the person of the physician at the present moment. Some of these transferences have a content which differs from that of their model in no respect whatever except for the substitution. These then—to keep to the same metaphor—are merely new impressions or reprints. Others are more ingeniously constructed; their content has been subjected to a moderating influence—to *sublimation*, as I call it and they may even become conscious, by cleverly taking advantage of some real peculiarity in the physician's person or circumstances and attaching themselves to that. These, then, will no longer be new impressions, but revised editions.

If the theory of analytic technique is gone into, it becomes evident that transference is an inevitable necessity. Practical experience, at all events, shows conclusively that there is no means of avoiding it, and that this latest creation of the disease must be combated like all the earlier ones. This happens, however, to be by far the hardest part of the whole task. It is easy to learn how to interpret dreams, to extract from the patient's associations his unconscious thoughts and memories, and to practise similar explanatory arts: for these the patient himself will always provide the text. Transference is the one thing the presence of which has to be detected almost without assistance and with only the slightest clues to go upon, while at the same time the risk of making arbitrary inferences has to be avoided. Nevertheless, transference cannot be evaded, since use is made of it in setting up all the obstacles that make the material inaccesible to treatment, and since it is only after the transference has been resolved that a patient arrives at a sense of conviction of the validity of the connections which have been constructed during the analysis.

Some people may feel inclined to look upon it as a serious objection to a method which is in any case troublesome enough that it itself should multiply the labours of the physician by creating a new species of pathological mental products. They may even be tempted to infer from the existence of transference that the patient will be injured by analytic treatment. Both these suppositions would be mistaken. The physician's labours are not multiplied by transference; it need make no difference to him whether he has to overcome any particular impulse of the patient's in connection with himself or with someone else. Nor does the treatment force upon the patient, in the shape of transference, any new task which he would not otherwise have performed. It is true that neuroses may be cured in institutions from which psycho-analytic treatment is excluded, that hysteria may be said to be cured not by the method but by the physician, and that there is usually a sort of blind dependence and a permanent bond between a patient and the physician who has removed his symptoms by hypnotic suggestion; but the scientific explanation of all these facts is to be found in the existence of 'transferences' such as are regularly directed by patients on to their physicians. Psycho-analytic treatment does not *create* transferences, it merely brings them to light, like so many other hidden psychical factors. The only difference is this—that spontaneously a patient will only call up affectionate and friendly transferences to help towards his recovery; if they cannot be called up, he feels the physician is 'antipathetic' to him, and breaks away from him as fast as possible and without having been influenced by him. In psycho-analysis, on the other hand, since the play of motives is different, all the patient's tendencies, including hostile ones, are aroused; they are then turned to account for the purposes of the analysis by being made conscious, and in this way the transference is constantly being destroyed. Transference, which seems ordained to be the greatest obstacle to psycho-analysis, becomes its most powerful ally, if its presence can be detected each time and explained to the patient.[8]

---

8. [*Footnote added* 1923:] A continuation of these remarks upon transference is contained in my technical paper on 'transference-love' (Freud, 1915a) [and in the earlier and more theoretical paper on "The Dynamics of Transference' (1912b). * * *

I have been obliged to speak of transference, for it is only by means of this factor that I can elucidate the peculiarities of Dora's analysis. Its great merit, namely, the unusual clarity which makes it seem so suitable as a first introductory publication, is closely bound up with its great defect, which led to its being broken off prematurely. I did not succeed in mastering the transference in good time. Owing to the readiness with which Dora put one part of the pathogenic material at my disposal during the treatment, I neglected the precaution of looking out for the first signs of transference, which was being prepared in connection with another part of the same material—a part of which I was in ignorance. At the beginning it was clear that I was replacing her father in her imagination, which was not unlikely, in view of the difference between our ages. She was even constantly comparing me with him consciously, and kept anxiously trying to make sure whether I was being quite straightforward with her, for her father 'always preferred secrecy and roundabout ways'. But when the first dream came, in which she gave herself the warning that she had better leave my treatment just as she had formerly left Herr K.'s house, I ought to have listened to the warning myself. 'Now,' I ought to have said to her, 'it is from Herr K. that you have made a transference on to me. Have you noticed anything that leads you to suspect me of evil intentions similar (whether openly or in some sublimated form) to Herr K.'s? Or have you been struck by anything about me or got to know anything about me which has caught your fancy, as happened previously with Herr K.?' Her attention would then have been turned to some detail in our relations, or in my person or circumstances, behind which there lay concealed something analogous but immeasurably more important concerning Herr K. And when this transference had been cleared up, the analysis would have obtained access to new memories, dealing, probably, with actual events. But I was deaf to this first note of warning, thinking I had ample time before me, since no further stages of transference developed and the material for the analysis had not yet run dry. In this way the transference took me unawares, and, because of the unknown quantity in me which reminded Dora of Herr K., she took her revenge on me as she wanted to take her revenge on him, and deserted me as she believed herself to have been deceived and deserted by him. Thus she *acted out* an essential part of her recollections and phantasies instead of reproducing it in the treatment. What this unknown quantity was I naturally cannot tell. I suspect that it had to do with money, or with jealousy of another patient who had kept up relations with my family after her recovery. When it is possible to work transferences into the analysis at an early stage, the course of the analysis is retarded and obscured, but its existence is better guaranteed against sudden and overwhelming resistances.

In Dora's second dream there are several clear allusions to transference. * * * {The message of these allusions, taken collectively} was, no doubt: 'Men are all so detestable that I would rather not marry. This is my revenge.'[9]

If cruel impulses and revengeful motives, which have already been used in the patient's ordinary life for maintaining her symptoms, become transferred on to the physician during treatment, before he has had time to detach them from himself by tracing them back to their sources, then it is not to be wondered at if the patient's condition is unaffected by his therapeutic efforts. For how could the patient take a more effective revenge than by demonstrating upon her own person the helplessness and incapacity of the physician? Nevertheless, I am not inclined to put too low a value on the therapeutic results even of such a fragmentary treatment as Dora's. * * *

---

9. The longer the interval of time that separates me from the end of this analysis, the more probable it seems to me that the fault in my technique lay in this omission: I failed to discover in time and to inform the patient that her homosexual (gynaecophilic) love for Frau K. was the strongest unconscious current in her mental life. I ought to have guessed that the main source of her knowledge of sexual matters could have been no one but Frau K.—the very person who later on charged her with being interested in those same subjects. Her knowing all about such things and, at the same time, her always pretending not to know where her knowledge came from was really too remarkable. I ought to have attached this riddle and looked for the motive of such an extraordinary piece of repression. * * * Before I had learnt the importance of the homosexual current of feeling in psychoneurotics, I was often brought to a standstill in the treatment of my cases or found myself in complete perplexity.

Three Essays on
The Theory of Sexuality

F reud's Three Essays on the Theory of Sexuality *is the touchstone for all his subsequent discussions of female psychology. He presented all his later statements as elaborations of or emendations to the views in this 1905 text.*

The prefaces (not included here), which Freud provided to the second (1910), third (1915) and fourth (1920) editions of his Three Essays on the Theory of Sexuality *stress that the essays deal with matters psychological and not biological, and that they are the product of psychoanalytic investigation, not of medical practice or observation. Freud notes (1915) that "the phylogenetic disposition can be seen at work behind the ontogenetic disposition," that is, that individuals have inherited traits, but his essays are not designed to take any characteristics of phylogeny or species formation into account.*

The three essays—one on sexual aberrations, one on infantile sexuality, and one on sexual life in puberty—have been abridged for this edition, and many notes added to the text both by Freud and Strachey have been eliminated. The remaining notes do, however, make clear how Freud's developing views were reflected in the various editions: and they particularly indicate how the changes in his instinct theory and his investigations of narcissism, discussed in my Introduction, influenced the 1915 and 1920 editions of the essays. It is important to remember that Freud did not revise Three Essays *to incorporate the conclusions he reached in his 1925, 1931, and 1933 papers dedicated specifically to female psychology.*

Essay I. The Sexual Aberrations

The fact of the existence of sexual needs in human beings and animals is expressed in biology by the assumption of a 'sexual instinct', on the analogy of the instinct of nutrition, that is of hunger. Everyday language possesses no counterpart to the word 'hunger', but science makes use of the word 'libido' for that purpose.

Popular opinion has quite definite ideas about the nature and characteristics of this sexual instinct. It is generally understood to be absent in childhood, to set in at the time of puberty in connection with the process of coming to maturity and to be revealed in the manifestations of an irresistible attraction exercised by one sex upon the other; while its aim is presumed to be sexual union, or at all events actions leading in that direction. We have every reason to believe, however, that these views give a very false picture of the true situation. If we look into them more closely we shall find that they contain a number of errors, inaccuracies and hasty conclusions.

I shall at this point introduce two technical terms. Let us call the person from whom sexual attraction proceeds the *sexual object* and the act towards which the instinct tends the *sexual aim*. Scientifically sifted observation, then, shows that numerous deviations occur in respect of both of these—the sexual object and the sexual aim. The relation between these deviations and what is assumed to be normal requires thorough investigation.

1. Deviations in Respect of the Sexual Object

The popular view of the sexual instinct is beautifully reflected in the poetic fable which tells how the original human beings were cut up into two halves—man and woman—and how these are always striving to unite again in love. It comes as a great surprise therefore to learn that there are men whose sexual object is a man and not a woman, and women whose sexual object is a woman and not a man. People of this kind are described as having 'contrary sexual feelings', or better, as being 'inverts', and the fact is described as 'inversion'. The number of such people is very considerable, though there are difficulties in establishing it precisely.

At the beginning of this subsection, Freud discusses three types of "in-verts": those who take as their exclusive sexual objects members of their own sex ("absolute inverts"): those whose objects may equally well be of their own or the opposite sex ("psychosexual hermaphrodites"): and those who take members of their own sex as objects only under certain limited circumstances, usually when opposite-sex objects are not available. In-verts have different attitudes of acceptance or rebellion in relation to their preferences; and both their preferences and their attitudes can os-cillate or change over time.

Freud's assessment of causality was careful. First he rejected the idea that inversion was a form of degeneracy, because it was so obvious that many—if not most—inverts functioned at a superior level intellectually, particularly in societies where inversion was not considered pathological. Then he indicated that only in absolute inverts can a constitutional or innate factor be argued as crucial, but even in these cases, it is likely that the innate factor is one common to all people, not just to inverts—namely, bisexuality. Freud's discussion of bisexuality and the remainder of this subsection follows.

* * * It is popularly believed that a human being is either a man or a woman. Science, however, knows of cases in which the sexual characters are obscured, and in which it is consequently difficult to determine the sex. This arises in the first instance in the field of anatomy. The genitals of the individuals concerned combine male and female characteristics. (This condition is known as her-maphroditism.) In rare cases both kinds of sexual apparatus are found side by side fully developed (true hermaphroditism); but far more frequently both sets of organs are found in an atrophied condition.

The importance of these abnormalities lies in the unexpected fact that they facilitate our understanding of normal development. For it appears that a certain degree of anatomical hermaphroditism occurs normally. In every normal male or female individual, traces are found of the apparatus of the opposite sex. These either persist without function as rudimentary organs or become mod-ified and take on other functions.

These long-familiar facts of anatomy lead us to suppose that an originally bisexual physical disposition has, in the course of evolution, become modified into a unisexual one, leaving behind only a few traces of the sex that has become atrophied.

It was tempting to extend this hypothesis to the mental sphere and to explain inversion in all its varieties as the expression of a

psychical hermaphroditism. All that was required further in order
to settle the question was that inversion should be regularly accompanied by the mental and somatic signs of hermaphroditism.

But this expectation was disappointed. It is impossible to demonstrate so close a connection between the hypothetical psychical
hermaphroditism and the established anatomical one. A general
lowering of the sexual instinct and a slight anatomical atrophy of
the organs is found frequently in inverts (cf. Havelock Ellis, 1915).
Frequently, but by no means regularly or even usually. The truth
must therefore be recognized that inversion and somatic hermaphroditism are on the whole independent of each other.

A great deal of importance, too, has been attached to what are
called the secondary and tertiary sexual characters and to the great
frequency of the occurrence of those of the opposite sex in inverts.
Much of this, again, is correct; but it should never be forgotten
that in general the secondary and tertiary sexual characters of one
sex occur very frequently in the opposite one. They are indications
of hermaphroditism, but are not attended by any change of sexual
object in the direction of inversion.

Psychical hermaphroditism would gain substance if the inversion of the sexual object were at least accompanied by a parallel
change-over of the subject's other mental qualities, instincts and
character traits into those marking the opposite sex. But it is only
in inverted women that character-inversion of this kind can be
looked for with any regularity. In men the most complete mental
masculinity can be combined with inversion. If the belief in
psychical hermaphroditism is to be persisted in, it will be necessary
to add that its manifestations in various spheres show only slight
signs of being mutually determined. Moreover the same is true
of somatic hermaphroditism: according to Halban (1903), occurrences of individual atrophied organs and of secondary sexual
characters are to a considerable extent independent of one
another.

The theory of bisexuality has been expressed in its crudest form
by a spokesman of the male inverts: 'a feminine brain in a masculine body'. But we are ignorant of what characterizes a feminine
brain * * * According to Krafft-Ebing, every individual's bisexual
disposition endows him with masculine and feminine brain
centres as well as with somatic organs of sex; these centres develop
only at puberty, for the most part under the influence of the sex-
gland, which is independent of them in the original disposition.

But what has just been said of masculine and feminine brains applies equally to masculine and feminine 'centres'; and incidentally we have not even any grounds for assuming that certain areas of the brain ('centres') are set aside for the functions of sex, as is the case, for instance, with those of speech.

Nevertheless, two things emerge from these discussions. In the first place, a bisexual disposition is somehow concerned in inversion, though we do not know in what that disposition consists, beyond anatomical structure. And secondly, we have to deal with disturbances that affect the sexual instinct in the course of its development.

Sexual Object of Inverts　The theory of psychical hermaphroditism presupposes that the sexual object of an invert is the opposite of that of a normal person. An inverted man, it holds, is like a woman in being subject to the charm that proceeds from masculine attributes both physical and mental: he feels he is a woman in search of a man.

But however well this applies to quite a number of inverts, it is, nevertheless, far from revealing a universal characteristic of inversion. There can be no doubt that a large proportion of male inverts retain the mental quality of masculinity, that they possess relatively few of the secondary characters of the opposite sex and that what they look for in their sexual object are in fact feminine mental traits. If this were not so, how would it be possible to explain the fact that male prostitutes who offer themselves to inverts—to-day just as they did in ancient times—imitate women in all the externals of their clothing and behaviour? Such imitation would otherwise inevitably clash with the ideal of the inverts. It is clear that in Greece, where the most masculine men were numbered among the inverts, what excited a man's love was not the *masculine* character of a boy, but his physical resemblance to a woman as well as his feminine mental qualities—his shyness, his modesty and his need for instruction and assistance. As soon as the boy became a man he ceased to be a sexual object for men and himself, perhaps, became a lover of boys. In this instance, therefore, as in many others, the sexual object is not someone of the same sex but someone who combines the characters of both sexes; there is, as it were, a compromise between an impulse that seeks for a man and one that seeks for a woman, while it remains a paramount condition that the object's body (i.e. genitals) shall be masculine. Thus the sexual object is a kind of reflection of the subject's own bisexual nature.[1]

The position in the case of women is less ambiguous; for among them the active inverts exhibit masculine characteristics, both physical and mental, with peculiar frequency and look for femininity in their sexual objects—though here again a closer knowledge of the facts might reveal greater variety.

1. [This last sentence was added in 1915.—*Footnote added* 1910:] It is true that psycho-analysis has not yet produced a complete explanation of the origin of inversion; nevertheless, it has discovered the psychical mechanism of its development, and has made essential contributions to the statement of the problems involved. In all the cases we have examined we have established the fact that the future inverts, in the earliest years of their childhood, pass through a phase of very intense but short-lived fixation to a woman (usually their mother), and that, after leaving this behind, they identify themselves with a woman and take *themselves* as their sexual object. That is to say, they proceed from a narcissistic basis, and look for a young man who resembles themselves and whom *they* may love as their mother loved *them*. Moreover, we have frequently found that alleged inverts have been by no means insusceptible to the charms of women, but have continually transposed the excitation aroused by women on to a male object. They have thus repeated all through their lives the mechanism by which their inversion arose. Their compulsive longing for men has turned out to be determined by their ceaseless flight from women.

[*Added* 1915:] Psycho-analytic research is most decidedly opposed to any attempt at separating off homosexuals from the rest of mankind as a group of a special character. By studying sexual excitations other than those that are manifestly displayed, it has found that all human beings are capable of making a homosexual object-choice and have in fact made one in their unconscious. Indeed, libidinal attachments to persons of the same sex play no less a part as factors in normal mental life, and a greater part as a motive force for illness, than do similar attachments to the opposite sex. On the contrary, psycho-analysis considers that a choice of an object independently of its sex—freedom to range equally over male and female objects—as it is found in childhood, in primitive states of society and early periods of history, is the original basis from which, as a result of restriction in one direction or the other, both the normal and the inverted types develop. Thus from the point of view of psycho-analysis the exclusive sexual interest felt by men for women is also a problem that needs elucidating and is not a self-evident fact based upon an attraction that is ultimately of a chemical nature. A person's final sexual attitude is not decided until after puberty and is the result of a number of factors, not all of which are yet known; some are of a constitutional nature but others are accidental. No doubt a few of these factors may happen to carry so much weight that they influence the results in their sense. But in general the multiplicity of determining factors is reflected in the variety of manifest sexual attitudes in which they find their issue in mankind. In inverted types, a predominance of

Sexual Aim of Inverts The important fact to bear in mind is that no one single aim can be laid down as applying in cases of inversion. Among men, intercourse *per anum* by no means coincides with inversion; masturbation is quite as frequently their exclusive aim, and it is even true that restrictions of sexual aim— to the point of its being limited to simple outpourings of emotion—are commoner among them than among heterosexual lovers. Among women, too, the sexual aims of inverts are various:

---

archaic constitutions and primitive psychical mechanisms is regularly to be found. Their most essential characteristics seem to be a coming into operation of narcissistic object-choice and a retention of the erotic significance of the anal zone. There is nothing to be gained, however, by separating the most extreme types of inversion from the rest on the basis of constitutional peculiarities of that kind. What we find as an apparently sufficient explanation of these types can be equally shown to be present, though less strongly, in the constitution of transitional types and of those whose manifest attitude is normal. The differences in the end-products may be of a qualitative nature, but analysis shows that the differences between their determinants are only quantitative. Among the accidental factors that influence object-choice we have found that frustration (in the form of an early deterrence, by fear, from sexual activity) deserves attention, and we have observed that the presence of both parents plays an important part. The absence of a strong father in childhood not infrequently favours the occurrence of inversion. Finally, it may be insisted that the concept of inversion in respect of the sexual object should be sharply distinguished from that of the occurrence in the subject of a mixture of sexual characters. In the relation between these two factors, too, a certain degree of reciprocal independence is unmistakably present.

[*Added* 1920:] Ferenczi (1914) has brought forward a number of interesting points on the subject of inversion. He rightly protests that, because they have in common the symptom of inversion, a large number of conditions, which are very different from one another and which are of unequal importance both in organic and psychical respects, have been thrown together under the name of 'homosexuality' (or, to follow him in giving it a better name, 'Homoerotism'). He insists that a sharp distinction should at least be made between two types: 'subject homo-erotics', who feel and behave like women, and 'object homo-erotics', who are completely masculine and who have merely exchanged a female for a male object. The first of these two types he recognizes as true 'sexual intermediates' in Hirschfeld's sense of the word; the second he describes, less happily, as obsessional neurotics. According to him, it is only in the case of object homo-erotics that there is any question of their struggling against their inclination to inversion or of the possibility of their being influenced psychologically. While granting the existence of these two types, we may add that there are many people in whom a certain quantity of subject homo-erotism is found in combination with a proportion of object homo-erotism. * * *

there seems to be a special preference for contact with the mucous membrane of the mouth.

Conclusion   It will be seen that we are not in a position to base a satisfactory explanation of the origin of inversion upon the material at present before us. Nevertheless our investigation has put us in possession of a piece of knowledge which may turn out to be of greater importance to us than the solution of that problem. It has been brought to our notice that we have been in the habit of regarding the connection between the sexual instinct and the sexual object as more intimate than it in fact is. Experience of the cases that are considered abnormal has shown us that in them the sexual instinct and the sexual object are merely soldered together—a fact which we have been in danger of overlooking in consequence of the uniformity of the normal picture, where the object appears to form part and parcel of the instinct. We are thus warned to loosen the bond that exists in our thoughts between instinct and object. It seems probable that the sexual instinct is in the first instance independent of its object; nor is its origin likely to be due to its object's attractions.

(B) Sexually Immature Persons and Animals as Sexual Objects
People whose sexual objects belong to the normally inappropriate sex—that is, inverts—strike the observer as a collection of individuals who may be quite sound in other respects. On the other hand, cases in which sexually immature persons (children) are chosen as sexual objects are instantly judged as sporadic aberrations. It is only exceptionally that children are the exclusive sexual objects in such a case. They usually come to play that part when someone who is cowardly or has become impotent adopts them as a substitute, or when an urgent instinct (one which will not allow of postponement) cannot at the moment get possession of any more appropriate object. Nevertheless, a light is thrown on the nature of the sexual instinct by the fact that it permits of so much variation in its objects and such a cheapening of them— which hunger, with its far more energetic retention of its objects, would only permit in the most extreme instances. A similar consideration applies to sexual intercourse with animals, which is by no means rare, especially among country people, and in which sexual attraction seems to override the barriers of species.

One would be glad on aesthetic grounds to be able to ascribe these and other severe aberrations of the sexual instinct to insanity; but that cannot be done. Experience shows that disturbances of the sexual instinct among the insane do not differ from those that occur among the healthy and in whole races or occupations. Thus the sexual abuse of children is found with uncanny frequency among school teachers and child attendants, simply because they have the best opportunity for it. The insane merely exhibit any such aberration to an intensified degree; or, what is particularly significant, it may become exclusive and replace normal sexual satisfaction entirely. * * *

The most general conclusion that follows from all these discussions seems, however, to be this. Under a great number of conditions and in surprisingly numerous individuals, the nature and importance of the sexual object recedes into the background. What is essential and constant in the sexual instinct is something else.[2]

2. Deviations in Respect of the Sexual Aim

The normal sexual aim is regarded as being the union of the genitals in the act known as copulation, which leads to a release of the sexual tension and a temporary extinction of the sexual instinct—a satisfaction analogous to the sating of hunger. But even in the most normal sexual process we may detect rudiments which, if they had developed, would have led to the deviations described as 'perversions'. For there are certain intermediate relations to the sexual object, such as touching and looking at it, which lie on the road towards copulation and are recognized as being preliminary sexual aims. On the one hand these activities are themselves accompanied by pleasure, and on the other hand they intensify the excitation, which should persist until the final sexual aim is attained. Moreover, the kiss, one particular contact

2. [*Footnote added* 1910:] The most striking distinction between the erotic life of antiquity and our own no doubt lies in the fact that the ancients laid the stress upon the instinct itself, whereas we emphasize its object. The ancients glorified the instinct and were prepared on its account to honour even an inferior object; while we despise the instinctual activity in itself, and find excuses for it only in the merits of the object. {Freud makes a similar point in the "Dora" case, 7:50}

of this kind, between the mucous membrane of the lips of the two people concerned, is held in high sexual esteem among many nations (including the most highly civilized ones), in spite of the fact that the parts of the body involved do not form part of the sexual apparatus but constitute the entrance to the digestive tract. Here, then, are factors which provide a point of contact between the perversions and normal sexual life and which can also serve as a basis for their classification. Perversions are sexual activities which either (*a*) extend, in an anatomical sense, beyond the regions of the body that are designed for sexual union, or (*b*) linger over the intermediate relations to the sexual object which should normally be traversed rapidly on the path towards the final sexual aim.

A. Anatomical Extensions

Overvaluation of the Sexual Object   It is only in the rarest instances that the psychical valuation that is set on the sexual object, as being the goal of the sexual instinct, stops short at its genitals. The appreciation extends to the whole body of the sexual object and tends to involve every sensation derived from it. The same overvaluation spreads over into the psychological sphere: the subject becomes, as it were, intellectually infatuated (that is, his powers of judgement are weakened) by the mental achievements and perfections of the sexual object and he submits to the latter's judgements with credulity. Thus the credulity of love becomes an important, if not the most fundamental, source of *authority*.

This sexual overvaluation is something that cannot be easily reconciled with a restriction of the sexual aim to union of the actual genitals and it helps to turn activities connected with other parts of the body into sexual aims.

The significance of the factor of sexual overvaluation can be best studied in men, for their erotic life alone has become accessible to research. That of women—partly owing to the stunting effect of civilized conditions and partly owing to their conventional secretiveness and insincerity—is still veiled in an impenetrable obscurity.[3]

---

3. [*Footnote added* 1920:] In typical cases women fail to exhibit any sexual overvaluation towards men; but they scarcely ever fail to do so towards their own children.

Sexual Use of the Mucous Membrane of the Lips and Mouth   The use of the mouth as a sexual organ is regarded as a perversion if the lips (or tongue) of one person are brought into contact with the genitals of another, but not if the mucous membranes of the lips of both of them come together. This exception is the point of contact with what is normal. Those who condemn the other practices (which have no doubt been common among mankind from primaeval times) as being perversions, are giving way to an unmistakable feeling of *disgust*, which protects them from accepting sexual aims of the kind. The limits of such disgust are, however, often purely conventional: a man who will kiss a pretty girl's lips passionately, may perhaps be disgusted at the idea of using her tooth-brush, though there are no grounds for supposing that his own oral cavity, for which he feels no disgust, is any cleaner than the girl's. Here, then, our attention is drawn to the factor of disgust, which interferes with the libidinal overvaluation of the sexual object but can in turn be overridden by libido. Disgust seems to be one of the forces which have led to a restriction of the sexual aim. These forces do not as a rule extend to the genitals themselves. But there is no doubt that the genitals of the opposite sex can in themselves be an object of disgust and that such an attitude is one of the characteristics of all hysterics, and especially of hysterical women. The sexual instinct in its strength enjoys overriding this disgust.

Sexual Use of the Anal Orifice   Where the anus is concerned it becomes still clearer that it is disgust which stamps that sexual aim as a perversion. I hope, however, I shall not be accused of partisanship when I assert that people who try to account for this disgust by saying that the organ in question serves the function of excretion and comes in contact with excrement—a thing which is disgusting in itself—are not much more to the point than hysterical girls who account for their disgust at the male genital by saying that it serves to void urine.

The playing of a sexual part by the mucous membrane of the anus is by no means limited to intercourse between men: preference for it is in no way characteristic of inverted feeling. On the contrary, it seems that *paedicatio*[4] with a male owes its origin

4. {Anal intercourse.}

to an analogy with a similar act performed with a woman; while mutual masturbation is the sexual aim most often found in intercourse between inverts. * * *

Unsuitable Substitutes for the Sexual Object—Fetishism There are some cases which are quite specially remarkable—those in which the normal sexual object is replaced by another which bears some relation to it, but is entirely unsuited to serve the normal sexual aim. From the point of view of classification, we should no doubt have done better to have mentioned this highly interesting group of aberrations of the sexual instinct among the deviations in respect of the sexual *object*. But we have postponed their mention till we could become acquainted with the factor of sexual overvaluation, on which these phenomena, being connected with an abandonment of the sexual aim, are dependent.

What is substituted for the sexual object is some part of the body (such as the foot or hair) which is in general very inappropriate for sexual purposes, or some inanimate object which bears an assignable relation to the person whom it replaces and preferably to that person's sexuality (e.g. a piece of clothing or underlinen). Such substitutes are with some justice likened to the fetishes in which savages believe that their gods are embodied.

B. Fixations of Preliminary Sexual Aims

Appearance of New Aims Every external or internal factor that hinders or postpones the attainment of the normal sexual aim (such as impotence, the high price of the sexual object or the danger of the sexual act) will evidently lend support to the tendency to linger over the preparatory activities and to turn them into new sexual aims that can take the place of the normal one. Attentive examination always shows that even what seem to be the strangest of these new aims are already hinted at in the normal sexual process.

Touching and Looking A certain amount of touching is indispensable (at all events among human beings) before the normal sexual aim can be attained. And everyone knows what a source of pleasure on the one hand and what an influx of fresh excitation on the other is afforded by tactile sensations of the skin of the sexual object. So that lingering over the stage of touching can scarcely be counted a perversion, provided that in the long run the sexual act is carried further.

The same holds true of seeing—an activity that is ultimately derived from touching. Visual impressions remain the most frequent pathway along which libidinal excitation is aroused; indeed, natural selection counts upon the accessibility of this pathway— if such a teleological form of statement is permissible—when it encourages the development of beauty in the sexual object. The progressive concealment of the body which goes along with civilization keeps sexual curiosity awake. This curiosity seeks to complete the sexual object by revealing its hidden parts. It can, however, be diverted ('sublimated') in the direction of art, if its interest can be shifted away from the genitals on to the shape of the body as a whole. It is usual for most normal people to linger to some extent over the intermediate sexual aim of a looking that has a sexual tinge to it; indeed, this offers them a possibility of directing some proportion of their libido on to higher artistic aims. On the other hand, this pleasure in looking [scopophilia] becomes a perversion (*a*) if it is restricted exclusively to the genitals, or (*b*) if it is connected with the overriding of disgust (as in the case of *voyeurs* or people who look on at excretory functions), or (*c*) if, instead of being *preparatory* to the normal sexual aim, it supplants it. This last is markedly true of exhibitionists, who, if I may trust the findings of several analyses, exhibit their own genitals in order to obtain a reciprocal view of the genitals of the other person.[5]

In the perversions which are directed towards looking and being looked at, we come across a very remarkable characteristic with which we shall be still more intensely concerned in the aberration that we shall consider next: in these perversions the sexual aim occurs in two forms, an *active* and a *passive* one.

The force which opposes scopophilia, but which may be overridden by it (in a manner parallel to what we have previously seen in the case of disgust), is *shame*.

---

5. [*Footnote added* 1920:] Under analysis, these perversions—and indeed most others—reveal a surprising variety of motives and determinants. The compulsion to exhibit, for instance, is also closely dependent on the castration complex: it is a means of constantly insisting upon the integrity of the subject's own (male) genitals and it reiterates his infantile satisfaction at the absence of a penis in those of women. {On the term "castration complex," see p. 122 below.}

Sadism and Masochism   The most common and the most significant of all the perversions—the desire to inflict pain upon the sexual object, and its reverse—received from Krafft-Ebing the names of 'sadism' and 'masochism' for its active and passive forms respectively * * *

As regards * * * sadism, the roots are easy to detect in the normal. The sexuality of most male human beings contains an element of *aggressiveness*—a desire to subjugate; the biological significance of it seems to lie in the need for overcoming the resistance of the sexual object by means other than the process of wooing. Thus sadism would correspond to an aggressive component of the sexual instinct which has become independent and exaggerated and, by displacement, has usurped the leading position.

In ordinary speech the connotation of sadism oscillates between, on the one hand, cases merely characterized by an active or violent attitude to the sexual object, and, on the other hand, cases in which satisfaction is entirely conditional on the humiliation and maltreatment of the object. Strictly speaking, it is only this last extreme instance which deserves to be described as a perversion.

Similarly, the term masochism comprises any passive attitude towards sexual life and the sexual object, the extreme instance of which appears to be that in which satisfaction is conditional upon suffering physical or mental pain at the hands of the sexual object. Masochism, in the form of a perversion, seems to be further removed from the normal sexual aim than its counterpart; it may be doubted at first whether it can ever occur as a primary phenomenon or whether, on the contrary, it may not invariably arise from a transformation of sadism.[6] It can often be shown that masochism is nothing more than an extension of sadism turned round upon the subject's own self, which thus, to begin with, takes the place of the sexual object. Clinical analysis of extreme cases of masochistic perversion show that a great number of factors (such as the castration complex and the sense of guilt) have combined to exaggerate and fixate the original passive sexual attitude.

6. [*Footnote added* 1924:] My opinion of masochism has been to a large extent altered by later reflection, based upon certain hypotheses as to the structure of the apparatus of the mind and the classes of instincts operating in it.

Pain, which is overriden in such cases, thus falls into line with disgust and shame as a force that stands in opposition and resistance to the libido.[7]

Sadism and masochism occupy a special position among the perversions, since the contrast between activity and passivity which lies behind them is among the universal characteristics of sexual life. * * *

But the most remarkable feature of this perversion is that its active and passive forms are habitually found to occur together in the same individual. A person who feels pleasure in producing pain in someone else in a sexual relationship is also capable of enjoying as pleasure any pain which he may himself derive from sexual relations. A sadist is always at the same time a masochist, although the active or the passive aspect of the perversion may be the more strongly developed in him and may represent his predominant sexual activity.

We find, then, that certain among the impulses to perversion occur regularly as pairs of opposites; and this, taken in conjunction with material which will be brought forward later, has a high theoretical significance. It is, moreover, a suggestive fact that the existence of the pair of opposites formed by sadism and masochism cannot be attributed merely to the element of aggressiveness. We should rather be inclined to connect the simultaneous presence of these opposites with the opposing masculinity and femininity which are combined in bisexuality—a contrast which often has to be replaced in psycho-analysis by that between activity and passivity.

3 The Perversions in General

Variation and Disease   It is natural that medical men, who first studied perversions in outstanding examples and under special conditions, should have been inclined to regard them, like inversion, as indications of degeneracy or disease. Nevertheless, it is even easier to dispose of that view in this case than in that of inversion. Everyday experience has shown that most of these ex-

---

7. [This short paragraph was in the first edition (1905), but the last two, as well as the next one, were only added in 1915.]

tensions, or at any rate the less severe of them, are constituents which are rarely absent from the sexual ife of healthy people, and are judged by them no differently from other intimate events. If circumstances favour such an occurrence, normal people too can substitute a perversion of this kind for the normal sexual aim for quite a time, or can find place for the one alongside the other. No healthy person, it appears, can fail to make some addition that might be called perverse to the normal sexual aim; and the universality of this finding is in itself enough to show how inappropriate it is to use the word perversion as a term of reproach. In the sphere of sexual life we are brought up against peculiar and, indeed, insoluble difficulties as soon as we try to draw a sharp line to distinguish mere variations within the range of what is physiological from pathological symptoms.

Nevertheless, in some of these perversions the quality of the new sexual aim is of a kind to demand special examination. Certain of them are so far removed from the normal in their content that we cannot avoid pronouncing them 'pathological'. This is especially so where (as, for instance, in cases of licking excrement or of intercourse with dead bodies) the sexual instinct goes to astonishing lengths in successfully overriding the resistances of shame, disgust, horror or pain. But even in such cases we should not be too ready to assume that people who act in this way will necessarily turn out to be insane or subject to grave abnormalities of other kinds. Here again we cannot escape from the fact that people whose behaviour is in other respects normal can, under the domination of the most unruly of all the instincts, put themselves in the category of sick persons in the single sphere of sexual life. On the other hand, manifest abnormality in the other relations of life can invariably be shown to have a background of abnormal sexual conduct.

In the majority of instances the pathological character in a perversion is found to lie not in the *content* of the new sexual aim but in its relation to the normal. If a perversion, instead of appearing merely *alongside* the normal sexual aim and object, and only when circumstances are unfavourable to *them* and favourable to *it*—if, instead of this, it ousts them completely and takes their place in *all* circumstances—if, in short, a perversion has the characteristics of exclusiveness and fixation—then we shall usually be justified in regarding it as a pathological symptom. * * *

In the last three subsections of the first essay, called "The Sexual Instinct in Neurotics," "Component Instincts and Erotogenic Zones," and "Intimation of the Infantile Character of Sexuality," Freud sets out what he has learned about sexuality from those of his patients in whom a neurosis existed as a "negative of the perversions," that is, who had mirror images in their unconscious minds of desires that are conscious and acted upon in the daily lives of "perverts." In non-neurotics perverse tendencies—part of the makeup of everyone—remain invisible, but neurotics have symptoms that reveal the perverse tendencies in their unconscious. An analyst can, then, show the nature of perversions more clearly in neurotics. Most apparent in such demonstrations will be (1) "the component instincts," chiefly two pairs of them—the scopophilic (love of looking) instinct and exhibitionism (love of being looked at) and the active and passive forms of the instinct for cruelty (sadism and masochism); and (2) "the erotogenic zones," those parts of the body which, in the perversions, have a sexual significance as great as or greater than the genitals. Analyzing psychoneurotics allows an analyst to see how frequently—indeed, universally—less obvious manifestations of the component instincts and of intense attention to the "erotogenic zones" are present in normal people's psychic lives. Freud advances the hypothesis that the sexuality of neurotics, which offers such clues to the sexuality of normal people, has remained in or been brought back to an infantile state. To explore this hypothesis, he turns his attention, in the second of the Three Essays, to infantile sexuality.

Essay II. Infantile Sexuality

Neglect of the Infantile Factor   One feature of the popular view of the sexual instinct is that it is absent in childhood and only awakens in the period of life described as puberty. This, however, is not merely a simple error but one that has had grave consequences, for it is mainly to this idea that we owe our present ignorance of the fundamental conditions of sexual life. A thorough study of the sexual manifestations of childhood would probably reveal the essential characters of the sexual instinct and would show us the course of its development and the way in which it is put together from various sources.

It is noticeable that writers who concern themselves with explaining the characteristics and reactions of the adult have devoted much more attention to the primaeval period which is comprised in the life of the individual's ancestors—have, that is, ascribed much more influence to heredity—than to the other primaeval

period, which falls within the lifetime of the individual himself—
that is, to childhood. One would surely have supposed that the
influence of this latter period would be easier to understand and
could claim to be considered before that of heredity.[8] It is true
that in the literature of the subject one occasionally comes across
remarks upon precocious sexual activity in small children—upon
erections, masturbation and even activities resembling coitus. But
these are always quoted only as exceptional events, as oddities or
as horrifying instances of precocious depravity. So far as I know,
not a single author has clearly recognized the regular existence
of a sexual instinct in childhood; and in the writings that have
become so numerous on the development of children, the chapter
on 'Sexual Development' is as a rule omitted.

Infantile Amnesia   The reason for this strange neglect is to be
sought, I think, partly in considerations of propriety, which the
authors obey as a result of their own upbringing, and partly in a
psychological phenomenon which has itself hitherto eluded explanation. What I have in mind is the peculiar amnesia which,
in the case of most people, though by no means all, hides the
earliest beginnings of their childhood up to their sixth or eighth
year. Hitherto it has not occurred to us to feel any astonishment
at the fact of this amnesia, though we might have had good
grounds for doing so. For we learn from other people that during
these years, of which at a later date we retain nothing in our
memory but a few unintelligible and fragmentary recollections,
we reacted in a lively manner to impressions, that we were capable
of expressing pain and joy in a human fashion, that we gave
evidence of love, jealousy and other passionate feelings by which
we were strongly moved at the time, and even that we gave ut-
terance to remarks which were regarded by adults as good evidence
of our possessing insight and the beginnings of a capacity for
judgement. And of all this we, when we are grown up, have no
knowledge of our own! Why should our memory lag so far behind
the other activities of our minds? We have, on the contrary, good
reason to believe that there is no period at which the capacity for
receiving and reproducing impressions is greater than precisely
during the years of childhood.

8. [*Footnote added* 1915:] Nor is it possible to estimate correctly the part played
   by heredity until the part played by childhood has been assessed.

On the other hand we must assume, or we can convince ourselves by a psychological examination of other people, that the very same impressions that we have forgotten have none the less left the deepest traces on our minds and have had a determining effect upon the whole of our later development. There can, therefore, be no question of any real abolition of the impressions of childhood, but rather of an amnesia similar to that which neurotics exhibit for later events, and of which the essence consists in a simple witholding of these impressions from consciousness, viz., in their repression. But what are the forces which bring about this repression of the impressions of childhood? Whoever could solve this riddle would, I think, have explained *hysterical* amnesia as well.

Meanwhile we must not fail to observe that the existence of infantile amnesia provides a new point of comparison between the mental states of children and psychoneurotics. We have already come across another such point in the formula to which we were led, to the effect that the sexuality of psycho-neurotics has remained at, or been carried back to, an infantile stage. Can it be, after all, that infantile amnesia, too, is to be brought into relation with the sexual impulses of childhood?

Moreover, the connection between infantile and hysterical amnesia is more than a mere play upon words. Hysterical amnesia, which occurs at the bidding of repression, is only explicable by the fact that the subject is already in possession of a store of memory-traces which have been withdrawn from conscious disposal, and which are now, by an associative link, attracting to themselves the material which the forces of repression are engaged in repelling from consciousness. It may be said that without infantile amnesia there would be no hysterical amnesia.

I believe, then, that infantile amnesia, which turns everyone's childhood into something like a prehistoric epoch and conceals from him the beginnings of his own sexual life, is responsible for the fact that in general no importance is attached to childhood in the development of sexual life. The gaps in our knowledge which have arisen in this way cannot be bridged by a single observer. As long ago as in the year 1896 I insisted on the significance of the years of childhood in the origin of certain important phenomena connected with sexual life, and since then I have never ceased to emphasize the part played in sexuality by the infantile factor.

1. *The Period of Sexual Latency in Childhood and Its Interruptions*

The remarkably frequent reports of what are described as irregular and exceptional sexual impulses in childhood, as well as the uncovering in neurotics of what have hitherto been unconscious memories of childhood, allow us to sketch out the sexual occurrences of that period in some such way as this.

There seems no doubt that germs of sexual impulses are already present in the new-born child and that these continue to develop for a time, but are then overtaken by a progressive process of suppression; this in turn is itself interrupted by periodical advances in sexual development or may be held up by individual peculiarities. Nothing is known for certain concerning the regularity and periodicity of this oscillating course of development. It seems, however, that the sexual life of children usually emerges in a form accessible to observation round about the third or fourth year of life.

Sexual Inhibitions   It is during this period of total or only partial latency that are built up the mental forces which are later to impede the course of the sexual instinct and, like dams, restrict its flow—disgust, feelings of shame and the claims of aesthetic and moral ideals. One gets an impression from civilized children that the construction of these dams is a product of education, and no doubt education has much to do with it.[9] But in reality this development is organically determined and fixed by heredity, and it can occasionally occur without any help at all from education. Education will not be trespassing beyond its appropriate domain if it limits itself to following the lines which have already been laid down organically and to impressing them somewhat more clearly and deeply.

Reaction-Formation and Sublimation   What is it that goes to the making of these constructions which are so important for the growth of a civilized and normal individual? They probably emerge at the cost of the infantile sexual impulses themselves.

---

9. {The latency period Freud is discussing follows the fourth year; that is, it comes at the time when children traditionally start school, so that it can be misconstrued as simply a product of education.}

Thus the activity of those impulses does not cease even during this period of latency, though their energy is diverted, wholly or in great part, from their sexual use and directed to other ends. Historians of civilization appear to be at one in assuming that powerful components are acquired for every kind of cultural achievement by this diversion of sexual instinctual forces from sexual aims and their direction to new ones—a process which deserves the name of 'sublimation'. To this we would add, accordingly, that the same process plays a part in the development of the individual and we would place its beginning in the period of sexual latency of childhood.

It is possible further to form some idea of the mechanism of this process of sublimation. On the one hand, it would seem, the sexual impulses cannot be utilized during these years of childhood, since the reproductive functions have been deferred—a fact which constitutes the main feature of the period of latency. On the other hand, these impulses would seem in themselves to be perverse—that is, to arise from erotogenic zones and to derive their activity from instincts which, in view of the direction of the subject's development, can only arouse unpleasurable feelings. They consequently evoke opposing mental forces (reacting impulses) which, in order to suppress this unpleasure effectively, build up the mental dams that I have already mentioned—disgust, shame and morality.

Interruptions of the Latency Period   We must not deceive ourselves as to the hypothetical nature and insufficient clarity of our knowledge concerning the processes of the infantile period of latency or deferment; but we shall be on firmer ground in pointing out that such an application of infantile sexuality represents an educational ideal from which individual development usually diverges at some point and often to a considerable degree. From time to time a fragmentary manifestation of sexuality which has evaded sublimation may break through; or some sexual activity may persist through the whole duration of the latency period until the sexual instinct emerges with greater intensity at puberty. In so far as educators pay any attention at all to infantile sexuality, they behave exactly as though they shared our views as to the construction of the moral defensive forces at the cost of sexuality, and as though they knew that sexual activity makes a child ineducable: for they stigmatize every sexual manifestation by children as a 'vice', without being able to do much against it. We, on the other hand, have every reason for turning our attention to these phenomena which are so much dreaded by education, for we may expect them to help us to discover the original configuration of the sexual instincts.

2. The Manifestations of Infantile Sexuality

Thumb-Sucking   For reasons which will appear later, I shall take thumb-sucking (or sensual sucking) as a sample of the sexual manifestations of childhood. * * *

Thumb-sucking appears already in early infancy and may continue into maturity, or even persist all through life. It consists in the rhythmic repetition of a sucking contact by the mouth (or lips). There is no question of the purpose of this procedure being the taking of nourishment. A portion of the lip itself, the tongue, or any other part of the skin within reach—even the big toe— may be taken as the object upon which this sucking is carried out. In this connection a grasping-instinct may appear and may manifest itself as a simultaneous rhythmic tugging at the lobes of the ears or a catching hold of some part of another person (as a rule the ear) for the same purpose. Sensual sucking involves a complete absorption of the attention and leads either to sleep or even to a motor reaction in the nature of an orgasm.[10] It is not infrequently combined with rubbing some sensitive part of the body such as the breast or the external genitalia. Many children proceed by this path from sucking to masturbation.

Lindner {a Hungarian pedatrician} clearly recognized the sexual nature of this activity and emphasized it without qualification. In the nursery, sucking is often classed along with the other kinds of sexual 'naughtiness' of children. This view has been most energetically repudiated by numbers of paediatricians and nerve-specialists, though this is no doubt partly due to a confusion between 'sexual' and 'genital'. Their objection raises a difficult question and one which cannot be evaded: what is the general

10. Thus we find at this early stage, what holds good all through life, that sexual satisfaction is the best soporific. Most cases of nervous insomnia can be traced back to lack of sexual satisfaction. It is well known that unscrupulous nurses put crying children to sleep by stroking their genitals.

characteristic which enables us to recognize the sexual manifestations of children? The concatenation of phenomena into which
we have been given an insight by psycho-analytic investigation
justifies us, in my opinion, in regarding thumb-sucking as a sexual
manifestation and in choosing it for our study of the essential
features of infantile sexual activity.

Auto-Erotism   We are in duty bound to make a thorough examination of this example. It must be insisted that the most
striking feature of this sexual activity is that the instinct is not
directed towards other people, but obtains satisfaction from the
subject's own body. It is 'auto-erotic', to call it by a happily chosen
term introduced by Havelock Ellis (1910).

Furthermore, it is clear that the behaviour of a child who
indulges in thumb-sucking is determined by a search for some
pleasure which has already been experienced and is now remembered. In the simplest case he proceeds to find this satisfaction
by sucking rhythmically at some part of the skin or mucous membrane. It is also easy to guess the occasions on which the child
had his first experiences of the pleasure which he is now striving
to renew. It was the child's first and most vital activity, his sucking
at his mother's breast, or at substitutes for it, that must have
familiarized him with this pleasure. The child's lips, in our view,
behave like an erotogenic zone, and no doubt stimulation by the
warm flow of milk is the cause of the pleasurable sensation. The
satisfaction of the erotogenic zone is associated, in the first instance, with the satisfaction of the need for nourishment. To begin
with, sexual activity attaches itself to functions serving the purpose
of self-preservation and does not become independent of them
until later. No one who has seen a baby sinking back satiated
from the breast and falling asleep with flushed cheeks and a blissful
smile can escape the reflection that this picture persists as a prototype of the expression of sexual satisfaction in later life. The
need for repeating the sexual satisfaction now becomes detached
from the need for taking nourishment—a separation which becomes inevitable when the teeth appear and food is no longer
taken in only by sucking, but is also chewed up. The child does
not make use of an extraneous body for his sucking, but prefers
a part of his own skin because it is more convenient, because it
makes him independent of the external world, which he is not
yet able to control, and because in that way he provides himself,

as it were, with a second erotogenic zone, though one of an inferior kind. The inferiority of this second region is among the reasons why at a later date he seeks the corresponding part—the lips—of another person. ('It's a pity I can't kiss myself', he seems to be saying.)

It is not every child who sucks in this way. It may be assumed that those children do so in whom there is a constitutional intensification of the erotogenic significance of the labial region. If that significance persists, these same children when they are grown up will become epicures in kissing, will be inclined to perverse kissing, or, if males, will have a powerful motive for drinking and smoking. If, however, repression ensues, they will feel disgust at food and will produce hysterical vomiting. The repression extends to the nutritional instinct owing to the dual purpose served by the labial zone. Many of my women patients who suffer from disturbances of eating, *globus hystericus*, constriction of the throat and vomiting, have indulged energetically in sucking during their childhood.

Our study of thumb-sucking or sensual sucking has already given us the three essential characteristics of an infantile sexual manifestation. At its origin it attaches itself to one of the vital somatic functions; it has as yet no sexual object, and is thus auto-erotic; and its sexual aim is dominated by an erotogenic zone. It is to be anticipated that these characteristics will be found to apply equally to most of the other activities of the infantile sexual instincts.

3. *The Sexual Aim of Infantile Sexuality*

Characteristics of Erotogenic Zones   The example of thumb-sucking shows us still more about what constitutes an erotogenic zone. It is a part of the skin or mucous membrane in which stimuli of a certain sort evoke a feeling of pleasure possessing a particular quality. There can be no doubt that the stimuli which produce the pleasure are governed by special conditions, though we do not know what those are. A rhythmic character must play a part among them and the analogy of tickling is forced upon our notice. It seems less certain whether the character of the pleasurable feeling evoked by the stimulus should be described as a 'specific' one—a 'specific' quality in which the sexual factor would precisely lie. Psychology is still so much in the dark in questions of pleasure and unpleasure that the most cautious assumption is the one most to be recommended. We may later come upon reasons which seem to support the idea that the pleasurable feeling does in fact possess a specific quality.

The character of erotogenicity can be attached to some parts of the body in a particularly marked way. There are predestined erotogenic zones, as is shown by the example of sucking. The same example, however, also shows us that any other part of the skin or mucous membrane can take over the functions of an erotogenic zone, and must therefore have some aptitude in that direction. Thus the quality of the stimulus has more to do with producing the pleasurable feeling than has the nature of the part of the body concerned. A child who is indulging in sensual sucking searches about his body and chooses some part of it to suck—a part which is afterwards preferred by him from force of habit; if he happens to hit upon one of the predestined regions (such as the nipples or genitals) no doubt it retains the preference. A precisely analogous tendency to displacement is also found in the symptomatology of hysteria. In that neurosis repression affects most of all the actual genital zones and these transmit their susceptibility to stimulation to other erotogenic zones (normally neglected in adult life), which then behave exactly like genitals. But besides this, precisely as in the case of sucking, any other part of the body can acquire the same susceptibility to stimulation as is possessed by the genitals and can become an erotogenic zone. Erotogenic and hysterogenic zones show the same characteristics.[11]

The Infantile Sexual Aim   The sexual aim of the infantile instinct consists in obtaining satisfaction by means of an appropriate stimulation of the erotogenic zone which has been selected in one way or another. This satisfaction must have been previously experienced in order to have left behind a need for its repetition; and we may expect that Nature will have made safe provisions so that this experience of satisfaction shall not be left to chance. We have already learnt what the contrivance is that fulfils this purpose

11. [*Footnote added* 1915:] After further reflection and after taking other observations into account, I have been led to ascribe the quality of erotogenicity to all parts of the body and to all the internal organs.

in the case of the labial zone: it is the simultaneous connection which links this part of the body with the taking in of food. We shall come across other, similar contrivances as sources of sexuality. The state of being in need of a repetition of the satisfaction reveals itself in two ways: by a peculiar feeling of tension, possessing, rather, the character of unpleasure, and by a sensation of itching or stimulation which is centrally conditioned and projected on to the peripheral erotogenic zone. We can therefore formulate a sexual aim in another way: it consists in replacing the projected sensation of stimulation in the erotogenic zone by an external stimulus which removes that sensation by producing a feeling of satisfaction. This external stimulus will usually consist in some kind of manipulation that is analogous to the sucking. * * *

4. Masturbatory Sexual Manifestations

Activity of the Anal Zone   * * * Like the labial zone, the anal zone is well suited by its position to act as a medium through which sexuality may attach itself to other somatic functions. It is to be presumed that the erotogenic significance of this part of the body is very great from the first. We learn with some astonishment from psycho-analysis of the transmutations normally undergone by the sexual excitations arising from this zone and of the frequency with which it retains a considerable amount of susceptibility to genital stimulation throughout life. The intestinal disturbances which are so common in childhood see to it that the zone shall not lack intense excitations. Intestinal catarrhs {or inflammations} at the tenderest age make children 'nervy', as people say, and in cases of later neurotic illness they have a determining influence on the symptoms in which the neurosis is expressed, and they put at its disposal the whole range of intestinal disturbances. If we bear in mind the erotogenic significance of the outlet of the intestinal canal, which persists, at all events in a modified form, we shall not be inclined to scoff at the influence of haemorrhoids, to which old-fashioned medicine used to attach so much importance in explaining neurotic conditions.

Children who are making use of the susceptibility to erotogenic stimulation of the anal zone betray themselves by holding back their stool till its accumulation brings about violent muscular contractions and, as it passes through the anus, is able to produce powerful stimulation of the mucous membrane. In so doing it must no doubt cause not only painful but also highly pleasurable sensations. One of the clearest signs of subsequent eccentricity or nervousness is to be seen when a baby obstinately refuses to empty his bowels when he is put on the pot—that is, when his nurse wants him to—and holds back that function till he himself chooses to exercise it. He is naturally not concerned with dirtying the bed, he is only anxious not to miss the subsidiary pleasure attached to defaecating. Educators are once more right when they describe children who keep the process back as 'naughty.'

The contents of the bowels,[12] which act as a stimulating mass upon a sexually sensitive portion of mucous membrane, behave like forerunners of another organ, which is destined to come into action after the phase of childhood. But they have other important meanings for the infant. They are clearly treated as a part of the infant's own body and represent his first 'gift': by producing them he can express his active compliance with his environment and, by witholding them, his disobedience. From being a 'gift' they later come to acquire the meaning of 'baby'—for babies, according to one of the sexual theories of children, are acquired by eating and are born through the bowels.

The retention of the faecal mass, which is thus carried out intentionally by the child to begin with, in order to serve, as it were, as a masturbatory stimulus upon the anal zone or to be employed in his relation to the people looking after him, is also one of the roots of the constipation which is so common among neuropaths. Further, the whole significance of the anal zone is reflected in the fact that few neurotics are to be found without their special scatological practices, ceremonies, and so on, which they carefully keep secret.[13]

12. [This paragraph was added in 1915.]

13. [*Footnote added* 1920:] Lou Andreas-Salomé (1916), in a paper which has given us a very much deeper understanding of the significance of anal erotism, has shown how the history of the first prohibition which a child comes across— the prohibition against getting pleasure from anal activity and its products— has a decisive effect on his whole development. This must be the first occasion on which the infant has a glimpse of an environment hostile to his instinctual impulses, on which he learns to separate his own entity from this alien one and on which he carries out the first 'repression' of his possibilities for pleasure. From that time on, what is 'anal' remains the symbol of everything that is to

Actual masturbatory stimulation of the anal zone by means of the finger, provoked by a centrally determined or peripherally maintained sensation of itching, is by no means rare among older children.

Activity of the Genital Zones   Among the erotogenic zones that form part of the child's body there is one which certainly does not play the opening part, and which cannot be the vehicle of the oldest sexual impulses, but which is destined to great things in the future. In both male and female children it is brought into connection with micturition {or urination} (in the glans and clitoris) and in the former is enclosed in a pouch of mucous membrane, so that there can be no lack of stimulation of it by secretions which may give an early start to sexual excitation. The sexual activities of this erotogenic zone, which forms part of the sexual organs proper, are the beginning of what is later to become 'normal' sexual life. The anatomical situation of this region, the secretions in which it is bathed, the washing and rubbing to which it is subjected in the course of a child's toilet, as well as accidental stimulation (such as the movement of intestinal worms in the case of girls), make it inevitable that the pleasurable feeling which this part of the body is capable of producing should be noticed by children even during their earliest infancy, and should give rise to a need for its repetition. If we consider this whole range of contrivances and bear in mind that both making a mess and measures for keeping clean are bound to operate in much the same way, it is scarcely possible to avoid the conclusion that the foundations for the future primacy over sexual activity exercised by this erotogenic zone are established by early infantile masturbation, which scarcely a single individual escapes. The action which disposes of the stimulus and brings about satisfaction consists in a rubbing movement with the hand or in the application of pressure (no doubt on the lines of a preexisting reflex) either from the hand or by bringing the thighs together. This last method

---

be repudiated and excluded from life. The clear-cut distinction between anal and genital processes which is later insisted upon is contradicted by the close anatomical and functional analogies and relations which hold between them. The genital apparatus remains the neighbour of the cloaca, and actually [to quote Lou Andreas-Salomé] 'in the case of women is only taken from it on lease'.

is by far the more common in the case of girls. The preference for the hand which is shown by boys is already evidence of the important contribution which the instinct for mastery is destined to make to masculine sexual activity.[14]

It will be in the interests of clarity[15] if I say at once that three phases of infantile masturbation are to be distinguished. The first of these belongs to early infancy, and the second to the brief efflorescence of sexual activity about the fourth year of life; only the third phase corresponds to pubertal masturbation, which is often the only kind taken into account.

Second Phase of Infantile Masturbation The masturbation of early infancy seems to disappear after a short time; but it may persist uninterruptedly until puberty, and this would constitute the first great deviation from the course of development laid down for civilized men. At some point of childhood after early infancy, as a rule before the fourth year, the sexual instinct belonging to the genital zone usually revives and persists again for a time until it is once more suppressed, or it may continue without interruption. This second phase of infantile sexual activity may assume a variety of different forms which can only be determined by a precise analysis of individual cases. But all its details leave behind the deepest (unconscious) impressions in the subject's memory, determine the development of his character, if he is to remain healthy, and the symptomatology of his neurosis, if he is to fall ill after puberty.[16] In the latter case we find that this sexual period has been forgotten and that the conscious memories that bear witness to it have been displaced. (I have already mentioned that

14. [*Footnote added* 1915:] Unusual techniques in carrying out masturbation in later years seem to point to the influence of a prohibition against masturbation which has been overcome.

15. {In 1915 Freud added this paragraph and made a number of changes in the following paragraphs in order to distinguish clearly the two phases of masturbation. See the 1912 "Discussion of Masturbation" anthologized below.}

16. [*Footnote added* 1915:] The problem of why the sense of guilt of neurotics is, as Bleuler [1913] recently recognized, regularly attached to the memory of some masturbatory activity, usually at puberty, still awaits an exhaustive analytic explanation. [*Added* 1920:] The most general and most important factor concerned must no doubt be that masturbation represents the executive agency of the whole of infantile sexuality and is, therefore, able to take over the sense of guilt attaching to it.

I am also inclined to relate normal infantile amnesia to this infantile sexual activity.) Psycho-analytic investigation enables us to make what has been forgotten conscious and thus do away with a compulsion that arises from the unconscious psychical material.

Return of Early Infantile Masturbation   During the years of childhood with which I am now dealing, the sexual excitation of early infancy returns, either as a centrally determined tickling stimulus which seeks satisfaction in masturbation, or as a process in the nature of a nocturnal emission which, like the nocturnal emissions of adult years, achieves satisfaction without the help of any action by the subject. The latter case is the more frequent with girls and in the second half of childhood; its determinants are not entirely intelligible and often, though not invariably, it seems to be conditioned by a period of earlier *active* masturbation. The symptoms of these sexual manifestations are scanty; they are mostly displayed on behalf of the still undeveloped sexual apparatus by the *urinary* apparatus, which thus acts, as it were, as the former's trustee. Most of the so-called bladder disorders of this period are sexual disturbances: nocturnal enuresis,[17] unless it represents an epileptic fit, corresponds to a nocturnal emission.

The reappearance of sexual activity is determined by internal causes and external contingencies, both of which can be guessed in cases of neurotic illness from the form taken by their symptoms and can be discovered with certainty by psycho-analytic investigation. I shall have to speak presently of the internal causes; great and lasting importance attaches at this period to the accidental *external* contingencies. In the foreground we find the effects of seduction, which treats a child as a sexual object prematurely and teaches him, in highly emotional circumstances, how to obtain satisfaction from his genital zones, a satisfaction which he is then usually obliged to repeat again and again by masturbation. An influence of this kind may originate either from adults or from other children. I cannot admit that in my paper on 'The Aetiology of Hysteria' (1896c) I exaggerated the frequency or importance of that influence, though I did not then know that persons who remain normal may have had the same experiences in their childhood, and though I consequently overrated the importance of

17. {Enuresis is involuntary bed-wetting.}

seduction in comparison with the factors of sexual constitution and development. Obviously seduction is not required in order to arouse a child's sexual life; that can also come about spontaneously from internal causes.

Polymorphously Perverse Disposition   It is an instructive fact that under the influence of seduction children can become polymorphously perverse, and can be led into all possible kinds of sexual irregularities. This shows that an aptitude for them is innately present in their disposition. There is consequently little resistance towards carrying them out, since the mental dams against sexual excesses—shame, disgust and morality—have either not yet been constructed at all or are only in course of construction, according to the age of the child. In this respect children behave in the same kind of way as an average uncultivated woman in whom the same polymorphously perverse disposition persists. Under ordinary conditions she may remain normal sexually, but if she is led on by a clever seducer she will find every sort of perversion to her taste, and will retain them as part of her own sexual activities. Prostitutes exploit the same polymorphous, that is, infantile, disposition for the purposes of their profession; and, considering the immense number of women who are prostitutes or who must be supposed to have an aptitude for prostitution without becoming engaged in it, it becomes impossible not to recognize that this same disposition to perversions of every kind is a general and fundamental human characteristic.

Component Instincts   Moreover, the effects of seduction do not help to reveal the early history of the sexual instinct; they rather confuse our view of it by presenting children prematurely with a sexual object for which the infantile sexual instinct at first shows no need. It must, however, be admitted that infantile sexual life, in spite of the preponderating dominance of erotogenic zones, exhibits components which from the very first involve other people as sexual objects. Such are the instincts of scopophilia, exhibitionism and cruelty, which appear in a sense independently of erotogenic zones; these instincts do not enter into intimate relations with genital life until later, but are already to be observed in childhood as independent impulses, distinct in the first instance from erotogenic sexual activity. Small children are essentially without shame, and at some periods of their earliest years show an unmistakable satisfaction in exposing their bodies, with special emphasis on the sexual parts. The counterpart of this supposedly perverse inclination, curiosity to see other people's genitals, probably does not become manifest until somewhat later in childhood, when the obstacle set up by a sense of shame has already reached a certain degree of development. Under the influence of seduction the scopophilic perversion can attain great importance in the sexual life of a child. But my researches into the early years of normal people, as well as of neurotic patients, force me to the conclusion that scopophilia can also appear in children as a spontaneous manifestation. Small children whose attention has once been drawn—as a rule by masturbation—to their own genitals usually take the further step without help from outside and develop a lively interest in the genitals of their playmates. Since opportunities for satisfying curiosity of this kind usually occur only in the course of satisfying the two kinds of need for excretion, children of this kind turn into *voyeurs*, eager spectators of the processes of micturition and defaecation. When repression of these inclinations sets in, the desire to see other people's genitals (whether of their own or the opposite sex) persists as a tormenting compulsion, which in some cases of neurosis later affords the strongest motive force for the formation of symptoms.

The cruel component of the sexual instinct develops in childhood even more independently of the sexual activities that are attached to erotogenic zones. Cruelty in general comes easily to the childish nature, since the obstacle that brings the instinct for mastery to a halt at another person's pain—namely a capacity for pity—is developed relatively late. The fundamental psychological analysis of this instinct has, as we know, not yet been satisfactorily achieved. It may be assumed that the impulse of cruelty arises from the instinct for mastery and appears at a period of sexual life at which the genitals have not yet taken over their later role. It then dominates a phase of sexual life which we shall later describe as a pregenital organization. Children who distinguish themselves by special cruelty towards animals and playmates usually give rise to a just suspicion of an intense and precocious sexual activity arising from erotogenic zones; and, though all the sexual instincts may display simultaneous precocity, *erotogenic* sexual activity seems, nevertheless, to be the primary one. The absence of the barrier of pity brings with it a danger that the connection between the cruel and the erotogenic instincts, thus established in childhood, may prove unbreakable in later life. Ever since Jean Jacques Rousseau's *Confessions*, it has been well known to all educationalists that the painful stimulation of the skin of the buttocks is one of the erotogenic roots of the *passive* instinct of cruelty (masochism). The conclusion has rightly been drawn by them that corporal punishment, which is usually applied to this part of the body, should not be inflicted upon any children whose libido is liable to be forced into collateral channels by the later demands of cultural education.

5. *The Sexual Researches of Childhood*[18]

The Instinct for Knowledge   At about the same time as the sexual life of children reaches its first peak, between the ages of three and five, they also begin to show signs of the activity which may be ascribed to the instinct for knowledge or research. This instinct cannot be counted among the elementary instinctual components, nor can it be classed as exclusively belonging to sexuality. Its activity corresponds on the one hand to a sublimated manner of obtaining mastery, while on the other hand it makes use of energy of scopophilia. Its relations to sexual life, however, are of particular importance, since we have learnt from psycho-analysis that the instinct for knowledge in children is attracted unexpectedly early and intensively to sexual problems and is in fact possibly first aroused by them.

The Riddle of the Sphinx   It is not by theoretical interests but by practical ones that activities of research are set going in children. The threat to the bases of a child's existence offered by the discovery or the suspicion of the arrival of a new baby and the fear that he may, as a result of it, cease to be cared for and loved, make him thoughtful and clear-sighted. And this history of the instinct's origin is in line with the fact that the first problem with which it deals is not the question of the distinction between the sexes but the riddle of where babies come from.[19] * * * On the

18. [The whole of this section on the sexual researches of children first appeared in 1915.] {See "The sexual theories of children" (1908), below, pp. 157–65.}
19. [In a later work, Freud (1925*j*) corrected this statement, saying that it is not true of girls, and not always true of boys.] {See "Some Psychical Consequences . . . ," p. 309 below.}

contrary, the existence of two sexes does not to begin with arouse any difficultics or doubts in children. It is self-evident to a male child that a genital like his own is to be attributed to everyone he knows, and he cannot make its absence tally with his picture of these other people.

Castration Complex and Penis Envy   This conviction is energetically maintained by boys, is obstinately defended against the contradictions which soon result from observation, and is only abandoned after severe internal struggles (the castration complex). The substitutes for this penis which they feel is missing in women play a great part in determining the form taken by many perversions. [20]

The assumption that all human beings have the same (male) form of genital is the first of the many remarkable and momentous sexual theories of children. It is of little use to a child that the science of biology justifies his prejudice and has been obliged to recognize the female clitoris as a true substitute for the penis.

Little girls do not resort to denial of this kind when they see that boys' genitals are formed differently from their own. They are ready to recognize them immediately and are overcome by envy for the penis—an envy culminating in the wish, which is so important in its consequences, to be boys themselves.

Theories of Birth   Many people can remember clearly what an intense interest they took during the prepubertal period in the question of where babies come from. The anatomical answers to the question were at the time very various: babies come out of the breast, or are cut out of the body, or the navel opens to let them through. Outside analysis, there are very seldom memories of any similar researches having been carried out in the *early* years of childhood. These earlier researches fell a victim to repression long since, but all their findings were of a uniform nature: people

---

20. [*Footnote added* 1920:] We are justified in speaking of a castration complex in women as well. Both male and female children form a theory that women no less than men originally had a penis, but that they have lost it by castration. The conviction which is finally reached by males that women have no penis often leads them to an enduringly low opinion of the other sex. {The "castration complex" is all of the conscious and unconscious desires, fears, sensations, and ideas that focus on the male genital and the possibility of castration.}

get babies by eating some particular thing (as they do in fairy tales) and babies are born through the bowel like a discharge of faeces. These infantile theories remind us of conditions that exist in the animal kingdom—and especially of the cloaca in types of animals lower than mammals.

Sadistic View of Sexual Intercourse   If children at this early age witness sexual intercourse between adults—for which an opportunity is provided by the conviction of grown-up people that small children cannot understand anything sexual—they inevitably regard the sexual act as a sort of ill-treatment or act of subjugation: they view it, that is, in a sadistic sense. Psycho-analysis also shows us that an impression of this kind in early childhood contributes a great deal towards a predisposition to a subsequent sadistic displacement of the sexual aim. Furthermore, children are much concerned with the problem of what sexual intercourse—or, as they put it, being married—consists in: and they usually seek a solution of the mystery in some common activity concerned with the function of micturition or defaecation.

Typical Failure of Infantile Sexual Researches   We can say in general of the sexual theories of children that they are reflections of their own sexual constitution and that in spite of their grotesque errors the theories show more understanding of sexual processes than one would have given their creators credit for. Children also perceive the alterations that take place in their mother owing to pregnancy and are able to interpret them correctly. The fable of the stork is often told to an audience that receives it with deep, though mostly silent, mistrust. There are, however, two elements that remain undiscovered by the sexual researches of children: the fertilizing role of semen and the existence of the female sexual orifice—the same elements, incidentally, in which the infantile organization is itself undeveloped. It therefore follows that the efforts of the childish investigator are habitually fruitless, and end in a renunciation which not infrequently leaves behind it a permanent injury to the instinct for knowledge. The sexual researches of these early years of childhood are always carried out in solitude. They constitute a first step towards taking an independent attitude in the world, and imply a high degree of alienation of the child from the people in his environment who formerly enjoyed his complete confidence.

6. The Phases of Development of the Sexual Organization[21]

The characteristics of infantile sexual life which we have hitherto emphasized are the facts that it is essentially autoerotic (i.e. that it finds its object in the infant's own body) and that its individual component instincts are upon the whole disconnected and independent of one another in their search for pleasure. The final outcome of sexual development lies in what is known as the normal sexual life of the adult, in which the pursuit of pleasure comes under the sway of the reproductive function and in which the component instincts, under the primacy of a single erotogenic zone, form a firm organization directed towards a sexual aim attached to some extraneous sexual object.

Pregenital Organizations   The study, with the help of psychoanalysis, of the inhibitions and disturbances of this process of development enables us to recognize abortive beginnings and preliminary stages of a firm organization of the component instincts such as this—preliminary stages which themselves constitute a sexual régime of a sort. These phases of sexual organization are normally passed through smoothly, without giving more than a hint of their existence. It is only in pathological cases that they become active and recognizable to superficial observation.

We shall give the name of 'pregenital' to organizations of sexual life in which the genital zones have not yet taken over their predominant part. We have hitherto identified two such organizations, which almost seem as though they were harking back to early animal forms of life.

The first of these is the oral or, as it might be called, cannibalistic pregenital sexual organization. Here sexual activity has not yet been separated from the ingestion of food; nor are opposite currents within the activity differentiated. The *object* of both activities is the same; the sexual *aim* consists in the incorporation of the object—the prototype of a process which, in the form of identification, is later to play such an important psychological part. A relic of this constructed phase of organization, which is forced upon our notice by pathology, may be seen in thumb-

---

21. [The whole of this section, too, first appeared in 1915.]

sucking, in which the sexual activity, detached from the nutritive activity, has substituted for the extraneous object one situated in the subject's own body.

A second pregenital phase is that of the sadistic-anal organization. Here the opposition between two currents, which runs through all sexual life, is already developed: they cannot yet, however, be described as 'masculine' and 'feminine', but only as 'active' and 'passive'. The *activity* is put into operation by the instinct for mastery through the agency of the somatic musculature; the organ which, more than any other, represents the *passive* sexual aim is the erotogenic mucous membrane of the anus. Both of these currents have objects, which, however, are not identical. Alongside these, other component instincts operate in an auto-erotic manner. In this phase, therefore, sexual polarity and an extraneous object are already observable. But organization and subordination to the reproductive function are still absent.

Ambivalence This form of sexual organization can persist throughout life and can permanently attract a large portion of sexual activity to itself. The predominance in it of sadism and the cloacal part played by the anal zone give it a quite peculiarly archaic colouring. It is further characterized by the fact that in it the opposing pairs of instincts are developed to an approximately equal extent, a state of affairs described by Bleuler's happily chosen term 'ambivalence'.

The assumption of the existence of pregenital organizations of sexual life is based on the analysis of the neuroses, and without a knowledge of them can scarcely be appreciated. Further analytic investigation may be expected to provide us with far more information on the structure and development of the normal sexual function.

In order to complete our picture of infantile sexual life, we must also suppose that the choice of an object, such as we have shown to be characteristic of the pubertal phase of development, has already frequently or habitually been effected during the years of childhood: that is to say, the whole of the sexual currents have become directed towards a single person in relation to whom they seek to achieve their aims. This then is the closest approximation possible in childhood to the final form taken by sexual life after puberty. The only difference lies in the fact that in childhood the combination of the component instincts and their subordination under the primacy of the genitals have been effected only very incompletely or not at all. Thus the establishment of that primacy in the service of reproduction is the last phase through which the organization of sexuality passes.[22]

Diphasic Choice of Object   It may be regarded as typical of the choice of an object that the process is diphasic, that is, that it occurs in two waves. The first of these begins between the ages of two and five, and is brought to a halt or to a retreat by the latency period; it is characterized by the infantile nature of the sexual aims. The second wave sets in with puberty and determines the final outcome of sexual life.

Although the diphasic nature of object-choice comes down in essentials to no more than the operation of the latency period, it is of the highest importance in regard to disturbances of that final outcome. The resultants of infantile object-choice are carried over into the later period. They either persist as such or are revived at the actual time of puberty. But as consequence of the repression which has developed between the two phases they prove unutilizable. Their sexual aims have become mitigated and they now represent what may be described as the 'affectionate current' of sexual life. Only psycho-analytic investigation can show that behind this affection, admiration and respect there lie concealed the old sexual longings of the infantile component instincts which have now become unserviceable. The object-choice of the pubertal period is obliged to dispense with the objects of childhood and to start afresh as a 'sensual current'. Should these two currents fail to converge, the result is often that one of the ideals of sexual life, the focusing of all desire upon a single object, will be unattainable.

7. The Sources of Infantile Sexuality

Our efforts to trace the origins of the sexual instinct have shown us so far that sexual excitation arises (*a*) as a reproduction of a satisfaction experienced in connection with other organic

22. {For Freud's later revision of this claim and his description of a third pregenital phase called "phallic," see "The Infantile Genital Organization" (1923), below pp. 267–71.}

processes, (*b*) through appropriate peripheral stimulation of erotogenic zones and (*c*) as an expression of certain 'instincts' (such as the scopophilic instinct and the instinct of cruelty) of which the origin is not yet completely intelligible. Psycho-analytic investigation, reaching back into childhood from a later time, and contemporary observation of children combine to indicate to us still other regularly active sources of sexual excitation.

Freud next offers a catalogue of the sources of infantile sexuality, which includes the following: general stimulation of the skin; rhythmic mechanical agitation of the body (passive movements); active movements in play and wrestling (and later verbal activity like quarreling); intense thrilling affects such as fear; a degree of pain; intellectual work. Excitation comes from these sources, but excitation can also spread back over the pathways from these sources. Thus disturbances of sexual pleasure often travel back to the nonsexual functions from whence excitation once came. Eating disorders and disturbances of oral sexual pleasure (at the time of weaning, for example) are linked. But, on the other hand, sublimations can also follow excitation pathways back to nonsexual functions.

Essay III. The Transformations of Puberty

With the arrival of puberty, changes set in which are destined to give infantile sexual life its final, normal shape. The sexual instinct has hitherto been predominantly auto-erotic; it now finds a sexual object. Its activity has hitherto been derived from a number of separate instincts and erotogenic zones, which, independently of one another, have pursued a certain sort of pleasure as their sole sexual aim. Now, however, a new sexual aim appears, and all the component instincts combine to attain it, while the erotogenic zones become subordinated to the primacy of the genital zone. Since the new sexual aim assigns very different functions to the two sexes, their sexual development now diverges greatly. That of males is the more straightforward and the more understandable, while that of females actually enters upon a kind of involution. A normal sexual life is only assured by an exact convergence of the affectionate current and the sensual current both being directed towards the sexual object and sexual aim. (The former, the affectionate current, comprises what remains over of the infantile efflorescence of sexuality.)[23] It is like the completion of a tunnel which has been driven through a hill from both directions.

The new sexual aim in men consists in the discharge of the sexual products. The earlier one, the attainment of pleasure, is by no means alien to it; on the contrary, the highest degree of pleasure is attached to this final act of the sexual process. The sexual instinct is now subordinated to the reproductive function; it becomes, so to say, altruistic. If this transformation is to succeed, the original dispositions and all the other characteristics of the instincts must be taken into account in the process. Just as on any other occasion on which the organism should by rights make new combinations and adjustments leading to complicated mechanisms, here too there are possibilities of pathological disorders if these new arrangements are not carried out. Every pathological disorder of sexual life is rightly to be regarded as an inhibition in development.

1. *The Primacy of the Genital Zones and Fore-Pleasure*

The starting-point and the final aim of the process which I have described are clearly visible. The intermediate steps are still in many ways obscure to us. We shall have to leave more than one of them as an unsolved riddle.

The most striking of the processes at puberty has been picked upon as constituting its essence: the manifest growth of the external genitalia. (The latency period of childhood is, on the other hand, characterized by a relative cessation of their growth.) In the meantime the development of the internal genitalia has advanced far enough for them to be able to discharge the sexual products or, as the case may be, to bring about the formation of a new living organism. Thus a highly complicated apparatus has been made ready and awaits the moment of being put into operation.

This apparatus is to be set in motion by stimuli, and observation shows us that stimuli can impinge on it from three directions: from the external world by means of the excitation of the erotogenic zones with which we are already familiar, from the organic

23. [This sentence was added in 1920.]

interior by ways which we have still to explore, and from mental life, which is itself a storehouse for external impressions and a receiving-post for internal excitations. All three kinds of stimuli produce the same effect, namely a condition described as 'sexual excitement', which shows itself by two sorts of indication, mental and somatic. The mental indications consist in a peculiar feeling of tension of an extremely compelling character; and among the numerous somatic ones are first and foremost a number of changes in the genitals, which have the obvious sense of being preparations for the sexual act—the erection of the male organ and the lubrication of the vagina.

Sexual Tension The fact that sexual excitement possesses the character of tension raises a problem the solution of which is no less difficult than it would be important in helping us to understand the sexual processes. In spite of all the differences of opinion that reign on the subject among psychologists, I must insist that a feeling of tension necessarily involves unpleasure. What seems to me decisive is the fact that a feeling of this kind is accompanied by an impulsion to make a change in the psychological situation, that it operates in an urgent way which is wholly alien to the nature of the feeling of pleasure. If, however, the tension of sexual excitement is counted as an unpleasurable feeling, we are at once brought up against the fact that it is also undoubtedly felt as pleasurable. In every case in which tension is produced by sexual processes it is accompanied by pleasure; even in the preparatory changes in the genitals a feeling of satisfaction of some kind is plainly to be observed. How, then, are this unpleasurable tension and this feeling of pleasure to be reconciled?

Everything relating to the problem of pleasure and unpleasure touches upon one of the sorest spots of present-day psychology. It will be my aim to learn as much as possible from the circumstances of the instance with which we are at present dealing, but I shall avoid any approach to the problem as a whole.[24]

Let us begin by casting a glance at the way in which the erotogenic zones fit themselves into the new arrangement. They have to play an important part in introducing sexual excitation. The

24. [*Footnote added* 1924:] I have made an attempt at solving this problem in the first part of my paper on 'The Economic Problem of Masochism' (1924*c*). {This paper is anthologized below.}

eye is perhaps the zone most remote from the sexual object, but it is the one which, in the situation of wooing an object, is liable to be the most frequently stimulated by the particular quality of excitation whose cause, when it occurs in a sexual object, we describe as beauty. (For the same reason the merits of a sexual object are described as 'attractions'.) This stimulation is on the one hand already accompanied by pleasure, while on the other hand it leads to an increase of sexual excitement or produces it if it is not yet present. If the excitation now spreads to another erotogenic zone—to the hand, for instance, through tactile sensations—the effect is the same: a feeling of pleasure on the one side, which is quickly intensified by pleasure arising from the preparatory changes [in the genitals], and on the other side an increase of sexual tension, which soon passes over into the most obvious unpleasure if it cannot be met by a further accession of pleasure. Another instance will perhaps make this even clearer. If an erotogenic zone in a person who is not sexually excited (e.g. the skin of a woman's breast) is stimulated by touch, the contact produces a pleasurable feeling, but it is at the same time better calculated than anything to arouse a sexual excitation that demands an increase of pleasure. The problem is how it can come about that an experience of pleasure can give rise to a need for greater pleasure.

The Mechanism of Fore-Pleasure   The part played in this by the erotogenic zones, however, is clear. What is true of one of them is true of all. They are all used to provide a certain amount of pleasure by being stimulated in the way appropriate to them. This pleasure then leads to an increase in tension which in its turn is responsible for producing the necessary motor energy for the conclusion of the sexual act. The penultimate stage of that act is once again the appropriate stimulation of an erotogenic zone (the genital zone itself, in the glans penis) by the appropriate object (the mucous membrane of the vagina); and from the pleasure yielded by this excitation the motor energy is obtained, this time by a reflex path, which brings about the discharge of the sexual substances. This last pleasure is the highest in intensity, and its mechanism differs from that of the earlier pleasure. It is brought about entirely by discharge: it is wholly a pleasure of satisfaction and with it the tension of the libido is for the time being extinguished.

This distinction between the one kind of pleasure due to the excitation of erotogenic zones and the other kind due to the discharge of the sexual substances deserves, I think, to be made more concrete by a difference in nomenclature. The former may be suitably described as 'fore-pleasure' in contrast to the 'end-pleasure' or pleasure of satisfaction derived from the sexual act. Fore-pleasure is thus the same pleasure that has already been produced, although on a smaller scale, by the infantile sexual instinct; end-pleasure is something new and is thus probably conditioned by circumstances that do not arise till puberty. The formula for the new function of the erotogenic zones runs therefore: they are used to make possible through the medium of the fore-pleasure which can be derived from them (as it was during infantile life), the production ot the greater pleasure of satisfaction. * * *

Dangers of Fore-Pleasure   The connection between fore-pleasure and infantile sexual life is, however, made clearer by the pathogenic part which it can come to play. The atainment of the normal sexual aim can clearly be endangered by the mechanism in which fore-pleasure is involved. This danger arises if at any point in the preparatory sexual processes the fore-pleasure turns out to be too great and the element of tension too small. The motive for proceeding further with the sexual process then disappears, the whole path is cut short, and the preparatory act in question takes the place of the normal sexual aim. Experience has shown that the precondition for this damaging event is that the erotogenic zone concerned or the corresponding component instinct shall already during childhood have contributed an unusual amount of pleasure. If further factors then come into play, tending to bring about a fixation, a compulsion may easily arise in later life which resists the incorporation of this particular fore-pleasure into a new context. Such is in fact the mechanism of many perversions, which consist in a lingering over the preparatory acts of the sexual process.

This failure of the function of the sexual mechanism owing to fore-pleasure is best avoided if the primacy of the genitals too is adumbrated in childhood; and indeed things seem actually arranged to bring this about in the second half of childhood (from the age of eight to puberty). During these years the genital zones already behave in much the same way as in maturity; they become the seat of sensations of excitation and or preparatory changes

whenever any pleasure is felt from the satisfaction of other erotogenic zones, though this result is still without a purpose—that
is to say, contributes nothing to a continuation of the sexual
process. Already in childhood, therefore, alongside of the pleasure
of satisfaction there is a certain amount of sexual tension, although
it is less constant and less in quantity. * * * It will be noticed
that in the course of our enquiry we began by exaggerating the
distinction between infantile and mature sexual life, and that we
are now setting this right. Not only the deviations from normal
sexual life but its normal form as well are determined by the
infantile manifestations of sexuality.

2. The Problem of Sexual Excitation

We remain in complete ignorance both of the origin and of
the nature of the sexual tension which arises simultaneously with
the pleasure when erotogenic zones are satisfied. The most obvious explanation, that this tension arises in some way out of the
pleasure itself, is not only extremely improbable in itself but becomes untenable when we consider that in connection with the
greatest pleasure of all, that which accompanies the discharge of
the sexual products, no tension is produced, but on the contrary
all tension is removed. Thus pleasure and sexual tension can only
be connected in an indirect manner.

Part Played by the Sexual Substances   Apart from the fact that
normally it is only the discharge of the sexual substances that
brings sexual excitation to an end, there are other points of contact
between sexual tension and the sexual products. In the case of a
man living a continent {or chaste} life, the sexual apparatus, at
varying intervals, which, however, are not ungoverned by rules,
discharges the sexual substances during the night, to the accompaniment of a pleasurable feeling and in the course of a dream
which hallucinates a sexual act. And in regard to this process
(nocturnal emission) it is difficult to avoid the conclusion that the
sexual tension, which succeeds in making use of the short cut of
hallucination as a substitute for the act iself, is a function of the
accumulation of semen in the vesicles containing the sexual products. Our experience in connection with the exhaustibility of the
sexual mechanism argues in the same sense. If the store of semen
is exhausted, not only is it impossible to carry out the sexual act,

but the susceptibility of the erotogenic zones to stimulus ceases, and their appropriate excitation no longer gives rise to any pleasure. We thus learn incidentally that a certain degree of sexual tension is required even for the excitability of the erotogenic zones. {On the other hand, the weakness of the theory that the sexual substances create and maintain sexual tension,} which we find accepted, for instance, in Krafft-Ebing's account of the sexual processes, lies in the fact that, having been designed to account for the sexual activity of adult males, it takes too little account of three sets of conditions in children, in females and in castrated males. In none of these three cases can there be any question of an accumulation of sexual products in the same sense as in males, and this makes a smooth application of the theory difficult. Nevertheless it may at once be admitted that it is possible to find means by which the theory may be made to cover these cases as well. In any case we are warned not to lay more weight on the factor of the accumulation of the sexual products than it is able to bear.

Freud follows this passage with several pages of reports about contemporary experiments with castrated males and with sex-change operations performed on animals. This biological excursion also includes his speculations about the "chemical basis" of sex, which he expects will one day be discovered—a remarkable anticipation of research into the "chemicals," we now call hormones.

3. The Libido Theory[25]

The conceptual scaffolding which we have set up to help us in dealing with the psychical manifestations of sexual life tallies well with these hypotheses as to the chemical basis of sexual excitation. We have defined the concept of libido as a quantitatively variable force which could serve as a measure of processes and transformations occurring in the field of sexual excitation. We distinguish this libido in respect of its special origin from the energy which must be supposed to underlie mental processes in general, and we thus also attribute a *qualitative* character to it. In thus distinguishing between libidinal and other forms of psychical energy we are giving expression to the presumption that the

25. [This whole section, except for its last paragraph, dates from 1915. It is largely based on Freud's paper on narcissism (1914c).]

sexual processes occuring in the organism are distinguished from the nutritive processes by a special chemistry. The analysis of the perversions and psychoneuroses has shown us that this sexual excitation is derived not from the so-called sexual parts alone, but from all the bodily organs. We thus reach the idea of a quantity of libido, to the mental representation of which we give the name of 'ego-libido', and whose production, increase or diminution, distribution and displacement should afford us possibilities for explaining the psychosexual phenomena observed.

This ego-libido is, however, only conveniently accessible to analytic study when it has been put to the use of cathecting sexual objects, that is, when it has become object-libido. We can then perceive it concentrating upon objects,[26] becoming fixed upon them or abandoning them, moving from one object to another and, from these situations, directing the subject's sexual activity, which leads to the satisfaction, that is, to the partial and temporary extinction, of the libido. The psycho-analysis of what are termed transference neuroses (hysteria and obsessional neurosis) affords us a clear insight at this point.

We can follow the object-libido through still further vicissitudes. When it is withdrawn from objects, it is held in suspense in peculiar conditions of tension and is finally drawn back into the ego, so that it becomes ego-libido once again. In contrast to object-libido, we also describe ego-libido as 'narcissistic' libido. From the vantage-point of psycho-analysis we can look across a frontier, which we may not pass, at the activities of narcissistic libido, and may form some idea of the relation between it and object-libido. Narcissistic or ego-libido seems to be the great reservoir from which the object-cathexes are sent out and into which they are withdrawn once more; the narcissistic libidinal cathexis of the ego is the original state of things, realized in earliest childhood, and is merely covered by the later extrusions of libido, but in essentials persists behind them.

It should be the task of a libido theory of neurotic and psychotic disorders to express all the observed phenomena and inferred processes in terms of the economics of the libido. It is easy to

---

26. [It is scarcely necessary to explain that here as elsewhere, in speaking of the libido concentrating on 'objects', withdrawing from 'objects', etc., Freud has in mind the mental presentations (*Vorstellungen*) of objects and not, of course, objects in the external world.]

guess that the vicissitudes of the ego-libido will have the major part to play in this connection, especially when it is a question of explaining the deeper psychotic disturbances. We are then faced by the difficulty that our method of research, psycho-analysis, for the moment affords us assured information only on the transformations that take place in the object-libido, but is unable to make any immediate distinction between the ego-libido and the other forms of energy operating in the ego.

For the present, therefore,[27] no further development of the libido theory is possible, except upon speculative lines. It would, however, be sacrificing all that we have gained hitherto from psycho-analytic observation, if we were to follow the example of C. G. Jung and water down the meaning of the concept of libido itself by equating it with psychical instinctual force in general. The distinguishing of the sexual instinctual impulses from the rest and the consequent restriction of the concept of libido to the former receives strong support from the assumption which I have already discussed that there is a special chemistry of the sexual function.

4. The Differentiation between Men and Women

As we all know, it is not until puberty that the sharp distinction is established between the masculine and feminine characters. From that time on, this contrast has a more decisive influence than any other upon the shaping of human life. It is true that the masculine and feminine dispositions are already easily recognizable in childhood. The development of the inhibitions of sexuality (shame, disgust, pity, etc.) takes place in little girls earlier and in the face of less resistance than in boys; the tendency to sexual repression seems in general to be greater; and, where the component instincts of sexuality appear, they prefer the passive form. The auto-erotic activity of the erotogenic zones is, however, the same in both sexes, and owing to this uniformity there is no possibility of a distinction between the two sexes such as arises after puberty. So far as the autoerotic and masturbatory manifestations of sexuality are concerned, we might lay it down that the sexuality of little girls is of a wholly masculine character.

27. [This paragraph was added in 1920.]

Indeed, if we were able to give a more definite connotation to the concepts of 'masculine' and 'feminine', it would even be possible to maintain that libido is invariably and necessarily of a masculine nature, whether it occurs in men or in women and irrespectively of whether its object is a man or a woman.[28]

Since I have become acquainted with the notion of bisexuality I have regarded it as the decisive factor, and without taking bisexuality into account I think it would scarcely be possible to arrive at an understanding of the sexual manifestations that are actually to be observed in men and women.

Leading Zones in Men and Women   Apart from this I have only the following to add. The leading erotogenic zone in female children is located at the clitoris, and is thus homologous to the masculine genital zone of the glans penis. All my experience concerning masturbation in little girls has related to the clitoris and not to the regions of the external genitalia that are important

28. [Before 1924 the words from 'libido' to the end of the sentence were printed in spaced type.—*Footnote added* 1915:] It is essential to understand clearly that the concepts of 'masculine' and 'feminine', whose meaning seems so unambiguous to ordinary people, are among the most confused that occur in science. It is possible to distinguish at least three uses. 'Masculine' and 'feminine' are used sometimes in the sense of activity and passivity, sometimes in a biological, and sometimes, again, in a sociological sense. The first of these three meanings is the essential one and the most serviceable in psychoanalysis. When, for instance, libido was described in the text above as being 'masculine,' the word was being used in this sense, for an instinct is always active even when it has a passive aim in view. The second, or biological, meaning of 'masculine' and 'feminine' is the one whose applicability can be determined most easily. Here 'masculine' and 'feminine' are characterized by the presence of spermatozoa or ova respectively and by the functions proceeding from them. Activity and its concomitant phenomena (more powerful muscular development, aggressiveness, greater intensity of libido) are as a rule linked with biological masculinity; but they are not necessarily so, for there are animal species in which these qualities are on the contrary assigned to the female. The third, or sociological, meaning receives its connotation from the observation of actually existing masculine and feminine individuals. Such observation shows that in human beings pure masculinity or femininity is not to be found either in a psychological or a biological sense. Every individual on the contrary displays a mixture of the character-traits belonging to his own and to the opposite sex; and he shows a combination of activity and passivity whether or not these last character-traits tally with his biological ones. [A later discussion of this point will be found in a footnote at the end of Chapter IV of *Civilization and its Discontents* (1930).]

in later sexual functioning. I am even doubtful whether a female child can be led by the influence of seduction to anything other than clitoridal masturbation. If such a thing occurs, it is quite exceptional. The spontaneous discharges of sexual excitement which occur so often precisely in little girls are expressed in spasms of the clitoris. Frequent erections of that organ make it possible for girls to form a correct judgement, even without any instruction, of the sexual manifestations of the other sex: they merely transfer on to boys the sensations derived from their own sexual processes.

If we are to understand how a little girl turns into a woman, we must follow the further vicissitudes of this excitability of the clitoris. Puberty, which brings about so great an accession of libido in boys, is marked in girls by a fresh wave of *repression*, in which it is precisely clitoridal sexuality that is affected. What is thus overtaken by repression is a piece of masculine sexuality. The intensification of the brake upon sexuality brought about by pubertal repression in women serves as a stimulus to the libido in men and causes an increase of its activity. Along with this heightening of libido there is also an increase of sexual overvaluation which only emerges in full force in relation to a woman who holds herself back and who denies her sexuality. When at last the sexual act is permitted and the clitoris itself becomes excited, it still retains a function: the task, namely, of transmitting the excitation to the adjacent female sexual parts, just as—to use a simile—pine shavings can be kindled in order to set a log of harder wood on fire. Before this transference can be effected, a certain interval of time must often elapse, during which the young woman is anaesthetic. This anaesthesia may become permanent if the clitoridal zone refuses to abandon its excitability, an event for which the way is prepared precisely by an extensive activity of that zone in childhood. Anaesthesia in women, as is well known, is often only apparent and local. They are anaesthetic at the vaginal orifice but are by no means incapable of excitement originating in the clitoris or even in other zones. Alongside these erotogenic determinants of anaesthesia must also be set the psychical determinants, which equally arise from repression.

When erotogenic susceptibility to stimulation has been successfully transferred by a woman from the clitoris to the vaginal orifice, it implies that she has adopted a new leading zone for the purposes of her later sexual activity. A man, on the other hand, retains his leading zone unchanged from childhood. The fact that women change their leading erotogenic zone in this way, together with the wave of repression at puberty, which, as it were, puts aside their childish masculinity, are the chief determinants of the greater proneness of woman to neurosis and especially to hysteria. These determinants, therefore, are intimately related to the essence of femininity.

5. *The Finding of an Object*

The processes at puberty thus establish the primacy of the genital zones; and, in a man, the penis, which has now become capable of erection, presses forward insistently towards the new sexual aim—penetration into a cavity in the body which excites his genital zone. Simultaneously on the psychical side the process of finding an object, for which preparations have been made from earliest childhood, is completed. At a time at which the first beginnings of sexual satisfaction are still linked with the taking of nourishment, the sexual instinct has a sexual object outside the infant's own body in the shape of his mother's breast. It is only later that the instinct loses that object, just at the time, perhaps, when the child is able to form a total idea of the person to whom the organ that is giving him satisfaction belongs. As a rule the sexual instinct then becomes auto-erotic, and not until the period of latency has been passed through is the original relation restored. There are thus good reasons why a child sucking at his mother's breast has become the prototype of every relation of love. The finding of an object is in fact a refinding of it.[29]

The Sexual Object during Early Infancy   But even after sexual activity has become detached from the taking of nourishment, an important part of this first and most significant of all sexual relations is left over, which helps to prepare for the choice of an

---

29. [*Footnote added* 1915:] Psycho-analysis informs us that there are two methods of finding an object. The first, described in the text, is the 'anaclitic' or 'attachment' one, based on attachment to early infantile prototypes. The second is the narcissistic one, which seeks for the subject's own ego and finds it again in other people. This latter method is of particularly great importance in cases where the outcome is a pathological one, but it is not relevant to the present context. {See p. 191 below.}

object and thus to restore the happiness that has been lost. All through the period of latency children learn to feel for other people who help them in their helplessness and satisfy their needs a love which is on the model of, and a continuation of, their relation as sucklings to their nursing mother. There may perhaps be an inclination to dispute the possibility of identifying a child's affection and esteem for those who look after him with sexual love. I think, however, that a closer psychological examination may make it possible to establish this identity beyond any doubt. A child's intercourse with anyone responsible for his care affords him an unending source of sexual excitation and satisfaction from his erotogenic zones. This is especially so since the person in charge of him, who, after all, is as a rule his mother, herself regards him with feelings that are derived from her own sexual life: she strokes him, kisses him, rocks him and quite clearly treats him as a substitute for a complete sexual object.[30] A mother would probably be horrified if she were made aware that all her marks of affection were rousing her child's sexual instinct and preparing for its later intensity. She regards what she does as asexual, 'pure' love, since, after all, she carefully avoids applying more excitations to the child's genitals than are unavoidable in nursery care. As we know, however, the sexual instinct is not aroused only by direct excitation of the genital zone. What we call affection will unfailingly show its effects one day on the genital zones as well. Moreover, if the mother understood more of the high importance of the part played by instincts in mental life as a whole—in all its ethical and psychical achievements—she would spare herself any self-reproaches even after her enlightenment. She is only fulfilling her task in teaching the child to love. After all, he is meant to grow up into a strong and capable person with vigorous sexual needs and to accomplish during his life all the things that human beings are urged to do by their instincts. It is true that an excess of parental affection does harm by causing precocious sexual maturity and also because, by spoiling the child, it makes him incapable in later life of temporarily doing without love or of being content with a smaller amount of it. One of the clearest indications that a child will later become neurotic is to be seen in an insatiable

---

30. Anyone who considers this 'sacrilegious' may be recommended to read Havelock Ellis's views [1913, 18] on the relation between mother and child, which agree almost completely with mine.

demand for his parents' affection. And on the other hand neu-
ropathic parents, who are inclined as a rule to display excessive
affection, are precisely those who are most likely by their caresses
to arouse the child's disposition to neurotic illness. Incidentally,
this example shows that there are ways more direct than inheritance by which neurotic parents can hand their disorder on to
their children.

Infantile Anxiety   Children themselves behave from an early age
as though their dependence on the people looking after them were
in the nature of sexual love. Anxiety in children is originally
nothing other than an expression of the fact that they are feeling
the loss of the person they love. It is for this reason that they are
frightened of every stranger. They are afraid in the dark because
in the dark they cannot see the person they love; and their fear
is soothed if they can take hold of that person's hand in the dark.
To attribute to bogeys and blood-curdling stories told by nurses
the responsibility for making children timid is to over-estimate
their efficacy. The truth is merely that children who are inclined
to be timid are affected by stories which would make no impression
whatever upon others, and it is only children with a sexual instinct
that is excessive or has developed prematurely or has become
vociferous owing to too much petting who are inclined to be
timid. In this respect a child, by turning his libido into anxiety
when he cannot satisfy it, behaves like an adult. On the other
hand an adult who has become neurotic owing to his libido being
unsatisfied behaves in his anxiety like a child: he begins to be
frightened when he is alone, that is to say when he is away from
someone of whose love he had felt secure, and he seeks to assuage
this fear by the most childish measures.[31]

31. For this explanation of the origin of infantile anxiety I have to thank a three-
     year-old boy whom I once heard calling out of a dark room: 'Auntie, speak
     to me! I'm frightened because it's so dark.' His aunt answered him: 'What
     good would that do? You can't see me.' 'That doesn't matter,' replied the
     child, 'if anyone speaks, it gets light.' Thus what he was afraid of was not
     the dark, but the absence of someone he loved; and he could feel sure of
     being soothed as soon as he had evidence of that person's presence. [*Added*
     1920:] One of the most important results of psycho-analytic research is this
     discovery that neurotic anxiety arises out of libido, that it is the product of a
     transformation of it, and that it is thus related to it in the same kind of way
     as vinegar is to wine. A further discussion of this problem will be found in

The Barrier against Incest We see, therefore, that the parents'
affection for their child may awaken his sexual instinct prematurely (i.e., before the somatic conditions of puberty are present)
to such a degree that the mental excitation breaks through in an
unmistakable fashion to the genital system. If, on the other hand,
they are fortunate enough to avoid this, then their affection can
perform its task of directing the child in his choice of a sexual
object when he reaches maturity. No doubt the simplest course
for the child would be to choose as his sexual objects the same
persons whom, since his childhood, he has loved with what may
be described as damped-down libido. But, by the postponing of
sexual maturation, time has been gained in which the child can
erect, among other restraints on sexuality, the barrier against incest, and can thus take up into himself the moral precepts which
expressly exclude from his object-choice, as being blood-relations,
the persons whom he has loved in his childhood. Respect for this
barrier is essentially a cultural demand made by society. Society
must defend itself against the danger that the interests which it
needs for the establishment of higher social units may be swallowed up by the family; and for this reason, in the case of every
individual, but in particular of adolescent boys, it seeks by all
possible means to loosen their connection with their family—a
connection which, in their childhood, is the only important
one.[32]

It is in the world of ideas, however, that the choice of an object
is accomplished at first; and the sexual life of maturing youth is
almost entirely restricted to indulging in phantasies, that is, in
ideas that are not destined to be carried into effect. In these
phantasies the infantile tendencies invariably emerge once more,

---

my *Introductory Lectures on Psycho-Analysis* (1916–17), Lecture XXV,
though even there it must be confessed, the question is not finally cleared
up. [For Freud's latest views on the subject of anxiety see his *Inhibitions,
Symptoms and Anxiety* (1926) and his *New Introductory Lectures* (1933),
Chapter XXXII.]

32. [*Footnote added* 1915:] The barrier against incest is probably among the
historical acquisitions of mankind, and, like other moral taboos, has no doubt
already become established in many persons by organic inheritance. (Cf. my
Totem and Taboo, 1912–13.) Psycho-analytic investigation shows, however,
how intensely the individual struggles with the temptation to incest during
his period of growth and how frequently the barrier is transgressed in phantasies
and even in reality.

but this time with intensified pressure from somatic sources. Among these tendencies the first place is taken with uniform frequency by the child's sexual impulses towards his parents, which are as a rule already differentiated owing to the attraction of the opposite sex—the son being drawn towards his mother and the daughter towards her father. At the same time as these plainly incestuous phantasies are overcome and repudiated, one of the most significant, but also one of the most painful, psychical achievements of the pubertal period is completed: detachment from parental authority, a process that alone makes possible the opposition, which is so important for the progress of civilization, between the new generation and the old. At every stage in the course of development through which all human beings ought by rights to pass, a certain number are held back; so there are some who have never got over their parents' authority and have withdrawn their affection from them either very incompletely or not at all. They are mostly girls, who, to the delight of their parents, have persisted in all their childish love far beyond puberty. It is most instructive to find that it is precisely these girls who in their later marriage lack the capacity to give their husbands what is due to them; they make cold wives and remain sexually anaesthetic. We learn from this that sexual love and what appears to be non-sexual love for parents are fed from the same sources; the latter, that is to say, merely corresponds to an infantile fixation of the libido.

The closer one comes to the deeper disturbances of psychosexual development, the more unmistakably the importance of incestuous object-choice emerges. In psychoneurotics a large portion or the whole of their psychosexual activity in finding an object remains in the unconscious as a result of their repudiation of sexuality. Girls with an exaggerated need for affection and an equally exaggerated horror of the real demands made by sexual life have an irresistible temptation on the one hand to realize the ideal of asexual love in their lives and on the other hand to conceal their libido behind an affection which they can express without self-reproaches, by holding fast throughout their lives to their infantile fondness, revived at puberty, for their parents or brothers and sisters. Psychoanalysis has no difficulty in showing persons of this kind that they are *in love*, in the everyday sense of the word, with these blood-relations of theirs; for, with the help of their symptoms and other manifestations of their illness, it traces their unconscious thoughts and translates them into conscious ones. In cases in which someone who has previously been healthy falls ill after an unhappy experience in love it is also possible to show with certainty that the mechanism of his illness consists in a turning-back of his libido on to those whom he preferred in his infancy.

After-Effects of Infantile Object-Choice Even a person who has been fortunate enough to avoid an incestuous fixation of his libido does not entirely escape its influence. It often happens that a young man falls in love seriously for the first time with a mature woman, or a girl with an elderly man in a position of authority; this is clearly an echo of the phase of development that we have been discussing, since these figures are able to re-animate pictures of their mother or father. There can be no doubt that every object-choice whatever is based, though less closely, on these prototypes. A man, especially, looks for someone who can represent his picture of his mother, as it has dominated his mind from his earliest childhood; and accordingly, if his mother is still alive, she may well resent this new version of herself and meet her with hostility. In view of the importance of a child's relations to his parents in determining his later choice of a sexual object, it can easily be understood that any disturbance of those relations will produce the gravest effects upon his adult sexual life. Jealousy in a lover is never without an infantile root or at least an infantile reinforcement. If there are quarrels between the parents or if their marriage is unhappy, the ground will be prepared in their children for the severest predisposition to a disturbance of sexual development or to a neurotic illness.

A child's affection for his parents is no doubt the most important infantile trace which, after being revived at puberty, points the way to his choice of an object; but it is not the only one. Other starting-points with the same early origin enable a man to develop more than one sexual line, based no less upon his childhood, and to lay down very various conditions for his object-choice.

Prevention of Inversion One of the tasks implicit in object-choice is that it should find its way to the opposite sex. This, as we know, is not accomplished without a certain amount of fumbling. Often enough the first impulses after puberty go astray, though without any permanent harm resulting. Dessoir [1894] has justly remarked upon the regularity with which adolescent boys and girls form sentimental friendships with others of their own sex. No doubt the strongest force working against a permanent inversion of the sexual object is the attraction which the opposing sexual characters exercise upon one another. Nothing can be said within the framework of the present discussion to throw light upon it. This factor is not in itself, however, sufficient to exclude inversion; there are no doubt a variety of other contributory factors. Chief among these is its authoritative prohibition by society. Where inversion is not regarded as a crime it will be found that it answers fully to the sexual inclinations of no small number of people. It may be presumed, in the next place, that in the case of men a childhood recollection of the affection shown them by their mother and others of the female sex who looked after them when they were children contributes powerfully to directing their choice towards women;[33] on the other hand their early experience of being deterred by their father from sexual activity and their competitive relation with him deflect them from their own sex. Both of these two factors apply equally to girls, whose sexual activity is particularly subject to the watchful guardianship of their mother. They thus acquire a hostile relation to their own sex which influences their object-choice decisively in what is regarded as the normal direction. The education of boys by male persons (by slaves, in antiquity) seems to encourage homosexuality. The frequency of inversion among the present-day aristocracy is made somewhat more intelligible by their employment of menservants, as well as by the fact that their mothers give less personal care to their children. In the case of some hysterics it is found that the early loss of one of their parents, whether by death, divorce or separation, with the result that the remaining parents absorbs the whole of the child's love, determines the sex of the person who is later to be chosen as a sexual object, and may thus open the way to permanent inversion.

33. [The rest of this sentence and the two following ones date from 1915. In the editions of 1905 and 1910 the following passage takes their place: 'while in the case of girls, who in any case enter a period of repression at puberty, impulses of rivalry play a part in discouraging them from loving members of their own sex.']

Freud concluded his Three Essays on the Theory of Sexuality *with a section called "Summary." He recapitulated the developmental theory presented in the essays and then made an effort to survey the factors that could interfere with or redirect development: constitution or heredity, repression, sublimation, accidental experiences ("first and foremost, seduction by other children or adults"), spontaneous sexual precocity, differences among individuals with respect to the onset and intensity of the developmental phases, and fixation. This list, Freud notes, simply shows how many areas of the biological foundation of sexuality remain unexplored.*

Hysterical Phantasies and Their Relation to Bisexuality

In a final footnote to his discussion of transference in the Dora case (above, p. 88), Freud candidly admitted: "Before I had learnt the importance of the homosexual current of feeling in psychoneurotics, I was often brought to a standstill in the treatment of my cases or found myself in complete perplexity." This short 1908 essay brings to the topic of fantasies his appreciation of the simultaneous presence of heterosexual and homosexual currents in all people. In the process, Freud offers an overview of the main ingredients—developed over nearly fifteen years of work—of his clinical theory of hysteria.

❧❧❧

We are all familiar with the delusional imaginings of the paranoic, which are concerned with the greatness and the sufferings of his own self and which appear in forms that are quite typical and almost monotonous. We have also become acquainted, through numerous accounts, with the strange performances with which certain perverts stage their sexual satisfaction, whether in idea or reality. Nevertheless, it may be new to some readers to hear that quite analogous psychical structures are regularly present in all the psychoneuroses, particularly in hysteria, and that these latter—which are known as hysterical phantasies—can be seen to have important connections with the causation of the neurotic symptoms.

A common source and normal prototype of all these creations of phantasy is to be found in what are called the day-dreams of

youth. These have already received some, though as yet insufficient, notice in the literature of the subject. They occur with
perhaps equal frequency in both sexes, though it seems that while
in girls and women they are invariably of an erotic nature, in
men they may be either erotic or ambitious. Nevertheless the
importance of the erotic factor in men, too, should not be given
a secondary rating; a closer investigation of a man's day-dreams
generally shows that all his heroic exploits are carried out and all
his successes achieved only in order to please a woman and to be
preferred by her to other men. These phantasies are satisfactions
of wishes proceeding from deprivation and longing. They are justly
called 'day-dreams', for they give us the key to an understanding
of night-dreams—in which the nucleus of the dream-formation
consists of nothing else than complicated day-time phantasies of
this kind that have been distorted and are misunderstood by the
conscious psychical agency.[1]

These day-dreams are cathected with a large amount of interest;
they are carefully cherished by the subject and usually concealed
with a great deal of sensitivity, as though they were among the
most intimate possessions of his personality. It is easy to recognize
a person who is absorbed in day-dreaming in the street, however,
by his sudden, as it were absent-minded, smile, his way of talking
to himself, or by the hastening of his steps which marks the climax
of the imagined situation. Every hysterical attack which I have
been able to investigate up to the present has proved to be an
involuntary irruption of day-dreams of this kind. For our observations no longer leave any room for doubt that such phantasies
may be unconscious just as well as conscious; and as soon as the
latter have become unconscious they may also become pathogenic—that is, they may express themselves in symptoms and
attacks. In favourable circumstances, the subject can still capture
an unconscious phantasy of this sort in consciousness. After I had
drawn the attention of one of my patients to her phantasies, she
told me that on one occasion she had suddenly found herself in
tears in the street and that, rapidly considering what it was she
was actually crying about, she had got hold of a phantasy to the
following effect. In her imagination she had formed a tender

1. Cf. *The Interpretation of Dreams* (1900a), 5: 491 ff. [The contents of this
paragraph had been stated more fully by Freud in his almost contemporary
paper 'Creative Writers and Day-Dreaming' (1908)].

attachment to a pianist who was well known in the town (though she was not personally acquainted with him); she had had a child by him (she was in fact childless); and he had then deserted her and her child and left them in poverty. It was at this point in her romance that she had burst into tears.

Unconscious phantasies have either been unconscious all along and have been formed in the unconscious; or—as is more often the case—they were once conscious phantasies, day-dreams, and have since been purposely forgotten and have become unconscious through 'repression.' Their content may afterwards either have remained the same or have undergone alterations, so that the present unconscious phantasies are derivatives of the once conscious ones. Now an unconscious phantasy has a very important connection with the subject's sexual life; for it is identical with the phantasy which served to give him sexual satisfaction during a period of masturbation. At that time the masturbatory act (in the widest sense of the term[2]) was compounded of two parts. One was the evocation of a phantasy and the other some active behaviour for obtaining self-gratification at the height of the phantasy. This compound, as we know, was itself merely soldered together. Originally the action was a purely auto-erotic procedure for the purpose of obtaining pleasure from some particular part of the body, which could be described as erotogenic. Later, this action became merged with a wishful idea from the sphere of object-love and served as a partial realization of the situation in which the phantasy culminated. When, subsequently, the subject renounces this type of satisfaction, composed of masturbation and phantasy, the action is given up, while the phantasy, from being conscious, becomes unconscious. If no other mode of sexual satisfaction supervenes, the subject remains abstinent; and if he does not succeed in sublimating his libido—that is, in deflecting his sexual excitation to higher aims—, the condition is now fulfilled for his unconscious phantasy to be revived and to proliferate, and, at least as regards some part of its content, to put itself into effect, with the whole force of his need for love, in the form of a pathological symptom.

In this way, unconscious phantasies are the immediate psych-

---

2. [I.e. not in its restricted literal sense of manual friction.]

ical precursors of a whole number of hysterical symptoms. Hysterical symptoms are nothing other than unconscious phantasies brought into view through 'conversion'; and in so far as the symptoms are somatic ones, they are often enough taken from the circle of the same sexual sensations and motor innervations as those which had originally accompanied the phantasy when it was still conscious. In this way the giving up of the habit of masturbation is in fact undone, and the purpose of the whole pathological process, which is a restoration of the original, primary sexual satisfaction, is achieved—though never completely, it is true, but always in a sort of approximation.

Anyone who studies hysteria, therefore, soon finds his interest turned away from its symptoms to the phantasies from which they proceed. The technique of psycho-analysis enables us in the first place to infer from the symptoms what those unconscious phantasies are and then to make them conscious to the patient. By this means it has been found that the content of the hysteric's unconscious phantasies corresponds completely to the situations in which satisfaction is consciously obtained by perverts; and if anyone is at a loss for examples of such situations he has only to recall the world-famous performances of the Roman Emperors, the wild excesses of which were, of course, determined only by the enormous and unrestrained power possessed by the authors of the phantasies. The delusions of paranoics are phantasies of the same nature, though they are phantasies which have become directly conscious. They rest on the sado-masochistic components of the sexual instinct, and they, too, may find their complete counterpart in certain unconscious phantasies of hysterical subjects. We also know of cases—cases which have their practical importance as well—in which hysterics do not give expression to their phantasies in the form of symptoms but as conscious realizations, and in that way devise and stage assaults, attacks or acts of sexual aggression.

This method of psycho-analytic investigation, which leads from the conspicuous symptoms to the hidden unconscious phantasies, tells us everything that can be known about the sexuality of psychoneurotics, including the fact which is to be the main subject-matter of this short preliminary publication.

Owing, probably, to the difficulties which the unconscious phantasies meet with in their endeavour to find expression, the relationship of the phantasies to the symptoms is not simple, but on the contrary, complicated in many ways.[3] As a rule—when, that is, the neurosis is fully developed and has persisted for some time—a particular symptom corresponds, not to a single unconscious phantasy, but to several such phantasies; and it does so not in an arbitary manner but in accordance with a regular pattern. At the beginning of the illness these complications are, no doubt, not all fully developed.

For the sake of general interest I will at this point go outside the framework of this paper and interpolate a series of formulas which attempt to give a progressively fuller description of the nature of hysterical symptoms. These formulas do not contradict one another, but some represnt an increasingly complete and precise approach to the facts, while others represent the application of different points of view:

1. Hysterical symptoms are mnemic symbols[4] of certain operative (traumatic) impressions and experiences.
2. Hysterical symptoms are substitutes, produced by 'conversion,' for the associative return of these traumatic experiences.
3. Hysterical symptoms are—like other psychical structures—an expression of the fulfilment of a wish.
4. Hysterical symptoms are the realization of an unconscious phantasy which serves the fulfilment of a wish.
5. Hysterical symptoms serve the purpose of sexual satisfaction and represent a portion of the subject's sexual life (a portion which corresponds to one of the constituents of his sexual instinct).
6. Hysterical symptoms correspond to a return of a mode of sexual satisfaction which was a real one in infantile life and has since been repressed.
7. Hysterical symptoms arise as a compromise between two opposite affective and instinctual impulses, of which one is attempting to bring to expression a component instinct or a

---

3. The same is true of the relation between the 'latent' dream-thoughts and the elements of the 'manifest' content of a dream. See the section of my *Interpretation of Dreams* [Chapter VI] which deals with the 'dream-work'.

4. {By "mnemic symbols" Freud means what we call "mnemonic devices": formulas, images, or other aids that help us remember—or keep us from forgetting.}

constituent of the sexual constitution, and the other is attempting to suppress it.
8. Hysterical symptoms may take over the representation of various unconscious impulses which are not sexual, but they can
never be without a sexual significance.

Among these various definitions the seventh brings out the
nature of hysterical symptoms most completely as the realization
of an unconscious phantasy; and the eighth recognizes the proper
significance of the sexual factor. Some of the proceding formulas
lead up to these two and are contained in them.

This connection between symptoms and phantasies makes it
easy to arrive from a psycho-analysis of the former at a knowledge
of the components of the sexual instincts which dominate the
individual, as I have demonstrated in my *Three Essays on the
Theory of Sexuality* [1905]. In some cases, however, investigation
by this means yields an unexpected result. It shows that there are
many symptoms where the uncovering of a sexual phantasy (or
of a number of phantasies, one of which, the most significant
and the earliest, is of a sexual nature) is not enough to bring about
a resolution of the symptoms. To resolve it one has to have *two*
sexual phantasies, of which one has a masculine and the other a
feminine character. Thus one of these phantasies springs from a
homosexual impulse. This new finding does not alter our seventh
formula. It remains true that a hysterical symptom must necessarily represent a compromise between a libidinal and a repressing
impulse; but it may also represent a union of two libidinal phantasies of an opposite sexual character.

I shall refrain from giving examples in support of this thesis
* * * {and} content myself with stating the following formula
and explaining its significance:
9. Hysterical symptoms are the expression on the one hand of a
masculine unconscious sexual phantasy, and on the other
hand of a feminine one.

I must expressly state that I cannot claim the same general
validity for this formula as I have done for the others. As far as I
can see, it applies neither to all the symptoms of a given case nor
to all cases. On the contrary, it is not hard to adduce cases in
which the impulses belonging to the opposite sexes have found
separate symptomatic expression, so that the symptoms of heterosexuality and those of homosexuality can be as clearly distin-

guished from each other as the phantasies concealed behind them. Nevertheless, the condition of things stated in the ninth formula is common enough, and, when it occurs, important enough to deserve special emphasis. It seems to me to mark the highest degree of complexity to which the determination of a hysterical symptom can attain, and one may therefore only expect to find it in a neurosis which has persisted for a long time and within which a great deal of organization has taken place.

The bisexual nature of hysterical symptoms, which can in any event be demonstrated in numerous cases, is an intersting confirmation of my view that the postulated existence of an innate bisexual disposition in man is especially clearly visible in the analysis of psychoneurotics. An exactly analogous state of affairs occurs in the same field when a person who is masturbating tries in his conscious phantasies to have the feelings both of the man and of the woman in the situation which he is picturing. Further counterparts are to be found in certain hysterical attacks in which the patient simultaneously plays both parts in the underlying sexual phantasy. In one case which I observed, for instance, the patient pressed her dress up against her body with one hand (as the woman), while she tried to tear it off with the other (as the man). This simultaneity of contradictory actions serves to a large extent to obscure the situation, which is otherwise so plastically portrayed in the attack, and it is thus well suited to conceal the unconscious phantasy that is at work.

In psycho-analytic treatment it is very important to be prepared for a symptom's having a bisexual meaning. We need not then be surprised or misled if a symptom seems to persist undiminished although we have already resolved one of its sexual meanings; for it is still being maintained by the—perhaps unsuspected—one belonging to the opposite sex. In the treatment of such cases, moreover, one may observe how the patient avails himself, during the analysis of the one sexual meaning, of the convenient possibility of constantly switching his associations, as though on to an adjoining track, into the field of the contrary meaning.

On the Sexual Theories of Children

The remarks on children's sexual theories that Freud added in 1915 to his Three Essays on the Theory of Sexuality (see above, pp. 121– 23) were first formulated in this 1908 essay. Much of the impetus for Freud's effort to catalogue children's theories came from a case study called "Analysis of a Phobia in a Five-Year-Old" (1909) but popularly known as "Little Hans" (10:3–148). The boy named "Little Hans" told many of his "sexual researches" to his father, who conducted the analysis in collaboration with Freud. Freud later questioned whether the riddle of conception and birth or the differences between females and males were of primary concern to children (see "Some Psychical Consequences of the Anatomical Distinction between the Sexes," below), but otherwise the views articulated here became staples in Freud's work and very important to the development, in the 1920s, of child analysis.

The essay begins with notes on sources of information—observations of children, adult memories related in analytic settings, and analytic reconstructions of neurotics' childhoods—and some methodological reflections. Freud remains reserved about exactly when children become intellectually concerned with sex, but he is convinced that all children start to think about sex before puberty. Similarly, he is convinced that there are few differences between the theories of healthy children and those of neurotic children, for all—in their various ways—go through the developmental phases that ground intellectual efforts. The main problem with the data, Freud says, is of another sort: "In consequence of the unfavorable circumstances, both of an internal and an external nature, the following observations apply chiefly to the sexual development of one sex only—that is, of males." These vaguely invoked circumstances were not further explored until Freud focused his attention on the particular difficulties encountered in analyzing women (see p. 324).

* * * If we could divest ourselves of our corporeal existence, and could view the things of this earth with a fresh eye as purely thinking beings, from another planet for instance, nothing perhaps would strike our attentions more forcibly than the fact of the existence of two sexes among human beings, who, though so much alike in other respects, yet mark the difference between them with such obvious external signs. But it does not seem that children choose this fundamental fact in the same way as the starting-point of their researches into sexual problems. Since they have known a father and mother as far back as they can remember in life, they accept their existence as a reality which needs no further enquiry, and a boy has the same attitude towards a little sister from whom he is separated by only a slight difference of age of one or two years. A child's desire for knowledge on this point does not in fact awaken spontaneously, prompted perhaps by some inborn need for established causes; it is aroused under the goad of the self-seeking instincts that dominate him, when— perhaps after the end of his second year—he is confronted with the arrival of a new baby. And a child whose own nursery has received no such addition is able, from observations made in other homes, to put himself in the same situation. The loss of his parents' care, which he actually experiences or justly fears, and the presentiment that from now on he must for evermore share all his possessions with the newcomer, have the effect of awakening his emotions and sharpening his capacities for thought. The elder child expresses unconcealed hostility towards his rival, which finds vent in unfriendly criticisms of it, in wishes that 'the stork should take it away again' and occasionally even in small attacks upon the creature lying helpless in the cradle. A wider difference in age usually softens the expression of this primary hostility. In the same way, at a rather later age, if no small brother or sister has appeared, the child's wish for a playmate, such as he has seen in other families, may gain the upper hand.

At the instigation of these feelings and worries, the child now comes to be occupied with the first, grand problem of life and asks himself the question: '*Where do babies come from?*'—a question which, there can be no doubt, first ran: 'Where did this particular, intruding baby come from?' We seem to hear the echoes of this first riddle in innumerable riddles of myth and legend. The question itself is, like all research, the product of a vital exigency, as though thinking were entrusted with the task of preventing the recurrence of such dreaded events. Let us assume, however, that the child's thinking soon becomes independent of this instigation, and henceforward goes on operating as a self-sustained instinct for research. Where a child is not already too much intimidated, he sooner or later adopts the direct method of demanding an answer from his parents or those in charge of him, who are in his eyes the source of all knowledge. This method, however, fails. The child receives either evasive answers or a rebuke for his curiosity, or he is dismissed with the mythologically significant piece of information which, in German countries, runs: 'The stork brings the babies; it fetches them out of the water.' I have reason to believe that far more children than their parents suspect are dissatisfied with this solution and meet it with energetic doubts, which, however, they do not always openly admit. I know of a three-year-old boy who, after receiving this piece of enlightenment, disappeared—to the terror of his nurse. He was found at the edge of the big pond adjoining the country house, to which he had hurried in order to see the babies in the water. I also know of another boy who could only allow his disbelief to find expression in a hesitant remark that he knew better, that it was not a stork that brought babies but a heron. It seems to me to follow from a great deal of information I have received that chidren refuse to believe the stork theory and that from the time of this first deception and rebuff they nourish a distrust of adults and have a suspicion of there being something forbidden which is being withheld from them by the 'grown-ups', and that they consequently hide their further researches under a cloak of secrecy. With this, however, the child also experiences the first occasion for a 'psychical conflict', in that views for which he feels an instinctual kind of preference, but which are not 'right' in the eyes of the grown-ups, come into opposition with other views, which are supported by the authority of the grown-ups without being acceptable to him himself. Such a psychical conflict may soon turn into a 'psychical dissociation'. The set of views which are bound up with being 'good', but also with a cessation of reflection, become the dominant and conscious views; while the other set, for which the child's work of research has meanwhile obtained fresh evidence, but which are not supposed to count, become the suppressed and 'unconscious' ones. The nuclear complex of a neurosis is in this way brought into being.

Recently, the analysis of a five-year-old boy, which his father undertook and which he has handed over to me for publication, has given me irrefutable proof of the correctness of a view towards which the psycho-analysis of adults had long been leading me. I now know that the change which takes place in the mother during pregnancy does not escape the child's sharp eyes and that he is very well able before long to establish the true connection between the increase in his mother's stoutness and the appearance of the baby. In the case just mentioned the boy was three and a half years old when his sister was born and four and three quarters when he showed his better knowledge by the most unmistakable allusions. This precocious discovery, however, is always kept secret, and later, in conformity with the further vicissitudes of the child's sexual researches, it is repressed and forgotten.

The 'stork fable', therefore, is not one of the sexual theories of children. On the contrary, it is the child's observation of animals, who hide so little of their sexual life and to whom he feels so closely akin, that strengthens his disbelief in it. With his knowledge, independently obtained, that babies grow inside the mother's body, he would be on the right road to solving the problem on which he first tries out his powers of thinking. But his further progress is inhibited by a piece of ignorance which cannot be made good and by false theories which the state of his own sexuality imposes on him.

These false sexual theories, which I shall now discuss, all have one very curious characteristic. Although they go astray in a grotesque fashion, yet each one of them contains a fragment of real truth; and in this they are analogous to the attempts of adults, which are looked at as strokes of genius, at solving the problems of the universe which are too hard for human comprehension. What is correct and hits the mark in such theories is to be explained by their origin from the components of the sexual instinct which are already stirring in the childish organism. For it is not owing to any arbitrary mental act or to chance impressions that those notions arise, but to the necessities of the child's psychosexual constitution; and this is why we can speak of sexual theories in children as being typical, and why we find the same mistaken beliefs in every child whose sexual life is accessible to us.

The first of these theories starts out from the neglect of the differences between the sexes on which I laid stress at the beginning of this paper as being characteristic of children. It consists in *attributing to everyone, including females, the possession of a penis*, such as the boy knows from his own body. It is precisely in what we must regard as the 'normal' sexual constitution that already in childhood the penis is the leading erotogenic zone and the chief auto-erotic sexual object; and the boy's estimate of its value is logically reflected in his inability to imagine a person like himself who is without this essential constituent. When a small boy sees his little sister's genitals, what he says shows that his prejudice is already strong enough to falsify his perception. He does not comment on the absence of a penis, but *invariably* says, as though by way of consolation and to put things right: 'Her ——'s still quite small. But when she gets bigger it'll grow all right.' The idea of a woman with a penis returns in later life, in the dreams of adults: the dreamer, in a state of nocturnal sexual excitation, will throw a woman down, strip her and prepare for intercourse—and then, in place of the female genitals, he beholds a well-developed penis and breaks off the dream and the excitation. The numerous hermaphrodites of classical antiquity faithfully reproduce this idea, universally held in childhood; one may observe that to most normal people they cause no offence, while the real hermaphroditic formations of the genitals which are permitted to occur by Nature nearly always excite the greatest abhorrence.

If this idea of a woman with a penis becomes 'fixated' in an individual when he is a child, resisting all the influences of later life and making him as a man unable to do without a penis in his sexual object, then, although in other respects he may lead a normal sexual life, he is bound to become a homosexual, and will seek his sexual object among men who, owing to some other physical and mental characteristics, remind him of women. Real women, when he comes to know them later, remain impossible as sexual objects for him, because they lack the essential sexual attraction; indeed, in connection with another impression of his childhood life, they may even become abhorrent to him. The child, having been mainly dominated by excitations in the penis, will usually have obtained pleasure by stimulating it with his hand; he will have been detected in this by his parents or nurse and terrorized by the threat of having his penis cut off. The effect of this 'threat of castration' is proportionate to the value set upon that organ and is quite extraordinarily deep and persistent. Legends and myths testify to the upheaval in the child's emotional life and to the horror which is linked with the castration complex—a complex which is subsequently remembered by consciousness with corresponding reluctance. The woman's genitalia, when seen later on, are regarded as a mutilated organ and recall this threat, and they therefore arouse horror instead of pleasure in the homosexual. This reaction cannot be altered in any way when the homosexual comes to learn from science that his childish assumption that women had a penis too was not so far wrong after all. Anatomy has recognized the clitoris within the female pudenda as being an organ that is homologous to the penis; and the physiology of the sexual processes has been able to add that this small penis which does not grow any bigger behaves in fact during childhood like a real and genuine penis—that it becomes the seat of excitations which lead to its being touched, that its excitability gives the little girl's sexual activity a masculine character and that a wave of repression in the years of puberty is needed in order for this masculine sexuality to be discarded and the woman to emerge. Since the sexual function of many women is crippled, whether by their obstinate clinging on to this excitability of the clitoris so that they remain anaesthetic in intercourse, or by such excessive repression occurring that its operation is partly replaced by hysterical compensatory formations—all this seems to show that there is some truth in the infantile sexual theory that women, like men, possess a penis.

It is easy to observe that little girls fully share their brother's opinion of it. They develop a great interest in that part of the boy's body. But this interest promptly falls under the sway of envy. They feel themselves unfairly treated. They make attempts to micturate in the posture that is made possible for boys by their possessing a big penis; and when a girl declares that 'she would rather be a boy,' we know what deficiency her wish is intended to put right.

If children could follow the hints given by the excitation of the penis they would get a little nearer to the solution of their problem. That the baby grows inside the mother's body is obviously not a sufficient explanation. How does it get inside? What starts its development? That the father has something to do with it seems likely; he says that the baby is *his* baby as well. Again, the penis certainly has a share, too, in these mysterious happenings; the excitation in it which accompanies all these activities of the child's thoughts bears witness to this. Attached to this excitation are impulses which the child cannot account for—obscure urges to do something violent, to press in, to knock to pieces, to tear open a hole somewhere. But when the child thus seems to be well on the way to postulating the existence of the vagina and to concluding that an incursion of this kind by his father's penis into his mother is the act by means of which the baby is created in his mother's body—at this juncture his enquiry is broken off in helpless perplexity. For standing in its way is his theory that his mother possesses a penis just as a man does, and the existence of the cavity which receives the penis remains undiscovered by him. It is not hard to guess that the lack of success of his intellectual efforts makes it easier for him to reject and forget them. This brooding and doubting, however, becomes the prototype of all later intellectual work directed towards the solution of problems, and the first failure has a crippling effect on the child's whole future.[1]

Their ignorance of the vagina also makes it possible for children to believe in the second of their sexual theories. If the baby grows in the mother's body and is then removed from it, this can only happen along the one possible pathway—the anal aperture. *The baby must be evacuated like a piece of excrement, like a stool.* When, in later childhood, the same question is the subject of solitary reflection or of a discussion between two children, the explanations probably arrived at are that the baby emerges from the navel, which comes open, or that the abdomen is slit up and the baby taken out—which was what happened to the wolf in the story of Little Red Riding-Hood. These theories are expressed aloud and also consciously remembered later on; they no longer contain anything objectionable. These same children have by then completely forgotten that in earlier years they believed in another theory of birth, which is now obstructed by the repression of the anal sexual components that has meanwhile occurred. At that time a {bowel movement} was something which could be talked about in the nursery without shame. The child was still not so distant from his constitutional coprophilic inclinations. There was nothing degraded about coming into the world like a heap of faeces, which had not yet been condemned by feelings of disgust. The cloacal theory, which, after all, is valid for so

---

1. {Freud's most extensive reflections on the relations between childhood sexual curiosity and adult intellectual/artistic work are in his 1910 essay on Leonardo da Vinci (11:59–138.}

many animals, was the most natural theory, and it alone could obtrude upon the child as being a probable one.[2]

This being so, however, it was only logical that the child should refuse to grant women the painful prerogative of giving birth to children. If babies are born through the anus, then a man can give birth just as well as a woman. It is therefore possible for a boy to imagine that he, too, has children of his own, without there being any need to accuse him on that account of having feminine inclinations.[3] He is merely giving evidence in this of the anal erotism which is still alive in him.

If the cloacal theory of birth is preserved in consciousness during later years of childhood, as occasionally happens, it is accompanied too by a solution—no longer, it is true, a primary one—of the problem of the origin of babies. Here it is like being in a fairy story; one eats some particular thing and gets a child from it. This infantile theory of birth is revived in cases of insanity. A manic woman, for instance, will lead the visiting doctor to a little heap of faeces which she has deposited in a corner of her cell, and say to him with a laugh: 'That's the baby I had to-day.'

The third of the typical sexual theories arises in children if, through some chance domestic occurrence, they become witnesses of sexual intercourse between their parents. Their perceptions of what is happening are bound, however, to be only very incomplete. Whatever detail it may be that comes under their observation—whether it is the relative positions of the two people, or the noises they make, or some accessory circumstance—children arrive in every case at the same conclusion. They adopt what may be called a *sadistic view of coition*. They see it as something that the stronger participant is forcibly inflicting on the weaker, and they (especially boys) compare it to the romping familiar to them from their childish experience—romping which, incidentally, is not without a dash of sexual excitation. I have not been able to ascertain that children recognize this behaviour which

2. {In birds, reptiles, amphibians, and many fishes, the cloaca is a common chamber for discharge from the intestinal, urinary, and reproductive canals. Coprophilia means, literally, love of excrement, and it is typical of children in the anal phases of development, as Freud noted in his *Three Essays*.}

3. [Cf. a similar remark in the case history of 'Little Hans', 10:93 *n*. It was only later, especially in the 'Wolf Man' analysis (1918), that Freud drew attention to the close connection that can exist between anal erotism and a feminine attitude. See, for instance, 17:81.]

they have witnessed between their parents as the missing link needed for solving the problem of babies; it appears more often that the connection is overlooked by them for the very reason that they have interpreted the act of love as an act of violence. But this view of it itself gives an impression of being a return of the obscure impulse towards cruel behaviour which became attached to the excitations of the child's penis when he first began to think about the problem of where babies came from. The possibility, too, cannot be excluded that this premature sadistic impulse, which might so nearly have led to the discovery of coition, itself first emerged under the influence of extremely obscure memories of parental intercourse, for which the child had obtained the material—though at the time he made no use of it—while he was still in his first years and was sharing his parents' bedroom.[4]

The sadistic theory of coitus which, taken in isolation, is misleading where it might have provided confirmatory evidence, is, once again, the expression of one of the innate components of the sexual instinct, any of which may be strongly marked to a greater or lesser degree in each particular child. For this reason the theory is correct up to a certain point; it has in part divined the nature of the sexual act and the 'sex-battle' that precedes it. Not infrequently, too, the child is in a position to support this view by accidental observations which he understands in part correctly, but also in part incorrectly and indeed in a reversed sense. In many marriages the wife does in fact recoil from her husband's embraces, which bring her no pleasure, but the risk of a fresh pregnancy. And so the child who is believed to be asleep (or who is pretending to be asleep) may receive an impression from his mother which he can only interpret as meaning that she is defending herself against an act of violence. At other times the whole marriage offers an observant child the spectacle of an unceasing quarrel, expressed in loud words and unfriendly gestures; so that he need not be surprised if the quarrel is carried on at night as well, and finally settled by the same method which he himself is accustomed to use in his relations with his brothers and sisters or playmates.

4. {For an example of a "primal scene" reconstructed in the analysis of a female, see Marie Bonaparte's report on her analysis with Freud: "Notes on the Analytical Discovery of a Primal Scene," in the Journal *The Psychoanalytic Study of the Child*, vol. 1, pp. 119–25.}

Moreover, if the child discovers spots of blood in his mother's bed or on her underclothes, he regards it as a confirmation of his view. It proves to him that his father has made another similar assault on his mother during the night (whereas we should rather take the fresh spots of blood to mean that there had been a temporary cessation of sexual intercourse). Much of the otherwise inexplicable 'horror of blood' shown by neurotics finds its explanation from this connection. Once again, however, the child's mistake contains a fragment of truth. For in certain familiar circumstances a trace of blood is in fact judged as a sign that sexual intercourse has been begun.[5]

A question connected somewhat indirectly with the insoluble problem of where babies come from also engages the child—the question as to the nature and content of the state called 'being married'; and he answers the question differently according as his chance perceptions in relation to his parents have coincided with instincts of his own which are still pleasurably coloured. All that these answers seem to have in common is that the child promises himself pleasurable satisfaction from being married and supposes that it involves a disregard of modesty. The notion I have most frequently met with is that *each of the married couple urinates in front of the other*. A variation of this, which sounds as if it was meant to indicate a greater knowledge symbolically, is that *the man urinates into the woman's chamber-pot*. In other instances the meaning of marriage is supposed to be that *the two people show their behinds to each other* (without being ashamed). In one case, in which education had succeeded in postponing sexual knowledge especially late, a fourteen-year-old girl, who had already begun to menstruate, arrived from the books she had read at the idea that being married consisted in a 'mixing of blood'; and since her own sister had not yet started her periods, the lustful girl made an assault on a female visitor who had confessed that she was just then menstruating, so as to force her to take part in this 'blood-mixing'.

Childhood opinions about the nature of marriage, which are not seldom retained by conscious memory, have great significance for the symptomatology of later neurotic illness. At first they find expression in children's games in which each child does with

---

5. {For further remarks on defloration and "horror of blood," see "The Taboo of Virginity" anthologized below.}

another whatever it is that in his view constitutes being married; and then, later on, the wish to be married may choose the infantile form of expression and so make its appearance in a phobia which is at first sight unrecognizable, or in some corresponding symptom.[6]

These seem to be the most important of the typical sexual theories that children produce spontaneously in early childhood, under the sole influence of the components of the sexual instinct. I know that I have not succeeded in making my material complete or in establishing an unbroken connection between it and the rest of infantile life. But I may add one or two supplementary observations, whose absence would otherwise be noticed by any well-informed person. Thus, for instance, there is the significant theory that a baby is got by a kiss—a theory which obviously betrays the predominance of the erotogenic zone of the mouth. In my experience this theory is exclusively feminine and is sometimes found to be pathogenic in girls whose sexual researches have been subjected to exceedingly strong inhibitions in childhood. Again, through an accidental observation, one of my women patients happened upon the theory of the 'couvade', which, as is well known, is a general custom among some races and is probably intended to contradict the doubts as to paternity which can never be entirely overcome.[7] A rather eccentric uncle of this patient's stayed at home for days after the birth of his child and received visitors in his dressing-gown, from which she concluded that both parents took part in the birth of their children and had to go to bed.

In about their tenth or eleventh year, children get to hear about sexual matters. A child who has grown up in a comparatively uninhibited social atmosphere, or who has found better opportunities for observation, tells other children what he knows, because this makes him feel mature and superior. What children learn in this way is mostly correct—that is, the existence of the vagina and its purpose is revealed to them; but otherwise the explanations they get from one another are not infrequently mixed with false ideas and burdened with remains of the older infantile

6. The games that are most significant for subsequent neuroses are playing at 'doctor' and at 'father and mother.'

7. {"Couvade" is a custom in various parts of the world: a man goes to bed and enacts a childbirth while his wife is giving birth.}

sexual theories. They are scarcely ever complete or sufficient to solve the primordial problem. Just as formerly it was ignorance of the vagina which prevented the whole process from being understood, so now is it ignorance of the semen. The child cannot guess that another substance besides urine is excreted from the male sexual organ, and occasionally an 'innocent' girl on her wedding night is still indignant at her husband 'urinating into her'. This information acquired in the years of pre-puberty is followed by a new access of sexual researches by the child. But the theories which he now produces no longer have the typical and original stamp which was characteristic of the primary theories of early childhood as long as the infantile sexual components could find expression in theories in an uninhibited and unmodified fashion. The child's later intellectual efforts at solving the puzzles of sex have not seemed to me worth collecting, nor can they have much claim to a pathogenic significance. Their multiplicity is of course mainly dependent on the nature of the enlightenment which a child receives; but their significance consists rather in the fact that they re-awaken the traces, which have since become unconscious, of his first period of sexual interest; so that it is not infrequent for masturbatory sexual activity and some degree of emotional detachment from his parents to be linked up with them. Hence the condemnatory judgement of teachers that enlightenment of such a kind at this age 'corrupts' children.

Let me give a few examples to show what elements often enter into these late speculations by children about sexual life. A girl had heard from her schoolmates that the husband gives his wife an egg, which she hatches out in her body. A boy, who had also heard of the egg, identified it with the testicle, which [in German] is vulgarly called by the word [*Ei*]; and he racked his brains to make out how the contents of the scrotum could be constantly renewed. The information given seldom goes far enough to prevent important uncertainties about sexual events. Thus a girl may arrive at an expectation that intercourse occurs on one occasion only, but that it lasts a very long time—twenty-four hours—and that all the successive babies come from this single occasion. One would suppose that this child had got her knowledge of the reproductive process from certain insects; but it turned out that this was not so and that the theory emerged as a spontaneous creation. Other girls are ignorant of the period of gestation, the life in the womb, and assume that the baby appears immediately after the first night of intercourse * * * These later sexual researches of children, or of adolescents who have been retarded at the stage of childhood, offer an almost inexhaustible theme and one which is perhaps not uninteresting in general; but it is more remote from my present interest. I must only lay stress on the fact that in this field children produce many incorrect ideas in order to contradict older and better knowledge which has become unconscious and is repressed.

The way in which children react to the information they are given also has its significance. In some, sexual repression has gone so far that they will not listen to anything; and these succeed in remaining ignorant even in later life—*apparently* ignorant, at least—until, in the psycho-analysis of neurotics, the knowledge that originated in early childhood comes to light. I also know of two boys between ten and thirteen years old who, though it is true that they listened to the sexual information, rejected it with the words: '*Your* father and other people may do something like that, but I know for certain *my* father never would.'[8] But however widely children's later reactions to the satisfaction of their sexual curiosity may vary, we may assume that in the first years of childhood their attitude was absolutely uniform, and we may feel certain that at that time all of them tried most eagerly to discover what it was that their parents did with each other so as to produce babies.

---

8. [This anecdote was repeated by Freud in his somewhat later paper on a special type of object-choice (1910), 11:170, where some further remarks on the present subject will be found.]

'Civilized' Sexual Morality and Modern Nervous Illness

I in this *1908 essay, more than in any other of his texts except* Civilization
and Its Discontents *(1930). Freud presented his stark view of human
social evolution and his dire tallying up of the cost of progress in the
sphere of sexual pleasure. His collective portrait of contemporary
women—including those who came to his consulting room—makes it
very clear how their inferior status and social restriction contributed to
their psychoneuroses. Freud might have concluded, as would a contemporary feminist, that "the personal is political" and that the emancipation
of women would have to include emancipation from neurosis-inducing
sexual and social roles and definitions. Freud's prescriptions were not,
however, social reformist or feminist; he remained very much a man of
his period as he praised traditional feminine virtues and Hausfrau behavior. For the frustration of sexual instinct that women and men experience in modern marriage, he suggests only one remedy: effective,
safe, and "dignified" contraception.*

*At the beginning of the essay (not included here), Freud surveys a
number of contemporary diagnoses of "modern nervous illness" and
applauds one, by the philosopher Christian von Ehrenfels, for its courageous achnowledgment that there is a difference between pleasurable
"natural" and unpleasurable "civilized" sexuality. All the other critics,
who bewailed the complexity and frantic pace of modern life, its cultural
degeneracy and rampant industrialization, had either neglected or underestimated the role of seuxality in modern nervous illness. Further, they
made no distinction between neurasthenia, which is caused by specific
and remediable "toxic" present conditions, and the psychoneuroses,
which arise from intrapsychic conflict, that is, from repressed wishes
clamoring to be free and meeting refusal from the ego or consciousness.*

*After making this distinction himself, Freud went on to offer his own
diagnosis of modern nervous illness in its psychoneurotic form.*

～✿～✿～✿～

* * * The reader who is prepared to agree with me in looking
for the aetiology of nervous illness pre-eminently in influences
which damage sexual life, will also be ready to follow the further
discussion, which is intended to set the theme of increasing nervous illness in a wider context.

Generally speaking, our civilization is built up on the suppression of instincts. Each individual has surrendered some part of
his possessions—some part of the sense of omnipotence or of the
aggressive or vindictive inclinations in his personality. From these
contributions has grown civilization's common possession of material and ideal property. Besides the exigencies of life, no doubt
it has been family feelings, derived from erotism, that have induced the separate individuals to make this renunciation. The
renunciation has been a progressive one in the course of the
evolution of civilization. The single steps in it were sanctioned
by religion; the piece of instinctual satisfaction which each person
had renounced was offered to Deity as a sacrifice, and the com-
munal property thus acquired was declared 'sacred'. The man
who, in consequence of his unyielding constitution, cannot fall
in with this suppression of instinct, becomes a 'criminal', an
'outlaw', in the face of society—unless his social position or his
exceptional capacities enable him to impose himself upon it as
great man, a 'hero'.

The sexual instinct—or, more correctly, the sexual instincts,
for analytic investigation teaches us that the sexual instinct is made
up of many separate constituents or component instincts—is probably more strongly developed in man than in most of the higher
animals; it is certainly more constant, since it has almost entirely
overcome the periodicity to which it is tied in animals. It places
extraordinarily large amounts of force at the disposal of civilized
activity, and it does this in virtue of its especially marked characteristic of being able to displace its aim without materially diminishing in intensity. This capacity to exchange its originally
sexual aim for another one, which is no longer sexual but which

is psychically related to the first aim, is called the capacity for *sublimation*. In contrast to this displacebility, in which its value for civilization lies, the sexual instinct may also exhibit a particularly obstinate fixation which renders it unserviceable and which sometimes causes it to degenerate into what are described as abnormalities. The original strength of the sexual instinct probably varies in each individual; certainly the proportion of it which is suitable for sublimation varies. It seems to us that it is the innate constitution of each individual which decides in the first instance how large a part of his sexual instinct it will be possible to sublimate and make use of. In addition to this, the effects of experience and the intellectual influences upon his mental apparatus succeed in bringing about the sublimation of a further portion of it. To extend this process of displacement indefinitely is, however, certainly not possible, any more than is the case with the transformation of heat into mechanical energy in our machines. A certain amount of direct sexual satisfaction seems to be indispensable for most organizations, and a deficiency in this amount, which varies from individual to individual, is visited by phenomena which, on account of their detrimental effects on functioning and their subjective quality of unpleasure, must be regarded as an illness.

Further propects are opened up when we take into consideration the fact that in man the sexual instinct does not originally serve the purposes of reproduction at all, but has as its aim the gaining of particular kinds of pleasure. It manifests itself in this way in human infancy, during which it attains its aim of gaining pleasure not only from the genitals but from other parts of the body (the erotogenic zones), and can therefore disregard any objects other than these convenient ones. We call this stage the stage of *auto-erotism*, and the child's upbringing has, in our view, the task of restricting it, because to linger in it would make the sexual instinct uncontrollable and unserviceable later on. The development of the sexual instinct then proceeds from atuo-erotism to object-love and from the autonomy of the erotogenic zones to their subordination under the primacy of the genitals, which are put at the service of reproduction. During this development a part of the sexual excitation which is provided by the subject's own body is inhibited as being unserviceable for the reproductive function and in favourable cases is brought to sublimation. The forces that can be employed for cultural activities are thus to a great extent obtained through the suppression of what are known as the *perverse* elements of sexual excitation.

If this evolution of the sexual instinct is borne in mind, three stages of civilization can be distinguished: a first one, in which the sexual instinct may be freely exercised without regard to the aims of reproduction; a second, in which all of the sexual instinct is suppressed except what serves the aims of reproduction; and a third, in which only *legitimate* reproduction is allowed as a sexual aim. This third stage is reflected in our present-day 'civilized' sexual morality.

If we take the second of these stages as an average, we must point out that a number of people are, on account of their organization, not equal to meeting its demands. In whole classes of individuals the development of the sexual instinct, as we have described it above, from auto-erotism to object-love with its aim of uniting the genitals, has not been carried out correctly and sufficiently fully. As a result of these disturbances of development two kinds of harmful deviation from normal sexuality—that is, sexuality which is serviceable to civilization—come about; and the relation between these two is almost that of positive and negative.[1]

In the first place (disregarding people whose sexual instinct is altogether excessive and uninhibitable) there are the different varieties of *perverts*, in whom an infantile fixation to a preliminary sexual aim has prevented the primacy of the reproductive function from being established, and the *homosexuals* or *inverts*, in whom, in a manner that is not quite understood, the sexual aim has been deflected away from the opposite sex. If the injurious effects of these two kinds of developmental disturbance are less than might be expected, this mitigation can be ascribed precisely to the complex way in which the sexual instinct is put together, which makes it possible for a person's sexual life to reach a serviceable final form even if one or more components of the instinct have been shut off from development. The constitution of people suffering from inversion—the homosexuals—is, indeed, often distinguished by their sexual instinct's possessing a special aptitude for cultural sublimation.

---

1. {Freud alludes here to the claim he made in *Three Essays* that the perversions are the negative of the neuroses (8:165); he explains the concept again on p. 171.}

More pronounced forms of the perversions and of homosexuality, especially if they are exclusive, do, it is true, make those
subject to them socially useless and unhappy, so that it must be
recognized that the cultural requirements even of the second stage
are a source of suffering for a certain proportion of mankind. The
fate of these people who differ constitutionally from the rest varies,
and depends on whether they have been born with a sexual instinct
which by absolute standards is strong or comparatively weak. In
the latter case—where the sexual instinct is in general weak—
perverts succeed in totally suppressing the inclinations which bring
them into conflict with the moral demands of their stage of civilization. But this, from the ideal point of view, is also the only
thing they succeed in achieving; for, in order to effect this suppression of their sexual instinct, they use up the forces which they
would otherwise employ in cultural activities. They are, as it were,
inwardly inhibited and outwardly paralysed. What we shall be
saying again later on about the abstinence demanded of men and
woman in the third stage of civilization applies to them too.

Where the sexual instinct is fairly intense, but perverse, there
are two possible outcomes. The first, which we shall not discuss
further, is that the person affected remains a pervert and has to
put up with the consequences of his deviation from the standard
of civilization. The second is far more interesting. It is that, under
the influence of education and social demands, a suppression of
the perverse instincts is indeed achieved, but it is a kind of suppression which is really no suppression at all. It can better be described
as a suppression that has failed. The inhibited sexual instincts
are, it is true, no longer expressed as such—and this constitutes
the success of the process—but they find expression in other ways,
which are quite as injurious to the subject and make him quite
as useless for society as satisfaction of the suppressed instincts in
an unmodified form would have done. This constitutes the failure
of the process, which in the long run more than counterbalances
its success. The substitutive phenomena which emerge in consequence of the suppression of the instinct amount to what we
call nervous illness, or, more precisely, the psychoneuroses. Neurotics are the class of people who, since they posses a recalcitrant
organization, only succeed, under the influence of cultural requirements, in achieving a suppression of their instincts which is
apparent and which becomes increasingly unsuccessful. They
therefore only carry on their collaboration with cultural activities

by a great expenditure of force and at the cost of an internal impoverishment, or are obliged at times to interrupt it and fall ill. I have described the neuroses as the 'negative' of the perversions because in the neuroses the perverse impulses, after being repressed, manifest themselves from the unconscious part of the mind—because the neuroses contain the same tendencies, though in a state of 'repression', as do the positive perversions.

Experience teaches us that for most people there is a limit beyond which their constitution cannot comply with the demands of civilization. All who wish to be more noble-minded than their constitution allows fall victims to neurosis; they would have been more healthy if it could have been possible for them to be less good. The discovery that perversions and neuroses stand in the relation of positive and negative is often unmistakably confirmed by observations made on the members of one generation of a family. Quite frequently a brother is a sexual pervert, while his sister, who, being a woman, possesses a weaker sexual instinct, is a neurotic whose symptoms express the same inclinations as the perversions of her sexuality more active brother. And correspondingly, in many families the men are healthy, but from a social point of view immoral to an undesirable degree, while the women are high-minded and over-refined, but severely neurotic.

It is one of the obvious social injustices that the standard of civilization should demand from everyone the same conduct of seuxal life—conduct which can be followed without any difficulty by some people, thanks to their organization, but which imposes the heaviest psychical sacrifices on others; though, indeed, the injustice is as a rule wiped out by disobedience to the injunctions of morality.

These considerations have been based so far as the requirement laid down by the second of the stages of civilization which we have postulated, the requirement that every sexual activity of the kind described as perserse is prohibited, while what is called normal sexual intercourse is freely permitted. We have found that even when the line between sexual freedom and restriction is drawn at this point, a number of individuals are ruled out as perverts, and a number of others, who make efforts not to be perverts whilst constitutionally they should be so, are forced into nervous illness. It is easy to predict the result that will follow if sexual freedom is still further circumscribed and the requirements of civilization are raised to the level of the third stage, which bans

all sexual activity outside legal marriage. The number of strong
natures who openly oppose the demands of civilization will increase enormously, and so will the number of weaker ones who,
faced with the conflict between the pressure of cultural influences
and the resistance of their constitution, take flight into neurotic
illness.

Let us now try to answer three questions that arise here:

1. What is the task that is set to the individual by the requirements
   of the third stage of civilization?
2. Can the legitimate sexual satisfaction that is permissible offer
   acceptable compensation for the renunciation of all other
   satisfactions?
3. In what relation do the possible injurious effects of this renunciation stand to its exploitation in the cultural field?

The answer to the first question touches on a problem which
has often been discussed and cannot be exhaustively treated here—
that of sexual abstinence. Our third stage of civilization demands
of individuals of both sexes that they shall practice abstinence
until they are married and that all who do not contract a legal
marriage shall remain abstinent throughout their lives. The position, agreeable to all the authorities, that sexual abstinence is
not harmful and not difficult to maintain, has also been widely
supported by the medical profession. It may be asserted, however,
that the task of mastering such a powerful impulse as that of the
sexual instinct by any other means than satisfying it is one which
can call for the whole of a man's forces. Mastering it by sublimation, by deflecting the sexual instinctual forces away from their
sexual aim to higher cultural aims, can be achieved by a minority
and then only intermittently, and least easily during the period
of ardent and vigorous youth. Most of the rest become neurotic
or are harmed in one way or another. Experience shows that the
majority of the people who make up our society are constitutionally unfit to face the task of abstinence. Those who would have
fallen ill under milder sexual restrictions fall ill all the more readily
and more severely before the demands of our cultural sexual
morality of to-day; for we know no better safeguard against the
threat to normal sexual life offered by defective innate dispositions
or disturbances of development than sexual satisfaction itself. The
more a person is disposed to neurosis, the less can he tolerate
abstinence; instincts which have been withdrawn from normal
development, in the sense in which it has been described above,

become at the same time all the more uninhibitable. But even those people who would have retained their health under the requirements of the second stage of civilization will now succumb to neurosis in great numbers. For the psychical value of sexual satisfaction increases with its frustration. The dammed-up libido is now put in a position to detect one or other of the weaker spots which are seldom absent in the structure of sexual life, and there to break through and obtain substitutive satisfaction of a neurotic kind in the form of pathological symptoms. Anyone who is able to penetrate the determinants of nervous illness will soon become convinced that its increase in our society arises from the intensification of sexual restrictions.

This brings us to the question whether sexual intercourse in legal marriage can offer full compensation for the restrictions imposed before marriage. There is such an abundance of material supporting a reply in the negative that we can give only the briefest summary of it. It must above all be borne in mind that our cultural sexual morality restricts sexual intercourse even in marriage itself, since it imposes on married couples the necessity of contenting themselves, as a rule, with a very few procreative acts. As a consequence of this consideration, satisfying sexual intercourse in marriage takes place only for a few years; and we must subtract from this, of course, the intervals of abstention necessitated by regard for the wife's health. After these three, four or five years, the marriage becomes a failure in so far as it has promised the satisfaction of sexual needs. For all the devices hitherto invented for preventing conception impair sexual enjoyment, hurt the fine susceptibilities of both partners and even actually cause illness. Fear of the consequences of sexual intercourse first brings the married couple's physical affection to an end; and then, as a remoter result, it usually puts a stop as well to the mental sympathy between them, which should have been the successor to their original passionate love. The spiritual disillusionment and bodily deprivation to which most marriages are thus doomed puts both partners back in the state they were in before their marriage, except for being the poorer by the loss of an illusion, and they must once more have recourse to their fortitude in mastering and deflecting their sexual instinct. We need not enquire how far men, by then in their maturer years, succeed in this task. Experience shows that they very frequently avail themselves of the degree of sexual freedom which is allowed them—although only with reluctance and under a veil of silence—by even the strictest sexual code. The 'double' sexual morality which is valid for men in our society is the plainest admission that society itself does not believe in the possibility of enforcing the precepts which it itself has laid down. But experience shows as well that women, who, as being the actual vehicle of the sexual interests of mankind, are only endowed in a small measure with the gift of sublimating their instincts, and who, though they may find a sufficient substitute for the sexual object in an infant at the breast, do not find one in a growing child—experience shows, I repeat, that women, when they are subjected to the disillusionments of marriage, fall ill of severe neuroses which permanently darken their lives. Under the cultural conditions of to-day, marriage has long ceased to be a panacea for the nervous troubles of women; and if we doctors still advise marriage in such cases, we are nevertheless aware that, on the contrary, a girl must be very healthy if she is to be able to tolerate it, and we urgently advise our male patients not to marry any girl who has had nervous trouble before marriage. On the contrary, the cure for nervous illness arising from marriage would be marital unfaithfulness. But the more strictly a woman has been brought up and the more sternly she has submitted to the demands of civilization, the more she is afraid of taking this way out; and in the conflict between her desires and her sense of duty, she once more seeks refuge in a neurosis. Nothing protects her virtue as securely as an illness. Thus the married state, which is held out as a consolation to the sexual instinct of the civilized person in his youth, proves to be inadequate even to the demands of the actual period of life covered by it. There is no question of its being able to compensate for the deprivation which precedes it.

But even if the damage done by civilized sexual morality is admitted, it may be argued in reply to our third question {p. 172} that the cultural gain derived from such an extensive restriction of sexuality probably more than balances these sufferings, which, after all, only affect a minority in any severe form. I must confess that I am unable to balance gain against loss correctly on this point, but I could advance a great many more considerations on the side of the loss. Going back to the subject of abstinence, which I have already touched on, I must insist that it brings in its train other noxae besides those involved in the neuroses and that the importance of the neuroses has for the most part not been fully appreciated.

The retardation of sexual development and sexual activity at which our education and civilization aim is certainly not injurious to begin with. It is seen to be a necessity, when one considers the late age at which young people of the educated classes reach independence and are able to earn a living. (This reminds one, incidentally, of the intimate interconnection between all our cultural institutions and of the difficulty of altering any part of them without regard to the whole.) But abstinence continued long after the age of twenty is no longer unobjectionable for a young man; and it leads to other damage even when it does not lead to neurosis. People say, to be sure, that the struggle against such a powerful instinct, and the strengthening of all the ethical and aesthetic forces which are necessary for this struggle, 'steel' the character; and this is true for a few specially favourably organized natures. It must be admitted that the differentiation of individual character, which is so marked in our day, has only become possible with the existence of sexual restriction. But in the vast majority of cases the struggle against sexuality eats up the energy available in a character and this at the very time when a young man is in need of all his forces in order to win his share and place in society. The relationship between the amount of sublimation possible and the amount of sexual activity necessary naturally varies very much from person to person and even from one calling to another. An abstinent artist is hardly conceivable; but an abstinent young *savant* is certainly no rarity. The latter can, by his self-restraint, liberate forces for his studies; while the former probably finds his artistic achievements powerfully stimulated by his sexual experience. In general I have not gained the impression that sexual abstinence helps to bring about energetic and self-reliant men of action or original thinkers or bold emancipators and reformers. Far more often it goes to produce well-behaved weaklings who later become lost in the great mass of people that tends to follow, unwillingly, the leads given by strong individuals.

The fact that the sexual instinct behaves in general in a self-willed and inflexible fashion is also seen in the results produced by efforts at abstinence. Civilized education may only attempt to suppress the instinct temporarily, till marriage, intending to give it free rein afterwards with the idea of then making use of it. But extreme measures are more successful against it than attempts at moderating it; thus the suppression often goes too far, with the unwished-for result that when the instinct is set free it turns out to be permanently impaired. For this reason complete abstinence in youth is often not the best preparation for marriage for a young man. Women sense this, and prefer among their suitors those who have already proved their masculinity with other women. The harmful results which the strict demand for abstinence before marriage produces in women's natures are quite especially apparent. It is clear that education is far from underestimating the task of suppressing a girl's sensuality till her marriage, for it makes use of the most drastic measures. Not only does it forbid sexual intercouse and set a high premium on the preservation of female chastity, but it also protects the young woman from temptation as she grows up, by keeping her ignorant of all the facts of the part she is to play and by not tolerating any impulse of love in her which cannot lead to marriage. The result is that when the girl's parental authorities suddenly allow her to fall in love, she is unequal to this psychical achievement and enters marriage uncertain of her own feelings. In consequence of this artificial retardation in her function of love, she has nothing but disappointments to offer the man who has saved up all his desire for her. In her mental feelings she is still attached to her parents, whose authority has brought about the suppression of her sexuality; and in her physical behaviour she shows herself frigid, which deprives the man of any high degree of sexual enjoyment. I do not know whether the anaesthetic type of woman exists apart from civilized education, though I consider it probable. But in any case such education actually breeds it, and these women who conceive without pleasure show little willingness afterwards to face the pains of frequent childbirth. In this way, the preparation for marriage frustrates the aims of marriage itself. When later on the retardation in the wife's development has been overcome and her capacity to love is awakened at the climax of her life as a woman, her relations to her husband have long since been ruined; and, as a reward for her previous docility, she is left with the choice between unappeased desire, unfaithfulness or a neurosis.

The sexual behaviour of a human being often *lays down the pattern* for all his other modes of reacting to life. If a man is energetic in winning the object of his love, we are confident that he will pursue his other aims with an equally unswerving energy;

but if, for all sorts of reasons, he refrains from satisfying his strong sexual instincts, his behaviour will be conciliatory and resigned rather than vigorous in other spheres of life as well. A special application of this proposition that sexual life lays down the pattern for the exercise of other functions can easily be recognized in the female sex as a whole. Their upbringing forbids their concerning themselves intellectually with sexual problems though they nevertheless feel extremely curious about them, and frightens them by condemning such curiosity as unwomanly and a sign of a sinful disposition. In this way they are scared away from *any* form of thinking, and knowlege loses its value for them. The prohibition of thought extends beyond the sexual field, partly through unavoidable association, partly automatically, like the prohibition of thought about religion among men, or the prohibition of thought about loyalty among faithful subjects. I do not believe that women's 'physiological feeble-mindedness' is to be explained by a biological opposition between intellectual work and sexual activity, as Moebius has asserted in a work which has been widely disputed. I think that the undoubted intellectual inferiority of so many women can rather be traced back to the inhibition of thought necessitated by sexual suppression.

In considering the question of abstinence, the distinction is not nearly strictly enough made between two forms of it—namely abstention from any sexual activity whatever and abstention from sexual intercourse with the opposite sex. Many people who boast of succeeding in being abstinent have only been able to do so with the help of masturbation and similar satisfactions which are linked with the auto-erotic sexual activities of early childhood. But precisely because of this connection such substitutive means of sexual satisfaction are by no means harmless; they predispose to the numerous varieties of neuroses and psychoses which are conditional on an involution of sexual life to its infantile forms. Masturbation, moreover, is far from meeting the ideal demands of civilized sexual morality, and consequently drives young people into the same conflicts with the ideals of education which they hoped to escape by abstinence. Furthermore, it vitiates the character through *indulgence*, and this is more than one way. In the first place, it teaches people to achieve important aims without taking trouble and by easy paths instead of through an energetic exertion of force—that is, it follows the principle that *sexuality lays down the pattern* of behaviour; secondly, in the phantasies that accompany satisfaction the sexual object is raised to a degree of excellence which is not easily found again in reality. A witty writer (Karl Kraus in the Vienna paper *Die Fackel*) once expressed this truth in reverse by cynically remarking: 'Copulation is no more than an unsatisfying substitute for masturbation.'

The sternness of the demands of civilization and the difficulty of the task of abstinence have combined to make avoidance of the union of the genitals of the two opposite sexes into the central point of abstinence and to favour other kinds of sexual activity, which, it might be said, are equivalent to semi-obedience. Since normal intercourse has been so relentlessly persecuted by morality—and also, on account of the possibilities of infection, by hygiene—what are known as the perverse forms of intercourse between the two sexes, in which other parts of the body take over the role of the genitals, have undoubtedly increased in social importance. These activities cannot, however, be regarded as being as harmless as analogous extensions [of the sexual aim] in love-relationships. They are ethically objectionable, for they degrade the relationships of love between two human beings from a serious matter to a convenient game, attended by no risk and no spiritual participation.[2] A further consequence of the aggravation of the difficulties of normal sexual life is to be found in the spread of homosexual satisfaction; in addition to all those who are homosexuals in virtue of their organization, or who became so in their childhood, there must be reckoned the great number of those in whom, in their maturer years, a blocking of the main stream of their libido has caused a widening in the side-channel of homosexuality.

All these unavoidable and unintended consequences of the requirement for abstinence converge in the one common result of completely ruining the preparation for marriage—marriage, which civilized sexual morality thinks should be the sole heir to the sexual impulses. Every man whose libido, as a result of masturbatory or perverse sexual practices, has become habituated

---

2. {It is important to note that Freud's "ethical" objection to homosexuality is that it is unserious, not that it is unnatural. Given the example of the Greeks, to which he often turns, Freud did not see even socially condoned homosexuality as anything but an initiatory prelude to marriage or a diversion from it; "serious" homosexual marriage was not, of course, an historically suggested possibility.}

to situations and conditions of satisfaction which are not normal, develops diminished potency in marriage. Women, too, who have been able to preserve their virginity with the help of similar measures, show themselves anaesthetic to normal intercourse in marriage. A marriage begun with a reduced capacity to love on both sides succumbs to the process of dissolution even more quickly than others. As a result of the man's weak potency, the woman is not satisfied, and she remains anaesthetic even in cases where her disposition to frigidity, derived from her education, could have been overcome by a powerful sexual experience. A couple like this finds more difficulties, too, in the prevention of children than a healthy one, since the husband's diminished potency tolerates the use of contraceptives badly. In this perplexity, sexual intercourse, as being the source of all their embarrassments, is soon given up, and with this the basis of married life is abandoned.

I ask any well-informed person to bear witness to the fact that I am not exaggerating but that I am describing a state of affairs of which equally bad instances can be observed over and over again. To the uninitiated it is hardly credible how seldom normal potency is to be found in a husband and how often a wife is frigid among married couples who live under the dominance of our civilized sexual morality, what a degree of renunciation, often on both sides, is entailed by marriage, and to what narrow limits married life—the happiness that is so ardently desired—is narrowed down. I have already explained that in these circumstances the most obvious outcome is nervous illness; but I must further point out the way in which a marriage of this kind continues to exercise its influence on the few children, or the only child born of it. At a first glance, it seems to be a case of transmission by inheritance; but closer inspection shows that it is really a question of the effect of powerful infantile impressions. A neurotic wife who is unsatisfied by her husband is, as a mother, over-tender and over-anxious towards her child, on to whom she transfers her need for love; and she awakens it to sexual precocity. The bad relations between its parents, moreover, excite its emotional life and cause it to feel love and hatred to an intense degree while it is still at a very tender age. Its strict upbringing, which tolerates no activity of the sexual life that has been aroused so early, lends support to the suppressing force and this conflict at such an age contains everything necessary for bringing about lifelong nervous illness.

I return now to my earlier assertion that, in judging the neuroses, their full importance is not as a rule taken into account. I
do not mean by this the undervaluation of these states shown in
their frivolous dismissal by relatives and in the boasting assurances
by doctors that a few weeks of cold water treatment or a few months
of rest and convalescence will cure the condition. These are
merely the opinions of quite ignorant doctors and laymen and
are mostly no more than words intended to give the sufferer a
short-lived consolation. It is, on the contrary, a well-known fact
that a chronic neurosis, even if is does not totally put an end to
the subject's capacity for existence, represents a severe handicap
in his life, of the same order, perhaps, as tuberculosis or a cardiac
defect. The situation would even be tolerable if neurotic illness
were to exclude from civilized activities only a number of individuals who were in any case of the weaker sort, and allowed the
rest to play their part in it at the cost of troubles that were merely
subjective. But, far from this being so, I must insist upon the
view that neuroses, whatever their extent and wherever they occur,
always succeed in frustrating the purposes of civilization, and in
that way actually perform the work of the suppressed mental forces
that are hostile to civilization. Thus, when society pays for obedience to its far-reaching regulations by an increase in nervous
illness, it cannot claim to have purchased a gain at the price of
sacrifices; it cannot claim a gain at all. Let us, for instance,
consider the very common case of a woman who does not love
her husband, because, owing to the conditions under which she
entered marriage, she has no reason to love him, but who very
much wants to love him, because that alone corresponds to the
ideal of marriage to which she has been brought up. She will in
that case suppress every impulse which would express the truth
and contradict her endeavours to fulfil her ideal, and she will
make special efforts to play the part of a loving, affectionate and
attentive wife. The outcome of this self-suppression will be a
neurotic illness; and this neurosis will in a short time have taken
revenge on the unloved husband and have caused him just as
much lack of satisfaction and worry as would have resulted from
an acknowledgement of the true state of affairs. This example is
completely typical of what a neurosis achieves. A similar failure
to obtain compensation is to be seen after the suppression of
impulses inimical to civilization which are not directly sexual. If
a man, for example, has become over-kind as a result of a violent

suppression of a constitutional inclination to harshness and cruelty, he often loses so much energy in doing this that he fails to carry out all that his compensatory impulses require, and he may, after all, do less good on the whole than he would have done without the suppression.

Let us add that a restriction of sexual activity in a community is quite generally accompanied by an increase of anxiety about life and of fear of death which interferes with the individual's capacity for enjoyment and does away with his readiness to face death for any purpose. A diminished inclination to beget children is the result, and the community or group of people in question is thus excluded from any share in the furture. In view of this, we may well raise the question whether our 'civilized' sexual morality is worth the sacrifice which it imposes on us, especially if we are still so much enslaved to hedonism as to include among the aims of our cultural development a certain amount of satisfaction of individual happiness. It is certainly not a physician's business to come forward with proposals for reform; but it seemed to me that I might support the urgency of such proposals if I were to amplify Von Ehrenfels's description of the injurious effects of our 'civilized' sexual morality by pointing to the important bearing of that morality upon the spread of modern nervous illness.

Contributions to a Discussion on Masturbation

F reud provided an introduction and the following concluding remarks
for a volume containing the 1912 Vienna Psychoanalytic Society
discussion on masturbation. This discussion, making clear that less was
known about female masturbation than male, was an important prelude
to Freud's 1919 essay " 'A Child Is Being Beaten' " (see below, pp.
215–40), where he notes for the first time that female sexual development
involves complexities he had not grasped.

Freud thought that masturbation, which he viewed as an incomplete
sexual discharge and an immature mode of sexuality, caused damage to
the sexual organs and led to neurasthenia. He advanced this view against
his Viennese colleague Wilhelm Stekel, who held that masturbation in
and of itself was a normal form of sexual gratification, one made problematic only by social prejudice and prohibition. Freud acknowledged
that libido which remained "damned up," without even the incomplete
discharge of masturbation, might also be damaging, but he wanted to
counter Stekel's simplification about the exclusively social origin of the
guilt feelings so often found associated with masturbation and so often
interfering with what release it could afford. In Freud's own work, as
well as in that of his followers, the idea that masturbation can lead straight
to neurasthenia did not persist. It was replaced with more complicated
formulations, and modified by the notion, preliminarily advanced in
1912, that for infants, children, and adolescents masturbation is normal,
ubiquitous, and not physically dangerous—although it could be emotionally dangerous if compulsive or guilt-ridden or constituting in one
or more ways an obstacle to loving other people. Masturbation in adults,
when it is preferred to intercourse (assuming that sexual partners are
available), is usually still regarded as a symptom.

That Freud, who was so courageous in his discovery of infantile sex-

*uality, should have exaggerated the danger arising from masturbation is another indication that he and his colleagues (except Stekel) were very much people of their period. Sexual mores have changed, and there have been periods in the history of psychoanalysis—starting in the late 1920s—when masturbation was heralded as an excellent way of overcoming sexual inhibition. This view has such wide popular currency now, particularly insofar as it seems to support sexual liberation for women, that whatever psychic conflicts still do surround masturbation are seldom discussed. For an important assessment of Freud's views in light of later psychoanalytic work, see Annie Reich, "The Discussion of 1912 on Masturbation and Our Present-Day Views" (1951) in her Psy*choanalytic Contributions *(New York: International Universities Press, 1973); and, more generally, the essays in I. M. Marcus and J. J. Francis, eds., Masturbation: From Infancy to Senescence (1975).*

～～～～

II Concluding Remarks

The older members of this group will be able to recall that some years ago we made a previous attempt at a collective discussion of this kind—a 'symposium', as our American colleagues call it—on the subject of masturbation.[1] At that time the opinions expressed showed such important divergences that we did not venture to lay our proceedings before the public. Since then the same group, together with some newcomers, having been uninterruptedly in touch with observed facts, and having had a constant interchange of ideas with one another, have so far clarified their views and arrived at common ground that the venture which we previously abandoned now no longer seems so rash. I really have an impression that the points on which we are agreed in connection with masturbation are now firmer and more deep-going than the disagreements—though these undeniably exist. Some of the apparent contradictions are only the result of the many different directions from which you have approached the subject, whereas in fact the opinions in question may quite well find a place alongside one another.

With your permission I will set before you a summary of the points on which we seem to be agreed or divided.

---

1. [This earlier discussion seems to have occurred on May 25 and June 1 and 8, 1910.]

We are all *agreed*, I feel,

a. on the importance of the phantasies which accompany or represent the act of masturbation,

b. on the importance of the sense of guilt, whatever its source may be, which is attached to masturbation, and

c. on the impossibility of assigning a qualitative determinant for the injurious effects of masturbation. (On this last point agreement is not unanimous.)

Unresolved differences of opinion have appeared

a. in respect to a denial of a somatic factor in the effects of masturbation,

b. in respect to a general denial of the injurious effects of masturbation,

c. with regard to the origin of the sense of guilt, which some of you wish to attribute directly to lack of satisfaction, while others adduce social factors in addition, or the attitude of the subject's personality at the moment, and

d. with regard to the ubiquity of masturbation in children.

Lastly, significant *uncertainties* exist

a. as to the mechanism of the injurious effects of masturbation, if there are any, and

b. as to the aetiological relation to masturbation to the 'actual neuroses'.

As regards the majority of the points of controversy among us, we have to thank the challenging criticisms of our colleague Wilhelm Stekel, based on his great and independent experience. There is no doubt that we have left very many points over to be established and clarified by some future band of observers and enquirers. But we may console ourselves with the knowledge that we have worked honestly and in no narrow spirit, and that in so doing we have opened up paths along which later research will be able to travel.

You must not expect much from my own contributions to the questions we are concerned with. You are aware of my preference for the fragmentary treatment of a subject, with emphasis on the points which seem to me best established. I have nothing new to offer—no solutions, only a few repetitions of things I have already maintained, a few words in defence of these old assertions against attacks made upon them by some of you, and, in addition, a few comments which must inevitably force themselves on anyone listening to your papers.

I have, as you know, divided masturbation according to the subject's age into (1) masturbation in infants, which includes all auto-erotic activities serving the purpose of sexual satisfaction, (2) masturbation in children, which arises directly out of the preceding kind and has already become fixed to certain erotogenic zones, and (3) masturbation at puberty, which is either continuous with childhood masturbation or is separated from it by the period of latency. In some of the accounts which I have heard you give, full justice has not quite been done to this temporal division. The ostensible unity of masturbation, which is fostered by the customary medical terminology, has given rise to some generalizations where a differentiation according to the three periods of life would have been better justified. It has been a matter for regret, too, that we have not been able to pay as much attention to female as to male masturbation; female masturbation, I believe, is deserving of a special study and in its case it is particularly true that a special emphasis lies on the modifications in it that arise in relation to the subject's age.

Freud takes up several minor topics and then comments on the relation between masturbation and neurasthenia or anxiety neurosis, the two clear types of "actual neurosis" (that is, neurosis with a specific, present, physical cause, as opposed to the overdetermined, past, psychological causes of the psychoneuroses). Freud reiterates his view advanced in the "Dora" case study (p. 71 above). Masturbation and an "actual neurosis" associated with it do not directly cause a psychoneurosis, but may provide the psychoneurosis with the necessary "somatic compliance" or habitually reenforced somatic pathway. The exact means by which masturbation may be injurious are difficult to analyze, but they must be considered, for it will not do simply to hope that when societal prejudice against masturbation disappears so will all its injurious effects.

* * * Masturbation corresponds essentially to infantile sexual activity and to its subsequent retention at a more mature age. We derive the neuroses from a conflict between a person's sexual urges and his other (ego) trends. Now someone might say: 'In my view the pathogenic factor in this aetiological relation lies solely in the ego's reaction to its sexuality.' By this he would be asserting that anyone could keep free of neurosis if only he were willing to allow unrestricted satisfaction to his sexual urges. But it is clearly arbitrary, and evidently pointless as well, to come to such a decision, and not to allow the sexual urges themselves to have any share in the pathogenic process. But if you admit that the sexual urges can have a pathogenic effect, you should no longer deny a similar significance to masturbation, which after all only consists in carrying out such sexual instinctual impulses. In every case which seems to show that masturbation is pathogenic, you will, no doubt, be able to trace the operation further back—to the instincts which manifest themselves in the masturbation and to the resistances which are directed against those instincts. Masturbation is not anything ultimate—whether somatically or psychologically— it is not a real 'agent', but merely the name for certain activities. Yet, however much we may trace things further back, our judgement on the causation of the illness will nevertheless rightly remain attached to this activity. And do not forget that masturbation is not to be equated with sexual activity in general: it is sexual activity subjected to certain limiting conditions. Thus it also remains possible that it is precisely these peculiarities of masturbatory activity which are the vehicles of its pathogenic effects.

We are therefore brought back once more from arguments to clinical observation, and we are warned by it not to strike out the heading 'Injurious Effects of Masturbation'. We are at all events confronted in the neuroses with cases in which masturbation has done damage.

This damage seems to occur in three different ways:

a. *Organic* injury may occur by some unknown mechanism. Here we must take into account the considerations of excess and of inadequate satisfaction, which have often been mentioned by you.

b. The injury may occur through the laying down of a *psychical pattern* according to which there is no necessity for trying to alter the external world in order to satisfy a great need. Where, however, a far-reaching reaction against this pattern develops, the most valuable character-traits may be initiated.

c. A *fixation of infantile sexual aims* may be made possible, and a persistence of psychical infantilism. Here we have the disposition for the occurrence of a neurosis. As psycho-analysts we cannot fail to be greatly interested in this result of masturbation—which in this case means, of course, masturbation occurring at puberty and continued afterwards. We must keep in mind the significance which masturbation acquires as a carrying into effect of phantasy—that half-way region interpolated between life in accordance with the pleasure principle and life in accordance with the reality principle; and we must remember how masturbation makes it possible to bring about sexual developments and sublimations in phantasy, which are nevertheless not advances but injurious compromises—though it is true, as an important remark of Stekel's has pointed out, that this same compromise renders severe perverse inclinations harmless and averts the worst consequences of abstinence.

On the basis of my medical experience, I cannot rule out a permanent reduction in potency as one among the results of masturbation, though I will grant to Stekel that in a number of cases it may turn out to be only apparent. This particular result of masturbation, however, cannot be classed unhesitatingly among the injurious ones. Some diminution of male potency and of the brutal aggressiveness involved in it is much to the purpose from the point of view of civilization. It facilitates the practice by civilized men of the virtues of sexual moderation and trustworthiness that are incumbent on them. Virtue accompanied by full potency is usually felt as a hard task.

This may strike you as cynical, but you may rest assured that it is not cynically meant. It sets out to be no more than a piece of dry description, without regard to whether it may cause satisfaction or annoyance. For masturbation, like so many other things, has *les défauts de ses vertus* and on the other hand *les vertus de ses défauts.*[2] If one is disentangling an involved and complex subject with a one-sided practical interest in its harmfulness and uses, one must put up with unwelcome discoveries.

Furthermore, I think we may with advantage distinguish what we may describe as the *direct* injuries caused by masturbation from those which arise *indirectly* from the ego's resistance and indignation against that sexual activity. I have not entered into these latter consequences.

And now I am obliged to add a few words on the second of the

2. {"the defects of his virtues" and vice versa.}

two painful questions we have been asked. Assuming that masturbation can be injurious, under what conditions and in what people does it prove to be so?

Like the majority of you, I am inclined to refuse to give a general answer to the question. It partly coincides with another, more comprehensive question: when does sexual activity in general become pathogenic for particular people? If we put this consideration on one side, we are left with a question of detail relating to the characteristics of masturbation in so far as it represents a special manner and form of sexual satisfaction. Here it would be to the point to repeat what is already known to us and has been discussed in other connections—to assess the influence of the *quantitative* factor and of the combined operation of several pathogenic factors. Above all, however, we should have to leave a wide field for what are known as an individual's constitutional dispositions. But it must be confessed that dealing with these is an awkward business. For we are in the habit of forming our opinion of individual dispositions *ex post facto*: we attribute this or that disposition to people after the event, when they have already fallen ill. We have no method of discovering it beforehand. We behave, in fact, like the Scottish King in one of Victor Hugo's novels, who boasted of an infallible method of recognizing witchcraft. He had the accused woman stewed in boiling water and then tasted the broth. He then judged according to the taste: 'Yes, that was a witch,' or 'No, that was not one.'

There is another question that I might draw your attention to, which has been dealt with too little in our discussions: that of 'unconscious' masturbation. I mean masturbation during sleep, during abnormal states, or fits. You will recall the many hysterical fits in which masturbatory acts recur in a disguised or unrecognizable way, after the subject has renounced that form of satisfaction, and the many symptoms in obsessional neurosis which seek to replace and repeat this kind of sexual activity, which has formerly been forbidden. We may also speak of a therapeutic return of masturbation. A number of you will have found on occasion, as I have, that it represents a great advance if during the treatment the patient ventures to take up masturbation once more, though he may have no intention of making a permanent stop at that infantile halting-place. In this connection I may remind you that a considerable number of precisely the most severe sufferers from neurosis have avoided all recollection of masturbation during historic times, while psycho-analysis is able to prove that that species of sexual activity had by no means been strange to them during the forgotten earliest period of their lives.

But I think the time has come to break off. For we are all agreed on one thing—that the subject of masturbation is quite inexhaustible.[3]

3. [In a letter to Fliess of December 22, 1897, Freud described masturbation as the 'primal addiction', for which later addictions (to alcohol, tobacco, morphine, etc.) are substitutes. He took up this idea very much later, in the discussion of gambling in his paper on Dostoevsky (1928).]

Selections from "On Narcissism: An Introduction"

The first major revision of Freud's libido theory appears in his 1914 essay "On Narcissism: An Introduction." As I noted in my Introduction, he added to his first notion of libido (instinctual drives focused on sexual objects and means of self-preservation—sex and hunger, for short) a notion of ego-libido or narcissism. Much of the theoretical argument of "On Narcissism" (not included here) is summarized in the section of the Three Essays called "The Libido Theory" (see pp. 133– 35 above). Freud additionally argues that ego-libido was harder to observe and analyze because in the psychoneuroses disturbances of object-libido obscured it from view. It is apparent in the psychoses, however, and it is particularly apparent in schizophrenia: a psychotic who has withdrawn from the world (withdrawn libido from objects) is living, as it were, in an inner world full of loved and hated imaginary objects. Children, too, Freud notes, are given to "omnipotence of thought" or the state in which mental representations and objects in the world are not firmly connected and in which it can seem that control over mental representations is control over "the world." Ego development brings an end to magical thinking: it is realistic connection to the object world.

In the section of the essay from which the following excerpt is taken, Freud turns his attention to three other spheres in which the distinction between object-libido and ego-libido can be studied. He first considers the withdrawal from the world that is typical of people suffering from painful organic diseases (and also of people asleep)—the "narcissism of illness." This withdrawal is then compared with its counterpart in hypochondria. Finally, Freud takes up object-libido and ego-libido in the erotic lives of men and women. In this section he draws a distinction between a characteristic masculine love, which involves a transference of early self-love or narcissism onto another person, who is then over-

valued, and a characteristic feminine love, which involves a perpetuation of early narcissism and a requirement that other people adoringly supplement the self-love. In this section, Freud emphasizes the perpetuation in women of their childhood narcissism (and anticipates that his emphasis will not win him many female friends—as it has not); in his late essays he emphasizes the perpetuation in women of their childhood mother-attachment. The two emphases were never explicitly reconciled, but Freud did note in his late essays how often women desire partners who will both worship them and succeed to their mother's role.

～～～～

* * * A third way in which we may approach the study of narcissism is by observing the erotic life of human beings, with its many kinds of differentiation in man and woman. Just as object-libido at first concealed ego-libido from our observation, so too in connection with the object-choice of infants (and of growing children) what we first noticed was that they derived their sexual objects from their experiences of satisfaction. The first auto-erotic sexual satisfactions are experienced in connection with vital functions which serve the purpose of self-preservation. The sexual instincts are at the outset attached to the satisfaction of the ego-instincts; only later do they become independent of these, and even then we have an indication of that original attachment in the fact that the persons who are concerned with a child's feeding, care, and protection become his earliest sexual objects; that is to say, in the first instance his mother or a substitute for her. Side by side, however, with this type and source of object-choice, which may be called the 'anaclitic' or 'attachment' type,[1] psycho-analytic research has revealed a second type, which we were not prepared for finding. We have discovered, especially clearly in people whose libidinal development has suffered some disturbance, such as perverts and homosexuals, that in their later choice of love-objects they have taken as a model not their mother but

---

1. ['*Anlehnungstypus.*' Literally, 'leaning-on type'. * * * This seems to be the first published appearance of the actual term '*Anlehnungstypus*'. The idea that a child arrives at its first sexual object on the basis of its nutritional instinct is to be found in the first edition of the *Three Essays* {p. 138 above} but the two or three explicit mentions in that work of the 'anaclitic type' were not added to it until the 1915 edition.

their own selves. They are plainly seeking *themselves* as a love-object, and are exhibiting a type of object-choice which must be termed 'narcissistic'. In this observation we have the strongest of the reasons which have led us to adopt the hypothesis of narcissism.

We have, however, not concluded that human beings are divided into two sharply differentiated groups, according as their object-choice conforms to the anaclitic or to the narcissistic type; we assume rather that both kinds of object-choice are open to each individual, though he may show a preference for one or the other. We say that a human being has originally two sexual objects—himself and the woman who nurses him—and in doing so we are postulating a primary narcissism in everyone, which may in some cases manifest itself in a dominating fashion in his object-choice.

A comparison of the male and female sexes then shows that there are fundamental differences between them in respect of their type of object-choice, although these differences are of course not universal. Complete object-love of the attachment type is, properly speaking, characteristic of the male. It displays the marked sexual overvaluation which is doubtless derived from the child's original narcissism and thus corresponds to a transference of that narcissism to the sexual object. This sexual overvaluation is the origin of the peculiar state of being in love, a state suggestive to a neurotic compulsion, which is thus traceable to an impoverishment of the ego as regards libido in favour of the love-object.[2] A different course is followed in the type of female most frequently met with, which is probably the purest and truest one. With the onset of puberty the maturing of the female sexual organs, which up till then have been in a condition of latency, seems to bring about an intensification of the original narcissism, and this is unfavourable to the development of a true object-choice with its accompanying sexual overvaluation. Women, especially if they grow up with good looks, develop a certain self-contentment which compensates them for the social restrictions that are imposed upon them in their choice of object. Strictly speaking, it is only themselves that such women love with an intensity comparable to that of the man's love for them. Nor does their need

---

2. [Freud returned to this in a discussion of being in love in Chapter VIII of his *Group Psychology* (1921), 18:112 f]

lie in the direction of loving, but of being loved; and the man who fulfils this condition is the one who finds favour with them. The importance of this type of woman for the erotic life of mankind is to be rated very high. Such women have the greatest fascination for men, not only for aesthetic reasons, since as a rule they are the most beautiful, but also because of a combination of interesting psychological factors. For it seems very evident that another person's narcissism has a great attraction for those who have renounced part of their own narcissism and are in search of object-love. The charm of a child lies to a great extent in his narcissism, his self-contentment and inaccessibility, just as does the charm of certain animals which seem not to concern themselves about us, such as cats and the large beasts of prey. Indeed, even great criminals and humorists, as they are represented in literature, compel our interest by the narcissistic consistency with which they manage to keep away from their ego anything that would diminish it. It is as if we envied them for maintaining a blissful state of mind—an unassailable libidinal position which we ourselves have since abandoned. The great charm of narcissistic women has, however, its reverse side; a large part of the lover's dissatisfaction, of his doubts of the woman's love, of his complaints of her enigmatic nature, has its root in this incongruity between the types of object-choice.

Perhaps it is not out of place here to give an assurance that this description of the feminine form of erotic life is not due to any tendentious desire on my part to depreciate women. Apart from the fact that tendentiousness is quite alien to me, I know that these different lines of development correspond to the differentiation of functions in a highly complicated biological whole; further, I am ready to admit that there are quite a number of women who love according to the masculine type and who also develop the sexual overvaluation proper to that type.

Even for narcissistic women, whose attitude towards men remains cool, there is a road which leads to complete object-love. In the child which they bear, a part of their own body confronts them like an extraneous object, to which, starting out from their narcissism, they can then give complete object-love. There are other women, again, who do not have to wait for a child in order to take the step in development from (secondary) narcissism to object-love. Before puberty they feel masculine and develop some way along masculine lines; after this trend has been cut short on their reaching female maturity, they still retain the capacity of longing for a masculine ideal—an ideal which is in fact a survival of the boyish nature that they themselves once possessed.

What I have so far said by way of indication may be concluded by a short summary of the paths leading to the choice of an object.

A person may love:—

1. According to the narcissistic type:
   a. what he himself is (i.e. himself),
   b. what he himself was,
   c. what he himself would like to be,
   d. someone who was once part of himself.

2. According to the anaclitic (attachment) type:
   a. the woman who feeds him,
   b. the man who protects him,

and the succession of substitutes who take their place. * * *

The primary narcissism of children which we have assumed and which forms one of the postulates of our theories of the libido, is less easy to grasp by direct observation than to confirm by inference from elsewhere. If we look at the attitude of affectionate parents towards their children, we have to recognize that it is a revival and reproduction of their own narcissism, which they have long since abandoned. The trustworthy pointer constituted by overvaluation, which we have already recognized as a narcissistic stigma in the case of object-choice, dominates, as we all know, their emotional attitude. Thus they are under a compulsion to ascribe every perfection to the child—which sober observation would find no occasion to do—and to conceal and forget all his shortcomings. (Incidentally, the denial of sexuality in children is connected with this.) Moreover, they are inclined to suspend in the child's favour the operation of all the cultural acquisitions which their own narcissism has been forced to respect, and to renew on his behalf the claims to privileges which were long ago given up by themselves. The child shall have a better time than his parents; he shall not be subject to the necessities which they have recognized as paramount in life. Illness, death, renunciation of enjoyment, restrictions on his own will, shall not touch him; the laws of nature and of society shall be abrogated in his favour; he shall once more really be the centre and core of creation— 'His Majesty the Baby', as we once fancied ourselves. The child shall fulfil those wishful dreams of the parents which they never carried out—the boy shall become a great man and a hero in his father's place, and the girl shall marry a prince as a tardy compensation for her mother. At the most touchy point in the narcissistic system, the immortality of the ego, which is so hard pressed by reality, security is achieved by taking refuge in the child. Parental love, which is so moving and at bottom so childish, is nothing but the parents' narcissism born again, which, transformed into object-love, unmistakably reveals its former nature.

On Transformations of Instinct as Exemplified in Anal Erotism

B oth in the pages of "On Narcissism" just presented and in this brief
1917 essay, Freud considered childhood "penis envy" as it becomes
a matter of adult female character. This train of thought grew from his
earlier investigations of how childhood anal erotism can shape adult
character. He concludes that in the female unconscious representations
of "faeces." "penis," and "baby" are virtually interchangeable: women
in analysis who do not, for example, reveal penis envy do reveal a wish
for a baby that is functionally equivalent as a compensatory wish. This
essay anticipates the much more thorough and innovative discussion of
the transformations of "penis envy" in "Some Psychical Consquences of
the Anatomical Distinction between the Sexes" (1925), below, pp.
304–14.

~~~~~~

Some years ago, observations made during psycho-analysis led
me to suspect that the constant co-existence in any one of the
three character-traits of *orderliness*, *parsimony* and *obstinacy* indicated an intensification of the anal-erotic components in his
sexual constitution, and that these modes of reaction, which were
favoured by his ego, had been established during the course of
his development through the assimilation of his anal erotism.[1]

In that publication my main object was to make known the
fact of this established relation; I was little concerned about its

1. 'Character and Anal Erotism' (1908*b*), 9:168.

theoretical significance. Since then there has been a general consensus of opinion that each one of the three qualities, avarice, pedantry and obstinacy, springs from anal-erotic sources—or, to express it more cautiously and more completely—draws powerful contributions from those sources. The cases in which these defects of character were combined and which in consequence bore a special stamp (the 'anal character') were merely extreme instances, which were bound to betray the particular connection that interests us here even to an unobservant eye.

As a result of numerous impressions, and in particular of one specially cogent analytical observation, I came to the conclusion a few years later that in the development of the libido in man the phase of genital primacy must be preceded by a 'pregenital organization' in which sadism and anal erotism play the leading parts.[2]

From that moment we had to face the problem of the later history of the anal-erotic instinctual impulses. What becomes of them when, owing to the establishment of a definitive genital organization, they have lost their importance in sexual life? Do they preserve their original nature, but in a state of repression? Are they sublimated or assimilated by transformation into character-traits? Or do they find a place within the new organization of sexuality characterized by genital primacy? Or, since none of these vicissitudes of anal erotism is likely to be the only one, to what extent and in what way does each of them share in deciding its fate? For the organic sources of anal erotism cannot of course be buried as a result of the emergence of the genital organization.

One would think that there could be no lack of material from which to provide an answer, since the processes of development and transformation in question must have taken place in everyone undergoing analysis. Yet the material is so obscure, the abundance of ever-recurring impressions so confusing, that even now I am unable to solve the problem fully and can do no more than make some contributions to its solution. In making them I need not refrain from mentioning, where the context allows it, other instinctual transformations besides anal-erotic ones. Finally, it scarcely requires to be emphasized that the developmental events here described—just as the others found in psycho-analysis—have

---

2. 'The Predisposition to Obsessional Neurosis' (1913), 12:313.

been inferred from the regressions into which they had been forced by neurotic processes.

As a starting-point for this discussion we may take the fact that it appears as if in the products of the unconscious—spontaneous ideas, phantasies and symptoms—the concepts *faeces* (money, gift),[3] *baby* and *penis* are ill-distinguished from one another and are easily interchangeable. We realize, of course, that to express oneself in this way is incorrectly to apply to the sphere of the unconscious terms which belong properly to other regions of mental life, and that we have been led astray by the advantages offered by an analogy. To put the matter in a form less open to objection, these elements in the unconscious are often treated as if they were equivalent and could replace one another freely.

This is most easily seen in the relation between 'baby' and 'penis'. It cannot be without significance that in the symbolic language of dreams, as well as of everyday life, both may be replaced by the same symbol; both baby and penis are called a 'little one', ['*das Kleine*'] It is a well-known fact that symbolic speech often ignores difference of sex. The 'little one', which originally meant the male genital organ, may thus have acquired a secondary application to the female genitals.

If we penetrate deeply enough into the neurosis of a woman, we not infrequently meet with the repressed wish to possess a penis like a man. We call this wish 'envy for a penis' and include it in the castration complex. Chance mishaps in the life of such a woman, mishaps which are themselves frequently the result of a very masculine disposition, have re-activated this infantile wish and, through the backward flow of libido, made it the chief vehicle of her neurotic symptoms. In other women we find no evidence of this wish for a penis; it is replaced by the wish for a baby, the frustration of which in real life can lead to the outbreak of a neurosis. It looks as if such women had understood (although this could not possibly have acted as a motive) that nature has given babies to women as a substitute for the penis that has been denied them. With other women, again, we learn that both wishes were present in their childhood and that one replaced the other. At first they had wanted a penis like a man; then at a later, though

3. [The relations between faeces and money, or gold, are discussed at some length in {"Character and Anal Eroticism"}.]

still childish, stage there appeared instead the wish for a baby. The impression is forced upon us that this variety in our findings is caused by accidental factors during childhood (e.g. the presence or absence of brothers or the birth of a new baby at some favourable time of life), so that the wish for a penis and the wish for a baby would be fundamentally identical.

We can say what the ultimate outcome of the infantile wish for a penis is in women in whom the determinants of a neurosis in later life are absent: it changes into the wish for a *man*, and thus puts up with the man as an appendage to the penis. This transformation, therefore, turns an impulse which is hostile to the female sexual function into one which is favourable to it. Such women are in this way made capable of an erotic life based on the masculine type of object-love, which can exist alongside the feminine one proper, derived from narcissism. We already know[4] that in other cases it is only a baby that makes the transition from narcissistic self-love to object-love possible. So that in this respect too a baby can be represented by the penis.

I have had occasional opportunities of being told women's dreams that had occurred after their first experience of intercourse. They revealed an unmistakable wish in the woman to keep for herself the penis which she had felt. Apart from their libidinal origin, then, these dreams indicated a temporary regression from man to penis as the object of her wish. One would certainly be inclined to trace back the wish for a man in a purely rationalistic way to the wish for a baby, since a woman is bound to understand sooner or later than there can be no baby without the co-operation of a man. It is, however, more likely that the wish for a man arises independently of the wish for a baby, and that when it arises—from understandable motives belonging entirely to ego-psychology—the original wish for a penis becomes attached to it as an unconscious libidinal reinforcement. The importance of the process described lies in the fact that a part of the young woman's narcissistic masculinity is thus changed into femininity, and so can no longer operate in a way harmful to the female sexual function.

Along another path, a part of the erotism of the pregenital

4. [See the later part of Section II of Freud's paper on narcissism, {above, p. 193}.]

phase, too, becomes available for use in the phase of genital primacy. The baby is regarded as 'lumf,'[5] as something which becomes detached from the body by passing through the bowel. A certain amount of libidinal cathexis which originally attached to the contents of the bowel can thus be extended to the baby born through it. Linguistic evidence of this identity of baby and faeces is contained in the expression 'to give someone a baby'. For its faeces are the infant's first gift, a part of his body which he will give up only on persuasion by someone he loves, to whom indeed, he will make a spontaneous gift of it as a token of affection; for, as a rule, infants do not dirty strangers. (There are similar if less intense reactions with urine.) Defaecation affords the first occasion on which the child must decide between a narcissistic and an object-loving attitude. He either parts obediently with his faeces, 'sacrifices' them to his love, or else retains them for purposes of auto-erotic satisfaction and later as a means of asserting his own will. If he makes the latter choice we are in the presence of defiance (obstinacy) which, accordingly, springs from a narcissistic clinging to anal erotism.

It is probable that the first meaning which a child's interest in faeces develops is that of 'gift' rather than 'gold or 'money'. The child knows no money apart from what is given him—no money acquired and none inherited of his own. Since his faeces are his first gift, the child easily transfers his interest from that substance to the new one which he comes across as the most valuable gift in life. Those who question this derivation of gifts should consider their experience of psycho-analytic treatment, study the gifts they receive as doctors from their patients, and watch the storms of transference which a gift from them can rouse in their patients.

Thus the interest in faeces is continued partly as interest in money, partly as a wish for a baby, in which latter an anal-erotic and a genital impulse ('envy for a penis') converge. But the penis has another anal-erotic significance apart from its relation to the interest in a baby. The relationship between the penis and the passage lined with mucous membrane which it fills and excites already has its prototype in the pregenital, anal-sadistic phase. The faecal mass, or as one patient called it, the faecal 'stick',

---

5. ['Little Hans's' word for faeces {in a case study Freud published in 1908—the first case study of a child} Cf. 10:54 and 68n.]

represents as it were the first penis, and the stimulated mucous membrane of the rectum represents that of the vagina. There are people whose anal erotism remains vigorous and unmodified up to the age preceding puberty (ten to twelve years); we learn from them that during the pregenital phase they had already developed in phantasy and in perverse play an organization analogous to the genital one, in which penis and vagina were presented by the faecal stick and the rectum. In other people—obsessional neurotics—we can observe the result of a regressive debasement of the genital organization. This is expressed in the fact that every phantasy originally conceived on the genital level is transposed to the anal level—the penis being replaced by the faecal mass and the vagina by the rectum.

As the interest in faeces recedes in a normal way, the organic analogy we have described here has the effect of transferring the interest on to the penis. When, later, in the course of the child's researches[6] he discovers that babies are born from the bowel, they inherit the greater part of his anal erotism; they have, however, been preceded by the penis in this as well as in another sense.

I feel sure that by this time the manifold interrelations of the series—faeces, penis, baby—have become totally unintelligible; so I will try to remedy the defect by presenting them diagramatically, and in considering the diagram [Fig. 1] we can review the same material in a different order. Unfortunately, this technical device is not sufficiently pliable for our purpose, or possibly we have not yet learned to use it with effect. In any case I hope the reader will not expect too much from it.

Anal erotism finds a narcissistic application in the production of defiance, which constitutes an important reaction on the part of the ego against demands made by other people. Interest in faeces is carried over first to interest in gifts, and then to interest in money. In girls, the discovery of the penis gives rise to envy for it, which later changes into the wish for a man as the possessor of a penis. Even before this the wish for a penis has changed into the wish for a baby, or the latter wish has taken the place of the former one. An organic analogy between penis and baby (dotted line) is expressed by the existence of a symbol ('little one') common

6. [See Freud's paper 'On the Sexual Theories of Children' {above, p. 159}.]

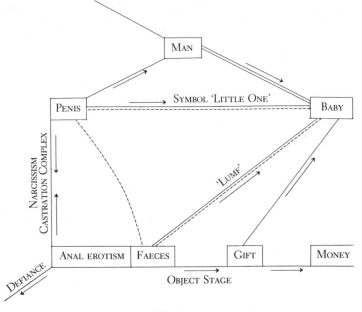

Figure 1.

to both. A rational wish (double line) then leads from the wish for a baby to the wish for a man: we have already appreciated the importance of this instinctual transformation.

Another part of the nexus of relations can be observed much more clearly in the male. It arises when the boy's sexual researches lead him to the discovery of the absence of a penis in women. He concludes that the penis must be a detachable part of the body, something analogous to faeces, the first piece of bodily substance the child had to part with. Thus the old anal defiance enters into the composition of the castration complex. The organic analogy which enabled the intestinal contents to be the forerunner of the penis during the pregenital phase cannot come into account as a motive; but the boy's sexual researches lead him to a psychical substitute for it. When a baby appears on the scene he regards it as 'lumf', in accordance with those researches, and he cathects it with powerful anal-erotic interest. When social experiences teach that a baby is to be regarded as a love-token, a gift, the wish for a baby receives a second contribution from the same source. Faeces, penis and baby are all three solid bodies; they all three, by forcible entry or expulsion, stimulate a membranous passage, i.e. the rectum and the vagina, the latter being as it were 'taken on lease' from the rectum, as Lou Andreas-Salomé aptly remarks.[7] Infantile sexual researches can only lead to the conclusion that the baby follows the same route as the faecal mass. The function of the penis is not usually discovered by those researches. But it is interesting to note that after so many détours an organic correspondence reappears in the psychical sphere as an unconscious identity.

7. In her paper ' "Anal" und "Sexual" ' (1916). [Freud added a footnote in 1920 to the second of his *Three Essays on Sexuality*, in which he summarized the contents of that paper. {p. 124 above}.]

The Taboo of Virginity

W hen psychoanalytic publishing resumed in 1918, after the dreadful interruption of the First World War, Freud issued this essay, which had been written in 1917 as the third in a series of "contributions to the psychology of love." The second essay in the series had focused on the topic of male psychical impotence, and this essay treats female frigidity. But this essay also continues Freud's interest—noted with reference to "On Transformations of Instinct as Exemplified in Anal Erotism"—in how childhood female sexuality becomes adult female sexuality.

In addition, "The Taboo of Virginity" is part of Freud's growing concern with social anthropology and with his idea that the stages of individual sexual development recapitulate in miniature the stages of social evolution. In a recent major work, Totem and Taboo (1912), Freud had explored similarities between types of neurotic behavior and "primitive" social taboos, on the assumption that a neurotic individual regresses to or remains fixated at his or her own equivalent of a "primitive" level. The taboo of virginity was a type of social taboo that Freud had not considered in Totem and Taboo, so he offers the present essay as a complement to the earlier book.

To the consternation of feminists, Freud often announces without any comment that women are or must be subordinated to men. In this essay (as in Totem and Taboo) he does present his rationale: subordination is required to support monogamy (and sexual fidelity), which is always in tension with "the polygamous tendency" in individuals and in societies. Male domination is only one of two possibilities (as Lou Andreas-Salomé pointed out in a letter cited at the end of this essay), but it is the only one that supports masculine claims to paternity, while feminine claims to maternity can be advanced without matriarchy. Defloration is like branding—it marks a woman as belonging to one man and as not available *to others, to bear their children. (But, Freud argued, insofar as defloration is felt by the woman as a wound to her narcissism, a defeat of her secret wish for a penis, it provokes her deep and often abiding hostility.) As in " 'Civilized' Sexual Morality and Modern Nervous Illness," Freud takes for granted the value of monogamy as an achievement of civilization— promiscuity arises from the unrelinquished past. And what else, Freud implicitly asks, could keep people with residual polygamous tendencies faithfully together than a system of subordination and branding? Among feminists, the main strand of reply has been: "equality and mutual respect." But both the value of monogamy and the idea that individual and social development evolve from :primitive" promiscuity to "civilized" pairing have also been hotly disputed.*

$\sim\!\!\sim\!\!\sim\!\!\sim$

Few details of the sexual life of primitive peoples are so alien to our own feelings as their estimate of virginity, the state in a woman of being untouched. The high value which her suitor places on a woman's virginity seems to us so firmly rooted, so much a matter of course, that we find ourselves almost at a loss if we have to give reasons for this opinion. The demand that a girl shall not bring to her marriage with a particular man any memory of sexual relations with another is, indeed, nothing other than a logical continuation of the right to exclusive possession of a woman, which forms the essence of monogamy, the extension of this monopoly to cover the past.

From this point we have no trouble in justifying what looked at first like a prejudice, by referring to our views on the erotic life of women. Whoever is the first to satisfy a virgin's desire for love, long and laboriously held in check, and who in doing so overcomes the resistances which have been built up in her through the influences of her milieu and education, that is the man she will take into a lasting relationship, the possibility of which will never again be open to any other man. This experience creates a state of bondage in the woman which guarantees that possession of her shall continue undisturbed and makes her able to resist new impressions and enticements from outside.

The expression 'sexual bondage' was chosen by von Krafft-Ebing (1892) to describe the phenomenon of a person's acquiring an unusually high degree of dependence and lack of self-reliance in relation to another person with whom he has a sexual rela-

tionship. This bondage can on occasion extend very far, as far as
the loss of all independent will and as far as causing a person to
suffer the greatest sacrifices of his own interests; the author, however, does not fail to remark that a certain measure of such dependence 'is absolutely necessary, if the tie is to last for any length
of time'. Some such measure of sexual bondage is, indeed, indispensable to the maintenance of civilized marriage and to holding at bay the polygamous tendencies which threaten it, and in
our social communities this factor is regularly reckoned upon.

Von Krafft-Ebing derives the formation of sexual bondage from
a conjunction of an 'uncommon degree of the state of being in
love and of weakness of character' in one person and unbounded
egoism in the other. Analytic experience, however, will not let
us rest satisifed with this simple attempt at explanation. We can
see, rather, that the decisive factor is the amount of sexual resistance that is overcome and in addition the fact that the process
of overcoming the resistance is concentrated and happens only
once. This state of bondage is, accordingly, far more frequent
and more intense in women than in men, though it is true it
occurs in the latter more often nowadays than it did in ancient
times. Wherever we have been able to study sexual bondage in
men it has shown itself as resulting from an overcoming of psychical impotence through one particular woman, to whom the man
in question has remained subsequently bound.[1] Many strange
marriages and not a few tragic events—even some with far-
reaching consequences—seem to owe their explanation to this
origin.

Turning to the attitude of primitive peoples, it is incorrect to
describe it by declaring that they set no value on virginity and to
submit as proof of this the fact that they perform the defloration
of girls outside marriage and before the first act of marital intercourse. On the contrary, it appears that for them, too, defloration
is a significant act; but is has become the subject of a taboo—of
a prohibition which may be described as religious. Instead of
reserving it for the girl's bridegroom and future partner in marriage, custom demands that *he shall shun the performance of it*.

It is no part of my purpose to make a full collection of the
literary evidence for the existence of this custom of prohibition,

---

1. [A remark on this will be found in a footnote at the end of Freud's late paper
'Analysis Terminable and Interminable' (1937).]

to pursue its geographical distribution and to enumerate all the forms in which it is expressed. I shall content myself, therefore, with stating the fact that the practice of rupturing the hymen in this way outside the subsequent marriage is very wide-spread among primitive races living to-day.   *   *   *

Freud presents a number of anthropologists' descriptions of defloration and mock-coitus ceremonies. Then he offers three explanations for why defloration is so often performed by someone other than the bridegroom: the association of defloration with the commonly reported horror of blood; general anxiety or sense of danger about novel situations or mysteries; a general taboo on women, combined with or involving "narcissism of minor differences" or a deep hostility toward persons who are "other." Finding each of these explanations partial and the three taken together not adequate to the clinical evidence he has gathered from his female patients—that is, from the female point of view—Freud leaves his anthropological speculations and returns to what psychoanalysis can offer about "the taboo on virginity."

We consider it to be the normal reaction for a woman after intercourse to embrace the man, pressing him to her at the climax of satisfaction, and we see this as an expression of her gratitude and a token of lasting bondage. But we know it is by no means the rule that the first occasion of intercourse should lead to this behaviour; very frequently it means only disappointment for the woman, who remains cold and unsatisfied, and it usually requires quite a long time and frequent repetition of the sexual act before she too begins to find satisfaction in it. There is an unbroken series from these cases of mere initial frigidity which soon vanishes, up to the cheerless phenomenon of permanent and obstinate frigidity which no tender efforts on the part of the husband can overcome. I believe this frigidity in women is not yet sufficiently understood and, except for those cases which must be blamed on the man's insufficient potency, calls for elucidation, possibly through allied phenomena.

I do not want to introduce at this point the attempts—which are so frequent—to take flight from the first occasion of sexual intercourse, because they are open to several interpretations and are in the main, although not altogether, to be understood as an expression of the general female tendency to take a defensive line. As against this, I do believe that light is thrown on the riddle of female frigidity by certain pathological cases in which, after the first and indeed after each repeated instance of sexual intercourse, the woman gives unconcealed expression to her hostility towards the man by abusing him, raising her hand against him or actually striking him. In one very clear case of this kind, which I was able to submit to a thorough analysis, this happened although the woman loved the man very much, used to demand intercourse herself and unmistakably found great satisfaction in it. I think that this strange, contradictory reaction is the result of the very same impulses which ordinarily can only find expression as frigidity—which, that is, can hold back the tender reaction without at the same time being able to put themselves into effect. In the pathological case we find separated so to speak into its two components what in the far more common instance of frigidity is united to produce an inhibiting effect. * * * The danger which is thus aroused through the defloration of a woman would consist in drawing her hostility down upon oneself, and the prospective husband is just the person who would have every reason to avoid such enmity.

Now analysis enables us to infer without difficulty which impulses in women take part in bringing about this paradoxical behaviour, in which I expect to find the explanation of frigidity. The first act of intercourse mobilizes a number of impulses which are out of place in the desired feminine attitude, some of which, incidentally, need not recur during subsequent intercourse. In the first place we think of the pain which defloration causes a virgin, and we are perhaps even inclined to consider this factor as decisive and to give up the search for any others. But we cannot well ascribe such importance to this pain; we must rather substitute for it the narcissistic injury which proceeds from the destruction of an organ and which is even represented in a rationalized form in the knowledge that loss of virginity brings a diminution of sexual value. The marriage customs of primitive peoples, however, contain a warning against over-estimating this. We have heard that in some cases the rite falls into two phases: after the hymen has been ruptured (by hand or with some instrument) there follows a ceremonial act of coitus or mock-intercourse with the representatives of the husband, and this proves to us that the purpose of the taboo observance is not fulfilled by avoiding anatomical defloration, that the husband is to be spared something else as well as the woman's reaction to the painful injury.

We find a further reason for the disappointment experienced in the first act of intercourse in the fact that, with civilized women at least, fulfilment cannot be in accordance with expectations. Before this, sexual intercourse has been associated in the strongest possible way with prohibitions; lawful and permissible intercourse is not, therefore, felt to be the same thing. Just how close this association can be is demonstrated in an almost comic fashion by the efforts of so many girls about to be married to keep their new love-relationship secret from everyone outside, and indeed even from their parents, where there is no real necessity to do so and no objection can be looked for. Girls often say openly that their love loses value for them if other people know of it. On occasion this feeling can become dominating and can completely prevent the development of any capacity for love in a marriage. The woman only recovers her susceptibility to tender feelings in an illicit relationship which has to be kept secret, and in which alone she knows for certain that her own will is uninfluenced.

However, this motive does not go deep enough either; besides, being bound up with civilized conditions, it fails to provide a satisfactory connection with the state of affairs among primitive people. All the more important, therefore, is the next factor, which is based on the evolution of the libido. We have learnt from analytic researches how universal and how powerful the earliest allocations of libido are. In these we are concerned with infantile sexual wishes which are clung to (in women usually a fixation of the libido on the father or a brother who takes his place)—wishes which frequently enough were directed towards other things than intercourse, or included it only as a dimly perceived goal. The husband is almost always so to speak only a substitute, never the right man; it is another man—in typical cases the father—who has first claim to a woman's love, the husband at most takes second place. It depends on how intense this fixation is and on how obstinately it is maintained whether the substitute is rejected as unsatisfying. Frigidity is thus among the genetic determinants of neuroses. The more powerful the psychical element in a woman's sexual life is, the greater will be the capacity for resistance shown by her distribution of libido to the upheaval of the first sexual act, and the less overpowering will be the effect which bodily possession of her can produce. Frigidity may then become established as a neurotic inhibition or provide the foundation for the development of other neuroses and even a moderate diminution of potency in the man will greatly contribute to help this process.

The customs of primitive peoples seem to take account of this *motif* of the early sexual wish by handing over the task of defloration to an elder, priest of holy man, that is, to a substitute for the father. * * * It agrees with our expectations, therefore, when we find the images of gods included among the father-surrogates entrusted with defloration. In some districts of India, the newly-married woman was obliged to sacrifice her hymen to the wooden lingam, and, according to St. Augustine's account, the same custom existed in the Roman marriage ceremony (of his time?), but modified so that the young wife only had to seat herself on the gigantic stone phallus of Priapus.[2]

There is another motive, reaching down into still deeper layers, which can be shown to bear the chief blame for the paradoxical reaction towards the man, and which, in my view, further makes its influence felt in female frigidity. The first act of intercourse activates in a woman other impulses of long standing as well as those already described, and these are in complete opposition to her womanly role and function.

We have learnt from the analysis of many neurotic women that they go through an early age in which they envy their brothers their sign of masculinity and feel at a disadvantage and humiliated because of the lack of it (actually because of its diminished size) in themselves. We include this 'envy for the penis' in the 'castration complex'. If we understand 'masculine' as including the idea of wishing to be masculine, then the designation 'masculine protest' fits this behaviour; the phrase was coined by Adler [1910] with the intention of proclaiming this factor as being responsible for neurosis in general. During this phase, little girls often make no secret of their envy, nor of the hostility towards their favoured brothers which arises from it. They even try to urinate standing upright like their brothers in order to prove the equality which they claim to. In the case already described in which the woman used to show uncontrolled aggression after intercourse towards her husband, whom otherwise she loved, I was able to establish that this phase had existed before that of object-choice. Only later

2. {Priapus is the fertility god in Greek and Roman mythology who personifies male phallic power; he was the son of Dionysus and Aphrodite.}

was the little girl's libido directed towards her father, and then, instead of wanting to have a penis, she wanted—a child.

I should not be surprised if in other cases the order in which these impulses occurred were reversed and this part of the castration complex only became effective after a choice of object had been successfully made. But the masculine phase in the girl in which she envies the boy for his penis is in any case developmentally the earlier, and it is closer to the original narcissism than it is to object-love.

Some time ago I chanced to have an opportunity of obtaining insight into a dream of a newly-married woman which was recognizable as a reaction to the loss of her virginity. It betrayed spontaneously the woman's wish to castrate her young husband and to keep his penis for herself. Certainly there was also room for the more innocent interpretation that what she wished for was the prolongation and repetition of the act, but several details of the dream did not fit into this meaning and the character as well as the subsequent behaviour of the woman who had the dream gave evidence in favour of the more serious view. Behind this envy for the penis, there comes to light the woman's hostile bitterness against the man, which never completely disappears in the relations between the sexes, and which is clearly indicated in the strivings and in the literary productions of 'emancipated' women. In a paleo-biological speculation, Ferenczi has traced back this hostility of women—I do not know if he is the first to do so—to the period in time when the sexes became differentiated. At first, in his opinion, copulation took place between two similar individuals, one of which, however, developed into the stronger and forced the weaker one to submit to sexual union. The feelings of bitterness arising from this subjection still persist in the present-day disposition of women. I do not think there is any harm in employing such speculations, so long as one avoids setting too much value on them.

After this enumeration of the motives for the paradoxical reaction of women to defloration, traces of which persist in frigidity, we may sum up by saying that a woman's *immature sexuality* is discharged on to the man who first makes her acquainted with the sexual act. This being so, the taboo of virginity is reasonable enough and we can understand the rule which decrees that precisely the man who is to enter upon a life shared with this woman shall avoid these dangers. At higher stages of civilization the importance attributed to this danger diminishes in face of her promise of bondage and no doubt of other motives and inducements; virginity is looked upon as a possession which the husband is not called upon to renounce. But analysis of disturbed marriages teaches us that the motives which seek to drive a woman to take vengeance for her defloration are not completely extinguished even in the mental life of civilized women. I think it must strike the observer in how uncommonly large a number of cases the woman remains frigid and feels unhappy in a first marriage, whereas after it has been dissolved she becomes a tender wife, able to make her second husband happy. The archaic reaction has, so to speak, exhausted itself on the first object. * * *

The taboo of virginity and something of its motivation has been depicted most powerfully of all in a well-known dramatic character, that of Judith in Hebbel's tragedy *Judith und Holofernes.* Judith is one of those women whose virginity is protected by a taboo. Her first husband was paralysed on the bridal night by a mysterious anxiety, and never again dared to touch her. 'My beauty is like belladonna,' she says. 'Enjoyment of it brings madness and death.' When the Assyrian general is besieging her city, she conceives the plan of seducing him by her beauty and of destroying him, thus employing a patriotic motive to conceal a sexual one. After she has been deflowered by this powerful man, who boasts of his strength and ruthlessness, she finds the strength in her fury to strike off his head, and thus becomes the liberator of her people. Beheading is well-known to us as a symbolic substitute for castrating; Judith is accordinly the woman who castrates the man who has deflowered her, which was just the wish of the newly-married woman expressed in the dream I reported. It is clear that Hebbel has intentionally sexualized the patriotic narrative from the Apocrypha of the Old Testament, for there Judith is able to boast after her return that she has not been defiled, nor is there in the biblical text any mention of her uncanny wedding night. But probably, with the fine perception of a poet, he sensed the ancient motive, which had been lost in the tendentious narrative, and has merely restored its earlier content to the material. * * *

It is interesting that in one's capacity as analyst one can meet with women in whom the opposed reactions of bondage and hostility both find expression and remain intimately associated with each other. There are women of this kind who seem to have fallen out with their husbands completely and who all the same can only make vain efforts to free themselves. As often as they try to direct their love towards some other man, the image of the first, although he is no longer loved, intervenes with inhibiting effect. Analysis then teaches us that these women, it is true, still cling to their first husbands in a state of bondage, but no longer through affection. They cannot get away from them, because they have not completed their revenge upon them, and in pronounced cases they have not even brought the impulses for vengeance to consciousness.

We may say, then, in conclusion that defloration has not only the one, civilized consequence of binding the woman lastingly to the man; it also unleashes an archaic reaction of hostility towards him, which can assume pathological forms that are frequently enough expressed in the appearance of inhibitions in the erotic side of married life, and to which we may ascribe the fact that second marriages so often turn out better than first. The taboo of virginity, which seems so strange to us, the horror with which, among primitive peoples, the husband avoids the act of defloration, are fully justified by this hostile reaction.

When she read Freud's essay, his friend and colleague Lou Andreas-Salomé wrote her response. This passage in her January 30, 1919, letter may have prompted Freud to think more about the "archaic" (and in individual terms "pre-Oedipal") forms of female existence. (See Sigmund Freud and Lou Andreas-Salomé Letters, edited by Ernst Pfeiffer, New York: Harcourt Brace Jovanovich, 1972, p. 89).

With regard to the short essay on 'The Taboo of Virginity' it occurred to me that this taboo may have been intensified by the fact that at one time (in a matriarchal society) the woman may have been the dominant partner. In this way, like the defeated deities, she acquired demonic properties, and was feared as an agent of retribution. Also her defloration by deity, priests, etc. points back to a time when she was not the 'private property' of the male, and in order to achieve this she had to shake off the shackles of her impressive past—which may still play its part as the earliest positive basis for the precautionary measures of the male.

Meanwhile, Karl Abraham wrote from Berlin on May 5, 1919, to send Freud birthday greetings and to report about a paper he was writing— "Manifestations of the Female Castration Complex"—which launched the extensive Berlin debates on female sexuality (see Bibliography):

Dear Professor,

This letter was meant to reach you on May 7th, but it will arrive some days later after all. My good wishes are nonetheless sincere. I had hoped to be able to send you a scientific contribution in honour of the day, as I have done several times previously. The paper in question will however be more extensive than I had anticipated and, because of my limited leisure, will not be ready for some weeks. It uses your recent publication on 'The Taboo of Virginity' as a point of departure and deals with the castration complex in women; I think it contributes something new. Some days ago I spoke in our Society about this topic. We have had regular meeting since the end of the war and they are far more productive than they used to be. * * *

'A Child Is Being Beaten,' A Contribution to the Study of the Origin of Sexual Perversions

As a contribution to the understanding of perversions, this long, complex clinical essay is a continuation of the first of the Three Essays. Specifically, it focuses on masochism—a topic to which Freud five years later devoted a summary or overview piece, "The Economic Problem of Masochism" (below, pages 283–93). The present essay also contains Freud's most extended discussion of repression considered from the angle of its motivation. He rejects two theoretical efforts to sexualize repression, one by his long-lost friend Fliess and another by his more recently lost colleague Alfred Adler. Fliess's notion that everyone, being bisexually constituted, is motivated to repress into the unconscious the mental sexual characteristics opposite to his or her anatomical sex is rejected because it too simply equates the dominant sexuality with anatomy. In this form, the adage "Anatomy is destiny" was completely unacceptable to Freud. Adler's more sociological theory of "masculine protest," on the other hand, is rejected because, while it has the virtue of simplicity—both men and women protest against the sexual line of inferior status, that is, femininity—it cannot explain differences in types of repression or failures of repression leading to symptom formation. Freud thought it was important to refute these theories because they obscured the centrality of the Oedipus complex in the formation of neuroses. In addition, the clinical data on beating fantasies had reaffirmed Freud in his conviction that the Oedipus complex was "the nuclear complex of the neuroses."

As a contribution to female psychology, this paper was a turning point.

The differences between the beating fantasies of males and females alerted Freud to developmental differences between the sexes that he had not focused on. He was once again concerned with the transformations instincts and object-relations undergo between childhood and adulthood, but his focus here was on a particular type of commonly occurring fantasy with the content "a child is being beaten." Because the fantasies had different histories and forms in males and females, Freud concluded that males and females repress differently. Male fantasies, originally rooted in a passive attitude toward the father (a homosexual current), remained masochistic even when mothers appeared in them as beaters, while female fantasies started out sadistic in relation to a sibling, then became passive and masochistic in relation to the father, and were finally transformed into sadistic scenes drained of any sexual quality. In this essay, Freud saw the differences in repression as part of the Oedipus complex; by 1925 he saw them as divergent consequences of relations with the same object, the mother, in the period he came to call "pre-Oedipal."

Much of the discussion of female psychology in this essay was based on Freud's analysis of his daughter Anna, and it is very instructive to read, in combination with his report, her own report: "Beating Fantasies and Daydreams," (1922), in The Writings of Anna Freud (New York: International Universities Press, 1974, volume 1). Anna Freud gives a very detailed and graphic indication of the content of her patient's (i.e., her own) beating fantasy, in contrast to her father's quite schematic approach in this essay. A summary of recent psychoanalytic work on beating fantasies is noted in the Bibliography, and it confirms that children with beating fantasies are seldom children who have actually been beaten or sexually abused. On the other hand, Oedipal-age children who develop beating fantasies that persist—that are not just transitory—do usually have depressed, preoccupied mothers who are unable to take pleasure in them during infancy and unable to tolerate or help contain their aggression in childhood. In line with Freud's underemphasis at this point on the "pre-Oedipal" period, neither he nor Anna Freud focused on the child-mother bond.

I.

It is surprising how often people who seek analytic treatment for hysteria or an obsessional neurosis confess to having indulged in the phantasy: 'A child is being beaten.' Very probably there are still more frequent instances of it among the far greater number of people who have not been obliged to come to analysis by manifest illness.

The phantasy has feelings of pleasure attached to it, and on their account the patient has reproduced it on innumerable occasions in the past or may even still be doing so. At the climax of the imaginary situation there is almost invariably a masturbatory satisfaction—carried out, that is to say, on the genitals. At first this takes place voluntarily, but later on it does so in spite of the patient's efforts, and with the characteristics of an obsession.

It is only with hesitation that this phantasy is confessed to. Its first appearance is recollected with uncertainty. The analytic treatment of the topic is met by unmistakable resistance. Shame and a sense of guilt are perhaps more strongly excited in this connection than when similar accounts are given of memories of the beginning of sexual life.

Eventually it becomes possible to establish that the first phantasies of the kind were entertained very early in life: certainly before school age, and not later than in the fifth or sixth year. When the child was at school and saw other children being beaten by the teacher, then, if the phantasies had become dormant, this experience called them up again, or, if they were still present, it reinforced them and noticeably modified their content. From that time forward it was 'an indefinite number' of children that were being beaten. The influence of the school was so clear that the patients concerned were at first tempted to trace back their beating-phantasies exclusively to these impressions of school life, which dated from later than their sixth year. But it was never possible for them to maintain that position; the phantasies had already been in existence before.

Though in the higher forms at school the children were no longer beaten, the influence of such occasions was replaced and more than replaced by the effects of reading, of which the importance was soon to be felt. In my patients' *milieu* it was almost always the same books whose contents gave a new stimulus to the beating-phantasies: those accessible to young people, such as what was known as the '*Bibliothèque rose*'[1], *Uncle Tom's Cabin*, etc. The child began to compete with these works of fiction by pro-

---

1. [A well-known series of books by Mme. de Ségur, of which *Les Malheurs de Sophie* was perhaps the most popular.]

ducing his own phantasies and by constructing a wealth of situations and institutions, in which children were beaten, or were punished and disciplined in some other way, because of their naughtiness and bad behaviour.

This phantasy—'a child is being beaten'—was invariably cathected with a high degree of pleasure and had its issue in an act of pleasurable auto-erotic satisfaction. It might therefore be expected that the sight of another child being beaten at school would also be a source of similar enjoyment. But as a matter of fact this was never so. The experience of real scenes of beating at school produced in the child who witnessed them a peculiarly excited feeling which was probably of a mixed character and in which repugnance had a large share. In a few cases the real experience of the scenes of beating was felt to be intolerable. Moreover, it was always a condition of the more sophisticated phantasies of later years that the punishment should do the children no serious injury.

The question was bound to arise of what relation there might be between the importance of the beating-phantasies and the part that real corporal punishment might have played in the child's bringing up at home. It was impossible, on account of the one-sidedness of the material, to confirm the first suspicion that the relation was an inverse one. The individuals from whom the data for these analyses were derived were very seldom beaten in their childhood, or were at all events not brought up by the help of the rod. Naturally, however, each of these children was bound to have become aware at one time or another of the superior physical strength of its parents or educators; the fact that in every nursery the children themselves at times come to blows requires no special emphasis.

As regards the early and simple phantasies which could not be obviously traced to the influence of school impressions or of scenes taken from books, further information would have been welcome. Who was the child that was being beaten? The one who was himself producing the phantasy or another? Was it always the same child or as often as not a different one? Who was it that was beating the child? A grown-up person? And if so, who? Or did the child imagine that he himself was beating another one? Nothing could be ascertained that threw any light upon all these questions—only the hesitant reply: 'I know nothing more about it: a child is being beaten.'

Enquiries as to the sex of the child that was being beaten met with more success, but none the less brought no enlightenment. Sometimes the answer was: 'Always boys', or 'Only girls'; more often it was: 'I don't know', or 'It doesn't matter which'. But the point to which the questions were directed, the discovery of some constant relation between the sex of the child producing the phantasy and that of the child that was being beaten, was never established. Now and again another characteristic detail of the content of the phantasy came to light: 'A small child is being beaten on its naked bottom.'

In these circumstances it was impossible at first even to decide whether the pleasure attaching to the beating-phantasy was to be described as sadistic or masochistic.

II.

A phantasy of this kind, arising, perhaps from accidental causes, in early childhood and retained for the purpose of auto-erotic satisfaction, can, in the light of our present knowledge, only be regarded as a primary trait of perversion. One of the components of the sexual function has, it seems, developed in advance of the rest, has made itself prematurely independent, has undergone fixation and in consequence been withdrawn from the later processes of development, and has in this way given evidence of a peculiar and abnormal constitution in the individual. We know that an infantile perversion of this sort need not persist for a whole lifetime; later on it can be subjected to repression, be replaced by a reaction-formation, or be transformed by sublimation. (It is possible that sublimation arises out of some special process which would be held back by repression.) But if these processes do not take place, then the perversion persists to maturity; and whenever we find a sexual aberration in adults—perversion, fetishism, inversion—we are justified in expecting that anamnestic investigation will reveal an event such as I have suggested, leading to a fixation in childhood. Indeed, long before the days of psycho-analysis, observers like Binet were able to trace the strange sexual aberrations of maturity back to similar impressions and to precisely the same period of childhood, namely, the fifth or sixth year. But at this point the enquiry was confronted with the limitations of our knowledge; for the impressions that brought about the fixation were without any traumatic force. They were for the most part commonplace and unexciting to other people. It was impossible to say why the sexual impulse had undergone fixation particularly upon them. It was possible, however, to look for their significance in the fact that they offered an occasion for fixation (even though it was an accidental one) to precisely that component which was prematurely developed and ready to press forward. We had in any case to be prepared to come to a provisional end somewhere or other in tracing back the train of causal connection; and the congenital constitution seemed exactly to correspond with what was required for a stopping-place of that kind.

If the sexual component which has broken loose prematurely is the sadistic one, then we may expect, on the basis of knowledge derived from other sources, that its subsequent repression will result in a disposition to an obsessional neurosis. This expectation cannot be said to be contradicted by the results of enquiry. The present short paper is based on the exhaustive study of six cases (four female and two male). Of these, two were cases of obsessional neurosis; one extremely severe and incapacitating, the other of moderate severity and quite well accessible to influence. There was also a third case which at all events exhibited clearly marked individual traits of obsessional neurosis. The fourth case, it must be admitted, was one of straightforward hysteria, with pains and inhibitions; and the fifth patient, who had come to be analysed merely on account of indecisiveness in life, would not have been classified at all by coarse clinical diagnosis, or would have been dismissed as 'psychasthenic'.[2] There is no need for feeling disappointed over these statistics. In the first place, we know that not every disposition is necessarily developed into a disorder; in the second place, we ought to be content to explain the facts before us, and ought as a rule to avoid the additional task of making it clear why something has *not* taken place.

The present state of our knowledge would allow us to make our way so far and no further towards the comprehension of beating-phantasies. In the mind of the analytic physician, it is true, there remains an uneasy suspicion that this is not a final solution of the problem. He is obliged to admit to himself that

---

2. [Nothing is said here of the sixth case.]

to a great extent these phantasies subsist apart from the rest of the content of a neurosis, and find no proper place in its structure. But impressions of this kind, as I know from my own experience, are only too willingly put on one side.

III.

Strictly considered—and why should this question not be considered with all possible strictness?—analytic work deserves to be recognized as genuine psycho-analysis only when it has succeeded in removing the amnesia which conceals from the adult his knowledge of his childhood from its beginning (that is, from about the second to the fifth year). This cannot be said among analysts too emphatically or repeated too often. The motives for disregarding this reminder are, indeed, intelligible. It would be desirable to obtain practical results in a shorter period and with less trouble. But at the present time theoretical knowledge is still far more important to all of us than therapeutic success, and anyone who neglects childhood analysis is bound to fall into the most disastrous errors. The emphasis which is laid here upon the importance of the earliest experiences does not imply any underestimation of the influence of later ones. But the later impressions of life speak loudly enough through the mouth of the patient, while it is the physician who has to raise his voice on behalf of the claims of childhood.

It is in the years of childhood between the ages of two and four or five that the congenital libidinal factors are first awakened by actual experiences and become attached to certain complexes. The beating-phantasies which are now under discussion show themselves only towards the end of this period or after its termination. So it may quite well be that they have an earlier history, that they go through a process of development, that they represent an end-product and not an initial manifestation.

This suspicion is confirmed by analysis. A systematic application of it shows that beating-phantasies have a historical development which is by no means simple, and in the course of which they are changed in most respects more than once—as regards their relation to the author of the phantasy, and as regards their object, their content and their significance.

In order to make it easier to follow these transformations in beating-phantasies I shall now venture to confine my descriptions to the female cases, which, since they are four as against two, in any case constitute the greater part of my material. Moreover, beating-phantasies in men are connected with another subject, which I shall leave on one side in this paper.[3] In my description I shall be careful to avoid being more schematic than is inevitable for the presentation of an average case. If then on further observation a greater complexity of circumstances should come to light, I shall nevertheless be sure of having before us a typical occurrence, and one, moreover that is not of an uncommon kind.

The first phase of beating-phantasies among girls, then, must belong to a very early period of childhood. Some features remain curiously indefinite, as though they were a matter of indifference. The scanty information given by the patients in their first statement, 'a child is being beaten', seems to be justified in respect to this phase. But another of their features can be established with certainty, and to the same effect in every case. The child being beaten is never the one producing the phantasy, but is invariably another child, most often a brother or a sister if there is any. Since this other child may be a boy or a girl, there is no constant relation between the sex of the child producing the phantasy and that of the child being beaten. The phantasy, then, is certainly not masochistic. It would be tempting to call it sadistic, but one cannot neglect the fact that the child producing the phantasy is never doing the beating herself. The actual identity of the person who does the beating remains obscure at first. Only this much can be established: it is not a child but an adult. Later on this indeterminate grown-up person becomes recognizable clearly and unambiguously as the (girl's) *father*.

This first phase of the beating-phantasy is therefore completely represented by the phrase: '*My father is beating the child.*' I am betraying a great deal of what is to be brought forward later when instead of this I say: 'My father is beating the child *whom I hate.*' Moreover, one may hesitate to say whether the characteristics of a 'phantasy' can yet be ascribed to this first step towards the later beating-phantasy. It is perhaps rather a question of recollections of events which have been witnessed, or of desires which have

3. [Freud does in fact discuss beating-phantasies in men below. Their specifically feminine basis is what he probably has in mind in speaking of 'another subject'.]

arisen on various occasions. But these doubts are of no importance.

Profound transformations have taken place between this first phase and the next. It is true that the person beating remains the same (that is, the father); but the child who is beaten has been changed into another one and is now invariably the child producing the phantasy. The phantasy is accompanied by a high degree of pleasure, and has now acquired a significant content, with the origin of which we shall be concerned later. Now, therefore, the wording runs: '*I am being beaten by my father.*' It is of an unmistakably masochistic character.

This second phase is the most important and the most momentous of all. But we may say of it in a certain sense that it has never had a real existence. It is never remembered, it has never succeeded in becoming conscious. It is a construction of analysis, but it is no less a necessity on that account.

The third phase once more resembles the first. It has the wording which is familiar to us from the patient's statement. The person beating is never the father, but is either left undetermined just as in the first phase, or turns in a characteristic way into a representative of the father, such as a teacher. The figure of the child who is producing the beating-phantasy no longer itself appears in it. In reply to pressing enquiries the patients only declare: 'I am probably looking on.' Instead of the one child that is being beaten, there are now a number of children present as a rule. Most frequently it is boys who are being beaten (in girls' phantasies), but none of them is personally known to the subject. The situation of being beaten, which was originally simple and monotonous, may go through the most complicated alterations and elaborations; and punishments and humiliations of another kind may be substituted for the beating itself. But the essential characteristic which distinguishes even the simplest phantasies of this phase from those of the first, and which establishes the connection with the intermediate phase, is this: the phantasy now has strong and unambiguous sexual excitement attached to it, and so provides a means for masturbatory satisfaction. But this is precisely what is puzzling. By what path has the phantasy of strange and unknown boys being beaten (a phantasy which has by this time become sadistic) found its way into the permanent possession of the little girl's libidinal trends?

Nor can we conceal from ourselves that the interrelations and sequence of the three phases of the beating-phantasy, as well as all its other peculiarities, have so far remained quite unintelligible.

IV.

If the analysis is carried through the early period to which the beating-phantasies are referred and from which they are recollected, it shows us the child involved in the agitations of its parental complex.

The affections of the little girl are fixed on her father, who has probably done all he could to win her love, and in this way has sown the seeds of an attitude of hatred and rivalry towards her mother. This attitude exists side by side with a current of affectionate dependence on her {mother}, and as years go on it may be destined to come into consciousness more and more clearly and forcibly, or else to give an impetus to an excessive reaction of devotion to her. But it is not with the girl's relation to her mother that the beating-phantasy is connected. There are other children in the nursery, only a few years older or younger, who are disliked on all sorts of other grounds, but chiefly because the parents' love has to be shared with them, and for this reason they are repelled with all the wild energy characteristic of the emotional life of those years. If the child in question is a younger brother or sister (as in three of my four cases) it is despised as well as hated; yet it attracts to itself the share of affection which the blinded parents are always ready to give the youngest child, and this is a spectacle the sight of which cannot be avoided. One soon learns that being beaten, even if it does not hurt very much, signifies a deprivation of love and a humiliation. And many children who believed themselves securely enthroned in the unshakable affection of their parents have by a single blow been cast down from all the heavens of their imaginary omnipotence. The idea of the father beating this hateful child is therefore an agreeable one, quite apart from whether he has actually been seen doing so. It means: 'My father does not love this other child, *he loves only me.*'

This then is the content and meaning of the beating-phantasy in its first phase. The phantasy obviously gratifies the child's jealousy and is dependent upon the erotic side of its life, but is also powerfully reinforced by the child's egoistic interests. Doubt remains, therefore, whether the phantasy ought to be described as purely 'sexual', nor can one venture to call it 'sadistic'.

As is well known, all the signs on which we are accustomed to base our distinctions tend to lose their clarity as we come nearer to the source. So perhaps we may say in terms recalling the prophecy made by the Three Witches to Banquo: 'Not clearly sexual, not in itself sadistic, but yet the stuff from which both will later come.'[4] In any case, however, there is no ground for suspecting that in this first phase the phantasy is already at the service of an excitation which involves the genitals and finds its outlet in a masturbatory act.

It is clear that the child's sexual life has reached the stage of genital organization, now that its incestuous love has achieved this premature choice of an object. This can be demonstrated more easily in the case of boys, but is also indisputable in the case of girls. Something like a premonition of what are later to be the final and normal sexual aims governs the child's libidinal trends. We may justly wonder why this should be so, but we may regard it as a proof of the fact that the genitals have already begun playing their part in the process of excitation. With boys the wish to beget a child from their mother is never absent, with girls the wish to have a child by their father is equally constant; and this in spite of their being completely incapable of forming any clear idea of the means for fulfilling these wishes. The child seems to be convinced that the genitals have something to do with the matter, even though in its constant brooding it may look for the essence of the presumed intimacy between its parents in relations of another sort, such as in their sleeping together, micturating in each other's presence, etc.; and material of the latter kind can be more easily apprehended in verbal images than the mystery that is connected with the genitals.

But the time comes when this early blossoming is nipped by the frost. None of these incestuous loves can avoid the fate of repression. They may succumb to it on the occasion of some discoverable external event which leads to disillusionment—such

---

4. {In Act 1, scene 3 of Shakespeare's *Macbeth*, the three witches tell Banquo he is "Lesser than Macbeth, and greater," "Thou shalt get kings, though thou be none." Freud had recently studied Lady Macbeth as one of the "character-types met with in psychoanalytic work" (14:311–315).}

as unexpected slights, the unwelcome birth of a new brother or sister (which is felt as faithlessness), etc.; or the same thing may happen owing to internal conditions apart from any such events, perhaps simply because their yearning remains unsatisfied too long. It is unquestionably true that such events are not the *effective* causes, but that these love-affairs are bound to come to grief sooner or later, though we cannot say on what particular stumbling block. Most probably they pass away because their time is over, because the children have entered upon a new phase of development in which they are compelled to recapitulate from the history of mankind the repression of an incestuous object-choice, just as at an earlier stage they were obliged to effect an object-choice of that very sort.[5] In the new phase no mental product of the incestuous love-impulses that is present unconsciously is taken over by consciousness; and anything that has already come into consciousness is expelled from it. At the same time as this process of repression takes place, a sense of guilt appears. This is also of unknown origin, but there is no doubt whatever that it is connected with the incestuous wishes, and that it is justified by the persistence of those wishes in the unconscious.[6]

The phantasy of the period of incestuous love had said: 'He (my father) loves only me, and not the other child, for he is beating it.' The sense of guilt can discover no punishment more severe than the reversal of this triumph: 'No, he does not love you, for he is beating you.' In this way the phantasy of the second phase, that of being beaten by her father, is a direct expression of the girl's sense of guilt, to which her love for her father has now succumbed. The phantasy, therefore, has become masochistic. So far as I know, this is always so; a sense of guilt is invariably the factor that transforms sadism into masochism. But this is certainly not the whole content of masochism. The sense of guilt cannot have won the field alone; a share must also fall to the love-impulse. We must remember that we are dealing with children in whom the sadistic component was able for constitutional reasons to develop prematurely and in isolation. We need not abandon this point of view. It is precisely such children who find it particularly easy to hark back to the pregenital, sadistic-

---

5. Compare the part played by Fate in the myth of Oedipus.
6. [*Footnote added* 1924:] See the continuation of this line of thought in 'The Dissolution of the Oedipus Complex' (1924). {See below, pp. 294–301.}

anal organization of their sexual life. If the genital organization, when it has scarcely been effected, is met by repression, the result is not only that every psychical representation of the incestuous love becomes unconscious, or remains so, but there is another result as well: a regressive debasement of the genital organization itself to a lower level. 'My father loves me' was meant in a genital sense; owing to the regression it is turned into 'My father is beating me (I am being beaten by my father)'. This being beaten is now a convergence of the sense of guilt and sexual love. *It is not only the punishment for the forbidden genital relation, but also the regressive substitute for that relation*, and from this latter source it derives the libidinal excitation which is from this time forward attached to it, and which finds its outlet in masturbatory acts. Here for the first time we have the essence of masochism.

This second phase—the child's phantasy of being itself beaten by its father—remains unconscious as a rule, probably in consequence of the intensity of the repression. I cannot explain why nevertheless in one of my six cases, that of a male, it was consciously remembered. This man, now grown up, had preserved the fact clearly in his memory that he used to employ the idea of being beaten by his mother for the purpose of masturbation, though to be sure he soon substituted for his own mother the mothers of his school-fellows or other women who in some way resembled her. It must not be forgotten that when a boy's incestuous phantasy is transformed into the corresponding masochistic one, one more reversal has to take place than in the case of a girl, namely the substitution of passivity for activity; and this additional degree of distortion may save the phantasy from having to remain unconscious as a result of repression. In this way the sense of guilt would be satisfied by regression instead of by repression. In the female cases the sense of guilt, in itself perhaps more exacting, could be appeased only by a combination of the two.

In two of my four female cases an elaborate superstructure of day-dreams, which was of great significance for the life of the person concerned, had grown up over the masochistic beating-phantasy. The function of this superstructure was to make possible a feeling of satisfied excitation, even though the masturbatory act was abstained from. In one of these cases the content—being beaten by the father—was allowed to venture again into consciousness, so long as the subject's own ego was made unrecognizable by a thin disguise. The hero of these stories was invariably beaten (or later only punished, humiliated, etc.) by his father.

I repeat, however, that as a rule the phantasy remains unconscious, and can only be reconstructed in the course of the analysis. This fact perhaps vindicates patients who say they remember that with them masturbation made its appearance before the third phase of the beating-phantasy (shortly to be discussed), and that this phase was only a later addition, made perhaps under the impression of scenes at school. Every time I have given credit to these statements I have felt inclined to assume that the masturbation was at first under the dominance of unconscious phantasies and that conscious ones were substituted for them later.

I look upon the beating-phantasy in its familiar third phase, which is its final form, as a substitute of this sort. Here the child who produces the phantasy appears almost as a spectator, while the father persists in the shape of a teacher or some other person in authority. The phantasy, which now resembles that of the first phase, seems to have become sadistic once more. It appears as though in the phrase, 'My father is beating the child, he loves only me,' the stress has been shifted back on to the first part after the second part has undergone repression. But only the *form* of this phantasy is sadistic; the satisfaction which is derived from it is masochistic. Its significance lies in the fact that it has taken over the libidinal cathexis of the repressed portion and at the same time the sense of guilt which is attached to the content of that portion. All of the many unspecified children who are being beaten by the teacher are, after all, nothing more than substitutes for the child itself.

We find here for the first time, too, something like a constancy of sex in the persons who play a part in the phantasy. The children who are being beaten are almost invariably boys, in the phantasies of boys just as much as in those of girls. This characteristic is naturally not to be explained by any rivalry between the sexes, as otherwise of course in the phantasies of boys it would be girls who would be being beaten; and it has nothing to do with the sex of the child who was hated in the first phase. But it points to a complication in the case of girls. When they turn away from their incestuous love for their father, with its genital significance, they easily abandon their feminine role. They spur their 'masculinity complex' (Van Ophuijsen, 1917) into activity, and from that time forward only want to be boys. For that reason the whipping-boys who represent them are boys too. In both the cases of day-dreaming—one of which almost rose to the level of a work of art—the heroes were always young men; indeed women used not to come into these creations at all, and only made their first appearance after many years, and then in minor parts.

V.

I hope I have brought forward my analytic observations in sufficient detail, and I should only like to add that the six cases I have mentioned so often do not exhaust my material. Like other analysts, I have at my disposal a far larger number of cases which have been investigated less thoroughly. These observations can be made use of along various lines: for elucidating the genesis of the perversions in general and of masochism in particular, and for estimating the part played by difference of sex in the dynamics of neurosis.

The most obvious result of such a discussion is its application to the origin of the perversions. The view which brought into the foreground in this connection the constitutional reinforcement or premature growth of a single sexual component is not shaken, indeed; but it is seen not to comprise the whole truth. The perversion is no longer an isolated fact in the child's sexual life, but falls into its place among the typical, not to say normal, processes of development which are familiar to us. It is brought into relation with the child's incestuous love-object, with its Oedipus complex. It first comes into prominence in the sphere of this complex, and after the complex has broken down it remains over, often quite by itself, the inheritor of the charge of libido from that complex and weighed down by the sense of guilt that was attached to it. The abnormal sexual constitution, finally, has shown its strength by forcing the Oedipus complex into a particular direction, and by compelling it to leave an unusual residue behind.

A perversion in childhood, as is well known, may become the basis for the construction of a perversion having a similar sense and persisting throughout life, one which consumes the subject's whole sexual life. On the other hand the perversion may be broken off and remain in the background of a normal sexual development, from which, however, it continues to withdraw a certain amount of energy. The first of these alternatives was already known before the days of analysis. Analytic investigation, however, of such fully-developed cases almost bridges the gulf between the two. For we find often enough with these perverts that they too made an attempt at developing normal sexual activity, usually at the age of puberty; but their attempt had not enough force in it and was abandoned in the face of the first obstacles which inevitably arise, whereupon they fell back upon their infantile fixation once and for all.

It would naturally be important to know whether the origin of infantile perversions from the Oedipus complex can be asserted as a general principle. While this cannot be decided without further investigation, it does not seem impossible. When we recall the anamneses which have been obtained in adult cases of perversion we cannot fail to notice that the decisive impression, the 'first experience', of all these perverts, fetishists, etc., is scarcely ever referred back to a time earlier than the sixth year. At this time, however, the dominance of the Oedipus complex is already over; the experience which is recalled, and which has been effective in such a puzzling way, may very well have represented the legacy of that complex. The connections between the experience and the complex which is by this time repressed are bound to remain obscure so long as analysis has not thrown any light on the time before the first 'pathogenic' impression. So it may be imagined how little value is to be attached, for instance, to an assertion that a case of homosexuality is congenital, when the ground given for this belief is that ever since his eighth or sixth year the person in question has felt inclinations only towards his own sex.

If, however, the derivation of perversions from the Oedipus complex can be generally established, our estimate of its importance will have gained added strength. For in our opinion the Oedipus complex is the actual nucleus of neuroses, and the infantile sexuality which culminates in this complex is the true determinant of neuroses. What remains of the complex in the unconscious represents the disposition to the later development of neuroses in the adult. In this way the beating-phantasy and other analogous perverse fixations would also only be precipitates of the Oedipus complex, scars, so to say, left behind after the process has ended, just as the notorious 'sense of inferiority' corresponds to a narcissistic scar of the same sort. * * *

Little light is thrown upon the genesis of masochism by our discussion of the beating-phantasy. To begin with, there seems to be a confirmation of the view that masochism is not the manifestation of a primary instinct, but originates from sadism which has been turned round upon the self—that is to say, by means of regression from an object to the ego.[7] Instincts with a passive aim must be taken for granted as existing, especially among women. But passivity is not the whole of masochism. The characteristic of unpleasure belongs to it as well,—a bewildering accompaniment to the satisfaction of an instinct. The transformation of sadism into masochism appears to be due to the influence of the sense of guilt which takes part in the act of repression. Thus repression is operative here in three ways: it renders the consequences of the genital organization unconscious, it compels that organization itself to regress to the earlier sadistic-anal stage, and it transforms the sadism of this stage into masochism, which is passive and again in a certain sense narcissistic. The second of these three effects is made possible by the weakness of the genital organization, which must be presupposed in these cases. The third becomes necessary because the sense of guilt takes as much objection to sadism as to incestuous object-choice genitally conceived. Again, the analyses do not tell us the origin of the sense of guilt itself. It seems to be brought along by the new phase upon which the child is entering, and, if it afterwards persists, it seems to correspond to a scar-like formation which is similar to the sense of inferiority. According to our present orientation in the structure of the ego, which is as yet uncertain, we should assign it to the agency in the mind which sets itself up as a critical conscience over against the rest of the ego[8] * * *

We may note too in passing that the analysis of the infantile perversion dealt with here is also of help in solving an old riddle—one which, it is true, has always troubled those who have not accepted psycho-analysis more than analysts themselves. Yet quite recently even Bleuler regarded it as a remarkable and inexplicable fact that neurotics make masturbation the central point of their sense of guilt. We have long assumed that this sense of guilt relates to the masturbation of early childhood and not to that of

7. {Freud changed his mind several times about whether or not there was "primary masochism." His affirmative answer is apparent in "The Economic Problem of Masochism," below, p. 287.}

8. {The agency Freud refers to came to be called the super-ego; see Chapter 3 of *The Ego and the Id* below, pp. 274–82.}

puberty, and that in the main it is to be connected not with the act of masturbation but with the phantasy which, although unconscious, lies at its root—that is to say, with the Oedipus complex.

As regards the third and apparently sadistic phase of the beating-phantasy, I have already discussed the significance that it gains as the vehicle of the excitation impelling towards masturbation; and I have shown how it arouses activities of the imagination which on the one hand continue the phantasy along the same line, and on the other hand neutralize it through compensation. Nevertheless the second phase, the unconscious and masochistic one, in which the child itself is being beaten by its father, is incomparably the more important. This is not only because it continues to operate through the agency of the phase that takes its place; we can also detect effects upon the character, which are directly derived from its unconscious form. People who harbour phantasies of this kind develop a special sensitiveness and irritability towards anyone whom they can include in the class of fathers. They are easily offended by a person of this kind, and in that way (to their own sorrow and cost) bring about the realization of the imagined situation of being beaten by their father. I should not be surprised if it were one day possible to prove that the same phantasy is the basis of the delusional litigiousness of paranoia.

VI.

It would have been quite impossible to give a clear survey of infantile beating-phantasies if I had not limited it, except in one or two connections, to the state of things in females. I will briefly recapitulate my conclusions. The little girl's beating-phantasy passes through three phases, of which the first and third are consciously remembered, the middle one remaining unconscious. The two conscious phases appear to be sadistic, whereas the middle and unconscious one is undoubtedly of a masochistic nature; its content consists in the child's being beaten by her father, and it carries with it the libidinal charge and the sense of guilt. In the first and third phantasies the child who is being beaten is always someone other than the subject; in the middle phase it is always the child herself; in the third phase it is almost invariably only boys who are being beaten. The person who does the beating is from the first her father, replaced later on by a substitute taken from the class of fathers. The unconscious phantasy of the middle phase had primarily a genital significance and developed by means of repression and regression out of an incestuous wish to be loved by the father. Another fact, though its connection with the rest does not appear to be close, is that between the second and third phases the girls change their sex, for in the phantasies of the latter phase they turn into boys.

I have not been able to get so far in my knowledge of beating-phantasies in boys, perhaps because my material was unfavourable. I naturally expected to find a complete analogy between the state of things in the case of boys and in that of girls, the mother taking the father's place in the phantasy. This expectation seemed to be fulfilled; for the content of the boy's phantasy which was taken to be the corresponding one was actually his being beaten by his mother (or later on by a substitute for her). But this phantasy, in which the boy's own self was retained as the person who was being beaten, differed from the second phase in girls in that it was able to become conscious. If on this account, however, we attempt to draw a parallel between it and the *third* phase of the girl's phantasy, a new difference is found, for the figure of the boy himself is not replaced by a number of unknown, and unspecified children, least of all by a number of girls. Therefore the expectation of there being a complete parallel was mistaken.

My male cases with an infantile beating-phantasy comprised only a few who did not exhibit some other gross injury to their sexual activities; again they included a fairly large number of persons who would have to be described as true masochists in the sense of being sexual perverts. They were either people who obtained their sexual satisfaction exclusively from masturbation accompanied by masochistic phantasies; or they were people who had succeeded in combining masochism with their genital activity in such a way that, along with masochistic performances and under similar conditions, they were able to bring about erection and emission or to carry out normal intercourse. In addition to this there was the rarer case in which a masochist is interfered with in his perverse activities by the appearance of obsessional ideas of unbearable intensity. Now perverts who can obtain satisfaction do not often have occasion to come for analysis. But as regards the three classes of masochists that have been mentioned there may be strong motives to induce them to go to an analyst.

The masochist masturbator finds that he is absolutely impotent if after all he does attempt intercourse with a woman; and the man who has hitherto effected intercourse with the help of a masochistic idea or performance may suddenly make the discovery that the alliance which was so convenient for him has broken down, his genital organs no longer reacting to the masochistic stimulus. We are accustomed confidently to promise recovery to psychically impotent patients who come to us for treatment; but we ought to be more guarded in making this prognosis so long as the dynamics of the disturbance are unknown to us. It comes as a disagreeable surprise if the analysis reveals the cause of the 'merely psychical' impotence to be a typically masochistic attitude, perhaps deeply embedded since infancy.

As regards these masochistic men, however, a discovery is made at this point which warns us not to pursue the analogy between their case and that of women any further at present, but to judge each independently. For the fact emerges that in their masochistic phantasies, as well as in the performances they go through for their realization, they invariably transfer themselves into the part of a woman; that is to say, their masochistic attitude coincides with a *feminine* one. This can easily be demonstrated from details of the phantasies; but many patients are even aware of it them-selves, and give expression to it as a subjective conviction. It makes no difference if in a fanciful embellishment of the masochistic scene they keep up the fiction that a mischievous boy, or page, or apprentice is going to be punished. On the other hand the persons who administer chastisement are always women, both in the phantasies and the performances. This is confusing enough; and the further question must be asked whether this feminine attitude already forms the basis of the masochistic element in the *infantile* beating-phantasy.[9]

Let us therefore leave aside consideration of the state of things in cases of adult masochism, which it is so hard to clear up, and turn to the infantile beating-phantasy in the male sex. Analysis of the earliest years of childhood once more allows us to make a surprising discovery in this field. The phantasy which has as its content being beaten by the mother, and which is conscious or can become so, is not a primary one. It possesses a preceding

9. [*Footnote added* 1924:] Further remarks on this subject will be found in 'The Economic Problem of Masochism' (1924).

stage which is invariably unconscious and has as its content: '*I am being beaten by my father.*' This preliminary stage, then, really corresponds to the second phase of the phantasy in the girl. The familiar and conscious phantasy: 'I am being beaten by my mother', takes the place of the third phase in the girl, in which, as has been mentioned already, unknown boys are the objects that are being beaten. I have not been able to demonstrate among boys a preliminary stage of a sadistic nature that could be set beside the first phase of the phantasy in girls, but I will not now express any final disbelief in its existence, for I can readily see the possibility of meeting with more complicated types.

In the male phantasy—as I shall call it briefly, and, I hope, without any risk of being misunderstood—the being beaten also stands for being loved (in a genital sense), though this has been debased to a lower level owing to regression. So the original form of the unconscious male phantasy was not the provisional one that we have hitherto given: 'I am being beaten by my father', but rather: '*I am loved by my father*'. The phantasy has been transformed by the processes with which we are familiar into the conscious phantasy: '*I am being beaten by my mother*'. The boy's beating-phantasy is therefore passive from the very beginning, and is derived from a feminine attitude towards his father. It corresponds with the Oedipus complex just as the female one (that of the girl) does; only the parallel relation which we expected to find between the two must be given up in favour of a common character of another kind. *In both cases the beating-phantasy has its origin in an incestuous attachment to the father.*

It will help to make matters clearer if at this point I enumerate the other similarities and differences between beating-phantasies in the two sexes. In the case of the girl the unconscious masochistic phantasy starts from the normal Oedipus attitude; in that of the boy it starts from the inverted attitude, in which the father is taken as the object of love. In the case of the girl the phantasy has a preliminary stage (the first phase), in which the beating bears no special significance and is performed upon a person who is viewed with jealous hatred. Both of these features are absent in the case of the boy, but this particular difference is one which might be removed by more fortunate observation. In her transition to the conscious phantasy [the third phase] which takes the place of the unconscious one, the girl retains the figure of her father, and in that way keeps unchanged the sex of the person beating; but she changes the figure and sex of the person being beaten, so that eventually a man is beating male children. The boy, on the contrary, changes the figure and sex of the person beating, by putting his mother in the place of his father; but he retains his own figure, with the result that the person beating and the person being beaten are of opposite sexes. In the case of the girl what was originally a masochistic (passive) situation is transformed into a sadistic one by means of repression, and its sexual quality is almost effaced. In the case of the boy the situation remains masochistic, and shows a greater resemblance to the original phantasy with its genital significance, since there is a difference of sex between the person beating and the person being beaten. The boy evades his homosexuality by repressing and remodelling his unconscious phantasy: and the remarkable thing about his later conscious phantasy is that it has for its content a feminine attitude without a homosexual object-choice. By the same process, on the other hand, the girl escapes from the demands of the erotic side of her life altogether. She turns herself in phantasy into a man, without herself becoming active in a masculine way, and is no longer anything but a spectator of the event which takes the place of a sexual act.

We are justified in assuming that no great change is effected by the *repression* of the original unconscious phantasy. Whatever is repressed from consciousness or replaced in it by something else remains intact and potentially operative in the unconscious. The effect of *regression* to an earlier stage of the sexual organization is quite another matter. As regards this we are led to believe that the state of things changes in the unconscious as well. Thus in both sexes the masochistic phantasy of being beaten by the father, though not the passive phantasy of being loved by him, lives on in the unconscious after repression has taken place. There are, besides, plenty of indications that the repression has only very incompletely attained its object. The boy, who has tried to escape from a homosexual object-choice, and who has not changed his sex, nevertheless feels like a woman in his conscious phantasies, and endows the women who are beating him with masculine attributes and characteristics. The girl, who has even renounced her sex, and who has on the whole accomplished a more thoroughgoing work of repression, nevertheless does not become freed from her father; she does not venture to do the beating herself; and since she has herself become a boy, it is principally boys whom she causes to be beaten.

I am aware that the differences that I have here described between the two sexes in regard to the nature of the beating-phantasy have not been cleared up sufficiently. But I shall not attempt to unravel these complications by tracing out their dependence on other factors, as I do not consider that the material for observation is exhaustive. So far as it goes, however, I should like to make use of it as a test for two theories. These theories stand in opposition to each other, though both of them deal with the relation between repression and sexual character, and each, according to its own view, represents the relation as a very intimate one. I may say at once that I have always regarded both theories as incorrect and misleading.

The first of these theories is anonymous. It was brought to my notice many years ago by a colleague {Fliess} with whom I was at that time on friendly terms. The theory is so attractive on account of its bold simplicity that the only wonder is that it should not have found its way into the literature of the subject except in a few scattered allusions. It is based on the fact of the bisexual constitution of human beings, and asserts that the motive force of repression in each individual is a struggle between the two sexual characters. The dominant sex of the person, that which is the more strongly developed, has repressed the mental representation of the subordinated sex into the unconscious. Therefore the nucleus of the unconscious (that is to say, the repressed) is in each human being that side of him which belongs to the opposite sex. Such a theory as this can only have an intelligible meaning if we assume that a person's sex is to be determined by the formation of his genitals; for otherwise it would not be certain which is a person's stronger sex and we should run the risk of reaching from the results of our enquiry the very fact which has to serve as its point of departure. To put the theory briefly: with men, what is unconscious and repressed can be brought down to feminine instinctual impulses; and conversely with women.

The second thory is of more recent origin. It is in agreement with the first one in so far as it too represents the struggle between the two sexes as being the decisive cause of repression. In other respects it comes into conflict with the former theory; moreover, it looks for support to sociological rather than biological sources. According to this theory of the 'masculine protest', formulated by Alfred Adler, every individual makes efforts not to remain on the inferior 'feminine line [of development]' and struggles towards the 'masculine line', from which satisfaction can alone be derived. Adler makes the masculine protest responsible for the whole formation both of character and of neuroses. Unfortunately he makes so little distinction between the two processes, which certainly have to be kept separate, and sets altogether so little store in general by the fact of repression, that to attempt to apply the doctrine of the masculine protest to repression brings with it the risk of misunderstanding. In my opinnion such an attempt could only lead us to infer that the masculine protest, the desire to break away from the feminine line, was in every case the motive force of repression. The repessing agency, therefore, would always be a masculine instinctual impulse, and the repressed would be a feminine one. But symptoms would also be the result of a feminine impulse, for we cannot discard the characteristic feature of symptoms—that they are substitutes for the repressed, substitutes that have made their way out in spite of repression.

Now let us take these two theories, which may be said to have in common a sexualization of the process of repression, and test them by applying them to the example of the beating-phantasies which we have been studying. The original phantasy, 'I am being beaten by my father', corresponds, in the case of the boy, to a feminine attitude, and is therefore an expression of that part of his disposition which belongs to the opposite sex. If this part of him undergoes repression, the first theory seems shown to be correct; for this theory set is up as a rule that what belongs to the opposite sex is identical with the repressed. It scarcely answers to our expectations, it is true, when we find that the conscious phantasy, which arises after repression has been accomplished, nevertheless exhibits the feminine attitude once more, though this time directed towards the mother. But we will not go into such doubtful points, when the whole question can be so quickly decided. There can be no doubt that the original phantasy in the case of the girl, 'I am being beaten (i.e. I am loved) by my father', represents a feminine attitude, and corresponds to her dominant and manifest sex; according to the theory, therefore, it ought to escape repression, and there would be no need for its becoming unconscious. But as a matter of fact it does become unconscious, and is replaced by a conscious phantasy which disavows the girl's manifest sexual character. The theory is therefore useless as an explanation of beating-phantasies, and is contradicted by the facts. It might be objected that it is precisely in unmanly boys and unwomanly girls that these beating-phantasies appeared and went through these vicissitudes; or that it was a trait of femininity in the boy and of masculinity in the girl which must be made responsible for the production of a passive phantasy in the boy, and its repression in the girl. We should be inclined to agree with this view, but it would not be any the less impossible to defend the supposed relation between manifest sexual character and the choice of what is destined for repression. In the last resort we can only see that both in male and female individuals masculine as well as feminine instinctual impulses are found, and that each can equally well undergo repression and so become unconscious.

The theory of the masculine protest seems to maintain its ground very much better on being tested in regard to the beating-phantasies. In the case of both boys and girls the beating-phantasy corresponds with a feminine attitude—one, that is, in which the individual is lingering on the 'feminine line'—and both sexes hasten to get free from this attitude by repressing the phantasy. Nevertheless, it seems to be only with the girl that the masculine protest is attended with complete success, and in that instance, indeed, an ideal example is to be found of the operation of the masculine protest. With the boy the result is not entirely satisfactory; the feminine line is not given up, and the boy is certainly not 'on top' in his conscious masochistic phantasy. It would therefore agree with the expectations derived from the theory if we were to recognize that this phantasy was a symptom which had come into existence through the failure of the masculine protest. It is a disturbing fact, to be sure, that the girl's phantasy, which owes its origin to the forces of repression, also has the value and meaning of a symptom. In this instance, where the masculine protest has completely achieved its object, surely the determining condition for the formation of a symptom must be absent.

Before we are led by this difficulty to a suspicion that the whole conception of the masculine protest is inadequate to meet the problem of neuroses and perversions, and that its application to them is unfruitful, we will for a moment leave the passive beating-phantasies and turn our attention to other instinctual manifestations of infantile sexual life—manifestations which have equally undergone repression. No one can doubt that there are also wishes and phantasies which keep to the masculine line from their very nature, and which are the expression of masculine instinctual impulses—sadistic tendencies, for instance, or a boy's lustful feelings towards his mother arising out of the normal Oedipus complex. It is no less certain that these impulses, too, are overtaken by repression. If the masculine protest is to be taken as having satisfactorily explained the repression of passive phantasies (which later become masochistic), then it becomes for that very reason totally inapplicable to the opposite case of active phantasies. That is to say, the doctrine of the masculine protest is altogether incompatible with the fact of repression. Unless we are prepared to throw away all that has been acquired in psychology since Breuer's first cathartic treatment and through its agency, we cannot expect that the principle of the masculine protest will acquire any significance in the elucidation of the neuroses and perversions.

The theory of psycho-analysis (a theory based on observation) holds firmly to the view that the motive forces of repression must not be sexualized. Man's archaic heritage forms the nucleus of the unconscious mind; and whatever part of that heritage has to be left behind in the advance to later phases of development, because it is unserviceable or incompatible with what is new and harmful to it, falls a victim to the process of repression. This selection is made more successfully with one group of instincts than with the other. In virtue of special circumstances which have often been pointed out already, the latter group, that of the sexual instincts, are able to defeat the intentions of repression, and to enforce their representation by substitutive formations of a disturbing kind. For this reason infantile sexuality, which is held under repression, acts as the chief motive force in the formation of symptoms; and the essential part of its content, the Oedipus complex, is the nuclear complex of neuroses. I hope that in this paper I have raised an expectation that the sexual aberrations of childhood, as well as those of mature life, are ramifications of the same complex.

The Psychogenesis of a Case of Homosexuality in a Woman

This is the only full case study of a woman that Freud wrote after the "Dora" case. Like that study of twenty years earlier, this one presents a treatment that was broken off. But "Dora" left her analysis, while Freud suggested to the homosexual young woman that she should seek a female analyst, someone not included in her "sweeping rejection of men," which Freud felt was baffling his therapeutic efforts. As the "Dora" case had ended with reflections on how new editions of old loves make up "transference," this one ends with reflections on how old "defense mechanisms" (unconscious strategies for protecting against intrapsychic or external sources of anxiety) can also be transferred or be part of the transference.

It is important to note that Freud did not view his patient's homosexuality as a disease in need of cure, because, as noted in my Introduction, he understood neuroses to be based on repressed, unconscious sexual desires, not sexual desires declared and ardently pursued, as in this case. The girl was "in no way ill," she had no "pathologically divided personality." But he did think that some homosexuals could be "in especially favorable circumstance" converted to "full bisexual functions," not to heterosexuality. Both homosexuality and heterosexuality are, in Freud's view, limitations of bisexuality—but one is socially acceptable and the other not (which of course means that conversions from heterosexuality to full bisexual functions are not in demand). Freud's recommendation that his patient seek a female analyst was in line with his liberal attitude, and also theoretically important for its acknowledgment that the "pre-Oedipal" period of mother-love was a territory where women analysts would be the best explorers—as they historically were, particularly in child psychoanalysis. In the essays he wrote on female psychology in the next decade, Freud again and again challenged his female trainees and colleagues to follow in the direction of this case, that is, to investigate the female's mother-bond.

This case also contains important remarks on psychoanalytic technique, all of which show Freud as a much less intrusive therapist than he was when he treated "Dora" twenty years earlier. He does not inflict his interpretations on the homosexual young woman, and he does not badger her until she accepts them. He is sympathetic to her frustrations and appreciative of her intellect.

Two years later, Freud wrote another essay—not anthologized here— in which homosexuality is also a central topic: "Some Neurotic Mechanisms in Jealousy, Paranoia and Homosexuality" (18:222–33). When compared with the present case study, this essay, which deals only with males, makes clear how little alike in psychic terms Freud thought male and female homosexuality are—another indication of how male and female development were becoming differentiated in Freud's thought.

～～～～

I.

Homosexuality in women, which is certainly not less common than in men, although much less glaring, has not only been ignored by the law, but has also been neglected by psycho-analytic research. The narration of a single case, not too pronounced in type, in which it was possible to trace its origin and development in the mind with complete certainty and almost without a gap may, therefore, have a certain claim to attention. If this presentation of it furnishes only the most general outlines of the various events concerned and of the conclusions reached from a study of the case, while suppressing all the characteristic details on which the interpretation is founded, this limitation is easily to be explained by the medical discretion necessary in discussing a recent case.

A beautiful and clever girl of eighteen, belonging to a family of good standing, had aroused displeasure and concern in her parents by the devoted adoration with which she pursued a certain 'society lady' who was about ten years older than herself. The parents asserted that, in spite of her distinguished name, this lady was nothing but a *cocotte*. It was well known, they said, that she lived with a friend, a married woman, and had intimate relations with her, while at the same time she carried on promiscuous affairs with a number of men. The girl did not contradict these evil reports, but neither did she allow them to interfere with her worship of the lady, although she herself was by no means lacking in a sense of decency and propriety. No prohibitions and no supervision hindered the girl from seizing every one of her rare opportunities of being together with her beloved, of ascertaining all her habits, of waiting for her for hours outside her door or at a tram-halt, of sending her gifts of flowers, and so on. It was evident that this one interest had swallowed up all others in the girl's mind. She did not trouble herself any further with educational studies, thought nothing of social functions or girlish pleasures, and kept up relations only with a few girl friends who could help her in the matter or serve as confidantes. The parents could not say to what lengths their daughter had gone in her relations with the questionable lady, whether the limits of devoted admiration had already been exceeded or not. They had never remarked in their daughter any interest in young men, nor pleasure in their attentions, while, on the other hand, they were sure that her present attachment to a woman was only a continuation, in a more marked degree, of a feeling she had displayed of recent years for other members of her own sex which had already aroused her father's suspicion and anger.

There were two details of her behaviour, in apparent contrast with each other, that most especially vexed her parents. On the one hand, she did not scruple to appear in the most frequented streets in the company of her undesirable friend, being thus quite neglectful of her own reputation; while, on the other hand, she disdained no means of deception, no excuses and no lies that would make meetings with her possible and cover them. She thus showed herself too open in one respect and full of deceitfulness in the other. One day it happened, indeed, as was sooner or later inevitable in the circumstances, that the father met his daughter in the company of the lady, about whom he had come to know. He passed them by with an angry glance which boded no good. Immediately afterwards the girl rushed off and flung herself over a wall down the side of a cutting on to the suburban railway line which ran close by. She paid for this undoubtedly serious attempt at suicide with a considerable time on her back in bed, though fortunately little permanent damage was done. After her recovery she found it easier to get her own way than before. The parents did not dare to oppose her with so much determination, and the lady, who up till then had received her advances coldly, was moved by such an unmistakable proof of serious passion and began to treat her in a more friendly manner.

About six months after this episode the parents sought medical advice and entrusted the physician with the task of bringing their daughter back to a normal state of mind. The girl's attempted suicide had evidently shown them that strong disciplinary measures at home were powerless to overcome her disorder. Before going further, however, it will be desirable to deal separately with the attitudes of her father and of her mother to the matter. The father was an earnest, worthy man, at bottom very tender-hearted, but he had to some extent estranged his children by the sternness he had adopted towards them. His treatment of his only daughter was too much influenced by consideration for his wife. When he first came to know of his daughter's homosexual tendencies he flew into a rage and tried to suppress them by threats. At that time perhaps he hesitated between different, though equally distressing, views—regarding her either as vicious, as degenerate, or as mentally afflicted. Even after the attempted suicide he did not achieve the lofty resignation shown by one of our medical colleagues who remarked of a similar irregularity in his own family: 'Well, it's just a misfortune like any other.' There was something about his daughter's homosexuality that aroused the deepest bitterness in him, and he was determined to combat it with all the means in his power. The low estimation in which psycho-analysis is so generally held in Vienna did not prevent him from turning to it for help. If this way failed he still had in reserve his strongest counter-measure: a speedy marriage was to awaken the natural instincts of the girl and stifle her unnatural tendencies.

The mother's attitude towards the girl was not so easy to grasp. She was still a youngish woman, who was evidently unwilling to give up her own claims to attractiveness. All that was clear was that she did not take her daughter's infatuation so tragically as did the father, nor was she so incensed at it. She had even for some time enjoyed her daughter's confidence concerning her passion. Her opposition to it seemed to have been aroused mainly by the harmful publicity with which the girl displayed her feelings. She had herself suffered for some years from neurotic troubles and enjoyed a great deal of consideration from her husband; she treated her children in quite different ways, being decidedly harsh towards her daughter and overindulgent to her three sons, the youngest of whom had been born after a long interval and was then not yet three years old. It was not easy to ascertain anything more definite about her character, for, owing to motives that will only later become intelligible, the patient was always reserved in what she said about her mother, whereas in regard to her father there was no question of this.

To a physician who was to undertake psycho-analytic treatment of the girl there were many grounds for misgiving. The situation he had to deal with was not the one that analysis demands, in which alone it can demonstrate its effectiveness. As is well known, the ideal situation for analysis is when someone who is otherwise his own master is suffering from an inner conflict which he is unable to resolve alone, so that he brings his trouble to the analyst and begs for his help. The physician then works hand in hand with one portion of the pathologically divided personality, against the other party in the conflict. Any situation which differs from this is to a greater or lesser degree unfavourable for psycho-analysis and adds fresh difficulties to the internal ones already present. Situations like that of a prospective house-owner who orders an architect to build him a villa according to his own tastes and requirements, or of a pious donor who commissions an artist to paint a sacred picture in the corner of which is to be a portrait of himself in adoration, are at bottom incompatible with the conditions necessary for psycho-analysis. Thus, it constantly happens that a husband instructs the physician as follows: 'My wife suffers from nerves, and for that reason gets on badly with me; please cure her, so that we may lead a happy married life again.' But often enough it turns out that such a request is impossible to fulfil—that is to say, the physician cannot bring about the result for which the husband sought the treatment. As soon as the wife is freed from her neurotic inhibitions she sets about getting a separation, for her neurosis was the sole condition under which the marriage could be maintained. Or else parents expect one to cure their nervous and unruly child. By a healthy child they mean one who never causes his parents trouble, and gives them nothing but pleasure. The physician may succeed in curing the child, but after that it goes its own way all the more decidedly, and the parents are now far more dissatisfed than before. In short, it is not a matter of indifference whether someone comes to analysis of his own accord or because he is brought to it—whether it is he himself who desires to be changed, or only his relatives, who love him (or who might be expected to love him).

Further unfavourable features in the present case were the facts that the girl was not in any way ill (she did not suffer from anything in herself, nor did she complain of her condition) and that the task to be carried out did not consist in resolving a neurotic conflict but in converting one variety of genital organization of sexuality into the other. Such an achievement—the removal of genital inversion or homosexuality—is in my experience never an easy matter. On the contrary, I have found success possible only in specially favourable circumstances, and even then the success essentially consisted in making access to the opposite sex (which had hitherto been barred) possible to a person restricted to homo-sexuality, thus restoring his full bisexual functions. After that it lay with him to choose whether he wished to abandon the path that is banned by society, and in some cases he has done so. One must remember that normal sexuality too depends upon a restric-tion in the choice of object. In general, to undertake to convert a fully developed homosexual into a heterosexual does not offer much more prospect of success than the reverse, except that for good practical reasons the latter is never attempted.

The number of successes achieved by psycho-analytic treatment of the various forms of homosexuality, which incidentally are manifold, is indeed not very striking. As a rule the homosexual is not able to give up the object which provides him with pleasure, and one cannot convince him that if he made the change he would rediscover in the other object the pleasure that he has renounced. If he comes to be treated at all, it is mostly through the pressure of external motives, such as the social disadvantages and dangers attaching to his choice of object, and such compo-nents of the instinct of self-preservation prove themselves too weak in the struggle against the sexual impulses. One then soon discovers his secret plan, namely, to obtain from the striking failure of his attempt a feeling of satisfaction that he has done everything possible against his abnormality, to which he can now resign himself with an easy conscience. The case is somewhat different when consideration for beloved parents and relatives has been the motive for his attempt to be cured. Here there really are libidinal impulses present which may put forth energies opposed to the homosexual choice of object; but their strength is rarely sufficient. It is only where the homosexual fixation has not yet become strong enough, or where there are considerable rudiments and vestiges of a heterosexual choice of object, i.e. in a still oscillating or in a definitely bisexual organization, that one may make a more favourable prognosis for psycho-analytic therapy.

For these reasons I refrained altogether from holding out to the parents any prospect of their wish being fulfilled. I merely said I was prepared to study the girl carefully for a few weeks or months, so as then to be able to pronounce how far a continuation of the analysis would be likely to influence her. In quite a number of cases, indeed, an analysis falls into two clearly distinguishable phases. In the first, the physician procures from the patient the necessary information, makes him familiar with the premises and postulates of psycho-analysis, and unfolds to him the reconstruction of the genesis of his disorder as deduced from the material brought up in the analysis. In the second phase the patient himself gets hold of the material put before him; he works on it, recollects what he can of the apparently repressed memories, and tries to repeat the rest as if he were in some way living it over again. In this way he can confirm, supplement, and correct the inferences made by the physician. It is only during this work that he experiences, through overcoming resistances, the inner change aimed at, and acquires for himself the convictions that make him independent of the physician's authority. These two phases in the course of the analytic treatment are not always sharply divided from each other; this can only happen when the resistance obeys certain conditions. But when this is so, one may bring up as an analogy the two stages of a journey. The first comprises all the necessary prepararations, to-day so complicated and hard to effect, before, ticket in hand, one can at last go on to the platform and secure a seat in the train. One then has the right, and the possibility, of travelling into a distant country; but after all these preliminary exertions one is not yet there—indeed, one is not a single mile nearer to one's goal. For this to happen one has to make the journey itself from one station to the other, and this part of the performance may well be compared with the second phase of the analysis.

The course of the present patient's analysis followed this two-phased pattern, but it was not continued beyond the beginning of the second phase. A special constellation of the resistance made it possible, nevertheless, to gain full confirmation of my constructions, and to obtain an adequate insight on broad lines into the way in which her inversion had developed. But before relating the findings of the analysis I must deal with a few points which have either been touched upon already by myself or which will have roused special interest in the reader.

I had made the prognosis partly dependent on how far the girl had succeeded in satisfying her passion. The information I obtained during the analysis seemed favourable in this respect. With none of the objects of her adoration had the patient enjoyed anything beyond a few kisses and embraces; her genital chastity, if one may use such a phrase, had remained intact. As for the *demi-mondaine* who had roused her most recent and by far her strongest emotions, she had always been treated coldly by her and never been allowed any greater favour than to kiss her hand. She was probably making a virtue of necessity when she kept insisting on the purity of her love and her physical repulsion against the idea of any sexual intercourse. But perhaps she was not altogether wrong when she boasted of her wonderful beloved that, being of good birth as she was, and forced into her present position only by adverse family circumstances, she had preserved, in spite of her situation, much nobility of character. For the lady used to recommend the girl every time they met to withdraw her affection from herself and from women in general, and she had persistently rejected the girl's advances up to the time of the attempted suicide.

A second point, which I at once tried to investigate, concerned any possible motives in the girl herself which might serve as a support for psycho-analytic treatment. She did not try to deceive me by saying that she felt any urgent need to be freed from her homosexuality. On the contrary, she said she could not conceive of any other way of being in love, but she added that for her parents' sake she would honestly help in the therapeutic attempt, for it pained her very much to be the cause of so much grief to them. To begin with, I could not but take this, too, as a propitious sign; for I could not guess the unconscious affective attitude that lay concealed behind it. What came to light later in this connection decisively influenced the course taken by the analysis and determined its premature conclusion.

Readers unversed in psycho-analysis will long have been awaiting an answer to two other questions. Did this homosexual girl show physical characteristics plainly belonging to the opposite sex, and did the case prove to be one of congenital or acquired (later-developed) homosexuality?

I am aware of the importance attaching to the first of these questions. But one should not exaggerate it and allow it to overshadow the fact that sporadic secondary characteristics of the opposite sex are very often present in normal individuals, and that well-marked physical characteristics of the opposite sex may be found in persons whose choice of object has undergone no change in the direction of inversion; in other words, that in both sexes *the degree of physical hermaphroditism is to a great extent independent of psychical hermaphroditism.* In modification of these statements it must be added that this independence is more evident in men than women, where bodily and mental traits belonging to the opposite sex are apt to coincide.[1] Still I am not in a position to give a satisfactory answer to the first of our questions about my patient. The psycho-analyst customarily forgoes a thorough physical examination of his patients in certain cases. Certainly there was no obvious deviation from the feminine physical type, nor any menstrual disturbance. The beautiful and well-made girl had, it is true, her father's tall figure, and her facial features were sharp rather than soft and girlish, traits which might be regarded as indicating a physical masculinity. Some of her intellectual attributes also could be connected with masculinity: for instance, her acuteness of comprehension and her lucid objectivity, in so far as she was not dominated by her passion. But these distinctions are conventional rather than scientific. What is certainly of greater importance is that in her behaviour towards her love-object she had throughout assumed the masculine part: that is to say, she displayed the humility and the sublime overvaluation of the sexual object so characteristic of the male lover, the renunciation of all narcissistic satisfaction, and the preference for being the lover rather than the beloved. She had thus not only chosen a feminine love-object, but had also developed a masculine attitude towards that object.

The second question, whether this was a case of congenital or acquired homosexuality, will be answered by the whole history of the patient's abnormality and its development. The study of

1. [Cf. the discussion of this point in *Three Essays* {above, p. 92}.]

this will show how far this question is a fruitless and inapposite one.

II.

After this highly discursive introduction I am only able to present a very concise summary of the sexual history of the case under consideration. In childhood the girl had passed through the normal attitude characteristic of the feminine Oedipus complex[2] in a way that was not at all remarkable, and had later also begun to substitute for her father a brother slightly older than herself. She did not remember any sexual traumas in early life, nor were any discovered by the analysis. Comparison of her brother's genital organs and her own, which took place about the beginning of the latency period (at five years old or perhaps a little earlier), left a strong impression on her and had far-reaching after-effects. There were very few signs pointing to infantile masturbation, or else the analysis did not go far enough to throw light on this point. The birth of a second brother when she was between five and six years old exercised no special influence upon her development. During the pre-pubertal years at school she gradually became acquainted with the facts of sex, and she received this knowledge with mixed feelings of lasciviousness and frightened aversion, in a way which may be called normal and was not exaggerated in degree. This amount of information about her seems meagre enough, nor can I guarantee that it is complete. It may be that the history of her youth was much richer in experiences; I do not know. As I have already said, the analysis was broken off after a short time, and therefore yielded an anamnesis not much more reliable than the other anamneses of homosexuals, which there is good cause to question. Further, the girl had never been neurotic, and came to the analysis without even one hysterical symptom, so that opportunities for investigating the history of her childhood did not present themselves so readily as usual.

At the age of thirteen to fourteen she displayed a tender and,

2. I do not see any advance or gain in the introduction of the term 'Electra complex', and do not advocate its use.

according to general opinion, exaggeratedly strong affection for a small boy, not quite three years old, whom she used to see regularly in a children's playground. She took to the child so warmly that in consequence a lasting friendship grew up between herself and his parents. One may infer from this episode that at that time she was possessed of a strong desire to be a mother herself and to have a child. However, after a short time she grew indifferent to the boy, and began to take an interest in mature, but still youthful, women. The manifestations of this interest soon brought upon her a severe chastisement at the hands of her father.

It was established beyond all doubt that this change occurred simultaneously with a certain event in the family, and one may therefore look to this for some explanation of the change. Before it happened, her libido was concentrated on a maternal attitude, while afterwards she became a homosexual attracted to mature women, and remained so ever since. The event which is so significant for our understanding of the case was a new pregnancy of her mother's, and the birth of a third brother when she was about sixteen.

The position of affairs which I shall now proceed to lay bare is not a product of my inventive powers; it is based on such trustworthy analytic evidence that I can claim objective validity for it. It was in particular a series of dreams, inter-related and easy to interpret, that decided me in favour of its reality.

The analysis revealed beyond all shadow of doubt that the lady-love was a substitute for—her mother. It is true that the lady herself was not a mother, but then she was not the girl's first love. The first objects of her affection after the birth of her youngest brother were really mothers, women between thirty and thirty-five whom she had met with their children during summer holidays or in the family circle of acquaintances in town. Motherhood as a *sine qua non* in her love-object was later on given up, because that precondition was difficult to combine in real life with another one, which grew more and more important. The specially intense bond with her latest love had still another basis which the girl discovered quite easily one day. Her lady's slender figure, severe beauty, and downright manner reminded her of the brother who was a little older than herself. Her latest choice corresponded, therefore, not only to her feminine but also to her masculine ideal; it combined satisfaction of the homosexual tendency with that of the heterosexual one. It is well known that analysis of male

homosexuals has in numerous cases revealed the same combination, which should warn us not to form too simple a conception
of the nature and genesis of inversion, and to keep in mind the
universal bisexuality of human beings.

But how are we to understand the fact that it was precisely the
birth of a child who came late in the family (at a time when the
girl herself was already mature and had strong wishes of her own)
that moved her to bestow her passionate tenderness upon the
woman who gave birth to this child, i.e. her own mother, and
to express that feeling towards a substitute for her mother? From
all that we know we should have expected just the opposite. In
such circumstances mothers with daughters of nearly a marriage-
able age usually feel embarrassed in regard to them, while the
daughters are apt to feel for their mothers a mixture of compassion,
contempt and envy which does nothing to increase their tenderness for them. The girl we are considering had in any case
altogether little cause to feel affection for her mother. The latter,
still youthful herself, saw in her rapidly developing daughter an
inconvenient competitor; she favoured the sons at her expense,
limited her independence as much as possible, and kept an especially strict watch against any close relation between the girl
and her father. A yearning from the beginning for a kinder mother
would, therefore, have been quite intelligible, but why it should
have flared up just then, and in the form of a consuming passion,
is hard to understand.

The explanation is as follows. It was just when the girl was
experiencing the revival of her infantile Oedipus complex at puberty that she suffered her great disappointment. She became
keenly conscious of the wish to have a child, and a male one;
that what she desired was her *father's* child and an image of *him*,
her consciousness was not allowed to know. And what happened
next? It was not *she* who bore the child, but her unconsciously
hated rival, her mother. Furiously resentful and embittered, she
turned away from her father and from men altogether. After this
first great reverse she forswore her womanhood and sought another
goal for her libido.

In doing so she behaved just as many men do who after a first
distressing experience turn their backs for ever upon the faithless
female sex and become woman-haters. It is related of one of the
most attractive and unfortunate princely figures of our time that
he became a homosexual because the lady he was engaged to

marry betrayed him with another man. I do not know whether this is true historically, but an element of psychological truth lies behind the rumour. In all of us, throughout life, the libido normally oscillates between male and female objects; the bachelor gives up his men friends when he marries, and returns to club-life when married life has lost its savour. Naturally, when the swing-over is fundamental and final, we suspect the presence of some special factor which definitely favours one side or the other, and which perhaps has only waited for the appropriate moment in order to turn the choice of object in its direction.

After her disappointment, therefore, this girl had entirely repudiated her wish for a child, her love of men, and the feminine role in general. It is evident that at this point a number of very different things might have happened. What actually happened was the most extreme case. She changed into a man and took her mother in place of her father as the object of her love.[3] Her relation to her mother had certainly been ambivalent from the beginning, and it proved easy to revive her earlier love for her mother and with its help to bring about an overcompensation for her current hostility towards her. Since there was little to be done with the real mother, there arose from this transformation of feeling the search for a substitute mother to whom she could become passionately attached.[4]

There was, in addition, a practical motive for this change, derived from her real relations with her mother, which served as a [secondary] gain from her illness. The mother herself still attached great value to the attentions and the admiration of men. If, then, the girl became homosexual and left men to her mother (in other words, 'retired in favour of' her mother), she would

---

3. It is by no means rare for a love-relation to be broken off through a process of identification on the part of the lover with the loved object, a process equivalent to a kind of regression to narcissism. After this has been accomplished, it is easy in making a fresh choice of object to direct the libido to a member of the sex opposite to that of the earlier choice.

4. The displacements of the libido here described are doubtless familiar to every analyst from investigation of the anamneses of neurotics. With the latter, however, they occur in early childhood, at the time of the early efflorescence of erotic life; with our patient, who was in no way neurotic, they took place in the first years following puberty, though, incidentally, they were just as completely unconscious. Perhaps one day this temporal factor may turn out to be of great importance.

remove something which had hitherto been partly responsible for her mother's dislike.[5]

This libidinal position of the girl's, thus arrived at, was greatly reinforced as soon as she perceived how much it displeased her father. After she had been punished for her over-affectionate attitude to a woman she realized how she could wound her father and take revenge on him. Henceforth she remained homosexual out of defiance against her father. Nor did she scruple to lie to him and to deceive him in every way. Towards her mother, indeed, she was only so far deceitful as was necessary to prevent her father from knowing things. I had the impression that her behaviour followed the principle of the talion: 'Since you have betrayed me, you must put up with my betraying you.' Nor can I come to any other conclusion about the striking lack of caution

---

5. As 'retiring in favour of someone else' has not previously been mentioned among the causes of homosexuality, or in the mechanism of libidinal fixation in general, I will adduce here another analytic observation of the same kind which has a special feature of interest. I once knew two twin brothers, both of whom were endowed with strong libidinal impulses. One of them was very successful with women, and had innumerable affairs with women and girls. The other went the same way at first, but it became unpleasant for him to be trespassing on his brother's preserves, and, owing to the likeness between them, to be mistaken for him on intimate occasions; so he got out of the difficulty by becoming homosexual. He left the women to his brother, and thus retired in his favour. Another time I treated a youngish man, an artist, unmistakably bisexual in disposition, in whom the homosexual trend had come to the fore simultaneously with a disturbance in his work. He fled from both women and work together. The analysis, which was able to bring him back to both, showed that fear of his father was the most powerful psychical motive for both the disturbances, which were really renunciations. In his imagination all women belonged to his father, and he sought refuge in men out of submission, so as to retire from the conflict with his father. Such a motivation of the homosexual object-choice must be by no means uncommon; in the primaeval ages of the human race all women presumably belonged to the father and head of the primal horde.

Among brothers and sisters who are not twins this 'retiring' plays a great part in other spheres as well as in that of erotic choice. For example, an elder brother studies music and is admired for it; the younger, far more gifted musically, soon gives up his own musical studies, in spite of his fondness for it, and cannot be persuaded to touch an instrument again. This is only one example of a very frequent occurrence, and investigation of the motives leading to this 'retirement' rather than to open rivalry discloses very complicated conditions in the mind.

displayed by this otherwise exceedingly shrewd girl, She *wanted* her father to know occasionally of her relations with the lady, otherwise she would be deprived of the satisfaction of her keenest desire—namely, revenge. So she saw to this by showing herself openly in the company of her adored one, by walking with her in the streets near her father's place of business, and the like. This maladroitness, moreover, was by no means unintentional. It was remarkable, too, that both parents behaved as if they understood their daughter's secret psychology. The mother was tolerant, as though she appreciated her daughter's 'retirement' as a favour to her; the father was furious, as though he realized the deliberate revenge directed against himself.

The girl's inversion, however, received its final reinforcement when she found in her 'lady' an object which promised to satisfy not only her homosexual trends, but also that part of her heterosexual libido which was still attached to her brother.

III.

Linear presentation is not a very adequate means of describing complicated mental processes going on in different layers of the mind. I am therefore obliged to pause in the discussion of the case and treat more fully and deeply some of the points brought forward above.

I mentioned the fact that in her behaviour to her adored lady the girl had adopted the characteristic masculine type of love. Her humility and her tender lack of pretensions, '*che poco spera e nulla chiede*',[6] her bliss when she was allowed to accompany the lady a little way and to kiss her hand on parting, her joy when she heard her praised as beautiful (while any recognition of her own beauty by another person meant nothing at all to her), her pilgrimages to places once visited by the loved one, the silence of all more sensual wishes—all these little traits in her resembled the first passionate adoration of a youth for a celebrated actress whom he regards as far above him, to whom he scarcely dares lift his bashful eyes. The correspondence with 'a special type of

6. ['Hoping little and asking for nothing.']

choice of object made by men' that I have described elsewhere (1910)[7] whose special features I traced to attachment to the mother, held good even to the smallest details. It may seem remarkable that she was not in the least repelled by the bad reputation of her beloved, although her own observations sufficiently confirmed the truth of such rumours. She was after all a well-brought-up and modest girl, who had avoided sexual adventures for herself, and who regarded coarsely sensual satisfactions as unaesthetic. But already her first passions had been for women who were not celebrated for specially strict propriety. The first protest her father made against her love-choice had been evoked by the pertinacity with which she sought the company of a film actress at a summer resort. Moreover, in all these affairs it had never been a question of women who had any reputation for homosexuality, and who might, therefore, have offered her some prospect of homosexual satisfaction; on the contrary, she illogically courted women who were coquettes in the ordinary sense of the word, and she rejected without hesitation the willing advances made by a homosexual friend of her own age. For her, the bad reputation of her 'lady', however, was positively a 'necessary condition for love'. All that is enigmatic in this attitude vanishes when we remember that in the case too of the *masculine* type of object-choice derived from the mother it is a necessary condition that the loved object should be in some way or other 'of bad repute' sexually—someone who really may be called a *cocotte*. When the girl learnt later how far her adored lady deserved this description and that she lived simply by giving her bodily favours, her reaction took the form of great compassion and of phantasies and plans for 'rescuing' her beloved from these ignoble circumstances. We were struck by the same urge to 'rescue' in the men of the type referred to above, and in my description of it I have tried to give the analytic derivation of this urge.

We are led into quite another realm of explanation by the analysis of the attempt at suicide, which I must regard as seriously intended, and which, incidentally, considerably improved her position both with her parents and with the lady she loved. She went for a walk with her one day in a part of the town and at an hour at which she was not unlikely to meet her father on his way

7. {Freud refers here to the first of his three "Contributions to the Psychology of Love," 11:163–76.}

from his office. So it turned out. Her father passed them in the street and cast a furious look at her and her companion, about whom he had by that time come to know. A few moments later she flung herself into the railway cutting. The explanation she gave of the immediate reasons determining her decision sounded quite plausible. She had confessed to the lady that the man who had given them such an irate glance was her father, and that he had absolutely forbidden their friendship. The lady became incensed at this and ordered the girl to leave her then and there, and never again to wait for her or to address her—the affair must now come to an end. In her despair at having thus lost her loved one for ever, she wanted to put an end to herself. The analysis, however, was able to disclose another and deeper interpretation behind the one she gave, which was confirmed by the evidence of her own dreams. The attempted suicide was, as might have been expected, determined by two other motives besides the one she gave: it was the fulfilment of a punishment (self-punishment), and the fulfilment of a wish. As the latter it meant the attainment of the very wish which, when frustrated, had driven her into homosexuality—namely, the wish to have a child by her father, for now she 'fell' through her father's fault.[8] The fact that at that moment the lady had spoken in just the same terms as her father, and had uttered the same prohibition, forms the connecting link between this deep interpretation and the superficial one of which the girl herself was conscious. From the point of view of self-punishment the girl's action shows us that she had developed in her unconscious strong death-wishes against one or other of her parents—perhaps against her father, out of revenge for impeding her love, but more probably against her mother too, when she was pregnant with the little brother. For analysis has explained the enigma of suicide in the following way: probably no one finds the mental energy required to kill himself unless, in the first place, in doing so he is at the same time killing an object with whom he has identified himself, and, in the second place, is turning

---

8. [In the text there is a play on the word *niederkommen*, which means both 'to fall' and 'to be delivered of a child'. There is in English, too, a colloquial use of the verb 'to fall', meaning pregnancy or childbirth.]—That the various methods of suicide can represent sexual wish-fulfilments has long been known to all analysts. (To poison oneself = to become pregnant; to drown = to bear a child; to throw oneself from a height = to be delivered of a child.)

against himself a death-wish which had been directed against someone else. Nor need the regular discovery of these unconscious death-wishes in those who have attempted suicide surprise us (any more than it ought to make us think that it confirms our deductions), since the unconscious of all human beings is full enough of such death-wishes, even against those they love. Since the girl identified herself with her mother, who should have died at the birth of the child denied to herself, this punishment-fulfilment itself was once again a wish-fulfilment. Finally, the discovery that several quite different motives, all of great strength, must have co-operated to make such a deed possible is only in accordance with what we should expect.

In the girl's account of her conscious motives the father did not figure at all; there was not even any mention of fear of his anger. In the motives laid bare by the analysis, on the other hand, he played the principal part. Her relation to her father had the same decisive importance for the course and outcome of the analytic treatment, or rather, analytic exploration. Behind her pretended consideration for her parents, for whose sake she had been willing to make the attempt to be transformed, lay concealed her attitude of defiance and revenge against her father which held her fast to her homosexuality. Secure under this cover, the resistance set a considerable region free to analytic investigation. The analysis went forward almost without any signs of resistance, the patient participating actively with her intellect, though absolutely tranquil emotionally. Once when I expounded to her a specially important part of the theory, one touching her nearly, she replied in an inimitable tone, 'How very interesting', as though she were a *grand dame* being taken over a museum and glancing through her lorgnon at objects to which she was completely indifferent. The impression one had of her analysis was not unlike that of a hypnotic treatment, where the resistance has in the same way withdrawn to a certain boundary line, beyond which it proves to be unconquerable. The resistance very often pursues similar tactics—Russian tactics, as they might be called—in cases of obsessional neurosis. For a time, consequently, these cases yield the clearest results and permit a deep insight into the causation of the symptoms. But presently one begins to wonder how it is that such marked progress in analytic understanding can be unaccompanied by even the slightest change in the patient's compulsions and inhibitions, until at last one perceives that everything that has been accomplished is subject to a mental reservation of doubt, and that behind this protective barrier the neurosis can feel secure. 'It would be all very fine', thinks the patient, often quite consciously, 'if I were obliged to believe what the man says, but there is no question of that, and so long as this is so I need change nothing.' Then, when one comes to close quarters with the motives for this doubt, the fight with the resistances breaks out in earnest.

In the case of our patient, it was not doubt but the affective factor of revenge against her father that made her cool reserve possible, that divided the analysis into two distinct phases, and rendered the results of the first phase so complete and perspicuous. It seemed, further, as though nothing resembling a transference to the physician had been effected. That, however, is of course absurd, or, at least, is a loose way of expressing things. For some kind of relation to the analyst must come into being, and this relation is almost always transferred from an infantile one. In reality she transferred to me the sweeping repudiation of men which had dominated her ever since the disappointment she had suffered from her father. Bitterness against men is as a rule easy to gratify upon the physician; it need not evoke any violent emotional manifestations, it simply expresses itself by rendering futile all his endeavours and by clinging to the illness. I know from experience how difficult it is to make a patient understand just precisely this mute kind of symptomatic behaviour and to make him aware of this latent, and often exceedingly strong, hostility without endangering the treatment. As soon, therefore, as I recognized the girl's attitude to her father, I broke off the treatment and advised her parents that if they set store by the therapeutic procedure it should be continued by a woman doctor. The girl had in the meanwhile promised her father that at any rate she would give up seeing the 'lady', and I do not know whether my advice, the reasons for which are obvious, will be followed.

There was a single piece of material in the course of this analysis which I could regard as a positive transference, as a greatly weakened revival of the girl's original passionate love for her father. Even this manifestation was not quite free from other motives, but I mention it because it brings up, in another direction, an interesting problem of analytic technique. At a certain period, not long after the treatment had begun, the girl brought a series of dreams which, distorted according to rule and couched in the usual dream-language, could nevertheless be easily translated with certainty. Their content, when interpreted, was, however, remarkable. They anticipated the cure of the inversion through the treatment, expressed her joy over the prospects in life that would then be opened before her, confessed her longing for a man's love and for children, and so might have been welcomed as a gratifying preparation for the desired change. The contradiction between them and the girl's utterances in waking life at the time was very great. She did not conceal from me that she meant to marry, but only in order to escape from her father's tyranny and to follow her true inclinations undisturbed. As for the husband, she remarked rather contemptuously, she would easily deal with him, and besides, one could have sexual relations with a man and a woman at one and the same time, as the example of the adored lady showed. Warned through some slight impression or other, I told her one day that I did not believe these dreams, that I regarded them as false or hypocritical, and that she intended to deceive me just as she habitually deceived her father. I was right; after I had made this clear, this kind of dream ceased. But I still believe that, beside the intention to mislead me, the dreams partly expressed the wish to win my favour; they were also an attempt to gain my interest and my good opinion—perhaps in order to disappoint me all the more thoroughly later on.

I can imagine that to point out the existence of lying dreams of this kind, 'obliging' dreams, will arouse a positive storm of helpless indignation in some readers who call themselves analysts. 'What!' they will exclaim, 'the unconscious, the real centre of our mental life, the part of us that is so much nearer the divine than our poor consciousness—it too can lie! Then how can we still build on the interpretations of analysis and the accuracy of our findings?' To which one must reply that the recognition of these lying dreams does not constitute any shattering novelty. I know, indeed, that the craving of mankind for mysticism is ineradicable, and that it makes ceaseless efforts to win back for mysticism the territory it has been deprived of by *The Interpretation of Dreams*, but surely in the case under consideration everything is simple enough. A dream is not the 'unconscious'; it is the form into which a thought left over from preconscious, or even from conscious, waking life, can, thanks to the favouring state of sleep, be recast. In the state of sleep this thought has been reinforced by unconscious wishful impulses and has thus experienced distortion through the dream-work, which is determined by the mechanisms prevailing in the unconscious. With our dreamer, the intention to mislead me, just as she did her father, certainly emanated from the preconscious, and may indeed have been conscious; it could come to expression by entering into connection with the unconscious wishful impulse to please her father (or father-substitute), and in this way it created a lying dream. The two intentions, to betray and to please her father, originated in the same complex; the former resulted from the repression of the latter, and the later one was brought back by the dream-work to the earlier one. There can therefore be no question of any devaluation of the unconscious, nor of a shattering of our confidence in the results of analysis.

I cannot neglect this opportunity of expressing for once my astonishment that human beings can go through such great and important moments of their erotic life without noticing them much, sometimes even, indeed, without having the faintest suspicion of their existence, or else, having become aware of those moments, deceive themselves so thoroughly in their judgement of them. This happens not only under neurotic conditions, where we are familiar with the phenomenon, but seems also to be common enough in ordinary life. In the present case, for example, a girl develops a sentimental adoration for women, which her parents at first find merely vexatious and hardly take seriously; she herself knows quite well that she is very much occupied with these relationships, but still she experiences few of the sensations of intense love until a particular frustration is followed by a quite excessive reaction, which shows everyone concerned that they have to do with a consuming passion of elemental strength. Nor had the girl ever perceived anything of the state of affairs which was a necessary preliminary to the outbreak of this mental storm. In other cases, too, we come across girls or women in a state of severe depression, who on being asked for a possible cause of their condition tell us that they have, it is true, had a slight feeling for a certain person, but that it was nothing deep and that they soon got over it when they had to give it up. And yet it was this renunciation, apparently so easily borne, that became the cause of serious mental disturbance. Again, we come across men who have passed through casual love-affairs and realize only from the subsequent effects that they had been passionatley in love with the person whom they had apparently regarded lightly. One is also amazed at the unexpected results that may follow an artificial abortion, the killing of an unborn child, which had been decided upon without remorse and without hesitation. It must be admitted that poets are right in liking to portray people who are in love without knowing it, or uncertain whether they do love, or who think that they hate when in reality they love. It would seem that the information received by our consciousness about our erotic life is especially liable to be incomplete, full of gaps, or falsified. Needless to say, in this discussion I have not omitted to allow for the part played by subsequent forgetting.

IV.

I now come back, after this digression, to the consideration of my patient's case. We have made a survey of the forces which led the girl's libido from the normal Oedipus attitude into that of homosexuality, and of the psychical paths traversed by it in the process. Most important in this respect was the impression made by the birth of her little brother, and we might from this be inclined to classify the case as one of late-acquired inversion.

But at this point we become aware of a state of things which also confronts us in many other instances in which light has been thrown by psycho-analysis on a a mental process. So long as we trace the development from its final outcome backwards, the chain of events appears continuous, and we feel we have gained an insight which is completely satisfactory or even exhaustive. But if we proceed the reverse way, if we start from the premises inferred from the analysis and try to follow these up to the final result, then we no longer get the impression of an inevitable sequence of events which could not have been otherwise determined. We notice at once that there might have been another result, and that we might have been just as well able to understand and explain the latter. The synthesis is thus not so satisfactory as the analysis; in other words, from a knowledge of the premises we could not have foretold the nature of the result.

It is very easy to account for this disturbing state of affairs. Even supposing that we have a complete knowledge of the aetiological factors that decide a given result, nevertheless what we know about them is only their quality, and not their relative strength. Some of them are suppressed by others because they are too weak, and they therefore do not affect the final result. But we never know beforehand which of the determining factors will prove the weaker or the stronger. We only say at the end that those which succeeded must have been the stronger. Hence the chain of causation can always be recognized with certainty if we follow the line of analysis, whereas to predict it along the line of synthesis is impossible.

We do not, therefore, mean to maintain that every girl who experiences a disappointment such as this of the longing for love that springs from the Oedipus attitude at puberty will necessarily on that account fall a victim to homosexuality. On the contrary, other kinds of reaction to this trauma are undoubtedly commoner. If so, however, there must have been present in this girl special factors that turned the scale, factors outside the trauma, probably of an internal nature. Nor is there any difficulty in pointing them out.

It is well known that even in a normal person it takes a certain time before the decision in regard to the sex of the love-object is finally made. Homosexual enthusiasms, exaggeratedly strong friendships tinged with sensuality, are common enough in both sexes during the first years after puberty. This was also so with our patient, but in her these tendencies undoubtedly showed themselves to be stronger, and lasted longer, than with others. In addition, these presages of later homosexuality had always occupied her *conscious* life, while the attitude arising from the Oedipus complex had remained *unconscious* and had appeared only in such signs as her tender behaviour to the little boy. As a schoolgirl she had been for a long time in love with a strict and unapproachable mistress, obviously a substitute mother. She had taken a specially lively interest in a number of young mothers long before her brother's birth and therefore all the more certainly long before the first reprimand from her father. From very early years, therefore, her libido had flowed in two currents, the one on the surface being one that we may unhesitatingly designate as homosexual. This latter was probably a direct and unchanged continuation of an infantile fixation on her mother. Possibly the analysis described here actually revealed nothing more than the process by which, on an appropriate occasion, the deeper heterosexual current of libido, too, was deflected into the manifest homosexual one.

The analysis showed, further, that the girl had brought along with her from her childhood a strongly marked 'masculinity complex'. A spirited girl, always ready for romping and fighting, she was not at all prepared to be second to her slightly older brother; after inspecting his genital organs she had developed a pronounced envy for the penis, and the thoughts derived from this envy still continued to fill her mind. She was in fact a feminist; she felt it to be unjust that girls should not enjoy the same freedom as boys, and rebelled against the lot of woman in general. At the time of the analysis the idea of pregnancy and child-birth was disagreeable to her, partly, I surmise, on account of the bodily disfigurement connected with them. Her girlish narcissism had fallen back on this defence, and indicated that she must formerly have had strong exhibitionist and scopophilic tendencies. Anyone who is anxious that the claims of acquired as opposed to hereditary factors should not be under-estimated in aetiology will call attention to the fact that the girl's behaviour, as described above, was exactly what would follow from the combined effect in a person with a strong mother-fixation of the two influences of her mother's neglect and her comparison of her genital organs with her brother's. It is possible here to attribute to the impress of the operation of external influence in early life something which one would have liked to regard as a constitutional peculiarity. On the other hand, a part even of this acquired disposition (if it *was* really acquired) has to be ascribed to inborn constitution. So we see in practice a con-tinual mingling and blending of what in theory we should try to separate into a pair of opposites—namely, inherited and acquired characters.

If the analysis had come to an earlier, still more premature end, it might have led to the view that this was a case of late-acquired homosexuality, but as it is, a consideration of the ma-terial impels us to conclude that it is rather a case of congenital homosexuality which, as usual, became fixed and unmistakably manifest only in the period following puberty. Each of these classifications does justice only to one part of the state of affairs ascertainable by observation, but neglects the other. It would be best not to attach too much value to this way of stating the problem.

The literature of homosexuality usually fails to distinguish clearly enough between the questions of the choice of object on the one hand, and of the sexual characteristics and sexual attitude of the subject on the other, as though the answer to the former necessarily involved the answers to the latter. Experience, how-

ever, proves the contrary: a man with predominantly male characteristics and also masculine in his erotic life may still be inverted
in respect to his object, loving only men instead of women. A
man in whose character feminine attributes obviously predomi-
nate, who may, indeed, behave in love like a woman, might be
expected, from this feminine attitude, to choose a man for his
love-object; but he may nevertheless be heterosexual, and show
no more inversion in respect to his object than an average normal
man. The same is true of women; here also mental sexual character and object-choice do not necessarily coincide. The mystery
of homosexuality is therefore by no means so simple as it is
commonly depicted in popular expositions—'a feminine mind,
bound therefore to love a man, but unhappily attached to a masculine body; a masculine mind, irresistibly attracted by women,
but, alas! imprisoned in a feminine body'. It is instead a question
of three sets of characteristics, namely—

> Physical sexual characters
> (physical hermaphroditism)
> Mental sexual characters
> (masculine or feminine attitude)
> Kind of object-choice

which, up to a certain point, vary independently of one another,
and are met with in different individuals in manifold permuta-
tions. Tendentious literature has obscured our view of this inter-
relationship by putting into the foreground, for practical reasons,
the third feature (the kind of object-choice), which is the only
one that strikes the layman, and in addition by exaggerating the
closeness of the association between this and the first feature.
Moreover, it blocks the way to a deeper insight into all that is
uniformly designated as homosexuality, by rejecting two fundamental facts which have been revealed by psycho-analytic investigation. The first of these is that homosexual men have
experienced a specially strong fixation on their mother; the second,
that, in addition to their manifest heterosexuality, a very considerable measure of latent or unconscious homosexuality can be
detected in all normal people. If these findings are taken into
account, then, clearly, the supposition that nature in a freakish
mood created a 'third sex' falls to the ground.

It is not for psycho-analysis to solve the problem of homosexuality. It must rest content with disclosing the psychical mech-

anisms that resulted in determining the object-choice, and with tracing back the paths from them to the instinctual dispositions. There its work ends, and it leaves the rest to biological research. * * * Psycho-analysis has a common basis with biology, in that it presupposes an original bisexuality in human beings (as in animals). But psycho-analysis cannot elucidate the intrinsic nature of what in conventional or in biological phraseology is termed 'masculine' and 'feminine': it simply takes over the two concepts and makes them the foundation of its work. When we attempt to reduce them further, we find masculinity vanishing into activity and femininity into passivity, and that does not tell us enough. I have already tried to explain how far we may reasonably expect, or how far experience has already proved, that the work of elucidation which is part of the task of analysis furnishes us with the means of effecting a modification of inversion. * * *

The Infantile Genital Organization *and* Medusa's Head

Freud inserted a summary of the contents of this 1923 essay into the 1924 edition of his Three Essays (see 7:199). In both texts, the emphasis is the same: what distinguishes the "genital organization" (or dominance of the genital erotogenic zone) in Oedipal children from that in adults is that for children of both sexes "only one genital, the male one, comes into account." Girls and boys in the Oedipal period consider that there are two sexual conditions: having a penis and being castrated.

This had been Freud's view since his survey of children's sexual theories in 1908 (pp. 157–65 above). But, even though he had held the theory for fifteen years, he remained able to describe the "phallic-genital" stage only in boys, for "the corresponding processes in the little girl are not known to us." This clinical and theoretical assymetry must have been one of the strongest impetuses to the review of psychoanalytic work on female psychology that Freud undertook in 1925 (see "Some Psychical Consequences of the Anatomical Distinction between the Sexes," below). The assymetry was certainly one of the main spurs to the storm of criticism that arose in the mid-1920s over Freud's claims about "penis envy."

Appended to this essay is a brief note on the symbolism of the Medusa's head, which Freud wrote in 1922, and which is alluded to in a footnote on p. 270.

～～～～

The difficulty of the work of research in psycho-analysis is clearly shown by the fact of its being possibly, in spite of whole decades of unremitting observation, to overlook features that are of general occurrence and situations that are characteristic, until at last they confront one in an unmistakable form. The remarks that follow are intended to make good a neglect of this sort in the field of infantile sexual development.

Readers of my *Three Essays on the Theory of Sexuality* (1905) will be aware that I have never undertaken any thorough remodelling of that work in its later editions, but have retained the original arrangement and have kept abreast of the advances made in our knowledge by means of interpolations and alterations in the text. In doing this, it may often have happened that what was old and what was more recent did not admit of being merged into an entirely uncontradictory whole. Originally, as we know, the accent was on a portrayal of the fundamental difference between the sexual life of children and of adults; later, the *pregenital organizations* of the libido made their way into the foreground, and also the remarkable and momentous fact of the *diphasic onset* of sexual development. Finally, our interest was engaged by the *sexual researches* of children; and from this we were able to recognize the far-reaching *approximation of the final outcome of sexuality in childhood* (in about the fifth year) to the definitive form taken by it in the adult. This is the point at which I left things in the last (1922) edition of my *Three Essays*.

On p. 63 of that volume[1] I wrote that 'the choice of an object, such as we have shown to be characteristic of the pubertal phase of development, has already frequently or habitually been effected during the years of childhood: that is to say, the whole of the sexual currents have become directed towards a single person in relation to whom they seek to achieve their aims. This then is the closest approximation possible in childhood to the final form taken by sexual life after puberty. The only difference lies in the fact that in childhood the combination of the component instincts and their subordination under the primacy of the genitals have been effected only very incompletely or not at all. Thus the establishment of that primacy in the service of reproduction is the last phase through which the organization of sexuality passes.'

To-day I should no longer be satisfied with the statement that in the early period of childhood the primacy of the genitals has

---

1. {See p. 125 above (7:199).}

been effected only very incompletely or not at all. The approximation of the child's sexual life to that of the adult goes much further and is not limited solely to the coming into being of the choice of an object. Even if a proper combination of the component instincts under the primacy of the genitals is not effected, nevertheless, at the height of the course of development of infantile sexuality, interest in the genitals and in their activity acquires a dominating significance which falls little short of that reached in maturity. At the same time, the main characteristic of this 'infantile genital organization' is its *difference* from the final genital organization of the adult. This consists in the fact that, for both sexes, only one genital, namely the male one, comes into account. What is present, therefore, is not a primacy of the genitals, but a primacy of the *phallus*.

Unfortunately we can describe this state of things only as it affects the male child; the corresponding processes in the little girl are not known to us. The small boy undoubtedly perceives the distinction between men and women, but to begin with he has no occasion to connect it with a difference in their genitals. It is natural for him to assume that all other living beings, humans and animals, possess a genital like his own; indeed, we know that he looks for an organ analogous to his own in inanimate things as well.[2] This part of the body, which is easily excitable, prone to changes and so rich in sensations, occupies the boy's interest to a high degree and is constantly setting new tasks to his instinct for research. He wants to see it in other people as well, so as to compare it with his own; and he behaves as though he had a vague idea that this organ could and should be bigger. The driving force which this male portion of the body will develop later at puberty expresses itself at this period of life mainly as an urge to investigate, as sexual curiosity. Many of the acts of exhibitionism and aggression which children commit, and which in later years would be judged without hesitation to be expressions of lust, prove in analysis to be experiments undertaken in the service of sexual research.

---

2. [Cf. the analysis of 'Little Hans' (1909), 10:9.]—It is, incidentally, remarkable what a small degree of attention the other part of the male genitals, the little sac with its contents, attracts in children. From all one hears in analyses, one would not guess that the male genitals consisted of anything more than the penis.

In the course of these researches the child arrives at the discovery that the penis is not a possession which is common to all creatures that are like himself. An accidental sight of the genitals of a little sister or playmate provides the occasion for this discovery. In unusually intelligent children, the observation of girls urinating will even earlier have aroused a suspicion that there is something different here. For they will have seen a different posture and heard a different sound, and will have made attempts to repeat their observations so as to obtain enlightenment. We know how children react to their first impressions of the absence of a penis. They disavow the fact and believe that they *do* see a penis, all the same. They gloss over the contradiction between observation and preconception by telling themselves that the penis is still small and will grow bigger presently; and they then slowly come to the emotionally significant conclusion that after all the penis had at least been there before and been taken away afterwards. The lack of a penis is regarded as a result of castration, and so now the child is faced with the task of coming to terms with castration in relation to himself. The further developments are too well known generally to make it necessary to recapitulate them here. But it seems to me that *the significance of the castration complex can only be rightly appreciated if its origin in the phase of phallic primacy is also taken into account.*[3]

We know, too, to what a degree depreciation of women, horror of women, and a disposition to homosexuality are derived from the final conviction that women have no penis. Ferenczi (1923) has recently, with complete justice, traced back the mythological symbol of horror—Medusa's head—to the impression of the female genitals devoid of a penis.[4]

It should not be supposed, however, that the child quickly and

---

3. It has been quite correctly pointed out that a child gets the idea of a narcissistic injury through a bodily loss from the experience of losing his mother's breast after sucking, from the daily surrender of his faeces and, indeed, even from his separation from the womb at birth. Nevertheless, one ought not to speak of a castration complex until this idea of a loss has become connected with the male genitals * * *

4. I should like to add that what is indicated in the myth is the *mother's* genitals. Athene, who carries Medusa's head on her armour, becomes in consequence the unapproachable woman, the sight of whom extinguishes all thought of a sexual approach. {See the 1922 note on the Medusa's head symbolism appended below, p. 272.}

readily makes a generalization from his observation that some women have no penis. He is in any case debarred from doing so by his assumption that the lack of a penis is the result of having been castrated as a punishment. On the contrary, the child believes that it is only unworthy female persons that have lost their genitals—females who, in all probability, were guilty of inadmissible impulses similar to his own. Women whom he respects, like his mother, retain a penis for a long time. For him, being a woman is not yet synonymous with being without a penis.[5] It is not till later, when the child takes up the problems of the origin and birth of babies, and when he guesses that only women can give birth to them—it is only then that the mother, too, loses her penis. And, along with this, quite complicated theories are built up to explain the exchange of the penis for a baby. In all this, the female genitals never seem to be discovered. The baby, we know, is supposed to live inside the mother's body (in her bowel) and to be born through the intestinal outlet. These last theories carry us beyond the stretch of time covered by the infantile sexual period.

It is not unimportant to bear in mind what transformations are undergone, during the sexual development of childhood, by the polarity of sex with which the choice of object, which, of course, presupposes a subject and an object. At the stage of the pregenital sadistic-anal organization, there is as yet no question of male and female; the antithesis between *active* and *passive* is the dominant one. At the following stage of infantile genital organization, which we now know about, *maleness* exists, but not femaleness. The antithesis here is between having *a male genital* and being *castrated*. It is not until development has reached its completion at puberty that the sexual polarity coincides with *male* and *female*. Maleness combines [the factors of] subject, activity and possession of the penis; femaleness takes over [those of] object and passivity. The vagina is now valued as a place of shelter for the penis; it enters into the heritage of the womb.

5. I learnt from the analysis of a young married woman who had no father but several aunts that she clung, until quite far on in the latency period, to the belief that her mother and her aunts had a penis. One of her aunts, however, was feeble-minded; and she regarded this aunt as castrated, as she felt herself to be.

Medusa's Head (1940 [1922])

We have not often attempted to interpret individual mythological themes, but an interpretation suggests itself easily in the case of the horrifying decapitated head of Medusa.

To decapitate = to castrate. The terror of Medusa is thus a terror of castration that is linked to the sight of something. Numerous analyses have made us familiar with the occasion for this: it occurs when a boy, who has hitherto been unwilling to believe the threat of castration, catches sight of the female genitals, probably those of an adult, surrounded by hair, and essentially those of his mother.

The hair upon Medusa's head is frequently represented in works of art in the form of snakes, and these once again are derived from the castration complex. It is a remarkable fact that, however frightening they may be in themselves, they nevertheless serve actually as a mitigation of the horror, for they replace the penis, the absence of which is the cause of the horror. This is a confirmation of the technical rule according to which a multiplication of penis symbols signifies castration.

The sight of Medusa's head makes the spectator stiff with terror, turns him to stone. Observe that we have here once again the same origin from the castration complex and the same transformation of affect! For becoming stiff means an erection. Thus in the original situation it offers consolation to the spectator: he is still in possession of a penis, and the stiffening reassures him of the fact.

This symbol of horror is worn upon her dress by the virgin goddess Athene. And rightly so, for thus she becomes a woman who is unapproachable and repels all sexual desires—since she displays the terrifying genitals of the Mother. Since the Greeks were in the main strongly homosexual, it was inevitable that we should find among them a representation of woman as a being who frightens and repels because she is castrated.

If Medusa's head takes the place of a representation of the female genitals, or rather if it isolates their horrifying effect from their pleasure-giving ones, it may be recalled that displaying the genitals is familiar in other connections as an apotropaic act. What arouses horror in oneself will produce the same effect upon the enemy against whom one is seeking to defend oneself. We read in Rabelais of how the Devil took to flight when the woman showed him her vulva.

The erect male organ also has an apotropaic {designed to avert evil} effect, but thanks to another mechanism. To display the penis (or any of its surrogates) is to say: 'I am not afraid of you. I defy you. I have a penis.' Here, then, is another way of intimidating the Evil Spirit.[6]

In order seriously to substantiate this interpretation it would be necessary to investigate the origin of this isolated symbol of horror in Greek mythology as well as parallels to it in other mythologies.

6. [It may be worth quoting a footnote added by Freud to a paper of Stekel's 'Zur Psychologie des Exhibitionismus', in *Zentralbl. Psychoanal.*, 1 (1911), 495: 'Dr. Stekel here proposes to derive exhibitionism from unconscious narcissistic motive forces. It seems to me probable that the same explanation can be applied to the apotropaic exhibiting found among the peoples of antiquity.']

An Excerpt from
Chapter III of
The Ego and the Id

In the late 1890s, when Freud was developing his first causal theory of hysteria, he operated with a relatively simple two-part image of the mind: a domain of consciousness, called the ego, which worked—more or less successfully—to control a domain of "the repressed," whose contents were unconscious. Over the next two decades, this topographical model was variously modified. Then in The Ego and the Id (1923), Freud recognized that psychoanalytic results had strained even the modified image, and proposed a clarifying new terminology.

The first two sections of this important text set out the rudiments of the new "structural theory." Freud speaks now of the id ("the reservoir of the libido"); the ego or control-center, which is partly conscious, partly unconscious; and the ego ideal or superego, an outgrowth of the id, which represents the history of the id's loves or object-choices and is the ego's partly conscious, partly unconscious "conscience." The third section of the text, an excerpt of which follows, focuses on the superego and presents the processes of "identification" through which the superego is built up.

Analyzing these identification processes brought Freud to a richer conception of the Oedipus complex. He notes here that for both females and males the Oedipus complex is both positive (made up of love for the opposite-sex parent and identification with the same-sex parent) and negative (love of the same-sex, identification with the opposite-sex parent). This line of thought, an elaboration of Freud's constant preoccupation with how infantile bisexuality is limited over time, is developed further in "The Dissolution of the Oedipus Complex" (1924: below, pp. 294–301), where it supports Freud's notion that the two sexes develop analogously—a notion he was on the verge of abandoning.

In his essays after 1925, Freud claims that the processes of superego *formation in the two sexes show how the developments of females and males are not analogous: the two sexes have superegos, he then argued, of differing strengths and flexibilities. Section 3 of The Ego and the Id is crucial for understanding this later argument, which I will comment on further (p. 304). But it is also crucial for understanding a new emphasis in Freud's later work. He had been paying more and more attention to the transformations that infantile desires and activities undergo as they shape adult character. With his "structural theory" he was able to sketch a more encompassing approach to character formation, so that he could speak very generally, for example, of "the feminine character."*

<hr>

III. The Ego and the Super-Ego (Ego Ideal)

* * * At this point we must widen our range a little. We succeeded in explaining the painful disorder of melancholia by supposing that [in those suffering from it] an object which was lost has been set up again inside the ego—that is, that an object-cathexis has been replaced by an identification.[1] At that time, however, we did not appreciate the full significance of this process and did not know how common and how typical it is. Since then we have come to understand that this kind of substitution has a great share in determining the form taken by the ego and that it makes an essential contribution towards building up what is called its 'character.'

At the very beginning, in the individual's primitive oral phase, object-cathexis and identification are no doubt indistinguishable from each other. We can only suppose that later on object-cathexes proceed from the id, which feels erotic trends as needs. The ego, which to begin with is still feeble, becomes aware of the object-cathexes, and either acquiesces in them or tries to fend them off by the process of repression.[2]

<hr>

1. 'Mourning and Melancholia' [(1917), 14:249].
2. An interesting parallel to the replacement of object-choice by identification is to be found in the belief of primitive peoples, and in the prohibitions based upon it, that the attributes of animals which are incorporated as nourishment persist as part of the character of those who eat them. As is well known, this belief is one of the roots of cannibalism and its effects have continued through the series of usages of the totem meal down to Holy Communion. [Cf. *Totem*

When it happens that a person has to give up a sexual object, there quite often ensues an alteration of his ego which can only be described as setting up of the object inside the ego, as it occurs in melancholia; the exact nature of this substitution is as yet unknown to us. It may be that by this introjection, which is a kind of regression to the mechanism of the oral phase, the ego makes it easier for the object to be given up or renders that process possible. It may be that this identification is the sole condition under which the id can give up its objects. At any rate the process, especially in the early phases of development, is a very frequent one, and it makes it possible to suppose that the character of the ego is a precipitate of abandoned object-cathexes and that it contains the history of those object-choices. It must, of course, be admitted from the outset that there are varying degrees of capacity for resistance, which decide the extent to which a person's character fends off or accepts the influences of the history of his erotic object-choices. In women who have had many experiences in love there seems to be no difficulty in finding vestiges of their object-cathexes in the traits of their character. We must also take into consideration cases of simultaneous object-cathexis and identification—cases, that is, in which the alteration in character occurs before the object has been given up. In such cases the alteration in character has been able to survive the object-relation and in a certain sense to conserve it.

From another point of view it may be said that this transformation of an erotic object-choice into an alteration of the ego is also a method by which the ego can obtain control over the id and deepen its relations with it—at the cost, it is true, of acquiescing to a large extent in the id's experiences. When the ego assumes the features of the object, it is forcing itself, so to speak, upon the id as a love-object and is trying to make good the id's loss by saying: 'Look, you can love me too—I am so like the object.'

The transformation of object-libido into narcissistic libido which thus takes place obviously implies an abandonment of sexual aims, a desexualization—a kind of sublimation, therefore. Indeed, the question arises, and deserves careful consideration,

---

and Taboo (1912–13), 13:82, 142, 154–5, etc.] The consequences ascribed by this belief to oral mastery of the object do in fact follow the case of the later sexual object-choice.

whether this is not the universal road to sublimation, whether all sublimation does not take place through the mediation of the ego, which begins by changing sexual object-libido into narcissistic libido and then, perhaps, goes on to give it another aim.[3]

Although it is a digression from our aim, we cannot avoid giving our attention for a moment longer to the ego's object-identifications. If they obtain the upper hand and become too numerous, unduly powerful and incompatible with one another, a pathological outcome will not be far off. It may come to a disruption of the ego in consequence of the different identifications becoming cut off from one another by resistances; perhaps the secret of the cases of what is described as 'multiple personality' is that the different identifications seize hold of consciousness in turn. Even when things do not go so far as this, there remains the question of conflicts between the various identifications into which the ego comes apart, conflicts which cannot after all be described as entirely pathological.

But, whatever the character's later capacity for resisting the influences of abandoned object-cathexes may turn out to be, the effects of the first identifications made in earliest childhood will be general and lasting. This leads us back to the origin of the ego ideal {or super-ego}; for behind it there lies hidden an individual's first and most important identification, his identification with the father in his own personal prehistory.[4] This is apparently not in the first instance the consequence or outcome of an object-cathexis; it is a direct and immediate identification and takes place earlier than any object-cathexis. But the object-choices belonging to the first sexual period and relating to the father and mother seem normally to find their outcome in an identification of this kind, and would thus reinforce the primary one.

The whole subject, however, is so complicated that it will be necessary to go into it in greater detail. The intricacy of the problem is due to two factors: the triangular character of the

---

3. Now that we have distinguished between the ego and the id, we must recognize the id as the great reservoir of libido indicated in my paper on narcissism [(1914), 14:75]. The libido which flows into the ego owing to the identifications described above brings about its 'secondary narcissism'.

4. Perhaps it would be safer to say 'with the parents'; for before a child has arrived at definite knowledge of the difference between the sexes, the lack of a penis, it does not distinguish in value between its father and its mother.

Oedipus situation and the constitutional bisexuality of each individual.

In its simplified form the case of a male child may be described as follows. At a very early age the little boy develops an object-cathexis for his mother, which originally related to the mother's breast and is the prototype of an object-choice on the anaclitic model;[5] the boy deals with his father by identifying himself with him. For a time these two relationships proceed side by side, until the boy's sexual wishes in regard to his mother become more intense and his father is perceived as an obstacle to them; from this the Oedipus complex originates. His identification with his father then takes on a hostile colouring and changes into a wish to get rid of his father in order to take his place with his mother. Henceforward his relation to his father is ambivalent; it seems as if the ambivalence inherent in the identification from the beginning had become manifest. An ambivalent attitude to his father and an object-relation of a solely affectionate kind to his mother make up the content of the simple positive Oedipus complex in a boy.

Along with the demolition of the Oedipus complex, the boy's object-cathexis of his mother must be given up. Its place may be filled by one of two things: either an identification with his mother or an intensification of his identification with his father. We are accustomed to regard the latter outcome as the more normal; it permits the affectionate relation to the mother to be in a measure retained. In this way the dissolution of the Oedipus complex[6] would consolidate the masculinity in a boy's character. In a precisely analogous way,[7] the outcome of the Oedipus attitude in a little girl may be an intensification of her identification with her mother (or the setting up of such an identification for the first time)—a result which will fix the child's feminine character.

These identifications are not what we should have expected [from the previous account (p. 276)], since they do not introduce

---

5. [See the paper on narcissism (1914), {p. 192 above.}

6. [Cf. the paper bearing this title (1924) in which Freud discussed the question more fully. (p. 294 below.)]

7. [The idea that the outcome of the Oedipus complex was 'precisely analogous' in girls and boys was abandoned by Freud not long after this. See 'Some Psychical Consequences of the Anatomical Distinction between the Sexes' (1925).]

the abandoned object into the ego; but this alternative outcome may also occur, and is easier to observe in girls than in boys. Analysis very often shows that a little girl, after she has had to relinquish her father as a love-object, will bring her masculinity into prominence and identify herself with her father (that is, with the object which has been lost), instead of with her mother. This will clearly depend on whether the masculinity in her disposition—whatever that may consist in—is strong enough.

It would appear, therefore that in both sexes the relative strength of the masculine and feminine sexual dispositions is what determines whether the outcome of the Oedipus situation shall be an identification with the father or with the mother. This is one of the ways in which bisexuality takes a hand in the subsequent vicissitudes of the Oedipus complex. The other way is even more important. For one gets an impression that the simple Oedipus complex is by no means its commonest form, but rather represents a simplification or schematization which, to be sure, is often enough justified for practical purposes. Closer study usually discloses the more complete Oedipus complex, which is twofold, positive and negative, and is due to the bisexuality originally present in children: that is to say, a boy has not merely an ambivalent attitude towards his father and an affectionate object-choice towards his mother, but at the same time he also behaves like a girl and displays an affectionate feminine attitude to his father and a corresponding jealousy and hostility towards his mother. It is this complicating element introduced by bisexuality that makes it so difficult to obtain a clear view of the facts in connection with the earliest object-choices and identifications, and still more difficult to describe them intelligibly. It may even be that the ambivalence displayed in the relations to the parents should be attributed entirely to bisexuality and that it is not, as I have represented above, developed out of identification in consequence of rivalry.

In my opinion it is advisable in general, and quite especially where neurotics are concerned, to assume the existence of the complete Oedipus complex. Analytic experience then shows that in a number of cases one or the other constitutent disappears, except for barely distinguishable traces; so that the result is a series with the normal positive Oedipus complex at one end and the inverted negative one at the other, while its intermediate members exhibit the complete form with one or other of its two components preponderating. At the dissolution of the Oedipus complex the four trends of which it consists will group themselves in such a way as to produce a father-identification and a mother-identification. The father-identification will preserve the object-relation to the mother which belonged to the positive complex and will at the same time replace the object-relation to the father which belonged to the inverted complex: and the same will be true, *mutatis mutandis*, of the mother-identification. The relative intensity of the two identifications in any individual will reflect the preponderance in him of one or other of the two sexual dispositions.

The broad general outcome of the sexual phase dominated by the Oedipus complex may, therefore, be taken to be the forming of a precipitate in the ego, consisting of these two identifications in some way united with each other. This modification of the ego retains its special position; it confronts the other contents of the ego as an ego ideal or super-ego.

The super-ego is, however, not simply a residue of the earliest object-choices of the id; it also represents an energetic reaction-formation against those choices. Its relation to the ego is not exhausted by the precept: 'You *ought to be* like this (like your father).' It also comprises the prohibition: 'You *may not be* like this (like your father)—that is, you may not do all that he does; some things are his prerogative.' This double aspect of the ego ideal derives from the fact that the ego ideal had the task of repressing the Oedipus complex; indeed, it is to that revolutionary event that it owes its existence. Clearly the repression of the Oedipus complex was no easy task. The child's parents, and especially his father, were perceived as the obstacle to a realization of his Oedipus wishes; so his infantile ego fortified itself for the carrying out of the repression by erecting this same obstacle within itself. It borrowed strength to do this, so to speak, from the father, and this loan was an extraordinarily momentous act. The super-ego retains the character of the father, while the more powerful the Oedipus complex was and the more rapidly it succumbed to repression (under the influence of authority, religious teaching, schooling and reading), the stricter will be the domination of the super-ego over the ego later on—in the form of conscience or perhaps of an unconscious sense of guilt. * * *

If we consider once more the origin of the super-ego as we have described it, we shall recognize that it is the outcome of two highly important factors, one of a biological and the other of a historical nature: namely, the lengthy duration in man of his childhood helplessness and dependence, and the fact of his Oedipus complex, the repression of which we have shown to be connected with the interruption of libidinal development by the latency period and so with the diphasic onset of man's sexual life. * * * We see, then, that the differentiation of the super-ego from the ego is no matter of chance; it represents the most important characteristics of the development both of the individual and of the species; indeed, by giving permanent expression to the influence of the parents it perpetuates the existence of the factors to which it owes its origin. * * *

The ego ideal is therefore the heir of the Oedipus complex, and thus it is also the expression of the most powerful impulses and most important libidinal vicissitudes of the id. By setting up this ego ideal, the ego has mastered the Oedipus complex and at the same time placed itself in subjection to the id. Whereas the ego is essentially the representative of the external world, of reality, the super-ego stands in contrast to it as the representative of the internal world, of the id. Conflicts between the ego and the ideal will, as we are now prepared to find, ultimately reflect the contrast between what is real and what is psychical, between the external world and the internal world.

Through the forming of the ideal, what biology and the vicissitudes of the human species have created in the id and left behind in it is taken over by the ego and re-experienced in relation to itself as an individual. Owing to the way in which the ego ideal is formed, it has the most abundant links with the phylogenetic acquisition of each individual—his archaic heritage. What has belonged to the lowest part of the mental life of each of us is changed, through the formation of the ideal, into what is highest in the human mind by our scale of values. It would be vain, however, to attempt to localize the ego ideal, even in the sense in which we have localized the ego, or to work it into any of the analogies with the help of which we have tried to picture the relation between the ego and the id.

It is easy to show that the ego ideal answers to everything that is expected of the higher nature of man. As a substitute for a longing for the father, it contains the germ from which all religions have evolved. The self-judgement which declares that the ego falls short of its ideal produces the religious sense of humility to which the believer appeals in his longing. As a child grows up, the role of father is carried on by teachers and others in authority; their injunctions and prohibitions remain powerful in the ego ideal and continue, in the form of conscience, to exercise the moral censorship. The tension between the demands of conscience and the actual performances of the ego is experienced as a sense of guilt. Social feelings rest on identifications with other people, on the basis of having the same ego ideal.

Religion, morality, and a social sense—the chief elements in the higher side of man[8]—were originally one and the same thing. According to the hypothesis which I put forward in *Totem and Taboo* they were acquired phylogenetically out of the father-complex: religion and moral restraint through the process of mastering the Oedipus complex itself, and social feeling through the necessity for overcoming the rivalry that then remained between the members of the younger generation. The male sex seems to have taken the lead in all these moral acquisitions; and they seem to have then been transmitted to women by cross-inheritance. Even to-day the social feelings arise in the individual as a super-structure built upon impulses of jealous rivalry against his brothers and sisters. Since the hostility cannot be satisfied, an identification with the former rival develops. The study of mild cases of homosexuality confirms the suspicion that in this instance, too, the identification is a substitute for an affectionate object-choice which has taken the place of the aggressive, hostile attitude.[9] * * *

8. I am at the moment putting science and art on one side.
9. Cf. *Group Psychology* (1921) [18:120] and 'Some Neurotic Mechanisms in Jealousy, Paranoia and Homosexuality' (1922) [ibid., 231]. {Both of these discussions concern male homosexuality.}

The Economic Problem of Masochism

It is commonly assumed that Freud counted masochism among the defining characteristics of femininity, "an expression of feminine nature," as he indeed wrote toward the beginning of this 1924 essay. But the remainder of his overpacked, complicated text should convince anyone that what he thought about women and masochism does not lend itself to simple summary.

Into the pool of this 1924 essay, two streams of Freud's major revisions of psychoanalytic theory poured. One was the revision of his instinct theory announced in the 1920 text Beyond the Pleasure Principle. Freud now speaks of two instincts, Eros (all sorts of libido) and the death instinct. The essay also received the newly articulated "structural theory" of id, ego, and superego, the last of which represents the external (and particularly parental) world in the psyche. In Chapter 4 of The Ego and the Id (not included in this volume), Freud had launched a discussion of how the dual-instinct theory and the structural theory would fit together, and the present essay continues that discussion.

Seeking theoretical cohesion and coherence now, Freud took a new look at "the economic problem of masochism." This effort went on while he was recuperating from the first radical operation on his cancerous jaw, certainly an unwelcome opportunity for thinking about pain. In Freud's terminology, assessing an "economic problem" means "taking into consideration the fact that the psychical processes aim at gaining pleasure and removing unpleasure" (6:270). Masochism is a puzzle because it contradicts the psyche's pleasure economy—unpleasure is its aim. To understand such a puzzling economy, the roles of the instincts and of the external world—as represented by the superego—must also be considered as possible sources of the contradiction.

Freud proceeds by distinguishing various types of masochism. After a dense general theoretical passage, not included here, he turns to "erotogenic masochism," the basic form of pleasure in pain, and its two derivatives, feminine masochism and moral masochism. Erotogenic masochism is presented as that portion of the death instinct that is not projected outward as aggression or (in combination with externalized libido) as sadism; it remains inside the individual, where some amount of it is fused with as yet unexternalized libido. (The rest of it remains unfused within the individual. Freud does not comment on the fate of this unmixed amount; he only says that it exists, untamed.)

Freud does not, it is important to note, relate erotogenic masochism specifically to female development. But in the 1932 lecture called "Femininity" (see p. 345 below) he does note that "the suppression of women's aggressiveness which is prescribed for them constitutionally and imposed on them socially favors the development of powerful masochistic impulses. . . ." Masochistic impulses are favored by a woman's constitution because her sexual apparatus is receptive, and she may feel "penis envy", and also by social conventions that provide little outlet for aggression, but masochistic impulses are not therefore inevitable.

The erotogenic masochism that accompanies the libido takes different forms in the different libidinal stages. The beating fantasies Freud had studied in 1919 arise with the anal-sadistic stage, the derivative masochism called "feminine" arises with the phallic or genital organization, and in both women and men it is bound up with fantasies of castration, copulation, or giving birth. Freud bases his description of this "feminine masochism" on male cases because these present the most extreme— and thus the most clear—cases of "feminine" fantasies. "Feminine masochism" in males is bound up with the castration complex, the boy's fear of losing his genital. Unfortunately, Freud does not say anything about the content of female phallic genital-stage fantasies (as opposed to the earlier beating fantasies), and his followers have been left to interpret him in various ways. Some, like Robert Waelder, for example, explicitly link masochism to the castration complex in females: ". . . masochism is, in the main, sexual enjoyment of playful castration: in the man of being treated like a woman; and in the woman of being rendered totally defenseless and being penetrated in any depth, i.e., of symbolic supercastration."[1]

Although beating fantasies are the link between erotogenic masochism and the desexualized moral masochism of people who (figuratively or literally) arrange to have themselves beaten for supposed moral failings, Freud's discussion of moral masochism at the end of this essay is not tied specifically to the distinctions between the sexes. He does distinguish

---

1. {Robert Waelder, Basic Theory of Psychoanalysis (New York: International Universities Press, 1960), p. 162.}

the unconscious need for punishment of the moral masochist from the conscious self-punishment of the person with a sadistic, overrigid superego, however. This distinction is important in relation to Freud's later claims about the relative lack of rigidity of the superego in females, which will be considered below, p. 304.

The fact that Freud commonly used male cases to illustrate his theoretical claims about men and women left his views on women open to very diverse interpretations, and also blinded him to problems and differences between the sexes. But after this essay and the next one ("The Dissolution of the Oedipus Complex"), both from 1924, he began to take stock of what this prejudice in favor of male cases had meant for his views on women.

* * * To return to masochism. Masochism comes under our observation in three forms: as a condition imposed on sexual excitation, as an expression of the feminine nature, and as a norm of behaviour. We may, accordingly, distinguish an *erotogenic*, a *feminine* and a *moral* masochism. The first, the erotogenic, masochism—pleasure in pain—lies at the bottom of the other two forms as well. Its basis must be sought along biological and constitutional lines and it remains incomprehensible unless one decides to make certain assumptions about matters that are extremely obscure. The third, and in some respects the most important, form assumed by masochism has only recently been recognized by psycho-analysis as a sense of guilt which is mostly unconscious; but it can already be completely explained and fitted into the rest of our knowledge. Feminine masochism, on the other hand, is the one that is most accessible to our observation and least problematical, and it can be surveyed in all its relations. We will begin our discussion with it.

We have sufficient acquaintance with this kind of masochism in men (to whom, owing to the material at my command, I shall restrict my remarks), derived from masochistic—and therefore often impotent—subjects whose phantasies either terminate in an act of masturbation or represent a sexual satisfaction in themselves. The real-life performances of masochistic perverts tally completely with these phantasies, whether the performances are carried out as an end in themselves or serve to induce potency and to lead to the sexual act. In both cases—for the performances are, after all, only a carrying-out of the phantasies in play—the manifest content is of being gagged, bound, painfully beaten, whipped, in some way maltreated, forced into unconditional obedience, dirtied and debased. It is far more rare for mutilations to be included in the content, and then only subject to strict limitations. The obvious interpretation, and one easily arrived at, is that the masochist wants to be treated like a small and helpless child, but, particularly, like a naughty child. It is unnecessary to quote cases to illustrate this; for the material is very uniform and is accessible to any observer, even to non-analysts. But if one has an opportunity of studying cases in which the masochistic phantasies have been especially richly elaborated, one quickly discovers that they place the subject in a characteristically female situation; they signify, that is, being castrated, or copulated with, or giving birth to a baby. For this reason I have called this form of masochism, *a potiori* as it were [i.e. on the basis of its extreme examples], the feminine form, although so many of its features point to infantile life. This superimposed stratification of the infantile and the feminine will find a simple explanation later on. Being castrated— or being blinded, which stands for it—often leaves a negative trace of itself in phantasies, in the condition that no injury is to occur precisely to the genitals or the eyes. (Masochistic tortures, incidentally, rarely make such a serious impression as the cruelties of sadism, whether imagined or performed.) A sense of guilt, too, finds expression in the manifest content of masochistic phantasies; the subject assumes that he has committed some crime (the nature of which is left indefinite) which is to be expiated by all these painful and tormenting procedures. This looks like a superficial rationalization of the masochistic subject-matter, but behind it there lies a connection with infantile masturbation. On the other hand, this factor of guilt provides a transition to the third, moral, form of masochism.

This feminine masochism which we have been describing is entirely based on the primary, erotogenic masochism, on pleasure in pain. This cannot be explained without taking our discussion very far back.

In my *Three Essays on the Theory of Sexuality*, in the section on the sources of infantile sexuality, I put forward the proposition that 'in the case of a great number of internal processes sexual excitation arises as a concomitant effect, as soon as the intensity of those processes passes beyond certain quantitative limits'. Indeed, 'it may well be that nothing of considerable importance can occur in the organism without contributing some component to the excitation of the sexual instinct'[2]. In accordance with this, the excitation of pain and unpleasure would be bound to have the same result, too. The occurrence of such a libidinal sympathetic excitation when there is tension due to pain and unpleasure would be an infantile physiological mechanism which ceases to operate later on. It would attain a varying degree of development in different sexual constitutions; but in any case it would provide the physiological foundation on which the psychical structure of erotogenic masochism would afterwards be erected.

The inadequacy of this explanation is seen, however, in the fact that it throws no light on the regular and close connections of masochism with its counterpart in instinctual life, sadism. If we go back a little further, to our hypothesis of the two classes of instincts which we regard as operative in the living organism, we arrive at another derivation of masochism, which, however, is not in contradiction with the former one. In (multicellular) organisms the libido meets the instinct of death, or destruction, which is dominant in them and which seeks to disintegrate the cellular organism and to conduct each separate unicellular organism [composing it] into a state of inorganic stability (relative though this may be). The libido has the task of making the destroying instinct innocuous, and it fulfils the task by diverting that instinct to a great extent outwards—soon with the help of a special organic system, the muscular apparatus—towards objects in the external world. The instinct is then called the destructive instinct, the instinct of mastery, or the will to power. A portion of the instinct is placed directly in the service of the sexual function, where it has an important part to play. This is sadism proper. Another portion does not share in this transposition outwards; it remains inside the organism and, with the help of the accompanying sexual excitation described above, becomes libidinally bound there. It is in this portion that we have to recognize the original, erotogenic masochism.

We are without any physiological understanding of the ways

2. [*Three Essays* (1905), 7:204–5.] {This section is not included above; see p. 127 for a summary of it.}

and means by which this taming of the death-instinct by the libido may be effected. So far as the psycho-analytic field of ideas is concerned, we can only assume that a very extensive fusion and amalgamation, in varying proportions, of the two classes of instincts takes place, so that we never have to deal with pure life instincts or pure death instincts but only with mixtures of them in different amounts. Corresponding to a fusion of instincts of this kind, there may, as a result of certain influences, be a *de*fusion of them. How large the portions of the death instincts are which refuse to be tamed in this way by being bound to admixtures of libido we cannot at present guess.

If one is prepared to overlook a little inexactitude, it may be said that the death instinct which is operative in the organism—primal sadism—is identical with masochism. After the main portion of it has been transposed outwards on to objects, there remains inside, as a residuum of it, the erotogenic masochism proper, which on the one hand has become a component of the libido and, on the other, still has the self as its object. This masochism would thus be evidence of, and a remainder from, the phase of development in which the coalescence, which is so important for life, between the death instinct and Eros took place. We shall not be surprised to hear that in certain circumstances the sadism, or instinct of destruction, which has been directed outwards, projected, can be once more introjected, turned inwards, and in this way regress to its earlier situation. If this happens, a secondary masochism is produced, which is added to the original masochism.

Erotogenic masochism accompanies the libido through all its developmental phases and derives from them its changing psychical coatings. The fear of being eaten up by the totem animal (the father) originates from the primitive oral organization; the wish to be beaten by the father comes from the sadistic-anal phase which follows it; castration, although it is later disavowed, enters into the content of masochistic phantasies as a precipitate of the phallic stage or organization; and from the final genital organization there arise, of course, the situations of being copulated with and of giving birth, which are characteristic of femaleness. The part played in masochism by the nates {buttocks}, too, is easily understandable, apart from its obvious basis in reality. The nates are the part of the body which is given erotogenic preference in the sadistic-anal phase, like the breast in the oral phase and the penis in the genital phase.

The third form of masochism, moral masochism, is chiefly remarkable for having loosened its connection with what we recognize as sexuality. All other masochistic sufferings carry with them the condition that they shall emanate from the loved person and shall be endured at his command. This restriction has been dropped in moral masochism. The suffering itself is what matters; whether it is decreed by someone who is loved or by someone who is indifferent is of no importance. It may even be caused by impersonal powers or by circumstances; the true masochist always turns his cheek whenever he has a chance of receiving a blow. It is very tempting, in explaining this attitude, to leave the libido out of account and to confine oneself to assuming that in this case the destructive instinct has been turned inwards again and is now raging against the self; yet there must be some meaning in the fact that linguistic usage has not given up the connection between this norm of behaviour and erotism and calls these self-injurers masochists too.

Let us keep to a habit of our technique and consider first the extreme and unmistakably pathological form of this masochism. I have described elsewhere[3] how in analytic treatment we come across patients to whom, owing to their behaviour towards its therapeutic influence, we are obliged to ascribe an 'unconscious' sense of guilt. I pointed out the sign by which such people can be recognized (a 'negative therapeutic reaction') and I did not conceal the fact that the strength of such an impulse constitutes one of the most serious resistances and the greatest danger to the success of our medical or educative aims. The satisfaction of this unconscious sense of guilt is perhaps the most powerful bastion in the subject's (usually composite) gain from illness—in the sum of forces which struggle against his recovery and refuse to surrender his state of illness. The suffering entailed by neuroses is precisely the factor that makes them valuable to the masochistic trend. It is instructive, too, to find, contrary to all theory and expectation, that a neurosis which has defied every therapeutic effort may vanish if the subject becomes involved in the misery

---

3. *The Ego and the Id* (1923) [Chapter V].

of an unhappy marriage, or loses all his money, or develops a dangerous organic disease. In such instances one form of suffering has been replaced by another; and we see that all that mattered was that it should be possible to maintain a certain amount of suffering.

Patients do not easily believe us when we tell them about the unconscious sense of guilt. They know only too well by what torments—the pangs of conscience—a conscious sense of guilt, a consciousness of guilt, expresses itself, and they therefore cannot admit that they could harbour exactly analogous impulses in themselves without being in the least aware of them. We may, I think, to some extent meet their objection if we give up the term 'unconscious sense of guilt', which is in any case psychologically incorrect,[4] and speak instead of a 'need for punishment', which covers the observed state of affairs just as aptly. We cannot, however, restrain ourselves from judging and localizing this unconscious sense of guilt in the same way as we do the conscious kind.

We have attributed the function of conscience to the superego and we have recognized the consciousness of guilt as an expression of a tension between the ego and the super-ego. The ego reacts with feelings of anxiety (conscience anxiety) to the perception that it has not come up to the demands made by its ideal, the super-ego. What we want to know is how the super-ego has come to play this demanding role and why the ego, in the case of a difference with its ideal, should have to be afraid.

We have said that the function of the ego is to unite and to reconcile the claims of the three agencies which it serves; and we may add that in doing so it also possesses in the super-ego a model which it can strive to follow. For this super-ego is as much a representative of the id as of the external world. It came into being through the introjection into the ego of the first objects of the id's libidinal impulses—namely, the two parents. In this process the relation to those objects was desexualized; it was diverted from its direct sexual aims. Only in this way was it possible for the Oedipus complex to be surmounted. The super-ego retained essential features of the introjected persons—their strength, their severity, their inclination to supervise and to punish. As I have said elsewhere,[5] it is easily conceivable that, thanks to the defusion of instinct

4. [Feelings cannot properly be described as 'unconscious'.]
5. *The Ego and the Id* {[Chapter IV]}.

which occurs along with this introduction into the ego, the severity was increased. The super-ego—the conscience at work in the ego—may then become harsh, cruel and inexorable against the ego which is in its charge * * *

But the same figures who continue to operate in the super-ego as the agency we know as conscience after they have ceased to be objects of the libidinal impulses of the id—these same figures also belong to the real external world. It is from there that they were drawn; their power, behind which lie hidden all the strongly-felt manifestations of reality. In virtue of this concurrence, the super-ego, the substitute for the Oedipus complex, becomes a representative of the real external world as well and thus also becomes a model for the endeavours of the ego.

In this way the Oedipus complex proves to be—as has already been conjectured in a historical sense—the source of our individual ethical sense, our morality. The course of childhood development leads to an ever-increasing detachment from parents, and their personal significance for the super-ego recedes into the background. To the imagos they leave behind there are then linked the influences of teachers and authorities, self-chosen models and publicly recognized heroes, whose figures need no longer be introjected by an ego which has become more resistant. The last figure in the series that began with the parents is the dark power of Destiny which only the fewest of us are able to look upon as impersonal. * * *

After these preliminaries we can return to our consideration of moral masochism. We have said that, by their behaviour during treatment and in life, the individuals in question give an impression of being morally inhibited to an excessive degree, of being under the domination of an especially sensitive conscience, although they are not conscious of any of this ultramorality. On closer inspection, we can see the difference there is between an unconscious extension of morality of this kind and moral masochism. In the former, the accent falls on the heightened sadism of the super-ego to which the ego submits; in the latter, it falls on the ego's own masochism which seeks punishment, whether from the super-ego or from the parental powers outside. We may be forgiven for having confused the two to begin with; for in both cases it is a question of a relationship between the ego and the super-ego (or powers that are equivalent to it), and in both cases what is involved is a need which is satisfied by punishment and suffering. It can hardly be an insignificant detail, then, that the sadism of the superego becomes for the most part glaringly conscious, whereas the masochistic trend of the ego remains as a rule concealed from the subject and has to be inferred from his behaviour.

The fact that moral masochism is unconscious leads us to an obvious clue. We were able to translate the expression 'unconscious sense of guilt' as meaning a need for punishment at the hands of a parental power. We now know that the wish, which so frequently appears in phantasies, to be beaten by the father stands very close to the other wish, to have a passive (feminine) sexual relation to him and is only a regressive distortion of it. If we insert this explanation into the content of moral masochism, its hidden meaning becomes clear to us. Conscience and morality have arisen through the overcoming, the desexualization, of the Oedipus complex; but through moral masochism morality becomes sexualized once more, the Oedipus complex is revived and the way is opened for a regression from morality to the Oedipus complex. This is to the advantage neither of morality nor of the person concerned. An individual may, it is true, have preserved the whole or some measure of ethical sense alongside of his masochism; but, alternatively, a large part of his conscience may have vanished into his masochism. Again, masochism creates a temptation to perform 'sinful' actions, which must then be expiated by the reproaches of the sadistic conscience (as is exemplified in so many Russian character-types) or by chastisement from the great parental power of Destiny. In order to provoke punishment from this last representative of the parents, the masochist must do what is inexpedient, must act against his own interests, must ruin the prospects which open out to him in the real world and must, perhaps, destroy his own real existence.

The turning back of sadism against the self regularly occurs where a *cultural suppression of the instincts* holds back a large part of the subject's destructive instinctual components from being exercised in life. We may suppose that this portion of the destructive instinct which has retreated appears in the ego as an intensification of masochism. The phenomena of conscience, however, lead us to infer that the destructiveness which returns from the external world is also taken up by the super-ego, without any such transformation, and increases its sadism against the ego. The sadism of the super-ego and the masochism of the ego supplement each other and unite to produce the same effects. It is only in this way, I think, that we can understand how the suppression of an instinct can—frequently or quite generally—result in a sense of guilt and how a person's conscience becomes more severe and more sensitive the more he refrains from aggression against others. * * *

Thus moral masochism becomes a classical piece of evidence for the existence of fusion of instinct. Its danger lies in the fact that it originates from the death instinct and corresponds to the part of that instinct which has escaped being turned outwards as an instinct of destruction. But since, on the other hand, it has the significance of an erotic component, even the subject's destruction of himself cannot take place without libidinal satisfaction.

The Dissolution of the Oedipus Complex

In this 1934 paper, the reader can almost feel Freud dislodging himself from his long-held conviction that females and males undergo analogous developments. The first part of the paper summarizes and combines the insights of "The Infantile Genital Organization" (above, pp. 267–71) and Chapter III of The Ego and the Id *(above, pp. 274–82), which discusses how identifications make up the superego. Then Freud pauses to note that the picture he has drawn will do only for male children: "How does the corresponding development take place in little girls?" In the remaining two pages of the essay, Freud tries to answer his own question, but the result is quite unsatisfactory. Despite the complex picture of mother identifications and father identifications given in* The Ego and the Id, *he drops back into his old habit of considering the little girl only in relation to her father. Nonetheless, his hesitancy left the theoretical door open to "Some Psychical Consequences of the Anatomical Distinction between the Sexes" (1925).*

At the end of the present essay, I have included some excerpts about early sexuality and the Oedipus complex taken from Freud's correspondence with Karl Abraham, leader of the Berlin Psychoanalytic Society. As Freud's views on female psychology shifted, Abraham's opinions were very important to him. (When Freud's correspondence with Ernest Jones is published, it will also provide illuminating glimpses of the 1920s debates.)

To an ever-increasing extent the Oedipus complex reveals its importance as the central phenomenon of the sexual period of eraly childhood. After that, its dissolution takes place; it succumbs to repression, as we say, and is followed by the latency period. It has not yet become clear, however, what it is that brings about its destruction. Analyses seem to show that it is the experience of painful disappointments. The little girl likes to regard herself as what her father loves above all else; but the time comes when she has to endure a harsh punishment from him and she is cast out of her fool's paradise. The boy regards his mother as his own property; but he finds one day that she has transferred her love and solicitude to a new arrival. Reflection must deepen our sense of the importance of those influences, for it will emphasize the fact that distressing experiences of this sort, which act in opposition to the content of the complex, are inevitable. Even when no special events occur, like those we have mentioned as examples, the absence of the satisfaction hoped for, the continued denial of the desired baby, must in the end lead the small lover to turn away from his hopeless longing. In this way the Oedipus complex would go to its destruction from its lack of success, from the effects of its internal impossibility.

Another view is that the Oedipus complex must collapse because the time has come for its disintegration, just as the milk-teeth fall out when the permanent ones begin to grow. Although the majority of human beings go through the Oedipus complex as an individual experience, it is nevertheless a phenomenon which is determined and laid down by heredity and which is bound to pass away according to programme when the next pre-ordained phase of development sets in. This being so, it is of no great importance what the occasions are which allow this to happen, or, indeed, whether any such occasions can be discovered at all.

The justice of both these views cannot be disputed. Moreover, they are compatible. There is room for the ontogenetic view side by side with the more far-reaching phylogenetic one. It is also true that even at birth the whole individual is destined to die, and perhaps his organic disposition may already contain the indication of what he is to die from. Nevertheless, it remains of interest to follow out how this innate programme is carried out and in what way accidental noxae exploit his disposition.

We have lately[1] been made more clearly aware than before that

---

1. [See 'The Infantile Genital Organization of the Libido'.]

a child's sexual development advances to a certain phase at which the genital organ has already taken over the leading role. But this genital is the male one only, or, more correctly, the penis; the female genital has remained undiscovered. This phallic phase, which is contemporaneous with the Oedipus complex, does not develop further to the definitive genital organization, but is submerged, and is succeeded by the latency period. Its termination, however, takes place in a typical manner and in conjunction with events that are of regular recurrence.

When the (male) child's interest turns to his genitals he betrays the fact by manipulating them frequently; and he then finds that the adults do not approve of this behaviour. More or less plainly, more or less brutally, a threat is pronounced that this part of him which he values so highly will be taken away from him. Usually it is from women that the threat emanates; very often they seek to strengthen their authority by a reference to the father or the doctor, who, so they say, will carry out the punishment. In a number of cases the women will themselves mitigate the threat in a symbolic manner by telling the child that what is to be removed is not his genital, which actually plays a passive part, but his hand, which is the active culprit. It happens particularly often that the little boy is threatened with castration, not because he plays with his penis with his hand, but because he wets his bed every night and cannot be got to be clean. Those in charge of him behave as if this nocturnal incontinence was the result and the proof of his being unduly concerned with his penis, and they are probably right. In any case, long-continued bed-wetting is to be equated with the emissions of adults. It is an expression of the same excitation of the genitals which has impelled the child to masturbate at this period.

Now it is my view that what brings about the destruction of the {male} child's phallic genital organization is this threat of castration. Not immediately, it is true, and not without other influences being brought to bear as well. For to begin with the boy does not believe in the threat or obey it in the least. Psychoanalysis has recently attached importance to two experiences which all children go through and which, it is suggested, prepare them for the loss of highly valued parts of the body. These experiences are the withdrawal of the mother's breast—at first intermittently and later for good—and the daily demand on them to give up the contents of the bowel. But there is no evidence to show that, when the threat of castration takes place, those experiences have any effect. It is not until a *fresh* experience comes his way that the child begins to reckon with the possibility of being castrated, and then only hesitatingly and unwillingly, and not without making efforts to depreciate the significance of something he has himself observed.

The observation which finally breaks down his unbelief is the sight of the female genitals. Sooner or later the child, who is so proud of his possession of a penis, has a view of the genital region of a little girl, and cannot help being convinced of the absence of a penis in a creature who is so like himself. With this, the loss of his own penis becomes imaginable, and the threat of castration takes its deferred effect.

We should not be as short-sighted as the person in charge of the child who threatens him with castration, and we must not overlook the fact that at this time masturbation by no means represents the whole of his sexual life. As can be clearly shown, he stands in the Oedipus attitude to his parents; his masturbation is only a genital discharge of the sexual excitation belonging to the complex, and throughout his later years will owe its importance to that relationship. The Oedipus complex offered the child two possibilities of satisfaction, an active and a passive one. He could put himself in his father's place in a masculine fashion and have intercourse with his mother as his father did, in which case he would soon have felt the latter as a hindrance; or he might want to take the place of his mother and be loved by his father, in which case his mother would become superfluous. The child may have had only very vague notions as to what constitutes a satisfying erotic intercourse; but certainly the penis must play a part in it, for the sensations in his own organ were evidence of that. So far he had had no occasion to doubt that women possessed a penis. But now his acceptance of the possibility of castration, his recognition that women were castrated, made an end of both possible ways of obtaining satisfaction from the Oedipus complex. For both of them entailed the loss of his penis—the masculine one as a resulting punishment and the feminine one as a precondition. If the satisfaction of love in the field of the Oedipus complex is to cost the child his penis, a conflict is bound to arise between his narcissistic interest in that part of his body and the

libidinal cathexis of his parental objects. In this conflict the first
of these forces normally triumphs: the child's ego turns away from
the Oedipus complex.

I have described elsewhere how this turning away takes place.[2]
The object-cathexes are given up and replaced by identifications.
The authority of the father or the parents is introjected into the
ego, and there it forms the nucleus of the super-ego, which takes
over the severity of the father and perpetuates his prohibition
against incest, and so secures the ego from the return of the
libidinal object-cathexis. The libidinal trends belonging to the
Oedipus complex are in part desexualized and sublimated (a thing
which probably happens with every transformation into an identification) and in part inhibited in their aim and changed into
impulses of affection. The whole process has, on the one hand,
preserved the genital organ—has averted the danger of its loss—
and, on the other, has paralysed it—has removed its function.
This process ushers in the latency period, which now interrupts
the child's sexual development.

I see no reason for denying the name of a 'repression' to the
ego's turning away from the Oedipus complex, although later
repressions come about for the most part with the participation
of the super-ego, which in this case is only just being formed.
But the process we have described is more than a repression. It
is equivalent, if it is ideally carried out, to a destruction and an
abolition of the complex. We may plausibly assume that we have
here come upon the borderline—never a very sharply drawn
one—between the normal and the pathological. If the ego has in
fact not achieved much more than a *repression* of the complex,
the latter persists in an unconscious state in the id and will later
manifest its pathogenic effect.

Analytic observation enables us to recognize or guess these
connections between the phallic organization, the Oedipus complex, the threat of castration, the formation of the super-ego and
the latency period. These connections justify the statement that
the destruction of the Oedipus complex is brought about by the
threat of castration. But this does not dispose of the problem; there
is room for a theoretical speculation which may upset the results
we have come to or put them in a new light. Before we start along

2. [In Chapter III of *The Ego and the Id*, above.]

this new path, however, we must turn to a question which has arisen in the course of this discussion and has so far been left on one side. The process which has been described refers, as has been expressly said, to male children only. How does the corresponding development take place in little girls?

At this point our material—for some incomprehensible reason[3]—becomes far more obscure and full of gaps. The female sex, too, develops an Oedipus complex, a super-ego and a latency period. May we also attribute a phallic organization and a castration complex to it? The answer is in the affirmative; but these things cannot be the same as they are in boys. Here the feminist demand for equal rights for the sexes does not take us far, for the morphological distinction is bound to find expression in differences of psychical development. 'Anatomy is Destiny', to vary a saying of Napoleon's. The little girl's clitoris behaves just like a penis to begin with; but, when she makes a comparison with a playfellow of the other sex, she perceives that she has 'come off badly'[4] and she feels this as a wrong done to her and as a ground for inferiority. For a while still she consoles herself with the expectation that later on, when she grows older, she will acquire just as big an appendage as the boy's. Here the masculinity complex of women branches off. A female child, however, does not understand her lack of a penis as being a sex character; she explains it by assuming that at some earlier date she had possessed an equally large organ and had then lost it by castration. She seems not to extend this inference from herself to other, adult females, but, entirely on the lines of the phallic phase, to regard them as possessing large and complete—that is to say, male—genitals. The essential difference thus comes about that the girl accepts castration as an accomplished fact, whereas the boy fears the possibility of its occurrence.

The fear of castration being thus excluded in the little girl, a powerful motive also drops out for the setting-up of a super-ego and for the breaking-off of the infantile genital organization. In her, far more than in the boy, these changes seem to be the result of upbringing and of intimidation from outside which threatens her with a loss of love. The girl's Oedipus complex is much simpler

---

3. [Freud suggested some explanation for this in Section I of his paper on 'Female Sexuality'.]
4. [Literally, 'come off too short'.]

than that of the small bearer of the penis; in my experience, it seldom goes beyond the taking of her mother's place and the adopting of a feminine attitude towards her father. Renunciation of the penis is not tolerated by the girl without some attempt at compensation. She slips—along the line of a symbolic equation, one might say—from the penis to a baby. Her Oedipus complex culminates in a desire, which is long retained, to receive a baby from her father as a gift—to bear him a child. One has an impression that the Oedipus complex is then gradually given up because this wish is never fulfilled. The two wishes—to possess a penis and a child—remain strongly cathected in the unconscious and help to prepare the female creature for her later sexual role. The comparatively lesser strength of the sadistic contribution to her sexual instinct, which we may no doubt connect with the stunted growth of her penis, makes it easier in her case for the direct sexual trends to be transformed into aim-inhibited trends of an affectionate kind. It must be admitted, however, that in general our insight into these developmental processes in girls is unsatisfactory, incomplete and vague.

I have no doubt that the chronological and causal relations described here between the Oedipus complex, sexual intimidation (the threat of castration), the formation of the super-ego and the beginning of the latency period are of a typical kind; but I do not wish to assert that this type is the only possible one. Variations in the chronological order and in the linking-up of these events are bound to have a very important bearing on the development of the individual. * * *

During the years 1923, 1924, and 1925, between "The Psychogenesis of a Case of Homosexuality in a Woman" and Freud's next major excursion into the "dark continent" (as he called it) of female sexuality, he was preoccupied with his own health and the disorder his withdrawal from public life caused in the little psychoanalytic community. Karl Abraham, in Berlin, was now emerging as the key leader organizationally and a crucial contributor scientifically. Freud regularly responded to suggestions that Abraham made by letter, in papers, and during his personal visits to Vienna. The following excerpts are from A Psychoanalytic Dialogue: The Letters of Sigmund Freud and Karl Abraham.

Abraham to Freud, October 7, 1923:

I have something pleasant to report in the scientific field. In my work on Melancholia,[5] of which Rank has the manuscript, I have assumed the presence of an early depression in infancy as a prototype for later melancholia. In the last few months Mrs Klein has skilfully conducted the psycho-analysis of a three-year-old with good therapeutic results. This child presented a true picture of the basic depression that I postulated in close combination with oral erotism. The case offers amazing insight into the infantile instinctual life.

I am pleased to see that my assumptions about the two stages in the anal-sadistic phase are confirmed by new material. I had a remarkable experience with one of my melancholics who is still in treatment with me. On my return from holiday, I found him at the beginning of a new depression following a disappointment connected with his fiancée. The depression had not set in with the same intensity as on previous occasions, but the rejection of the love-object was visible in its characteristic form. Quick intervention resulted in the melancholia changing within a fortnight, and more clearly on each subsequent day, into an obsessional neurosis with the main obsessional idea of strangling the mother (fiancée). In contrast to previous times, no cannibalistic-oral sadism, but manual sadism. The patient has already resumed work and my impression is that it has been possible to divert a melancholia *in statu nascendi* into a relatively more favourable form of illness.

May I go on talking about my work? What I said in Lavarone about the stages of object-love, and particularly about partial incorporation, is being very nicely confirmed at present. I had assumed that in paranoid and related psychoses regression to this phase could be demonstrated. The analysis of a psychosis which was presented at our first meeting supplied excellent confirmatory material. The patient had, among other delusional ideas, the idea that a monkey was inside her. This monkey could be shown with absolute clarity to be her father's penis.

This is all for today.

5. Karl Abraham, 'A Short Study of the Development of the Libido, viewed in the Light of Mental Disorders', *Selected Papers on Psycho-Analysis*, London, 1927.

Abraham to Freud, December 3, 1924:

I have another theoretical question but there is no urgency for a reply and you should not write or dictate a letter for this purpose alone. The question concerns a point in the theory of sexuality. Your concept of a change of erotogenic zones in the woman at puberty has always proved correct in practice. I have recently wondered whether in early infancy there may be an early vaginal awakening of the female libido, which is destined to be repressed and which is subsequently followed by clitoral primacy as the expression of the phallic phase. A number of observations seem to bear this out. If my assumption is correct it would have one advantage for us: we would be better able to understand the female Oedipus complex as the result of an early vaginal reaction to the father's penis (possibly in the form of spontaneous contractions) and the change of the erotogenic zone in puberty would then be a resumption of the original position. One could justifiably follow up this idea some time, since it is based on a number of observations. It could be fitted into our present theory which it does not contradict in any way and to which it might make a small addition. If it seems worth your while, I could report some of my observations which gave me the idea. It has not yet been clarified and the relationship to the phallic phase in particular is so far unclear.

Freud to Abraham, December 12, 1924:

Finally, your latest theme, the assumed vaginal share in the early infantile flourishing of the libido, interests me greatly. I do not know anything about it. As I gladly admit, the female side of the problem is extraordinarily obscure to me. If your ideas and observations on the subject already permit communication, I should very much like to hear about them, but I can wait. According to my preconceived ideas on the subject, the vaginal share would tend to be expressed anally. The vagina, as we know, is a later acquisition by separation from the cloaca.

Abraham to Freud, December 26, 1924:

The suggestions about the female erotogenic zones that I made in my last letter are far from ready to be incorporated into our theory of sexuality as it stands. In recent months I have felt that some of our theories about the erotogenic zones appeared incomplete. I have for a long time questioned whether the displacement from the clitoris to the vagina could have occurred in an earlier version though in an inverse direction. We have had to convince ourselves in so many other contexts that the psycho-sexual processes of puberty are repetitions. This assumed sexual stage would have to have as a sexual aim the reception of the penis. The opening intended for this seems to me, too, to have cloacal characteristics; that is to say, one has to assume vaginal sensations are conducted from the anal zone and that pleasurable contractions of the vagina must somehow be linked with contractions of the anal sphincter. The ease with which little girls can be seduced to coitus-like actions, as well as the tendency to vaginal masturbation and, in particular, the introduction of foreign bodies, must all rest on such processes. Two neurotic symptoms have forced me to assume something which we could call an early vaginal-anal stage: frigidity and *vaginismus*. In the light of all my psychoanalytic experience, I cannot believe that frigidity is merely based on the failure of the libido to pass from the clitoris to the vagina. There must be a prohibition which has an immediate and local basis; this is even more valid for *vaginismus*. Why should the vagina react so negatively to the first attempts at coitus unless something positive has preceded this? Similarly, hysterical vomiting is preceded by a positive and pleasurable experience in early infancy.

As I mentioned last time, such an assumption would also throw light on the obscure origin of the female Oedipus complex.

Freud to Abraham, December 29, 1924:

As for the two scientific questions mentioned in your letter, my attitude is different in each. In the first, the question of the female leading zone, I am eager to learn, look forward to your novelties in the matter, and have no preconceived ideas.

Some Psychical Consequences of the Anatomical Distinction Between the Sexes

In this 1925 essay Freud finally acknowledges that his view of female infantile psychology has been—to use Ernest Jones's term—"phallocentric," that is, based on the model of the male child. He sets out to correct this situation by admitting that when he treated women who were strongly attached to their fathers the male model seemed appropriate: girls, like boys, were chiefly and decisively attached to the opposite-sex parent. But this analogy obscured the "prehistory" of the Oedipus complex in girls, the period—often quite long, and always very intense—of their mother-love.

After he has recapitulated the main lines of the male child's development—relying on the formulations of "The Dissolution of the Oedipus Complex" (1924)—Freud turns his attention first to the mother-daughter bond in the pre-Oedipal period and then to how this bond gives way—more or less—to father-love. Penis envy, always an important element of Freud's theory of female development, carries the burden of explanation as Freud considers why and how girls turn toward their fathers. His discussion culminates in a contrast: the dissolution of the Oedipus complex in boys was equivalent to the formation, by means of identifications, of a severe superego; in girls "the motive for the dissolution of the Oedipus complex is lacking" because they do not fear castration. The female superego is, thus less rigid and stringent. Considering all that Freud had said in The Ego and the Id and "The Economic Problem of Masochism" about how disruptive to psychic harmony a severe or sadistic superego can be, one might have thought that women should be counted fortunate (unless their freedom meant that they received their punishment anyway, as masochists with oversevere egos; see p. 291 above). But on

the final page of this essay Freud comes to the opposite conclusion, and
seems to fault women for their flexible superegos (see also p. 314 below).

Among Freud's feminist critics, most have objected to his general—
overgeneral—scheme of differentiation, with its pejorative connotations.
But recently there have emerged critics who accept the differentiation
he makes between masculine and feminine superego development but
insist that the feminine conscience and sense of justice are not less but
simply different, speaking "in a different voice" (to use psychologist Carol
Gilligan's phrase).

With this essay, Freud began to revise his ideas about female psy-
chology, but it is important to note that he focused his attention only
on "object-relations," that is the girl's love of her mother, newly em-
phasized, and then her turn toward her father. He did not feel it necessary
to reconsider the whole of his theory of stages— oral, anal, phallic, and
genital—or any events of puberty or adolescence (where he located the
shift from clitoris to vagina as leading erotogenic zone) or the theory of
bisexuality as it applied to females. Because Freud placed so much stress
on penis envy as he revised his theory, his critics tended to focus on that
topic—and the full range of stages and issues in female development was
obscured.

~~~~~

In my own writings and in those of my followers more and more
stress is laid on the necessity that the analyses of neurotics shall
deal thoroughly with the remotest period of their childhood, the
time of the early efflorescence of sexual life. It is only by examining
the first manifestations of the patient's innate instinctual constitution and the effects of his earliest experiences that we can accurately gauge the motive forces that have led to his neurosis and
can be secure against the errors into which we might be tempted
by the degree to which things have become remodelled and overlaid in adult life. This requirement is not only of theoretical but
also of practical importance, for it distinguishes our efforts from
the work of those physicians whose interests are focused exclusively
on therapeutic results and who employ analytic methods, but only
up to a certain point. An analysis of early childhood such as we
are considering is tedious and laborious and makes demands both
upon the physician and upon the patient which cannot always be
met. Moreover, it leads us into dark regions where there are as
yet no signposts. Indeed, analysts may feel reassured, I think, that

there is no risk of their work becoming mechanical, and so of losing its interest, during the next few decades.

In the following pages I bring forward some findings of analytic research which would be of great importance if they could be proved to apply universally. Why do I not postpone publication of them until further experience has given me the necessary proof, if such proof is obtainable? Because the conditions under which I work have undergone a change, with implications which I cannot disguise. Formerly, I was not one of those who are unable to hold back what seems to be a new discovery until it has been either confirmed or corrected. My *Interpretation of Dreams* (1900) and my 'Fragment of an Analysis of a Case of Hysteria' (1905) (the case of Dora) were suppressed by me—if not for the nine years enjoined by Horace—at all events for four or five years before I allowed them to be published. But in those days I had unlimited time before me—'oceans of time' as an amiable author puts it— and material poured in upon me in such quantities that fresh experiences were hardly to be escaped. Moreover, I was the only worker in a new field, so that my reticence involved no danger to myself and no loss to others.

But now everything has changed. The time before me is limited. The whole of it is no longer spent in working, so that my opportunities for making fresh observations are not so numerous. If I think I see something new, I am uncertain whether I can wait for it to be confirmed. And further, everything that is to be seen upon the surface has already been exhausted; what remains has to be slowly and laboriously dragged up from the depths. Finally, I am no longer alone. An eager crowd of fellow-workers is ready to make use of what is unfinished or doubtful, and I can leave to them that part of the work which I should otherwise have done myself. On this occasion, therefore, I feel justified in publishing something which stands in urgent need of confirmation before its value or lack of value can be decided.

In examining the earliest mental shapes assumed by the sexual life of children we have been in the habit of taking as the subject of our investigations the male child, the little boy. With little girls, so we have supposed, things must be similar, though in some way or other they must nevertheless be different. The point in development at which this difference lay could not be clearly determined.

In boys the situation of the Oedipus complex is the first stage that can be recognized with certainty. It is easy to understand, because at that stage a child retains the same object which he previously cathected with his libido—not as yet a genital one—during the preceding period while he was being suckled and nursed. The fact, too, that in this situation he regards his father as a disturbing rival and would like to get rid of him and take his place is a straightforward consequence of the actual state of affairs. I have shown elsewhere how the Oedipus attitude in little boys belongs to the phallic phase, and how its destruction is brought about by the fear of castration—that is, by narcissistic interest in their genitals. The matter is made more difficult to grasp by the complicating circumstance that even in boys the Oedipus complex has a double orientation, active and passive, in accordance with their bisexual constitution; a boy also wants to take his *mother's* place as the love-object of his *father*—a fact which we describe as the feminine attitude.

As regards the prehistory of the Oedipus complex in boys we are far from complete clarity. We know that that period includes an identification of an affectionate sort with the boy's father, an identification which is still free from any sense of rivalry in regard to his mother. Another element of that stage is invariably, I believe, a masturbatory activity in connection with the genitals, the masturbation of early childhood, the more or less violent suppression of which by those in charge of the child sets the castration complex in action. It is to be assumed that this masturbation is attached to the Oedipus complex and serves as a discharge for the sexual excitation belonging to it. It is, however, uncertain whether the masturbation has this character from the first, or whether on the contrary it makes its first appearance spontaneously as an activity of a bodily organ and is only brought into relation with the Oedipus complex at some later date; this second possibility is by far the more probable. Another doubtful question is the part played by bed-wetting and by the breaking of that habit through the intervention of training measures. We are inclined to make the simple connection that continued bed-wetting is a result of masturbation and that its suppression is regarded by boys as an inhibition of their genital activity—that is, as having the meaning of a threat of castration; but whether we are always right in supposing this remains to be seen. Finally, analysis shows us in a shadowy way how the fact of a child at a very early age listening to his parents copulating may set up his first sexual excitation, and how that event may, owing to its after-effects, act as a starting-point for the child's whole sexual development. Masturbation, as well as the two attitudes in the Oedipus complex, later on become attached to this early experience, the child having subsequently interpreted its meaning. It is impossible, however, to suppose that these observations of coitus are of universal occurrence, so that at this point we are faced with the problem of 'primal phantasies'. Thus the prehistory of the Oedipus complex, even in boys, raises all of these questions for sifting and explanation; and there is the further problem of whether we are to suppose that the process invariably follows the same course, or whether a great variety of different preliminary stages may not converge upon the same terminal situation.

In little girls the Oedipus complex raises one problem more than in boys. In both cases the mother is the original object; and there is no cause for surprise that boys retain that object in the Oedipus complex. But how does it happen that girls abandon it and instead take their father as an object? In pursuing this question I have been able to reach some conclusions which may throw light precisely on the prehistory of the Oedipus relation in girls.

Every analyst has come across certain women who cling with especial intensity and tenacity to the bond with their father and to the wish in which it culminates of having a child by him. We have good reason to suppose that the same wishful phantasy was also the motive force of their infantile masturbation, and it is easy to form an impression that at this point we have been brought up against an elementary and unanalysable fact of infantile sexual life. But a through analysis of these very cases brings something different to light—namely, that here the Oedipus complex has a long prehistory and is in some respects a secondary formation.

The old paediatrician Lindner once remarked that a child discovers the genital zones (the penis or the clitoris) as a source of pleasure while indulging in sensual sucking (thumb-sucking). I shall leave it an open question whether it is really true that the child takes the newly found source of pleasure in exchange for the recent loss of the mother's nipple—a possibility to which later phantasies (fellatio) seem to point. Be that as it may, the genital zone is discovered at some time or other, and there seems no justification for attributing any psychical content to the first activities in connection with it. But the first step in the phallic phase which begins in this way is not the linking-up of the masturbation with the object-cathexes of the Oedipus complex, but a momentous discovery which little girls are destined to make. They notice the penis of a brother or playmate, strikingly visible and of large proportions, at once recognize it as the superior counterpart of their own small and inconspicuous organ, and from that time forward fall a victim to envy for the penis.

There is an interesting contrast between the behaviour of the two sexes. In the analogous situation, when a little boy first catches sight of a girl's genital region, he begins by showing irresolution and lack of interest; he sees nothing or disavows what he has seen, he softens it down or looks about for expedients for bringing it into line with his expectations. It is not until later, when some threat of castration has obtained a hold upon him, that the observation becomes important to him: if he then recollects or repeats it, it arouses a terrible storm of emotion in him and forces him to believe in the reality of the threat which he has hitherto laughed at. This combination of circumstances leads to two reactions, which may become fixed and will in that case, whether separately or together or in conjunction with other factors, permanently determine the boy's relations to women: horror of the mutilated creature or triumphant contempt for her. These developments, however, belong to the future, though not to a very remote one.

A little girl behaves differently. She makes her judgement and her decision in a flash. She has seen it and knows that she is without it and wants to have it.[1]

Here what has been named the masculinity complex of women branches off. It may put great difficulties in the way of their regular development towards femininity, if it cannot be got over soon enough. The hope of some day obtaining a penis in spite of everything and so of becoming like a man may persist to an

---

1. This is an opportunity for correcting a statement which I made many years ago. I believed that the sexual interest of children, unlike that of pubescents, was aroused, not by the difference between the sexes, but by the problem of where babies come from. We now see that, at all events with girls, this is certainly not the case. With boys it may no doubt happen sometimes one way and sometimes the other; or with both sexes chance experiences may determine the event.

incredibly late age and may become a motive for strange and otherwise unaccountable actions. Or again, a process may set in which I should like to call a 'disavowal', a process which in the mental life of children seems neither uncommon nor very dangerous but which in an adult would mean the beginning of a psychosis. Thus a girl may refuse to accept the fact of being castrated, may harden herself in the conviction that she *does* possess a penis, and may subsequently be compelled to behave as though she were a man.

The psychical consequences of envy for the penis, in so far as it does not become absorbed in the reaction-formation of the masculinity complex, are various and far-reaching. After a woman has become aware of the wound to her narcissism, she develops, like a scar, a sense of inferiority. When she has passed beyond her first attempt at explaining her lack of a penis as being a punishment personal to herself and has realized that that sexual character is a universal one, she begins to share the contempt felt by men for a sex which is the lesser in so important a respect, and, at least in holding that opinion, insists on being like a man.[2]

Even after penis-envy has abandoned its true object, it continues to exist: by an easy displacement it persists in the character-trait of *jealousy*. Of course, jealousy is not limited to one sex and has a wider foundation than this, but I am of opinion that it plays a far larger part in the mental life of women than of men and that that is because it is enormously reinforced from the direction of displaced penis-envy. While I was still unaware of this source of jealousy and was considering the phantasy 'a child is being

---

2. In my first critical account of the 'History of the Psycho-Analytic Movement' (1914) [14:54–5], I recognized that this fact represents the core of truth contained in Adler's theory. That theory has no hesitation in explaining the whole world by this single point ('organ-inferiority', the 'masculine protest', 'breaking away from the feminine line') and prides itself upon having in this way robbed sexuality of its importance and put the desire for power in its place! Thus the only organ which could claim to be called 'inferior' without any ambiguity would be the clitoris. On the other hand, one hears of analysts who boast that, though they have worked for dozens of years, they have never found a sign of the existence of a castration complex. We must bow our heads in recognition of the greatness of this achievement, even though it is only a negative one, a piece of virtuosity in the art of overlooking and mistaking. The two theories form an interesting pair of opposites: in the latter not a trace of a castration complex, in the former nothing else than its consequences. {On Adler, see pp. 237–40 above.}

beaten', which occurs so commonly in girls, I constructed a first phase for it in which its meaning was that another child, a rival of whom the subject was jealous, was to be beaten.[3] This phantasy seems to be a relic of the phallic period in girls. The peculiar rigidity which struck me so much in the monotonous formula 'a child is being beaten' can probably be interpreted in a special way. The child which is being beaten (or caressed) may ultimately be nothing more nor less than the clitoris itself, so that at its very lowest level the statement will contain a confession of mastur-bation, which has remained attached to the content of the formula from its beginning in the phallic phase till later life.

A third consequence of penis-envy seems to be a loosening of the girl's relation with her mother as a love-object. The situation as a whole is not very clear, but it can be seen that in the end the girl's mother, who sent her into the world so insufficiently equipped, is almost always held responsible for her lack of a penis. The way in which this comes about historically is often that soon after the girl has discovered that her genitals are unsatisfactory she begins to show jealousy of another child on the ground that her mother is fonder of it than of her, which serves as a reason for her giving up her affectionate relation to her mother. It will fit in with this if the child which has been preferred by her mother is made into the first object of the beating-phantasy which ends in masturbation.

There is yet another surprising effect of penis-envy, or of the discovery of the inferiority of the clitoris, which is undoubtedly the most important of all. In the past I had often formed an impression that in general women tolerate masturbation worse than men, that they more frequently fight against it and that they are unable to make use of it in circumstances in which a man would seize upon it as a way of escape without any hesitation. Experience would no doubt elicit innumerable exceptions to this statement, if we attempted to turn it into a rule. The reactions of human individuals of both sexes are of course made up of masculine and feminine traits. But it appeared to me nevertheless as though masturbation were further removed from the nature of women than of men, and the solution of the problem could be assisted by the reflection that masturbation, at all events of the

---

3. ' "A Child is Being Beaten," ' {p. 224 above}.

clitoris, is a masculine activity and that the elimination of clitoridal sexuality is a necessary precondition for the development
of femininity. Analyses of the remote phallic period have now
taught me that in girls, soon after the first signs of penis-envy, an
intense current of feeling against masturbation makes its appearance, which cannot be attributed exclusively to the educational
influence of those in charge of the child. This impulse is clearly
a forerunner of the wave of repression which at puberty will do
away with a large amount of the girl's masculine sexuality in order
to make room for the development of her femininity. It may
happen that this first opposition to auto-erotic activity fails to attain
its end. And this was in fact the case in the instances which I
analysed. The conflict continued, and both then and later the
girl did everything she could to free herself from the compulsion
to masturbate. Many of the later manifestations of sexual life in
women remain unintelligible unless this powerful motive is
recognized.

I cannot explain the opposition which is raised in this way by
little girls to phallic masturbation except by supposing that there
is some concurrent factor which turns her violently against that
pleasurable activity. Such a factor lies close at hand. It cannot
be anything else than her narcissistic sense of humiliation which
is bound up with penis-envy, the reminder that after all this is a
point on which she cannot compete with boys and that it would
therefore be best for her to give up the idea of doing so. Thus the
little girl's recognition of the anatomical distinction between the
sexes forces her away from masculinity and masculine masturbation on to new lines while lead to the development of femininity.

So far there has been no question of the Oedipus complex, nor
has it up to this point played any part. But now the girl's libido
slips into a new position along the line—there is no other way of
putting it—of the equation 'penis-child'. She gives up her wish
for a penis and puts in place of it a wish for a child: and *with
that purpose in view* she takes her father as a love-object. Here
mother becomes the object of her jealousy. The girl has turned
into a little woman. If I am to credit a single analytic instance,
this new situation can give rise to physical sensations which would
have to be regarded as a premature awakening of the female genital
apparatus. When the girl's attachment to her father comes to grief
later on and has to be abandoned, it may give place to an iden-

tification with him and the girl may thus return to her masculinity complex and perhaps remain fixated in it.

I have now said the essence of what I had to say: I will stop, therefore, and cast an eye over our findings. We have gained some insight into the prehistory of the Oedipus complex in girls. The corresponding period in boys is more or less unknown. In girls the Oedipus complex is a secondary formation. The operations of the castration complex precede it and prepare for it. As regards the relation between the Oedipus and castration complexes there is a fundamental contrast between the two sexes. *Whereas in boys the Oedipus complex is destroyed by the castration complex, in girls it is made possible and led up to by the castration complex.* This contradiction is cleared up if we reflect that the castration complex always operates in the sense implied in its subject-matter: it inhibits and limits masculinity and encourages femininity. The difference between the sexual development of males and females at the stage we have been considering is an intelligible consequence of the anatomical distinction between their genitals and of the psychical situation involved in it; it corresponds to the difference between a castration that has been carried out and one that has merely been threatened. In their essentials, therefore, our findings are self-evident and it should have been possible to foresee them.

The Oedipus complex, however, is such an important thing that the manner in which one enters and leaves it cannot be without its effects. In boys * * * the complex is not simply repressed, it is literally smashed to pieces by the shock of threatened castration. Its libidinal cathexes are abandoned, desexualized and in part sublimated; its objects are incorporated into the ego, where they form the nucleus of the super-ego and give that new structure its characteristic qualities. In normal, or, it is better to say, in ideal cases, the Oedipus complex exists no longer, even in the unconscious; the super-ego has become its heir. Since the penis (to follow Ferenczi) owes its extraordinarily high narcissistic cathexis to its organic significance for the propagation of the species, the catastrophe to the Oedipus complex (the abandonment of incest and the institution of conscience and morality) may be regarded as a victory of the race over the individual. This is an interesting point of view when one considers that neurosis is based upon a struggle of the ego against the demands of the sexual function. But to leave the standpoint of individual psychology is not of any immediate help in clarifying this complicated situation.

In girls the motive for the demolition of the Oedipus complex is lacking. Castration has already had its effect, which was to force the child into the situation of the Oedipus complex. Thus the Oedipus complex escapes the fate which it meets with in boys: it may be slowly abandoned or dealt with by repression, or its effects may persist far into women's normal mental life. I cannot evade the notion (though I hesitate to give it expression) that for women the level of what is ethically normal is different from what it is in men. Their super-ego is never so inexorable, so impersonal, so independent of its emotional origins as we require it to be in men. Character-traits which critics of every epoch have brought up against women—that they show less sense of justice than men, that they are less ready to submit to the great exigencies of life, that they are more often influenced in their judgements by feelings of affection or hostility—all these would be amply accounted for by the modification in the formation of their super-ego which we have inferred above. We must not allow ourselves to be deflected from such conclusions by the denials of the femininsts, who are anxious to force us to regard the two sexes as completely equal in position and worth; but we shall, of course, willingly agree that the majority of men are also far behind the masculine ideal and that all human individuals, as a result of their bisexual disposition and of cross-inheritance, combine in themselves both masculine and feminine characteristics, so that pure masculinity and femininity remain theoretical constructions of uncertain content.

I am inclined to set some value on the considerations I have brought forward upon the psychical consequences of the anatomical distinction between the sexes. I am aware, however, that this opinion can only be maintained if my findings, which are based on a handful of cases, turn out to have general validity and to be typical. If not, they would remain no more than a contribution to our knowledge of the different paths along which sexual life develops.

In the valuable and comprehensive studies on the masculinity and castration complexes in women by Abraham (1921), Horney (1923) and Helen Deutsch (1925) there is much that touches closely on what I have written but nothing that coincides with it completely, so that here again I feel justified in publishing this paper.

Libidinal Types

T his brief reflection, written in 1931, shows Freud trying to expand
and systematize his work on character types. We have seen Freud
arguing that adult sexuality presupposes a delimitation of infantile bisexuality into two extreme types—masculine and feminine—and many
intermediary, mixed ones. Here we see him suggesting that adult character presupposes delimitation of the child psyche in which id, ego, and
superego struggle for power into one in which one of the three structures
has gained ascendency. Id-ruled people (erotics), ego-ruled people (narcissists), and super-ego-ruled people (obsessionals), as well as mixtures
of these types, each have strengths and weaknesses in love and work.

Two relatively pure libidinal types, Freud argues, make great contributions to civilization: the obsessionals, who are conservative, and the
narcissists, who are revolutionary—like Freud himself. No contrast is
drawn in this essay between male types and female types, but it is obvious
that the narcissistic type described here is not the female narcissist we
met in "On Narcissism" (above, p. 192), but rather her lover, the male
narcissist who projects his self-love outward, who loves in an idealizing,
overvaluing way someone who supports his self-love. Similarly, given
Freud's newly articulated concept of the superego and the conclusion of
"Some Psychical Consequences of the Anatomical Distinction between
the Sexes," it seems reasonable to say that the narcissistic type described
here, who experiences little conflict between ego and superego after the
superego is formed (p. 318 below), must be male. From a female with
no such strict superego to be at peace with, no leadership and cultural
achievement is to be expected.

But this pejorative-sounding conclusion would only hold, in Freud's
scheme, for women at the purely feminine end of the bisexuality scale.
In the two essays that follow this one, Freud did, in fact, argue that

*cultural achievement among women would come from those with a
pronounced "masculinity complex" (and, one might guess, a strong
superego—but Freud never speculates about how this might come about
if girls do not experience the "dissolution of the Oedipus complex" as
boys do). Freud's claim meant, in other words, that bisexuality in women
supports cultural creativity, and it complements his argument that homosexuality or bisexuality is especially common among culturally creative
men (see 11:69 ff.).*

*During the early 1930s, when Freud was often speculating about the
conditions for cultural achievement and about the conditions that destroy
civilizations (he and Albert Einstein exchanged letters in 1932 on the
question "Why War?"), he stressed again and again how discontented
humans are with their sexuality. Cultural achievement is the special
province not of erotics, but of obsessionals and narcissists. But, further,
such achievement is generally linked to the fate of human sexuality,
which "give the impression of being in a process of involution as function,
just as our hair and teeth are as organs," "which denies us full satisfaction
and urges us along other paths," as Freud noted in* Civilization and Its
Discontents. *A long footnote from this text (21:105–106) is cited below
after "Libidinal Types": it links Freud's melancholy thread of speculation
about the troubled human sexual function to his old theme of bisexuality.*

Observation teaches us that individual human beings realize the
general picture of humanity in an almost infinite variety of ways.
If we yield to the legitimate need to distinguish particular types
in this multiplicity, we shall at the start have the choice as to
what characteristics and what points of view we shall take as the
basis of our differentiation. For that purpose physical qualities
will doubtless serve no less well than mental ones; the most valuable distinctions will be those which promise to present a regular
combination of physical and mental characteristics.

It is doubtful whether we are as yet in a position to discover
types to fulfil this requirement—as we shall no doubt be able to
do later, on some basis of which we are still ignorant. If we confine
our effort to setting up purely psychological types, the libidinal
situation will have a first claim to serve as a basis for our classification. It may fairly be demanded that this classification should
not merely be deduced from our knowledge or our hypotheses
about the libido, but that it should be easily confirmed in actual
experience and that it should contribute to the clarification of the

mass of our observations and help us to grasp them. It may at once be admitted that these libidinal types need not be the only possible ones even in the psychical field, and that, if we proceeded from other qualities, we might perhaps establish a whole set of other psychological types. But it must be required of all such types that they shall not coincide with clinical pictures. On the contrary, they must comprehend all the variations which according to our practical judgement fall within the limits of the normal. In their extreme developments, however, they may well approximate to clinical pictures and in that way help to bridge the gulf that is supposed to lie between the normal and the pathological.

According, then, as the libido is predominantly allocated to the provinces of the mental apparatus, we can distinguish three main libidinal types. To give names to these types is not particularly easy; following the lines of our depth-psychology, I should like to call them the *erotic*, the *narcissistic* and the *obsessional* types.[1]

The *erotic* type is easily characterized. Erotics are those whose main interest—the relatively largest part of whose libido—is turned towards love. Loving, but above all being loved, is the most important thing for them. They are dominated by the fear of loss of love and are therefore especially dependent on others who may withhold their love from them. Even in its pure form this type is very common one. Variants of it occur according as it is blended with another type and in proportion to the amount of aggressiveness present in it. From the social and cultural standpoint this type represents the elementary instinctual demands of the id, to which the other psychical agencies have become compliant.

The second type is what I have termed the *obsessional* type—a name which may at first seem strange. It is distinguished by the predominance of the super-ego, which is separated from the ego under great tension. People of this type are dominated by fear of their conscience instead of fear of losing love. They exhibit, as it were, an internal instead of an external dependence. They develop a high degree of self-reliance; and, from the social standpoint, they are true, pre-eminently conservative vehicles of civilization.

The third type, justly called the *narcissistic* type, is mainly to

---

1. [Freud had approached this classification of types in Chapter II of *Civilization and its Discontents* (1930).]

be described in negative terms. There is no tension between ego and super-ego (indeed, on the strength of this type one would scarcely have arrived at the hypothesis of a super-ego), and there is no preponderance of erotic needs. The subject's main interest is directed to self-preservation; he is independent and not open to intimidation. His ego has a large amount of aggressiveness at its disposal, which also manifests itself in readiness for activity. In his erotic life loving is preferred above being love. People belonging to this type impress others as being 'personalities'; they are especially suited to act as a support for others, to take on the role of leaders and to give a fresh stimulus to cultural development or to damage the established state of affairs.

These pure types will hardly escape the suspicion of having been deduced from the theory of the libido. But we feel ourselves on the firm ground of experience when we turn to the mixed types, which are to be observed so much more frequently than the unmixed ones. These new types—the *erotic-obsessional*, the *erotic-narcissistic* and the *narcissistic-obsessional*—seem in fact to afford a good classification of the individual psychical structures which we have come to know through analysis. If we study these mixed types we find in them pictures of characters with which we have long been familiar. In the *erotic-obsessional* type it appears that the preponderance of instinctual life is restricted by the influence of the super-ego. In this type, dependence at once on contemporary human objects and on the residues of parents, educators and exemplars, is carried to its highest pitch. The *erotic-narcissistic* type is perhaps the one we must regard as the commonest of all. It unites opposites, which are able to moderate one another in it. One may learn from this type, as compared with the two other erotic ones, that aggressiveness and activity go along with a predominance of narcissism. Finally, the *narcissistic-obsessional* type produces the variation which is most valuable from a cultural standpoint; for it adds to independence of the external world and a regard for the demands of conscience a capacity for vigorous action, and it strengthens the ego against the super-ego.

One might think one was making a jest if one asked why no mention has been made here of another mixed type which is theoretically possible—namely, the *erotic-obsessional-narcissistic* type. But the answer to this jest is serious. Such a type would no longer be a type at all: it would be the absolute norm, the ideal harmony. We thus realize that the phenomenon of types arises precisely from the fact that, of the three main ways of employing the libido in the economy of the mind, one or two have been favoured at the expense of the others.

The question may also be raised of what the relation is of these libidinal types to pathology—whether some of them have a special disposition to pass over into neurosis, and if so, which types lead to which forms of neurosis. The answer is that the setting-up of these libidinal types throws no new light on the genesis of the neuroses. Experience shows that all these types can exist without any neurosis. The pure types, marked by the undisputed preponderance of a single mental agency, seem to have a better chance of manifesting themselves as pure characterological pictures, while we might expect that mixed types would provide a more favourable soil for conditions leading to a neurosis. But I think we should not make up our minds on these matters till they have been submitted to a careful and specially directed examination.

It seems easy to infer that when people of the erotic type fall ill they will develop hysteria, just as those of the obsessional type will develop obsessional neurosis; but these inferences, too, share the uncertainty which I have just stressed. People of the narcissistic type who are exposed to a frustration from the external world, though otherwise independent, are peculiarly disposed to psychosis; and they also present essential preconditions for criminality.

It is a familiar fact that the aetiological preconditions of neurosis are not yet known with certainty. The precipitating causes of it are frustrations and internal conflicts: conflicts between the three major psychical agencies, conflicts arising within the libidinal economy in consequence of our bisexual disposition and conflicts between the erotic and the aggressive instinctual components. It is the endeavour of the psychology of the neuroses to discover what makes these processes, which belong to the normal course of mental life, become pathogenic.

The footnote below from Civilization and Its Discontents *(1930) links Freud's old theory of bisexuality to his current speculations on the "involution" over time of the human sexual function.*

* * * The view expressed above is supported by the following considerations. Man is an animal organism with (like others) an unmistakably bisexual disposition.

The individual corresponds to a fusion of two symmetrical halves, of which, according to some investigators, one is purely male and the other female. It is equally possible that each half was originally hermaphrodite. Sex is a biological fact which, although it is of extraordinary importance in mental life, is hard to grasp psychologically. We are accustomed to say that every human being displays both male and female instinctual impulses, needs and attributes; but though anatomy, it is true, can point out the characteristic of maleness and femaleness, psychology cannot. For psychology the contrast between the sexes fades away into one between activity and passivity, in which we far too readily identify activity with maleness and passivity with femaleness, a view which is by no means universally confirmed in the animal kingdom. The theory of bisexuality is still surrounded by many obscurities and we cannot but feel it as a serious impediment in psychoanalysis that it has not yet found any link with the theory of the instincts. However this may be, if we assume it as a fact that each individual seeks to satisfy both male and female wishes in his sexual life, we are prepared for the possibility that those [two sets of] demands are not fulfilled by the same object, and that they interfere with each other unless they can be kept apart and each impulse guided into a particular channel that is suited to it. Another difficulty arises from the circumstance that there is so often associated with the erotic relationship, over and above its own sadistic components, a quota of plain inclination to aggression. The love-object will not always view these complications with the degree of understanding and tolerance shown by the peasant woman who complained that her husband did not love her any more, since he had not beaten her for a week.

The conjecture which goes deepest, however, is the one which takes its start from what I have said * * * to the effect that, with the assumption of an erect posture by man and with the depreciation of his sense of smell, it was not only his anal erotism which threatened to fall a victim to organic repression, but the whole of his sexuality; so that since this, the sexual function has been accompanied by a repugnance which cannot further be accounted for, and which prevents its complete satisfaction and forces it away from the sexual aim into sublimations and libidinal displacements. I know that Bleuler (1913) once pointed to the existence of a primary repelling attitude like this towards sexual life. All neurotics, and many others besides, take exception to the fact that 'inter urinas et faeces nascimur [we are born between urine and faeces].' The genitals, too, give rise to strong sensations of smell which many people cannot tolerate and which spoil sexual intercourse for them. Thus we should find that the deepest root of the sexual repression which advances along with civilization is the organic defence of the new form of life achieved with man's erect gait against his earlier animal existence. This result of scientific research coincides in a remarkable way with commonplace prejudices that have often made themselves heard. Nevertheless, these things are at present no more than unconfirmed possibilities which have not been substantiated by science. Nor should we forget that, in spite of the undeniable depreciation of olfactory stimuli, there exist even in Europe peoples among whom the strong genital odours which are so repellent to us are highly prized as sexual stimulants and who refuse to give them up. * * *

Female Sexuality

Afber "Some Psychical Consequences of the Anatomical Distinction between the Sexes" was published in 1925, discussions of female psychology went on in all the European centers of psychoanalysis. Freud was moved to take these discussions into account in his 1931 essay "Female Sexuality." The essay also contains Freud's review of his own early work Three Essays on the Theory of Sexuality. He wanted to consider what his new view of the little girl's bond with her mother implied for the picture of female development in his 1905 work, to which he had not added any text or footnotes since 1924.

When he looked back to the Three Essays, Freud stressed again his basic conclusions about female bisexuality: the girl has two sexual organs, her "masculine" clitoris and her "feminine" vagina, and two phases in her sexual life. He looks for ways to coordinate these familiar conclusions with his current stress on her two childhood love-objects—first her mother and then her father. Freud's established terminology of "active" and "passive" libidinal aims is coordinated with the more recent distinction between two phases of phallic sexuality articulated in The Ego and the Id: the girl has an active negative (related to the mother) and a passive positive (to the father) Oedipal configuration. Freud himself seems startled by how much "masculine" and "active" love for the mother he is willing to attribute to the little girl in her negative Oedipal mode. And it is obvious from his review of the recent psychoanalytic literature that his critics—particularly Karen Horney and Ernest Jones—were even more skeptical.

Freud's closing review of the recent literature is very unusual. After 1925, when his younger Viennese colleague Otto Rank left the psychoanalytic fold, most of Freud's exchanges with his critics took place in the privacy of his correspondences, rather than in publications. Ernest

Jones, who supported the work of both Karen Horney and Melanie Klein, received letters from Freud about the dissents of both—Horney's on the topic of penis envy and Klein's on the timing and consequences of the Oedipus complex in females and males. These letters are currently unavailable, but they are being prepared for a publication of the complete Freud/Jones correspondence. I have appended to the present essay a letter on female sexuality that Freud wrote in 1935 to one of Horney's colleagues in Berlin, Carl Mueller-Braunschweig.

The contentious, abrupt, and sometimes annoyed tone of "Female Sexuality" is related to the fact that Freud felt divisions among his followers outside of Vienna growing—precisely over the topic of female sexuality. He stated his position strongly, assuming that the controversy would work itself out after his death, with his influence restricted to the written word. Contemporary readers, even those with knowledge of the essay's polemical context and of the complex theoretical developments that had preceded it, often find it shocking; many feel that it is antifeminist, an assault on visons of equality between women and men—and Freud himself in a footnote to the text made it clear that he anticipated just this response.

I.

During the phase of the normal Oedipus complex we find the child tenderly attached to the parent of the opposite sex, while its relation to the parent of its own sex is predominantly hostile. In the case of a boy there is no difficulty in explaining this. His first love-object was his mother. She remains so; and, with the strengthening of his erotic desires and his deeper insight into the relations between his father and mother, the former is bound to become his rival. With the small girl it is different. Her first object, too, was her mother. How does she find her way to her father? How, when and why does she detach herself from her mother? We have long understood that the development of female sexuality is complicated by the fact that the girl has the task of giving up what was originally her leading genital zone—the clitoris—in favour of a new zone—the vagina. But it now seems to us that there is a second change of the same sort which is no less characteristic and important for the development of the female: the exchange of her original object—her mother—for her father.

The way in which the two tasks are connected with each other is not yet clear to us.

It is well known that there are many women who have a strong attachment to their father; nor need they be in any way neurotic. It is upon such women that I have made the observations which I propose to report here and which have led me to adopt a particular view of female sexuality. I was struck, above all, by two facts. The first was that where the woman's attachment to her father was particularly intense, analysis showed that it had been preceded by a phase of exclusive attachment to her mother which had been equally intense and passionate. Except for the change of her love-object, the second phase had scarcely added any new feature to her erotic life. Her primary relation to her mother had been built up in a very rich and many-sided manner. The second fact taught me that the *duration* of this attachment had also been greatly underestimated. In several cases it lasted until well into the fourth year—in one case into the fifth year—so that it covered by far the longer part of the period of early sexual efflorescence. Indeed, we had to reckon with the possibility that a number of women remain arrested in their original attachment to their mother and never achieve a true change-over towards men. This being so, the pre-Oedipus phase in women gains an importance which we have not attributed to it hitherto.

Since this phase allows room for all the fixations and repressions from which we trace the origin of the neuroses, it would seem as though we must retract the universality of the thesis that the Oedipus complex is the nucleus of the neuroses. But if anyone feels reluctant about making this correction, there is no need for him to do so. On the one hand, we can extend the content of the Oedipus complex to include all the child's relations to both parents; or, on the other, we can take due account of our new findings by saying that the female only reaches the normal positive Oedipus situation after she has surmounted a period before it that is governed by the negative complex.[1] And indeed during that phase a little girl's father is not much else for her than a troublesome rival, although her hostility towards him never reaches the pitch which is characteristic of boys. We have, after all, long

1. [The positive and negative Oedipus complexes were discussed by Freud in Chapter III of *The Ego and the Id* {above, pp. 277–79}.]

given up any expectation of a neat parallelism between male and female sexual development.

Our insight into this early, pre-Oedipus, phase in girls comes to us as a surprise, like the discovery, in another field, of the Minoan-Mycenean civilization behind the civilization of Greece.

Everything in the sphere of this first attachment to the mother seemed to me so difficult to grasp in analysis—so grey with age and shadowy and almost impossible to revivify—that it was as if it had succumbed to an especially inexorable repression. But perhaps I gained this impression because the women who were in analysis with me were able to cling to the very attachment to the father in which they had taken refuge from the early phase that was in question. It does indeed appear that women analysts—as, for instance, Jeanne Lampl-de Groot and Helene Deutsch—have been able to perceive these facts more easily and clearly because they were helped in dealing with those under their treatment by the transference to a suitable mother-substitute. Nor have I succeeded in seeing my way through any case completely, and I shall therefore confine myself to reporting the most general findings and shall give only a few examples of the new ideas which I have arrived at. Among these is a suspicion that this phase of attachment to the mother is especially intimately related to the aetiology of hysteria, which is not surprising when we reflect that both the phase and the neurosis are characteristically feminine, and further, that in this dependence on the mother we have the germ of later paranoia in women.[2] For this germ appears to be the surprising, yet regular, fear of being killed (? devoured) by the mother. It is plausible to assume that this fear corresponds to a hostility which develops in the child towards her mother in consequence of the manifold restrictions imposed by the latter in the course of training and bodily care and that the mechanism of projection is favoured by the early age of the child's psychical organization.[3]

---

2. In the well-known case of delusional jealousy reported by Ruth Mack Brunswick (1928), the direct source of the disorder was the patient's pre-Oedipus fixation (to her sister). [Cf. also Freud's own 'Case of Paranoia Running Contrary to the Psycho-Analytic Theory of the Disease' (1915), {14:261–274.}]
3. [The girl's fear of being killed by her mother is discussed further below on p. 334.]

II.

I began by stating the two facts which have struck me as new: that a woman's strong dependence on her father merely takes over the heritage of an equally strong attachment to her mother, and that this earlier phase has lasted for an unexpectedly long period of time. I shall now go back a little in order to insert these new findings into the picture of female sexual development with which we are familiar. In doing this, a certain amount of repetition will be inevitable. It will help our exposition if, as we go along, we compare the state of things in women with that in men.

First of all, there can be no doubt that the bisexuality, which is present, as we believe, in the innate disposition of human beings, comes to the fore much more clearly in women than in men. A man, after all, has only one leading sexual zone, one sexual organ, whereas a woman has two: the vagina—the female organ proper—and the clitoris, which is analogous to the male organ. We believe we are justified in assuming that for many years the vagina is virtually non-existent and possibly does not produce sensations until puberty. It is true that recently an increasing number of observers report that vaginal impulses are present even in these early years. In women, therefore, the main genital occurrences of childhood must take place in relation to the clitoris. Their sexual life is regularly divided into two phases, of which the first has a masculine character, while only the second is specifically feminine. Thus in female development there is a process of transition from the one phase to the other, to which there is nothing analogous in the male. A further complication arises from the fact that the clitoris, with its virile character, continues to function in later female sexual life in a manner which is very variable and which is certainly not yet satisfactorily understood. We do not, of course, know the biological basis of these peculiarities in women; and still less are we able to assign them any teleological purpose.

Parallel with this first great difference there is the other, concerned with the finding of the object. In the case of a male, his mother becomes his first love-object as a result of her feeding him and looking after him, and she remains so until she is replaced by someone who resembles her or is derived from her. A female's first object, too, must be her mother: the primary conditions for a choice of object are, of course, the same for all children. But at the end of her development, her father—a man—should have become her new love-object. In other words, to the change in her own sex there must correspond a change in the sex of her object. The new problems that now require investigating are in what way this change takes place, how radically or how incompletely it is carried out, and what the different possibilities are which present themselves in the course of this development.

We have already learned, too, that there is yet another difference between the sexes, which relates to the Oedipus complex. We have an impression here that what we have said about the Oedipus complex applies with complete strictness to the male child only and that we are right in rejecting the term 'Electra complex'[4] which seeks to emphasize the analogy between the attitude of the two sexes. It is only in the male child that we find the fateful combination of love for the one parent and simultaneous hatred for the other as a rival. In his case it is the discovery of the possibility of castration, as proved by the sight of the female genitals, which forces on him the transformation of his Oedipus complex, and which leads to the creation of his super-ego and thus initiates all the processes that are designed to make the individuals find a place in the cultural community. After the paternal agency has been internalized and become a super-ego, the next task is to detach the latter from the figures of whom it was originally the psychical representative. In this remarkable course of development it is precisely the boy's narcissistic interest in his genitals—his interest in preserving his penis—which is turned round into a curtailing of his infantile sexuality.

One thing that is left over in men from the influence of the Oedipus complex is a certain amount of disparagement in their attitude towards women, whom they regard as being castrated. In extreme cases this gives rise to an inhibition in their choice of object, and, if it is supported by organic factors, to exclusive homosexuality.

Quite different are the effects of the castration complex in the female. She acknowledges the fact of her castration, and with it, too, the superiority of the male and her own inferiority; but she

4. [See 'The Psychogenesis of a Case of Homosexuality in a Woman' {p. 250}.]

rebels against this unwelcome state of affairs. From this divided
attitude three lines of development open up. The first leads to a
general revulsion from sexuality. The little girl, frightened by the
comparison with boys, grows dissatisfied with her clitoris, and
gives up her phallic activity and with it her sexuality in general
as well as a good part of her masculinity in other fields. The
second line leads her to cling with defiant self-assertiveness to her
threatened masculinity. To an incredibly late age she clings to
the hope of getting a penis some time. That hope becomes her
life's aim; and the phantasy of being a man in spite of everything
often persists as a formative factor over long periods. This 'masculinity complex' in women can also result in a manifest homosexual choice of object. Only if her development follows the third,
very circuitous, path does she reach the final normal female attitude, in which she takes her father as her object and so finds
her way to the feminine form of the Oedipus complex. Thus in
women the Oedipus complex is the end-result of a fairly lengthy
development. It is not destroyed, but created, by the influence of
castration; it escapes the strongly hostile influences which, in the
male, have a destructive effect on it, and indeed it is all too often
not surmounted by the female at all. For this reason, too, the
cultural consequences of its break-up are smaller and of less importance in her. We should probably not be wrong in saying that
it is this difference in the reciprocal relation between the Oedipus
and the castration complex which gives its special stamp to the
character of females as social beings.[5]

We see, then, that the phase of exclusive attachment to the
mother, which may be called the *pre-Oedipus* phase, possesses a
far greater importance in women than it can have in men. Many
phenomena of female sexual life which were not properly understood before can be fully explained by reference to this phase.

---

5. It is to be anticipated that men analysts with feminist views, as well as our
women analysts, will disagree with what I have said here. They will hardly
fail to object that such notions spring from the 'masculinity complex' of the
male and are designed to justify on theoretical grounds his innate inclination
to disparage and suppress women. But this sort of psycho-analytic argumen-
tation reminds us here, as it so often does, of Dostoevsky's famous 'knife that
cuts both ways'. The opponents of those who argue in this way will on their
side think it quite natural that the female sex should refuse to accept a view
which appears to contradict their eagerly coveted equality with men. The use
of analysis as a weapon of controversy can clearly lead to no decision. * * *

Long ago, for instance, we noticed that many women who have chosen their husband on the model of their father, or have put him in their father's place, nevertheless repeat towards him, in their married life, their bad relations with their mother.[6] The husband of such a woman was meant to be the inheritor of her relation to her father, but in reality he became the inheritor of her relation to her mother. This is easily explained as an obvious case of regression. Her relation to her mother was the original one, and her attachment to her father was built up on it, and now, in marriage, the original relation emerges from repression. For the main content of her development to womanhood lay in the carrying over of her affective object attachments from her mother to her father.

With many women we have the impression that their years of maturity are occupied by a struggle with their husband, just as their youth was spent in a struggle with their mother. In the light of the previous discussions we shall conclude that their hostile attitude to their mother is not a consequence of the rivalry implicit in the Oedipus complex, but originates from the preceding phase and has merely been reinforced and exploited in the Oedipus situation. And actual analytic examination confirms this view. Our interest must be directed to the mechanisms that are at work in her turning away from the mother who was an object so intensely and exclusively loved. We are prepared to find, not a single factor, but a whole number of them operating together towards the same end.

Among these factors are some which are determined by the circumstances of infantile sexuality in general, and so hold good equally for the erotic life of boys. First and foremost we may mention jealousy of other people—of brothers and sisters, rivals, among whom the father too has a place. Childhood love is boundless; it demands exclusive possession, it is not content with less than all. But it has a second characteristic: it has, in point of fact, no aim and is incapable of obtaining complete satisfaction; and principally for that reason it is doomed to end in disappointment and to give place to a hostile attitude. Later on in life the lack of an ultimate satisfaction may favour a different result. This very factor may ensure the uninterrupted continuance of the libidinal

6. [See 'The Taboo of Virginity' {above, p. 210}.]

cathexis, as happens with love-relations that are inhibited in their aim. But in the stress of the processes of development it regularly happens that the libido abandons its unsatisfying position in order to find a new one.

Another, much more specific motive for turning away from the mother arises from the effect of the castration complex on the creature who is without a penis. At some time or other the little girl makes the discovery of her organic inferiority—earlier and more easily, of course, if there are brothers or other boys about. We have already taken note of the three paths which diverge from this point: (*a*) the one which leads to a cessation of her whole sexual life, (*b*) the one which leads to a defiant over-emphasis of her masculinity, and (*c*) the first steps towards definitive femininity. It is not easy to determine the exact timing here or the typical course of events. Even the point of time when the discovery of castration is made varies, and a number of other factors seem to be inconstant and to depend on chance. The state of the girl's own phallic activity plays a part; and so too does the question whether this activity was found out or not, and how much interference with it she experienced afterwards.

Little girls usually discover for themselves their characteristic phallic activity—masturbation of the clitoris; and to begin with this is no doubt unaccompanied by phantasy. The part played in starting it by nursery hygiene is reflected in the very common phantasy which makes the mother or nurse into a seducer.[7] Whether little girls masturbate less frequently and from the first less energetically than little boys is not certain; quite possibly it is so. Actual seduction, too, is common enough; it is initiated either by other children or by someone in charge of the child who wants to soothe it, or send it to sleep or make it dependent on them. Where seduction intervenes it invariably disturbs the natural course of the developmental process, and it often leaves behind extensive and lasting consequences.

A prohibition of masturbation, as we have seen, becomes an incentive for giving it up; but it also becomes a motive for rebelling against the person who prohibits it—that is to say, the mother, or the mother-substitute who later regularly merges with her. A defiant persistence in masturbation appears to open the way to

---

7. [Cf. a fuller discussion of this below, {p. 335}.]

masculinity. Even where the girl has not succeeded in suppressing her masturbation, the effect of the apparently vain prohibition is seen in her later efforts to free herself at all costs from a satisfaction which has been spoilt for her. When she reaches maturity her object-choice may still be influenced by this persisting purpose. Her resentment at being prevented from free sexual activity plays a big part in her detachment from her mother. The same motive comes into operation again after puberty, when her mother takes up her duty of guarding her daughter's chastity. We shall, of course, not forget that the mother is similarly opposed to a boy's masturbating and thus provides him, too, with a strong motive for rebellion.

When the little girl discovers her own deficiency, from seeing a male genital, it is only with hesitation and reluctance that she accepts the unwelcome knowledge. As we have seen, she clings obstinately to the expectation of one day having a genital of the same kind too, and her wish for it survives long after her hope has expired. The child invariably regards castration in the first instance as a misfortune peculiar to herself; only later does she realize that it extends to certain other children and lastly to certain grown-ups. When she comes to understand the general nature of this characteristic, it follows that femaleness—and with it, of course, her mother—suffers a great depreciation in her eyes.

This account of how girls respond to the impression of castration and the prohibition against masturbation will very probably strike the reader as confused and contradictory. This is not entirely the author's fault. In truth, it is hardly possible to give a description which has general validity. We find the most different reactions in different individuals, and in the same individual the contrary attitudes exist side by side. With the first intervention of the prohibition, the conflict is there, and from now on it will accompany the development of the sexual function. Insight into what takes place is made particularly difficult by the fact of its being so hard to distinguish the mental processes of this first phase from later ones by which they are overlaid and are distorted in memory. Thus, for instance, a girl may later construe the fact of castration as a punishment for her masturbatory activity, and she will attribute the carrying out of this punishment to her father, but neither of these ideas can have been a primary one. Similarly, boys regularly fear castration from their father, although in their case, too, the threat most usually comes from their mother.

However this may be, at the end of this first phase of attachment to the mother, there emerges, as the girl's strongest motive for turning away from her, the reproach that her mother did not give her a proper penis—that is to say, brought her into the world as a female. A second reproach, which does not reach quite so far back, is rather a surprising one. It is that her mother did not give her enough milk, did not suckle her long enough. Under the conditions of modern civilization this may be true often enough, but certainly not so often as is asserted in analyses. It would seem rather that this accusation gives expression to the general dissatisfaction of children, who, in our monogamous civilization, are weaned from the breast after six or nine months, whereas the primitive mother devotes herself exclusively to her child for two or three years. It is as though our children had remained for ever unsated, as though they had never sucked long enough at their mother's breast. But I am not sure whether, if one analysed children who had been suckled as long as the children of primitive peoples, one would not come upon the same complaint. Such is the greed of a child's libido!

When we survey the whole range of motives for turning away from the mother which analysis brings to light—that she failed to provide the little girl with the only proper genital, that she did not feed her sufficiently, that she compelled her to share her mother's love with others, that she never fulfilled all the girl's expectations of love, and, finally, that she first aroused her sexual activity and then forbade it—all these motives seem nevertheless insufficient to justify the girl's final hostility. Some of them follow inevitably from the nature of infantile sexuality; others appear like rationalizations devised later to account for the uncomprehended change in feeling. Perhaps the real fact is that the attachment to the mother is bound to perish, precisely because it was the first and was so intense; just as one can often see happen in the first marriages of young women which they have entered into when they were most passionately in love. In both situations the attitude of love probably comes to grief from the disappointments that are unavoidable and from the accumulation of occasions for aggression. As a rule, second marriages turn out much better.

We cannot go so far as to assert that the ambivalence of emotional cathexes is a universally valid law, and that it is absolutely impossible to feel great love for a person without its being accompanied by a hatred that is perhaps equally great, or vice versa.

Normally adults do undoubtedly succeed in separating those two attitudes from each other, and do not find themselves obliged to hate their love-objects and to love their enemy as well as hate him. But this seems to be the result of later developments. In the first phases of erotic life, ambivalence is evidently the rule. Many people retain this archaic trait all through their lives. It is characteristic of obsessional neurotics that in their object-relationships love and hate counterbalance each other. In primitive races, too, we may say that ambivalence predominates.[8] We shall conclude, then, that the llittle girl's intense attachment to her mother is strongly ambivalent, and that it is in consequence precisely of this ambivalence that (with the assistance of the other factors we have adduced) her attachment is forced away from her mother— once again, that is to say, in consequence of a general characteristic of infantile sexuality.

The explanation I have attempted to give is at once met by a question: 'How is it, then, that boys are able to keep intact their attachment to their mother, which is certainly no less strong than that of girls?' The answer comes equally promptly: 'Because boys are able to deal with their ambivalent feelings towards their mother by directing all their hostility on to their father.' But, in the first place, we ought not to make this reply until we have made a close study of the pre-Oedipus phase in boys, and, in the second place, it is probably more prudent in general to admit that we have as yet no clear understanding of these processes, with which we have only just become acquainted.

III.

A further question arises: 'What does the little girl require of her mother? What is the nature of her sexual aims during the time of exclusive attachment to her mother?' The answer we obtain from the analytic material is just what we should expect. The girl's sexual aims in regard to her mother are active as well as passive and are determined by the libidinal phases through which the child passes. Here the relation of activity to passivity is especially interesting. It can easily by observed that in every

---

8. [See *Totem and Taboo* (1912–13) passim, and especially the second essay.]

field of mental experience, not merely that of sexuality, when a child receives a passive impression it has a tendency to produce an active reaction. It tries to do itself what has just been done to it. This is part of the work imposed on it of mastering the external world and can even lead to its endeavouring to repeat an impression which it would have reason to avoid on account of its distressing content. Children's play, too, is made to serve this purpose of supplementing a passive experience with an active piece of behaviour and of thus, as it were, annulling it. When a doctor has opened a child's mouth, in spite of his resistance, to look down his throat, the same child, after the doctor had gone, will play at being the doctor himself, and will repeat the assault upon some small brother or sister who is as helpless in his hands as he was in the doctor's.[9] Here we have an unmistakable revolt against passivity and a preference for the active role. This swing-over from passivity to activity does not take place with the same regularity or vigour in all children; in some it may not occur at all. A child's behaviour in this respect may enable us to draw conclusions as to the relative strength of the masculinity and femininity that it will exhibit in its sexuality.

The first sexual and sexually coloured experiences which a child has in relation to its mother are naturally of a passive character. It is suckled, fed, cleaned, and dressed by her, and taught to perform all its functions. A part of its libido goes on clinging to those experiences and enjoys the satisfactions bound up with them; but another part strives to turn them into activity. In the first place, being suckled at the breast gives place to active sucking. As regards the other experiences the child contents itself either with becoming self-sufficient—that is, with itself successfully carrying out what had hitherto been done for it—or with repeating its passive experiences in an active form in play; or else it actually makes its mother into the object and behaves as the active subject towards her. For a long time I was unable to credit this last behaviour, which takes place in the field of real action, until my observations removed all doubts on the matter.

We seldom hear of a little girl's wanting to wash or dress her

9. [Cf. the similar passage near the end of Chapter II of *Beyond the Pleasure Principle* (1920g), 18:17.] {After Anna Freud's *The Ego and the Mechanisms of Defense* was published in 1936, her term for this mechanism prevailed: "identification with the aggressor."}

mother, or tell her to perform her excretory functions. Sometimes, it is true, she says: 'Now let's play that I'm the mother and you're the child's but generally she fulfils these active wishes in an indirect way, in her play with her doll, in which she represents the mother and the doll the child. The fondness girls have for playing with dolls, in contrast to boys, is commonly regarded as a sign of early awakened femininity. Not unjustly so; but we must not overlook the fact that what finds expression here is the *active* side of femininity, and that the little girl's preference for dolls is probably evidence of the exclusiveness of her attachment to her mother, with complete neglect of her father-object.

The very surprising sexual activity of little girls in relation to their mother is manifested chronologically in oral, sadistic, and finally even in phallic trends directed towards her. It is difficult to give a detailed account of these because they are often obscure instinctual impulses which it was impossible for the child to grasp psychically at the time of their occurrence, which were therefore only interpreted by her later, and which then appear in the analysis in forms of expression that were certainly not the original ones. Sometimes we come across them as transferences on to the later, father-object, where they do not belong and where they seriously interfere with our understanding of the situation. We find the little girl's aggressive oral and sadistic wishes in a form forced on them by early repression, as a fear of being killed by her mother— a fear which, in turn, justifies her death-wish against her mother, if that becomes conscious. It is impossible to say how often this fear of the mother is supported by an unconscious hostility on the mother's part which is sensed by the girl. (Hitherto, it is only in men that I have found the fear of being eaten up. This fear is referred to the father, but it is probably the product of a transformation of oral aggressivity directed to the mother. The child wants to eat up its mother from whom it has had its nourishment; in the case of the father there is no such obvious determinant for the wish.)

The women patients showing a strong attachment to their mother in whom I have been able to study the pre-Oedipus phase have all told me that when their mother gave them enemas or rectal douches they used to offer the greatest resistance and react with fear and screams of rage. This behaviour may be very frequent or even the habitual thing in children. I only came to understand the reason for such a specially violent opposition from a remark made by Ruth Mack Brunswick, who was studying these problems at the same time as I was, to the effect that she was inclined to compare the outbreak of anger after an enema to the orgasm following genital excitation. The accompanying anxiety should, she thought, be construed as a transformation of the desire for aggression which had been stirred up. I believe that this is really so and that, at the sadistic-anal level, the intense passive stimulation of the intestinal zone is responded to by an outbreak of desire for aggression which is manifested either directly as rage, or, in consequence of its suppression, as anxiety. In later years this reaction seems to die away.

In regard to the passive impulses of the phalllic phase, it is noteworthy that girls regularly accuse their mother of seducing them. This is because they necessarily received their first, or at any rate their strongest, genital sensations when they were being cleaned and having their toilet attended to by their mother (or by someone such as a nurse who took her place). Mothers have often told me, as a matter of observation, that their little daughters of two and three years old enjoy these sensations and try to get their mothers to make them more intense by repeated touching and rubbing. The fact that the mother thus unavoidably initiates the child into the phallic phase is, I think, the reason why, in phantasies of later years, the father so regularly appears as the sexual seducer. When the girl turns away from her mother, she also makes over to her father her introduction into sexual life.[10]

Lastly, intense *active* wishful impulses directed towards the mother also arise during the phallic phase. The sexual activity of this period culminates in clitoridal masturbation. This is probably accompanied by ideas of the mother, but whether the child at-

10. [This is the last phase of a long story. When, in his early analyses, Freud's hysterical patients told him that they had been seduced by their father in childhood, he accepted these tales as the truth and regarded the traumas as the cause of their illness. It was not long before he recognized his mistake, and he admitted it in a letter to Fliess of September 21, 1897 {See above, p. 53}. He soon grasped the important fact that these apparently false memories were wishful phantasies, which pointed the way to the existence of the Oedipus complex. An account of his contemporary reactions to these discoveries is given in Chapter III of his *Autobiographical Study* (1925), 20:34–5. It was only in the present passage that Freud gave his full explanation of these ostensible memories. He discusses this whole episode at greater length in Lecture XXXIII of his *New Introductory Lectures* (1933).]

taches a sexual aim to the idea, and what the aim is, I have not been able to discover from my observations. It is only when all her interests have received a fresh impetus through the arrival of a baby brother or sister that we can clearly recognize such an aim. The little girl wants to believe that she has given her mother the new baby, just as the boy wants to; and her reaction to this event and her behaviour to the baby is exactly the same as his. No doubt this sounds quite absurd, but perhaps that is only because it sounds so unfamiliar.

The turning-away from her mother is an extremely important step in the course of a little girl's development. It is more than a mere change of object. We have already described what takes place in it and the many motives put forward for it; we may now add that hand in hand with it there is to be observed a marked lowering of the active sexual impulses and a rise of the passive ones. It is true that the active trends have been affected by frustration more strongly; they have proved totally unrealizable and are therefore abandoned by the libido more readily. But the passive trends have not escaped disappointment either. With the turning-away from the mother clitoridal masturbation frequently ceases as well; and often enough when the small girl represses her previous masculinity a considerable portion of her sexual trends in general is permanently injured too. The transition to the father-object is accomplished with the help of the passive trends in so far as they have escaped the catastrophe. The path to the development of femininity now lies open to the girl, to the extent to which it is not restricted by the remains of the pre-Oedipus attachment to her mother which she has surmounted.

If we now survey the stage of sexual development in the female which I have been describing, we cannot resist coming to a definite conclusion about female sexuality as a whole. We have found the same libidinal forces at work in it as in the male child and we have been able to convince ourselves that for a period of time these forces follow the same course and have the same outcome in each.

Biological factors subsequently deflect those libidinal forces [in the girl's case] from their original aims and conduct even active and in every sense masculine trends into feminine channels. Since we cannot dismiss the notion that sexual excitation is derived from the operation of certain chemical substances, it seems plausible at first to expect that biochemistry will one day disclose a substance to us whose presence produces a male sexual excitation and another substance which produces a female one. But this hope seems no less naïve than the other one—happily obsolete to-day—that it may be possible under the microscope to isolate the different exciting factors of hysteria, obsessional neurosis, melancholia, and so on.

Even in sexual chemistry things must be rather more complicated. For psychology, however, it is a matter of indifference whether there is a single sexually exciting substance in the body or two or countless numbers of them. Psycho-analysis teaches us to manage with a single libido, which, it is true, has both active and passive aims (that is, modes of satisfaction). This antithesis and, above all, the existence of libidinal trends with passive aims, contains within itself the remainder of our problem.

IV.

An examination of the analytic literature on the subject shows that everything that has been said by me here is already to be found in it.[11] It would have been superfluous to publish this paper if it were not that in a field of research which is so difficult of access every account of first-hand experiences or personal views may be of value. Moreover, there are a number of points which I have defined more sharply and isolated more carefully. In some of the other papers on the subject the description is obscured because they deal at the same time with the problems of the super-ego and the sense of guilt. This I have avoided doing. Also, in describing the various outcomes of this phase of development, I have refrained from discussing the complications which arise when a child, as a result of disappointment from her father, returns to the attachment to her mother which she had abandoned, or when, in the course of her life, she repeatedly changes over from one position to the other. But precisely because my paper is only one contribution among others, I may be spared an exhaustive survey of the literature, and I can confine myself to bringing out

---

11. {A bibliography of the literature Freud surveys in this section (IV) can be found below, pp. 370–75.}

the more important points on which I agree or disagree with these other writings.

Abraham's (1921) description of the manifestations of the castration complex in the female is still unsurpassed; but one would be glad if it had included the factor of the girl's original exclusive attachment to her mother. I am in agreement with the principal points in Jeanne Lampl-de Groot's (1927) important paper. In this the complete identity of the pre-Oedipus phase in boys and girls is recognized, and the girl's sexual (phallic) activity towards her mother is affirmed and substantiated by observations. The turning-away from the mother is traced to the influence of the girl's recognition of castration, which obliges her to give up her sexual object, and often masturbation along with it. The whole development is summed up in the formula that the girl goes through a phase of the 'negative' Oedipus complex before she can enter the positive one. A point on which I find the writer's account inadequate is that it represents the turning-away from the mother as being merely a change of object and does not discuss the fact that it is accompanied by the plainest manifestations of hostility. To this hostility full justice is done in Helene Deutsch's latest paper, on feminine masochism and its relation to frigidity (1930), in which she also recognizes the girl's phallic activity and the intensity of her attachment to her mother. Helene Deutsch states further that the girl's turning towards her father takes place *viâ* her passive trends (which have already been awakened in relation to her mother). In her earlier book (1925) the author had not yet set herself free from the endeavour to apply the Oedipus pattern to the pre-Oedipus phase, and she therefore interpreted the little girl's phallic activity as an identification with her father.

Fenichel (1930) rightly emphasizes the difficulty of recognizing in the material produced in analysis what parts of it represent the unchanged content of the pre-Oedipus phase and what parts have been distorted by regression (or in other ways). He does not accept Jeanne Lampl-de Groot's assertion of the little girl's active attitude in the phallic phase. He also rejects the 'displacement backwards' of the Oedipus complex proposed by Melanie Klein (1928), who places its beginnings as early as the commencement of the second year of life. This dating of it, which would also necessarily imply a modification of our view of all the rest of the child's development, does not in fact correspond to what we learn from the analyses of adults, and it is especially incompatible with my findings as to the long duration of the girl's pre-Oedipus attachment to her mother. A means of softening this contradiction is afforded by the reflection that we are not as yet able to distinguish in this field between what is rigidly fixed by biological laws and what is open to movement and change under the influence of accidental experience. The effect of seduction has long been familiar to us and in just the same way other factors—such as the date at which the child's brothers and sisters are born or the time when it discovers the difference between the sexes, or again its direct observations of sexual intercourse or its parents' behaviour in encouraging or repelling it—may hasten the child's sexual development and bring it to maturity.

Some writers are inclined to reduce the importance of the child's first and most original libidinal impulses in favour of later developmental processes, so that—to put this view in its most extreme form—the only role left to the former is merely to indicate certain paths, while the [psychical] intensities[12] which flow along those paths are supplied by later regressions and reaction-formations. Thus, for instance, Karen Horney (1926) is of the opinion that we greatly over-estimate the girl's primary penis-envy and that the strength of the masculine trend which she develops later is to be attributed to a *secondary* penis-envy which is used to fend off her feminine impulses and, in particular, her feminine attachment to her father. This does not tally with my impressions. Certain as is the occurrence of later reinforcements through regressions and reaction-formation, and difficult as it is to estimate the relative strength of the confluent libidinal components, I nevertheless think that we should not overlook the fact that the first libidinal impulses have an intensity of their own which is superior to any that come later and which may indeed be termed incommensurable. It is undoubtedly true that there is an antithesis between the attachment to the father and the masculinity complex; it is the general antithesis that exists between activity and passivity, masculinity and femininity. But this gives us no right to assume that only one of them is primary and that the other owes its strength merely to the force of defence. And if the defence against femininity is so energetic, from what other source can it draw its strength than from the masculine trend which found its first

12. {That is, intensities of psychic representations of instinctual energy.}

expression in the child's penis-envy and therefore deserves to be named after it?

A similar objection applies to Ernest Jones's view (1927) that the phallic phase in girls is a secondary, protective reaction rather than a genuine developmental stage. This does not correspond either to the dynamic or the chronological position of things.

This letter to Carl Mueller-Braunschweig was made available by his colleague Dr. Edith Weigert to the American journal Psychiatry, *where it was published in a translation by Dr. Helm Stierlin (vol. 34, 1971, p. 329).*

Wien, XIX, Strassberg. 47

21.7.1935

Lieber Herr Doktor,

I gratefully confirm the receipt of your manuscript and continue to ponder the question as to what its further fate should be. Until I shall reach a decision in this matter, I shall keep it with me.

There is no need to get back once more to the joke about generous cursing. However, in what I had to say critically, I felt, after all, inhibited. Your work fits into that of authors such as Horney, Jones, [Sandor] Rado, etc., who do not come to grips with the bisexuality of women and who, in particular, object to the phallic stage. The frequency [of such writings] seems in itself proof that something is missing, undiscovered or unsaid at this point. I think I have now found an answer as to what needs to be supplemented. However, I cannot tell it to you; it would require a lengthy treatise and would represent also an unjustified authoritarian attempt to interfere with the evaluation of your work. Therefore, I limit myself to some comments which pertain to all of you and add a few others which concern your work only.

I object to all of you to the extent that you do not distinguish more clearly and cleanly between what is psychic and what is biological, that you try to establish a neat parallelism between the two and that you, motivated by such intent, unthinkingly construe psychic facts which are unprovable and that you, in the process of so doing, must declare as reactive or regressive much that without doubt is primary. Of course, these reproaches must remain obscure. In addition, I would only like to emphasize that we must keep psychoanalysis separate from biology just as we have kept it separate from anatomy and physiology; at the present, sexual biology seems to lead us to two substances which attract each other.

We deal only with one libido which behaves in a male way.

For you alone: (a) The existence of characteristics in the little girl which can be called feminine is no argument whatsoever for a corresponding early role of the vagina. (b) The point of view of narcissistic hurt is my own, not Rado's. For years I have been reducing to this one point the only kernel of truth to be found in Adler's theory (inferiority feeling and organic masculine protest). (c) Your notion of a precocious genitality appears to me particularly unfortunate. After all, your little girl, too, complains about the fact that she has no penis for the mother, and not that the mother has no penis for her. It seems evident that she has believed in the penis of the mother for a long time. (d) It is correct that the sight of the penis and its function of urination cannot be the motive, only the trigger of the child's envy. However, no one has stated this.

With many apologies because of the inevitable obscurity of this critique, I remain

Yours cordially,
/s/ Freud.

Femininity

This lecture is the fifth of the seven New Introductory Lectures Freud composed in 1932. Up to its final section it is a digest of "Some Psychical Consequences . . ." (1925) and "Female Sexuality" (1931). The findings of those two essays are simply reworked and resynthesized.

In the final pages, however, Freud turns to adult female psychology. He offers no new observations, but he does try to coordinate his descriptions of adult women with the new emphasis on the pre-Oedipal mother-daughter bond and its eventual disruption. As he sets out his summaries, Freud is also testing whether the libido theory of the Three Essays—the idea that there is one libido, active and "masculine"—needs to be revised. The answer was negative, even though Freud had to keep reminding himself not to fall into a facile equation of activity with masculinity, passivity with femininity.

* * * To-day's lecture * * * may serve to give you an example of a detailed piece of analytic work, and I can say two things to recommend it. It brings forward nothing but observed facts, almost without any speculative additions, and it deals with a subject which has a claim on your interest second almost to no other. Throughout history people have knocked their heads against the riddle of the nature of femininity—

> Häupter in Hieroglyphenmützen,
> Häupter in Turban und schwarzem Barett,

Perückenhäupter und tausend andre
Arme, schwitzende Menschenhäupter. . . .[1]

Nor will *you* have escaped worrying over this problem—those of you who are men; to those of you who are women this will not apply—you are yourselves the problem. When you meet a human being, the first distinction you make is 'male or female?' and you are accustomed to make the distinction with unhesitating certainty. Anatomical science shares your certainty at one point and not much further. The male sexual product, the spermatozoon, and its vehicle are male; the ovum and the organism that harbours it are female. In both sexes organs have been formed which serve exclusively for the sexual functions; they were probably developed from the same [innate] disposition into two different forms. Besides this, in both sexes the other organs, the bodily shapes and tissues, show the influence of the individual's sex, but this is inconstant and its amount variable; these are what are known as the secondary sexual characters. Science next tells you something that runs counter to your expectations and is probably calculated to confuse your feelings. It draws your attention to the fact that portions of the male sexual apparatus also appear in women's bodies, though in an atrophied state, and vice versa in the alternative case. It regards their occurrence as indications of *bisexuality*, as though an individual is not a man or a woman but always both—merely a certain amount more the one than the other. You will then be asked to make yourselves familiar with the idea that the proportion in which masculine and feminine are mixed in an individual is subject to quite considerable fluctuations. Since, however, apart from the very rarest cases, only one kind of sexual product—ova or semen—is nevertheless present in one person, you are bound to have doubts as to the decisive significance of those elements and must conclude that what constitutes masculinity or femininity is an unknown characteristic which anatomy cannot lay hold of.

* * *

1. Heads in hieroglyphic bonnets,
   Heads in turbans and black birettas,
   Heads in wigs and thousand other
   Wretched, sweating heads of humans. . . .
   (Heine, *Nordsee* [Second Cycle, VII, 'Fragen'].)

Can psychology do so perhaps? We are accustomed to employ 'masculine' and 'feminine' as mental qualities as well, and have in the same way transferred the notion of bisexuality to mental life. Thus we speak of a person, whether male or female, as behaving in a masculine way in one connection and in a feminine way in another. But you will soon perceive that this is only giving way to anatomy or to convention. You cannot give the concepts of 'masculine' and 'feminine' *any* new connotation. The distinction is not a psychological one; when you say 'masculine', you usually mean 'active', and when you say 'feminine', you usually mean 'passive'. Now it is true that a relation of the kind exists. The male sex-cell is actively mobile and searches out the female one, and the latter, the ovum, is immobile and waits passively. This behaviour of the elementary sexual organisms is indeed a model for the conduct of sexual individuals during intercourse. The male pursues the female for the purpose of sexual union, seizes hold of her and penetrates into her. But by this you have precisely reduced the characteristic of masculinity to the factor of aggressiveness so far as psychology is concerned. You may well doubt whether you have gained any real advantage from this when you reflect that in some classes of animals the females are the stronger and more aggressive and the male is active only in the single act of sexual union. This is so, for instance, with the spiders. Even the functions of rearing and caring for the young, which strike us as feminine *par excellence*, are not invariably attached to the female sex in animals. In quite high species we find that the sexes share the task of caring for the young between them or even that the male alone devotes himself to it. Even in the sphere of human sexual life you soon see how inadequate it is to make masculine behaviour coincide with activity and feminine with passivity. A mother is active in every sense towards her child; the act of lactation itself may equally be described as the mother suckling the baby or as her being sucked by it. The further you go from the narrow sexual sphere the more obvious will the 'error of superimposition'[2] become. Women can display great activity in various directions, men are not able to live in company with their own kind unless they develop a large amount of passive adaptability. If you now tell me that these facts go to prove pre-

---

2. [I.e. mistaking two different things for a single one. The term was explained in *Introductory Lectures*, XX, 16:304.]

cisely that both men and women are bisexual in the psychological sense, I shall conclude that you have decided in your own minds to make 'active' coincide with 'masculine' and 'passive' with 'feminine'. But I advise you against it. It seems to me to serve no useful purpose and adds nothing to our knowledge.

One might consider characterizing femininity psychologically as giving preference to passive aims. This is not, of course, the same thing as passivity; to achieve a passive aim may call for a large amount of activity. It is perhaps the case that in a woman, on the basis of her share in the sexual function, a preference for passive behaviour and passive aims is carried over into her life to a greater or lesser extent, in proportion to the limits, restricted or far-reaching, within which her sexual life thus serves as a model. But we must beware in this of underestimating the influence of social customs, which similarly force women into passive situations. All this is still far from being cleared up. There is one particularly constant relation between femininity and instinctual life which we do not want to overlook. The suppression of women's aggressiveness which is prescribed for them constitutionally and imposed on them socially favours the development of powerful masochistic impulses, which succeed, as we know, in binding erotically the destructive trends which have been diverted inwards. Thus masochism, as people say, is truly feminine. But if, as happens so often, you meet with masochism in men, what is left to you but to say that these men exhibit very plain feminine traits?

And now you are already prepared to hear that psychology too is unable to solve the riddle of femininity. The explanation must no doubt come from elsewhere, and cannot come till we have learnt how in general the differentiation of living organisms into two sexes came about. We know nothing about it, yet the existence of two sexes is a most striking characteristic of organic life which distinguishes it sharply from inanimate nature. However, we find enough to study in those human individuals who, through the possession of female genitals, are characterized as manifestly or predominantly feminine. In conformity with its peculiar nature, psycho-analysis does not try to describe what a woman is—that would be a task it could scarcely perform—but sets about enquiring how she comes into being, how a woman develops out of a child with a bisexual disposition. In recent times we have begun to learn a little about this, thanks to the circumstance that several of our excellent women colleagues in analysis have begun to work at the question. The discussion of this has gained special attractiveness from the distinction between the sexes. For the ladies, whenever some comparison seemed to turn out unfavourable to their sex, were able to utter a suspicion that we, the male analysts, had been unable to overcome certain deeply-rooted prejudices against what was feminine, and that this was being paid for in the partiality of our researches. We, on the other hand, standing on the ground of bisexuality, had no difficulty in avoiding impoliteness. We had only to say: 'This doesn't apply to *you*. You're the exception; on this point you're more masculine than feminine.'

We approach the investigation of the sexual development of women with two expectations. The first is that here once more the constitution will not adapt itself to its function without a struggle. The second is that the decisive turning-points will already have been prepared for or completed before puberty. Both expectations are promptly confirmed. Furthermore, a comparison with what happens with boys tells us that the development of a little girl into a normal woman is more difficult and more complicated, since it includes two extra tasks, to which there is nothing corresponding in the development of a man. Let us follow the parallel lines from their beginning. Undoubtedly the material is different to start with in boys and girls: it did not need the psychoanalysis to establish that. The difference in the structure of the genitals is accompanied by other bodily differences which are too well known to call for mention. Differences emerge too in the instinctual disposition which give a glimpse of the later nature of women. A little girl is as a rule less aggressive, defiant and self-sufficient; she seems to have a greater need for being shown affection and on that account to be more dependent and pliant. It is probably only as a result of this pliancy that she can be taught more easily and quicker to control her excretions: urine and faeces are the first gifts that children make to those who look after them, and controlling them is the first concession to which the instinctual life of children can be induced. One gets an impression, too, that little girls are more intelligent and livelier than boys of the same age; they go out more to meet the external world and at the same time form stronger object-cathexes. I cannot say whether this lead in development has been confirmed by exact observations, but in any case there is no question that girls cannot be described as intellectually backward. These sexual differences are not, however, of great consequence: they can be outweighed by individual variations. For our immediate purposes they can be disregarded.

Both sexes seem to pass through the early phases of libidinal development in the same manner. It might have been expected that in girls there would already have been some lag in aggressiveness in the sadistic-anal phase, but such is not the case. Analysis of children's play has shown our women analysts that the aggressive impulses of little girls leave nothing to be desired in the way of abundance and violence. With their entry into the phallic phase the differences between the sexes are completely eclipsed by their agreements. We are now obliged to recognize that the little girl is a little man. In boys, as we know, this phase is marked by the fact that they have learnt how to derive pleasurable sensations from their small penis and connect its excited state with their ideas of sexual intercourse. Little girls do the same thing with their still smaller clitoris. It seems that with them all their masturbatory acts are carried out on this penis-equivalent, and that the truly feminine vagina is still undiscovered by both sexes. It is true that there are a few isolated reports of early vaginal sensations as well, but it could not be easy to distinguish these from sensations in the anus or vestibulum; in any case they cannot play a great part. We are entitled to keep to our view that in the phallic phase of girls the clitoris is the leading erotogenic zone. But it is not, of course, going to remain so. With the change to femininity the clitoris should wholly or in part hand over its sensitivity, and at the same time its importance, to the vagina. This would be one of the two tasks which a woman has to perform in the course of her development, whereas the more fortunate man has only to continue at the time of his sexual maturity the activity that he has previously carried out at the period of the early efflorescence of his sexuality.

We shall return to the part played by the clitoris; let us now turn to the second task with which a girl's development is burdened. A boy's mother is the first object of his love, and she remains so too during the formation of his Oedipus complex, and in essence, all through his life. For a girl too her first object must be her mother (and the figures of wet-nurses and foster-mothers that merge into her). The first object-cathexes occur in attachment to the satisfaction of the major and simple vital needs, and the circumstanes of the care of children are the same for both sexes. But in the Oedipus situation the girl's father has become her love-object, and we expect that in the normal course of development she will find her way from this paternal object to her final choice of an object. In the course of time, therefore, a girl has to change her erotogenic zone and her object—both of which a boy retains. The question then arises of how this happens: in particular, how does a girl pass from her mother to an attachment to her father? or, in other words, how does she pass from her masculine phase to the feminine one to which she is biologically destined?

It would be a solution of ideal simplicity if we could suppose that from a particular age onwards the elementary influence of the mutual attraction between the sexes makes itself felt and impels the small woman towards men, while the same law allows the boy to continue with his mother. We might suppose in addition that in this the children are following the pointer given them by the sexual preference of their parents. But we are not going to find things so easy; we scarcely know whether we are to believe seriously in the power of which poets talk so much and with such enthusiasm but which cannot be further dissected analytically. We have found an answer of quite another sort by means of laborious investigations, the material for which at least was easy to arrive at. For you must know that the number of women who remain till a late age tenderly dependent on a paternal object, or indeed on their real father, is very great. We have established some surprising facts about these women with an intense attach-ment of long duration to their father. We knew, of course, that there had been a preliminary stage of attachment to the mother, but we did not know that it could be so rich in content and so long-lasting, and could leave behind so many opportunities for fixations and dispositions. During this time the girl's father is only a troublesome rival; in some cases the attachment to her mother lasts beyond the fourth year of life. Almost everything that we find later in her relation to her father was already present in this earlier attachment and has been transferred subsequently on to her father. In short, we get an impression that we cannot under-stand women unless we appreciate this phase of their pre-Oedipus attachment to their mother.

We shall be glad, then, to know the nature of the girl's libidinal relations to her mother. The answer is that they are of very many different kinds. Since they persist through all three phases of infantile sexuality, they also take on the characteristics of the different phases and express themselves by oral, sadistic-anal and phallic wishes. These wishes represent active as well as passive impulses; if we relate them to the differentiation of the sexes which is to appear later—though we should avoid doing so as far as possible—we may call them masculine and feminine. Besides this, they are completely ambivalent, both affectionate and of a hostile and aggressive nature. The latter often only come to light after being changed into anxiety ideas. It is not always easy to point to a formulation of these early sexual wishes; what is most clearly expressed is a wish to get the mother with child and the corresponding wish to bear her a child—both belonging to the phallic period and sufficiently surprising, but established beyond doubt by analytic observation. The attractiveness of these investigations lies in the surprising detailed findings which they bring us. Thus, for instance, we discover the fear of being murdered or poisoned, which may later form the core of a paranoic illness, already present in this pre-Oedipus period, in relation to the mother. Or another case: you will recall an interesting episode in the history of analytic research which caused me many distressing hours. In the period in which the main interest was directed to discovering infantile sexual traumas, almost all my women patients told me that they had been seduced by their father. I was driven to recognize in the end that these reports were untrue and so came to understand that hysterical symptoms are derived from phantasies and not from real occurrences. It was only later that I was able to recognize in this phantasy of being seduced by the father the expression of the typical Oedipus complex in women. And now we find the phantasy of seduction once more in the pre-Oedipus prehistory of girls; but the seducer is regularly the mother. Here, however, the phantasy touches the ground of reality, for it was really the mother who by her activities over the child's bodily hygiene inevitably stimulated, and perhaps even roused for the first time, pleasurable sensations in her genitals.

I have no doubt you are ready to suspect that this portrayal of the abundance and strength of a little girl's sexual relations with her mother is very much overdrawn. After all, one has opportunities of seeing little girls and notices nothing of the sort. But the objection is not to the point. Enough can be seen in the children if one knows how to look. And besides, you should consider how little of its sexual wishes a child can bring to pre-conscious expression or communicate at all. Accordingly we are only within our rights if we study the residues and consequences of this emotional world in retrospect, in people in whom these processes of development had attained a specially clear and even excessive degree of expansion. Pathology has always done us the service of making discernible by isolation and exaggeration conditions which would remain concealed in a normal state. And since our investigations have been carried out on people who were by no means seriously abnormal, I think we should regard their outcome as deserving belief.

We will now turn our interest on to the single question of what it is that brings this powerful attachment of the girl to her mother to an end. This, as we know, is its usual fate: it is destined to make room for an attachment to her father. Here we come upon a fact which is a pointer to our further advance. This step in development does not involve only a simple change of object. The turning away from the mother is accompanied by hostility; the attachment to the mother ends in hate. A hate of that kind may become very striking and last all through life; it may be carefully overcompensated later on; as a rule one part of it is overcome while another part persists. Events of later years naturally influence this greatly. We will restrict ourselves, however, to studying it at the time at which the girl turns to her father and to enquiring into the motives for it. We are then given a long list of accusations and grievances against the mother which are supposed to justify the child's hostile feelings; they are of varying validity which we shall not fail to examine. A number of them are obvious rationalizations and the true sources of enmity remain to be found. I hope you will be interested if on this occasion I take you through all the details of a psycho-analytic investigation.

The reproach against the mother which goes back furthest is that she gave the child too little milk—which is construed against her as a lack of love. Now there is some justification for this reproach in our families. Mothers often have insufficient nourishment to give their children and are content to suckle them for a few months, for half or three-quarters of a year. Among primitive peoples children are fed at their mother's breast for two or three years. The figure of the wet-nurse who suckles the child is as a rule merged into the mother; when this has not happened, the reproach is turned into another one—that the nurse, who fed the child so willingly, was sent away by the mother too early. But whatever the true state of affairs may have been, it is impossible that the child's reproach can be justified as often as it is met with. It seems, rather, that the child's avidity for its earliest nourishment is altogether insatiable, that it never gets over the pain of losing its mother's breast. I should not be surprised if the analysis of a primitive child, who could still suck at its mother's breast when it was already able to run about and talk, were to bring the same reproach to light. The fear of being poisoned is also probably connected with the withdrawal of the breast. Poison is nourishment that makes one ill. Perhaps children trace back their early illnesses too to this frustration. A fair amount of intellectual education is a prerequisite for believing in chance; primitive people and uneducated ones, and no doubt children as well, are able to assign a ground for everything that happens. Perhaps originally it was a reason on animistic lines. Even to-day in some strata of our population no one can die without having been killed by someone else—preferably by the doctor. And the regular reaction of a neurotic to the death of someone closely connected with him is to put the blame on himself for having caused the death.

The next accusation against the child's mother flares up when the next baby appears in the nursery. If possible the connection with oral frustration is preserved: the mother could not or would not give the child any more milk because she needed the nourishment for the new arrival. In cases in which the two children are so close in age that lactation is prejudiced by the second pregnancy, this reproach acquires a real basis, and it is a remarkable fact that a child, even with an age difference of only 11 months, is not too young to take notice of what is happening. But what the child grudges the unwanted intruder and rival is not only the suckling but all the other signs of maternal care. It feels that it has been dethroned, despoiled, prejudiced in its rights; it casts a jealous hatred upon the new baby and develops a grievance against the faithless mother which often finds expression in a disagreeable change in its behaviour. It becomes 'naughty', perhaps, irritable and disobedient and goes back on the advances it has made towards controlling its excretions. All of this has been very long familiar and is accepted as self-evident; but we rarely form a correct idea of the strength of these jealous impulses, of the tenacity with which they persist and of the magnitude of their influence on later development. Especially as this jealousy is constantly receiving fresh nourishment in the later years of childhood and the whole shock is repeated with the birth of each new brother or sister. Nor does it make much difference if the child happens to remain the mother's preferred favourite. A child's demands for love are immoderate, they make exclusive claims and tolerate no sharing.

An abundant source of a child's hostility to its mother is provided by its multifarious sexual wishes, which alter according to the phase of the libido and which cannot for the most part be satisfied. The strongest of these frustrations occur at the phallic period, if the mother forbids pleasurable activity with the genitals—often with severe threats and every sign of displeasure— activity to which, after all, she herself had introduced the child. One would think these were reasons enough to account for a girl's turning away from her mother. One would judge, if so, that the estrangement follows inevitably from the nature of children's sexuality, from the immoderate character of their demand for love and the impossibility of fulfilling their sexual wishes. It might be thought indeed that this first love-relation of the child's is doomed to dissolution for the very reason that it is the first, for these early object-cathexes are regularly ambivalent to a high degree. A powerful tendency to aggressiveness is always present beside a powerful love, and the more passionately a child loves its object the more sensitive does it become to disappointments and frustrations from that object; and in the end the love must succumb to the accumulated hostility. Or the idea that there is an original ambivalence such as this in erotic cathexes may be rejected, and it may be pointed out that it is the special nature of the mother-child relation that leads, with equal inevitability, to the destruction of the child's love; for even the mildest upbringing cannot avoid using compulsion and introducing restrictions, and any such intervention in the child's liberty must provoke as a reaction an inclination to rebelliousness and aggressiveness. A discussion of these possibilities might, I think, be most interesting; but an objection suddenly emerges which forces our interest in another direction. All these factors—the slights, the disappointments in love, the jealousy, the seduction followed by prohibition—are, after all, also in operation in the relation of a *boy* to his mother and are yet unable to alienate him from the maternal object. Unless we can find something that is specific for girls and is not present or not in the same way present in boys, we shall not have explained the termination of the attachment of girls to their mother.

I believe we have found this specific factor, and indeed where we expected to find it, even though in a surprising form. Where we expected to find it, I say, for it lies in the castration complex. After all, the anatomical distinction [between the sexes] must express itself in psychical consequences. It was, however, a surprise to learn from analyses that girls hold their mother responsible for their lack of a penis and do not forgive her for their being thus put at a disadvantage.

As you hear, then, we ascribe a castration complex to women as well. And for good reasons, though its content cannot be the same as with boys. In the latter the castration complex arises after they have learnt from the sight of the female genitals that the organ which they value so highly need not necessarily accompany the body. At this the boy recalls to mind the threats he brought on himself by his doings with that organ, he begins to give credence to them and falls under the influence of fear of castration, which will be the most powerful motive force in his subsequent development. The castration complex of girls is also started by the sight of the genitals of the other sex. They at once notice the difference and, it must be admitted, its significance too. They feel seriously wronged, often declare that they want to 'have something like it too', and fall a victim to 'envy for the penis', which will leave ineradicable traces on their development and the formation of their character and which will not be surmounted in even the most favourable cases without a severe expenditure of psychical energy. The girl's recognition of the fact of her being without a penis does not by any means imply that she submits to the fact easily. On the contrary, she continues to hold on for a long time to the wish to get something like it herself and she believes in that possibility for improbably long years; and analysis can show that, at a period when knowledge of reality has long since rejected the fulfilment of the wish as unattainable, it persists in the unconscious and retains a considerable cathexis of energy. The wish to get the longed-for penis eventually in spite of everything may contribute to the motives that drive a mature woman to analysis, and what she may reasonably expect from analysis—a capacity, for instance, to carry on an intellectual profession—may often be recognized as a sublimated modification of this repressed wish.

One cannot very well doubt the importance of envy for the penis. You may take it as an instance of male injustice if I assert that envy and jealousy play an even greater part in the mental life of women than of men. It is not that I think these characteristics are absent in men or that I think they have no other roots in women than envy for the penis; but I am inclined to attribute their greater amount in women to this latter influence. Some analysts, however, have shown an inclination to depreciate the importance of this first instalment of penis-envy in the phallic phase. They are of opinion that what we find of this attitude in women is in the main a secondary structure which has come about on the occasion of later conflicts by regression to this early infantile impulse. This, however, is a general problem of depth psychology. In many pathological—or even unusual—instinctual attitudes (for instance, in all sexual perversions) the question arises of how much of their strength is to be attributed to early infantile fixations and how much to the influence of later experiences and developments. In such cases it is almost always a matter of complemental series such as we put forward in our discussion of the aetiology of the neuroses. Both factors play a part in varying amounts in the causation; a less on the one side is balanced by a more on the other. The infantile factor sets the pattern in all cases but does not always determine the issue, though it often does. Precisely in the case of penis-envy I should argue decidedly in favour of the preponderance of the infantile factor.

The discovery that she is castrated is a turning-point in a girl's growth. Three possible lines of development start from it: one leads to sexual inhibition or to neurosis, the second to change of character in the sense of a masculinity complex, the third, finally, to normal femininity. We have learnt a fair amount, though not everything, about all three.

The essential content of the first is as follows: the little girl has hitherto lived in a masculine way, has been able to get pleasure by the excitation of her clitoris and has brought this activity into relation with her sexual wishes directed towards her mother, which are often active ones; now, owing to the influence of her penis-envy, she loses her enjoyment in her phallic sexuality. Her self-love is mortified by the comparison with the boy's far superior equipment and in consequence she renounces her masturbatory satisfaction from her clitoris, repudiates her love for her mother and at the same time not infrequently represses a good part of her sexual trends in general. No doubt her turning away from her mother does not occur all at once, for to begin with the girl regards her castration as an individual misfortune, and only gradually extends it to other females and finally to her mother as well. Her love was directed to her *phallic* mother; with the discovery that her mother is castrated it becomes possible to drop her as an object, so that the motives for hostility, which have long been accumulating, gain the upper hand. This means, therefore, that as a result of the discovery of women's lack of a penis they are debased in value for girls just as they are for boys and later perhaps for men.

You all know the immense aetiological importance attributed by our neurotic patients to their masturbation. They make it responsible for all their troubles and we have the greatest difficulty in persuading them that they are mistaken. In fact, however, we ought to admit to them that they are right, for masturbation is the executive agent of infantile sexuality, from the faulty development of which they are indeed suffering. But what neurotics mostly blame is the masturbation of the period of puberty; they have mostly forgotten that of early infancy, which is what is really in question. I wish I might have an opportunity some time of explaining to you at length how important all the factual details of early masturbation become for the individual's subsequent neurosis or character: whether or not it was discovered, how the parents struggled against it or permitted it, or whether he succeeded in suppressing it himself. All of this leaves permanent traces on his development. But I am on the whole glad that I need not do this. It would be a hard and tedious task and at the end of it you would put me in an embarrassing situation by quite certainly asking me to give you some practical advice as to how a parent or educator should deal with the masturbation of small children. From the development of girls, which is what my present lecture is concerned with, I can give you the example of a child herself trying to get free from masturbating. She does not always suceed in this. If envy for the penis has provoked a powerful impulse against clitoridal masturbation but this nevertheless refuses to give way, a violent struggle for liberation ensues in which the girl, as it were, herself takes over the role of her deposed mother and gives expression to her entire dissatisfaction with her inferior clitoris in her efforts against obtaining satisfaction from it. Many years later, when her masturbatory activity has long since been suppressed, an interest still persists which we must interpret as a defence against a temptation that is still dreaded. It manifests inself in the emergence of sympathy for those to whom similar difficulties are attributed, it plays a part as a motive in contracting a marriage, and, indeed, it may determine the choice of a husband or lover. Disposing of early infantile masturbation is truly no easy or indifferent business.

Along with the abandonment of clitoridal masturbation a certain amount of activity is renounced. Passivity now has the upper hand, and the girl's turning to her father is accomplished principally with the help of passive instinctual impulses. You can see that a wave of development like this, which clears the phallic activity out of the way, smooths the ground for femininity. If too much is not lost in the course of it through repression, this femininity may turn out to be normal. The wish with which the girl turns to her father is no doubt originally the wish for the penis which her mother has refused her and which she now expects from her father. The feminine situation is only established, however, if the wish for a penis is replaced by one for a baby, if, that is, a baby takes the place of a penis in accordance with an ancient symbolic equivalence. It has not escaped us that the girl has wished for a baby earlier, in the undisturbed phallic phase: that, of course, was the meaning of her playing with dolls. But that play was not in fact an expression of her femininity; it served as an identification with her mother with the intention of substituting activity for passivity. *She* was playing the part of her mother and the doll was herself: now she could do with the baby everything that her mother used to do with her. Not until the emergence of the wish for a penis does the doll-baby become a baby from the girl's father, and thereafter the aim of the most powerful feminine wish. Her happiness is great if later on this wish for a baby finds fulfilment in reality, and quite especially so if the baby is a little boy who brings the longed-for penis with him. Often enough in her combined picture of 'a baby from her father' the emphasis is laid on the baby and her father left unstressed. In this way the ancient masculine wish for the possession of a penis is still faintly visible through the femininity now achieved. But perhaps we ought rather to recognize this wish for a penis as being *par excellence* a feminine one.

With the transference of the wish for a penis-baby on to her father, the girl has entered the situation of the Oedipus complex.

Her hostility to her mother, which did not need to be freshly created, is now greatly intensified, for she becomes the girl's rival, who receives from her father everything that she desires from him. For a long time the girl's Oedipus complex concealed her pre-Oedipus attachment to her mother from our view, though it is nevertheless so important and leaves such lasting fixations behind it. For girls the Oedipus situation is the outcome of a long and difficult development; it is a kind of preliminary solution, a position of rest which is not soon abandoned, especially as the beginning of the latency period is not far distant. And we are now struck by a difference between the two sexes, which is probably momentous, in regard to the relation of the Oedipus complex to the castration complex. In a boy the Oedipus complex, in which he desires his mother and would like to get rid of his father as being a rival, develops naturally from the phase of his phallic sexuality. The threat of castration compels him, however to give up that attitude. Under the impression of the danger of losing his penis, the Oedipus complex is abandoned, repressed and, in the most normal cases, entirely destroyed, and a severe super-ego is set up as its heir. What happens with a girl is almost the opposite. The castration complex prepares for the Oedipus complex instead of destroying it; the girl is driven out of her attachment to her mother through the influence of her envy for the penis and she enters the Oedipus situation as though into a haven of refuge. In the absence of fear of castration the chief motive is lacking which leads boys to surmount the Oedipus complex. Girls remain in it for an indeterminate length of time; they demolish it late and, even so, incompletely. In these circumstances the formation of the super-ego must suffer; it cannot attain the strength and independence which give it its cultural significance, and feminists are not pleased when we point out to them the effects of this factor upon the average feminine character.

To go back a little. We mentioned as the second possible reaction to the discovery of female castration the development of a powerful masculinity complex. By this we mean that the girl refuses, as it were, to recognize the unwelcome fact and, defiantly rebellious, even exaggerates her previous masculinity, clings to her clitoridal activity and takes refuge in an identification with her phallic mother or her father. What can it be that decides in favour of this outcome? We can only suppose that it is a constitutional factor, a greater amount of activity, such as is ordinarily characteristic of a male. However that may be, the essence of this process is that at this point in development the wave of passivity is avoided which opens the way to the turn towards femininity. The extreme achievement of such a masculinity complex would appear to be the influencing of the choice of an object in the sense of manifest homosexuality. Analytic experience teaches us, to be sure, that female homosexuality is seldom or never a direct continuation of infantile masculinity. Even for a girl of this kind it seems necessary that she should take her father as an object for some time and enter the Oedipus situation. But afterwards, as a result of her inevitable disappointments from her father, she is driven to regress into her early masculinity complex. The significance of these disappointments must not be exaggerated; a girl who is destined to become feminine is not spared them, though they do not have the same effect. The predominance of the constitutional factor seems indisputable; but the two phases in the development of female homosexuality are well mirrored in the practices of homosexuals, who play the parts of mother and baby with each other as often and as clearly as those of husband and wife.

What I have been telling you here may be described as the prehistory of women. It is a product of the very last few years and may have been of interest to you as an example of detailed analytic work. Since its subject is woman, I will venture on this occasion to mention by name a few of the women who have made valuable contributions to this investigation. Dr. Ruth Mack Brunswick [1928] was the first to describe a case of neurosis which went back to a fixation in the pre-Oedipus stage and had never reached the Oedipus situation at all. The case took the form of jealous paranoia and proved accessible to therapy. Dr. Jeanne Lampl-de Groot [1927] has established the incredible phallic activity of girls towards their mother by some assured observations, and Dr. Helene Deutsch [1932] has shown that the erotic actions of homosexual women reproduce the relations between mother and baby.

It is not my intention to pursue the further behaviour of femininity through puberty to the period of maturity. Our knowledge, moreover, would be insufficient for the purpose. But I will bring a few features together in what follows. Taking its prehistory as a starting-point, I will only emphasize here that the development of femininity remains exposed to disturbance by the residual phenomena of the early masculine period. Regressions to the fixations of the pre-Oedipus phases very frequently occur; in the course of some women's lives there is a repeated alternation between periods in which masculinity or femininity gains the upper hand. Some portion of what we men call 'the enigma of women' may perhaps be derived from this expression of bisexuality in women's lives. But another question seems to have become ripe for judgement in the course of these researches. We have called the motive force of sexual life 'the libido'. Sexual life is dominated by the polarity of masculine-feminine; thus the notion suggests itself of considering the relation of the libido to this antithesis. It would not be surprising if it were to turn out that each sexuality had its own special libido appropriated to it, so that one sort of libido would pursue the aims of a masculine sexual life and another sort those of a feminine one. But nothing of the kind is true. There is only one libido, which serves both the masculine and the feminine sexual functions. To it itself we cannot assign any sex; if, following the conventional equation of activity and masculinity, we are inclined to describe it as masculine, we must not forget that it also covers trends with a passive aim. Nevertheless the juxtaposition 'feminine libido' is without any justification. Furthermore, it is our impression that more constraint has been applied to the libido when it is pressed into the service of the feminine function, and that—to speak teleologically—Nature takes less careful account of its [that function's] demands than in the case of masculinity. And the reason for this may lie—thinking once again teleologically—in the fact that the accomplishment of the aim of biology has been entrusted to the aggressiveness of men and has been made to some extent independent of women's consent.

The sexual frigidity of women, the frequency of which appears to confirm this disregard, is a phenomenon that is still insufficiently understood. Sometimes it is psychogenic and in that case accessible to influence; but in other cases it suggests the hypothesis of its being constitutionally determined and even of there being a contributory anatomical factor.

I have promised to tell you of a few more psychical peculiarities of mature femininity, as we come across them in analytic observation. We do not lay claim to more than an average validity for these assertions; nor is it always easy to distinguish what should be ascribed to the influence of the sexual function and what to social breeding. Thus, we attribute a larger amount of narcissism to femininity, which also affects women's choice of object, so that to be loved is a stronger need for them than to love. The effect of penis-envy has a share, further, in the physical vanity of women, since they are bound to value their charms more highly as a late compensation for their original sexual inferiority. Shame, which is considered to be a feminine characteristic *par excellence* but is far more a matter of convention than might be supposed, has as its purpose, we believe, concealment of genital deficiency. We are not forgetting that at a later time shame takes on other functions. It seems that women have made few contributions to the discoveries and inventions in the history of civilization; there is, however, one technique which they may have invented—that of plaiting and weaving. If that is so, we should be tempted to guess the unconscious motive for the achievement. Nature herself would seem to have given the model which this achievement imitates by causing the growth at maturity of the pubic hair that conceals the genitals. The step that remained to be taken lay in making the threads adhere to one another, while on the body they stick into the skin and are only matted together. If you reject this idea as fantastic and regard my belief in the influence of lack of a penis on the configuration of femininity as an *idée fixe*, I am of course defenceless.

The determinants of women's choice of an object are often made unrecognizable by social conditions. Where the choice is able to show itself freely, it is often made in accordance with the narcissistic ideal of the man whom the girl had wished to become. If the girl has remained in her attachment to her father—that is, in the Oedipus complex—her choice is made according to the paternal type. Since, when she turned from her mother to her father, the hostility of her ambivalent relation remained with her mother, a choice of this kind should guarantee a happy marriage. But very often the outcome is of a kind that presents a general threat to such a settlement of the conflict due to ambivalence. The hostility that has been left behind follows in the train of the positive attachment and spreads over on to the new object. The woman's husband, who to begin with inherited from her father, becomes after a time her mother's heir as well. So it may easily happen that the second half of a woman's life may be filled by the struggle against her husband, just as the shorter first half was filled by her rebellion against her mother. When this reaction has been lived through, a second marriage may easily turn out

very much more satisfying. Another alteration in a woman's nature, for which lovers are unprepared, may occur in a marriage
after the first child is born. Under the influence of a woman's
becoming a mother herself, an identification with her own mother
may be revived, against which she had striven up till the time of
her marriage, and this may attract all the available libido to itself,
so that the compulsion to repeat reproduces an unhappy marriage
between her parents. The difference in a mother's reaction to the
birth of a son or a daughter shows that the old factor of lack of a
penis has even now not lost its strength. A mother is only brought
unlimited satisfaction by her relation to a son; this is altogether
the most perfect, the most free from ambivalence of all human
relationships.[3] A mother can transfer to her son the ambition
which she has been obliged to suppress in herself, and she can
expect from him the satisfaction of all that has been left over in
her of her masculinity complex. Even a marriage is not made
secure until the wife has succeeded in making her husband her
child as well and in acting as a mother to him.

A woman's identification with her mother allows us to distinguish two strata: the pre-Oedipus one which rests on her affectionate attachment to her mother and takes her as a model, and
the later one from the Oedipus complex which seeks to get rid of
her mother and take her place with her father. We are no doubt
justified in saying that much of both of them is left over for the
future and that neither of them is adequately surmounted in the
course of development. But the phase of the affectionate pre-
Oedipus attachment is the decisive one for a woman's future:
during it preparations are made for the acquisition of the characteristics with which she will later fulfil her role in the sexual
function and perform her invaluable social tasks. It is in this
identification too that she acquires her attractiveness to a man,
whose Oedipus attachment to his mother it kindles into passion.
How often it happens, however, that it is only his son who obtains
what he himself aspired to! One gets an impression that a man's
love and a woman's are a phase apart psychologically.

The fact that women must be regarded as having little sense of
justice is no doubt related to the predominance of envy in their

3. [This point seems to have been made by Freud first in a footnote to Chapter
VI of *Group Psychology* (1921), 18:101 *n*. He repeated it in the *Introductory
Lectures*, XIII, 15:206 and in *Civilization and its Discontents* (1930), 21:113.]

mental life; for the demand for justice is a modification of envy and lays down the condition subject to which one can put envy aside. We also regard women as weaker in their social interests and as having less capacity for sublimating their instincts than men. The former is no doubt derived from the dissocial quality which unquestionably characterizes all sexual relations. Lovers find sufficiency in each other, and families too resist inclusion in more comprehensive associations.[4] The aptitude for sublimation is subject to the greatest individual variations. On the other hand I cannot help mentioning an impression that we are constantly receiving during analytic practice. A man of about thirty strikes us as a youthful, somewhat unformed individual, whom we expect to make powerful use of the possibilities for development opened up to him by analysis. A woman of the same age, however, oftens frightens us by her psychical rigidity and unchangeability. Her libido has taken up final positions and seems incapable of exchanging them for others. There are no paths open to further development; it is as though the whole process had already run its course and remains thenceforward insusceptible to influence—as though, indeed, the difficult development to femininity had exhausted the possibilities of the person concerned. As therapists we lament this state of things, even if we succeed in putting an end to our patient's ailment by doing away with her neurotic conflict.

That is all I had to say to you about femininity. It is certainly incomplete and fragmentary and does not always sound friendly. But do not forget that I have only been describing women in so far as their nature is determined by their sexual function. It is true that that influence extends very far; but we do not overlook the fact that an individual woman may be a human being in other respects as well. If you want to know more about femininity, enquire from your own experiences of life, or turn to the poets, or wait until science can give you deeper and more coherent information.

4. [Cf. some remarks on this in Chapter XII (D) of *Group Psycholgy* (1921), 18:140.]

Selection from Chapter VII of *An Outline of Psycho-Analysis*

After his summary lecture "Femininity," Freud made one more effort to review his conclusions about the distinct developmental courses of the two sexes. This review was contained in Chapters 3 and 7 of a book he was writing in the last year of his life and left unfinished: An Outline of Psychoanalysis. In the excerpt from Chapter 7 that follows, Freud retraces the developmental divergence of the sexes, starting with a discussion of the Oedipus complex:

❧❧❧❧

* * * A this point we must give separate accounts of the development of boys and girls (of males and females), for it is now that the difference between the sexes finds psychological expression for the first time. We are faced here by the great enigma of the biological fact of the duality of the sexes: it is an ultimate fact for our knowledge, it defies every attempt to trace it back to something else. Psycho-analysis has contributed nothing to clearing up this problem, which clearly falls wholly within the province of biology. In mental life we only find reflections of this great antithesis; and their interpretation is made more difficult by the fact, long suspected, that no individual is limited to the modes of reaction of a single sex but always finds some room for those of the opposite one, just as his body bears, alongside of the fully developed organs of one sex, atrophied and often useless rudiments of those of the other. For distinguishing between male and female in mental life we make use of what is obviously an inadequate empirical and conventional equation: we call everything that is strong and active male, and everthing that is weak and passive female. This fact of psychological bisexuality, too, embarrasses all our enquiries into the subject and makes them harder to describe.

A child's first erotic object is the mother's breast that nourishes it; love has its origin in attachment to the satisfied need for nourishment. There is no doubt that, to begin with, the child does not distinguish between the breast and its own body; when the breast has to be separated from the body and shifted to the '*outside*' because the child so often finds it absent, it carries with it as an '*object*' a part of the original narcissistic libidinal cathexis. This first object is later completed into the person of the child's mother, who not only nourishes it but also looks after it and thus arouses in it a number of other physical sensations, pleasurable and unpleasurable. By her care of the child's body she becomes its first seducer. In these two relations lies the root of a mother's importance, unique, without parallel, established unalterably for a whole lifetime as the first and strongest love-object and as the prototype of all later love-relations—for both sexes. In all this the phylogenetic foundation has so much the upper hand over personal accidental experience that it makes no difference whether a child has really sucked at the breast or has been brought up on the bottle and never enjoyed the tenderness of a mother's case. In both cases the child's development takes the same path; it may be that in the second case its later longing grows all the greater. And for however long it is fed at its mother's breast, it will always be left with a conviction after it has been weaned that its feeding was too short and too little.

This preface is not superfluous, for it can heighten our realization of the intensity of the Oedipus complex. When a boy (from the age of two or three) has entered the phallic phase of his libidinal development, is feeling pleasurable sensations in his sexual organ and has learnt to procure these at will by manual stimulation, he becomes his mother's lover. He wishes to possess her physically in such ways as he has divined from his observations and intuitions about sexual life, and he tries to seduce her by showing her the male organ which he is proud to own. In a word, his early awakened masculinity seeks to take his father's place with her; his father has hitherto in any case been an envied model to the boy, owing to the physical strength he perceives in him and the authority with which he finds him clothed. His father now becomes a rival who stands in his way and whom he would like to get rid of. If while his father is away he is allowed to share his mother's bed and if when his father returns he is once more banished from it, his satisfaction when his father disappears and his disappointment when he emerges again are deeply felt experiences. This is the subject of the Oedipus complex, which the Greek legend has translated from the world of a child's phantasy into pretended reality. Under the conditions of our civilization it is invariably doomed to a frightening end.

The boy's mother has understood quite well that his sexual excitation relates to herself. Sooner or later she reflects that it is not right to allow it to continue. She thinks she is doing the correct thing in forbidding him to handle his genital organ. Her prohibition has little effect; at the most it brings about some modification in his method of obtaining satisfaction. At last his mother adopts the severest measures; she threatens to take away from him the thing he is defying her with. Usually, in order to make the threat more frightening and more credible, she delegates its execution to the boy's father, saying that she will tell him and that he will cut the penis off. Strange to say, this threat operates only if another condition is fulfilled before or afterwards. In itself it seems too inconceivable to the boy that such a thing could happen. But if at the time of the threat he can recall the appearance of female genitals or if shortly afterwards he has a sight of them—of genitals, that is to say, which really lack this supremely valued part, then he takes what he has heard seriously and, coming under the influence of the *castration complex*, experiences the severest trauma of his young life.[1]

---

1. Castration has a place too in the Oedipus legend, for the blinding with which Oedipus punishes himself after the discovery of his crime is, by the evidence of dreams, a symbolic substitute for castration. The possibility cannot be excluded that a phylogenetic memory-trace may contribute to the extraordinarily terrifying effect of the threat—a memory-trace from the prehistory of the primal family, when the jealous father actually robbed his son of his genitals if the latter became troublesome to him as a rival with a woman. The primaeval custom of circumcision, another symbolic substitute for castration, can only be understood as an expression of submission to the father's will. (Cf. the puberty rites of primitive peoples.) No investigation has yet been made of the form taken by the events described above among people and in civilizations which do not suppress masturbation in children.

The results of the threat of castration are multifarious and incalculable; they affect the whole of a boy's relations with his father and mother and subsequently with men and women in general. As a rule the child's masculinity is unable to stand up to this first shock. In order to preserve his sexual organ he renounces the possession of his mother more or less completely; his sexual life often remains permanently encumbered by the prohibition. If a strong feminine component, as we call it, is present in him, its strength is increased by this intimidation of his masculinity. He falls into a passive attitude to his father, such as he attributes to his mother. It is true that as a result of the threat he has given up masturbation, but not the activities of his imagination accompaying it. On the contrary, since these are now the only form of sexual satisfaction remaining to him, he indulges in them more than before and in these phantasies, though he still continues to identify himself with his father, he also does so, simultaneously and perhaps predominantly, with his mother. Derivatives and modified products of these early masturbatory phantasies usually make their way into his later ego and play a part in the formation of his character. Apart from this encouragement of his femininity, fear and hatred of his father gain greatly in intensity. The boy's masculinity withdraws, as it were, into a defiant attitude towards his father, which will dominate his later behaviour in human society in a compulsive fashion. A residue of his erotic fixation to his mother is often left in the form of an excessive dependence on her, and this persists as a kind of bondage to women.[2] He no longer ventures to love his mother, but he cannot risk not being loved by her, for in that case he would be in danger of being betrayed by her to his father and handed over to castration. The whole experience, with all its antecedents and consequences, of which my account has only been able to give a selection, is subjected to a highly energetic repression, and, as is made possible by the laws operating in the unconscious id, all the mutually contending emotional impulses and reactions which are set going at that time are preserved in the unconscious and ready to disturb the later development of the ego after puberty. When the somatic process of sexual maturation puts fresh life into the old libidinal fixations which had apparently been surmounted, sexual life will

2. [Cf. a footnote to Section VIII of 'Analysis Terminable and Interminable' (1937).]

turn out to be inhibited, without homogeneity and fallen apart into mutually conflicting urges.

It is no doubt true that the impact of the threat of castration upon a boy's budding sexual life does not always have these dreaded consequences. It will depend once again on *quantitative* relations how much damage is done and how much avoided. The whole occurrence, which may probably be regarded as the central experience of the years of childhood, the greatest problem of early life and the strongest source of later inadequacy, is so completely forgotten that its reconstruction during the work of analysis is met in adults by the most decided disbelief. Indeed, aversion to it is so great that people try to silence any mention of the proscribed subject and the most obvious reminders of it are overlooked by a strange intellectual blindness. One may hear it objected, for instance, that the legend of Kind Oedipus has in fact no connection with the construction made by analysis: the cases are quite different, since Oedipus did not know that it was his father that he killed and his mother that he married. What is overlooked in this is that a distortion of this kind is inevitable if an attempt is made at a poetic handling of the material, and that there is no introduction of extraneous material but only a skilful employment of the factors presented by the theme. The ignorance of Oedipus is a legitimate representation of the unconscious state into which, for adults, the whole experience has fallen; and the coercive power of the oracle, which makes or should make the hero innocent, is a recognition of the inevitability of the fate which has condemned every son to live through the Oedipus complex. Again it was pointed out from psycho-analytic quarters how easily the riddle of another dramatic hero, Shakespeare's procrastinator, Hamlet, can be solved by reference to the Oedipius complex, since the prince came to grief over the task of punishing someone else for what coincided with the substance of his own Oedipus wish—whereupon the general lack of understanding on the part of the literary world showed how ready is the mass of mankind to hold fast to its infantile repressions. * * *

The effects of the castration complex in little girls are more uniform and no less profound. A female child has, of course, no need to fear the loss of a penis; she must, however, react to the fact of not having received one. From the very first she envies boys its possession; her whole development may be said to take place under the colours of envy for the penis. She begins by making vain attempts to do the same as boys and later, with greater success, makes efforts to compensate for her defect—efforts which may lead in the end to a normal feminine attitude. If during the phallic phase she tries to get pleasure like a boy by the manual stimulation of her genitals, it often happens that she fails to obtain sufficient satisfaction and extends her judgement of inferiority from her stunted penis to her whole self. As a rule she soon gives up masturbating, since she has no wish to be reminded of the superiority of her brother or playmate, and turns away from sexuality altogether.

If a little girl persists in her first wish—to grow into a boy—in extreme cases she will end as a manifest homosexual, and otherwise she will exhibit markedly masculine traits in the conduct of her later life, will choose a masculine vocation, and so on. The other path leads by way of abandoning the mother she has loved: the daughter, under the influence of her envy for the penis, cannot forgive her mother for having sent her into the world so insufficiently equipped. In her resentment over this she gives up her mother and puts someone else in her place as the object of her love—her father. If one has lost a love-object, the most obvious reaction is to identify oneself with it, to replace it from within, as it were, by identification. This mechanism now comes to the little girls' help. Identification with her mother can take the place of attachment to her mother. The little daughter puts herself in her mother's place, as she has always done in her games; she tries to take her mother's place with her father, and begins to hate the mother she used to love, and from two motives: from jealousy as well as from mortification over the penis she has been denied. Her new relation to her father may start by having as its content a wish to have his penis at her disposal, but it culminates in another wish—to have a baby from him as a gift. The wish for a baby has thus taken the place of the wish for a penis, or has at all events split off from it.

It is an interesting thing that the relation between the Oedipus complex and the castration complex should take such a different shape—an opposite one, in fact—in the case of females as compared to that of males. In males, as we have seen, the threat of castration brings the Oedipus complex to an end; in females we find that, on the contrary, it is their lack of a penis that forces them into their Oedipus complex. It does little harm to a woman if she remains in her feminine Oedipus attitude. She will in that case choose her husband for his paternal characteristics and be ready to recognize his authority. Her longing to possess a penis, which is in fact unappeasable, may find satisfaction if she can succeed in completing her love for the organ by extending it to the bearer of the organ, just as happened earlier when she progressed from her mother's breast to her mother as a whole person.

If we ask an analyst what his experience has shown to be the mental structures least accessible to influence in his patients, the answer will be: in a woman her wish for a penis, in a man his feminine attitude towards his own sex, a precondition of which would, of course, be the loss of his penis.[3]

---

3. [Freud had discussed this at much greater length in Section VIII of 'Analysis Terminable and Interminable' (1937).]

Annotated
Bibliography

There is an enormous library of Freud studies and biographies, including the most important, Ernest Jones's three-volume *The Life and Work of Sigmund Freud* (1953–57). The highlights of this library have been surveyed in Peter Gay's recent very thorough *Freud: A Life for Our Times* (1988).

Freud's letters to Fliess have been published in two English editions: Marie Bonaparte, Anna Freud, and Ernst Kris, eds., *The Origins of Psychoanalysis* (1954), which has a fine introduction by Ernst Kris; and Jeffrey M. Masson, ed., *The Complete Letters of Sigmund Freud to Wilhelm Fliess* (1985), the edition from which the excerpts presented in this volume have been drawn. Masson's tendentious notes to the complete edition, and a book he wrote called *The Assault on Truth: Freud's Suppression of the Seduction Theory* (1984), have been at the center of a recent controversy over whether Freud suppressed—rather than found good reasons to supersede—the seduction theory and over whether psychoanalysis ignores the realities of sexual abuse by focusing on Oedipal fantasies. This controversy first arose in the 1930s in the socialist critique of psychoanalysis (see Russell Jacoby, *The Repression of Psychoanalysis* (1983), but the recent version has also involved feminist writers. The controversy has unfortunately ignored important psychoanalytic work on child abuse, for example, H. Kempe and P. Mrazek, eds., *Sexually Abused Children and Their Families* (1981), and particularly Anna Freud's paper "A Psychoanalyst's View of Sexual Abuse by Parents."

The literature on the Dora case grows larger all the time: see the relevant essays in M. Kanzer and J. Glenn, *Freud and His Patients* (1980) and *Revue Française de Psychanalyse* XXXVII (1973). There is a collection of literary critical and feminist pieces as well : C. Bernheimer and C. Kahane, eds., *In Dora's Case: Freud—Hysteria—Feminism* (1985).

As Freud revised the text of his 1905 *Three Essays on the Theory of Sexuality* up to the 1924 edition, he was stimulated by the work of his closest colleagues Karl Abraham, Sandor Ferenczi, and Ernest Jones. Only his letters to and from Abraham have been published, and some of these are cited in this anthology (pp. 300–303). The following Abraham papers, from *The Selected Papers of Karl Abraham* (1954), are particularly important: "The First Pregenital Stage of the Libido" (1916), "The Infantile Theory of the Origin of the Female Sex" (1923), and "Manifestations of the Female Castration Complex" (1920). In 1924 Ferenczi published a book he had been working on for some time, which was not translated into English until 1938: *Thalassa, A Theory of Genitality*. Freud also knew well his earlier "The Nosology of Male Homosexuality (Homoerotism)" (1914), and "Stages in the Development of the Sense of Reality" (1913), both in his *Contributions to Psychoanalysis* (1916). (I will note the relevant papers by Jones below.) The paper by Lou Andreas-Salomé mentioned in my Introduction is " 'Anal' and 'Sexuel' " in *Imago*, 1917; it has not been translated into English (in French, see the anthology of her work, *L'amour du narcissisme*), but there is a résumé of its contents in Freud's *Three Essays* (7:187).

The revisions that Freud made in his instinct theory have been succinctly presented by E. Bibring, "The Development and Problems of the Theory of Instincts," *International Journal of Psychoanalysis* XXII (1934), as well as in more elaborate psychoanalytic studies. One of the most important papers from within Freud's circle relating to his ideas on female narcissism was Lou Andreas-Salomé's "The Dual Orientation of Narcissism," translated for *Psychoanalytic Quarterly* XIII (1962). See also Annie Reich, "Narcissistic Object Choice in Women," in her *Psychoanalytic Contributions* (1973). In the 1970s, particularly, Freud's work on narcissism came in for a great deal of reconsideration. For a survey of the terrain at the beginning of this wave, see Sydney Pulver, "Narcissism: The Term and the Concept," *Journal of the American Psychoanalytic Association* XVIII (1970), and the important book by Heinz Kohut, *The Analysis of the Self* (1971). Freud's remarks on female narcissism were not a focus of attention in this country, rather they became part of a larger cultural review: see C. Lasch, *The Culture of Narcissism* (1978) and S. Sobo, "Narcissism and Social Disorder," *Yale Review* 64 (1975). In France, female narcissism has been quite a topic: see Sarah Kofman, *The Enigma of Woman* (trans. 1985) for her quarrel with René Girard.

A review of Freud's theory is contained in Bela Grunberger, "Outline for a Study of Narcissism in Female Sexuality," in J. Chasseguet-Smirgel, ed., *Female Sexuality: New Psychoanalytic Views* (trans. 1970).

Freud's excursions into anthropology, and the essay "The Taboo of Virginity," have been considered from an anthropological point of view, particularly by Margaret Mead, *Male and Female* (1949). More recently: Rayne Reiter, ed., *Toward an Anthropology of Women* (1975), and M. Z. Rosaldo and L. Lamphere, eds., *Women, Culture and Society* (1974). For a superficial summary view, see Edwin Wallace, *Freud and Anthropology: A History and Reappraisal* (1983).

There is an extensive recent psychoanalytic literature on beating fantasies that refers back to Freud's " 'A Child is Being Beaten' " and Anna Freud's essay. Bibliographies can be found with two recent contributions stemming from child analytic work: K. K. Novick and J. Novick, "Beating Fantasies in Children," *International Journal of Psychoanalysis* 53 (1972); and "The Essence of Masochism," *Psychoanalytic Study of the Child* (1981).

Freud's case study of a female homosexual was the focus of the psychoanalytic literature on female homosexuality until after the Second World War. See Ernest Jones, "The Early Development of Female Sexuality" (1927), which concluded that intense oral eroticism and unusually strong sadism are involved in female homosexuality, as is an intense identification with the father. Jones began to make a typology of female homosexuals: those who wish to be accepted by men as a man; those whose libido is centered on women, and who enjoy their own femininity vicariously through their partners; those whose feminine desires are satisfied by a woman who behaves sexually like a man. Raymond de Sausure, "Homosexual Fixations among Neurotic Women," (1929), emphasized the narcissism of neurotic female homosexuals. Helene Deutsch wrote "Female Homosexuality" in 1932 (it is available in R. Fliess, *The Psychoanalytic Reader*, (1948, 1962) with other papers on female sexuality) to emphasize the pre-Oedipal mother-daughter bond that Freud had pointed to at the end of his case study. In recent years, when psychoanalysts have—with a few exceptions—returned to Freud's disassociation of homosexuality and neurosis, the work of Freud's contemporaries has been referred to but refocused. See, for example, J. McDougall, *A Plea for a Measure of Abnormality* (1978); the relevant (but usually more conservative) papers in J. Marmor, ed., *Homosexual Behavior* (1975). Outside of psychoanalysis, psychological approaches to female homosexuality focus much more on social factors and on homophobia, while the quest for a biological basis for male and female homosexuality goes on in some medical and psychiatric circles.

After Freud's *The Ego and the Id* was published, the development of the superego in females became a topic among his followers: Carl Mueller-Braunschweig, "The Genesis of the Feminine Superego," *International Journal of Psychoanalysis* 7 (1926); Hanns Sachs, "On the Formation of the Superego in Women," *Internation Journal of Psychoanalysis* 60 (1929); Edith Jacobson, "Ways of Female Superego Formation and the Female Castration Conflict" (1937), reprinted in *Psychoanalytic Quarterly* 45 (1976); Phyllis Greenacre, "Anatomical Structure and Superego Development," in her *Trauma, Growth and Personality* (1952). The topic is taken up in many of the anthologies of recent work that will be cited below, and see also Catherine Millot, "The Feminine Superego" in *m/f: a feminist journal* 10 (1985).

Helene Deutsch wrote on female masochism in 1930: "The Significance of Masochism in the Mental Life of Women," *International Journal of Psychoanalysis* 11 (1930). More than any other single paper, this one by Deutsch promoted the notion that women are naturally masochistic. Horney's "The Problem of Feminine Masochism" (1935), is in her collection *Feminine Psychology* (1967). Jeanne Lampl-De Groot, "Masochism and Narcissism" (1937) is in her collection *The Development of the Mind* (1965). Muriel Gardiner's "Feminie Masochism and Passivity" is in *Bulletin of the Philadelphia Association for Psychoanalysis* 5 (1955). Masochism is a recurrent topic in Annie Reich's collection *Psychoanalytic Contributions* (1973). Rudolph Loewenstein, "A Contribution to the Psychoanalytic Theory of Masochism" (1957) is in his *Selected Papers* (1982). Marie Bonaparte's 1935 essay "Passivity, Masochism, Femininity" is responded to by Ethel Person, "Some New Observations on the Origins of Femininity" in Jean Strouse, ed., *Women and Analysis*. Person's article has a bibliography of further recent readings, as does Paula Caplan's "The Myth of Women's Masochism," *American Psychologist* 39 (1984).

Janine Chasseguet-Smirgel introduces her collection of essays, *Female Sexuality: New Psychoanalytic Views* (trans. 1970), with a survey and summaries of the papers from the late 1920s and early 1930s supporting Freud's late views on female psychology (Lampl-de Groot, Deutsch, Mack Brunswick, Bonaparte) and opposing them (Mueller, Horney, Klein, Jones). Some of the supporters' papers are collected in R. Fliess, *The Psychoanalytic Reader* (1948, 1962) and all are in the collections by the individual authors noted above. Josine Mueller's "The Problem of the Libidinal Development of the Genital Phase in Girls" (1925) appeared in *International Journal of Psychoanalysis* 13 (1932). Horney's papers are in the collection noted above, *Feminine Psychology*. Klein's *The Psychoanalysis of Children* (trans. 1932) and the later four-volume *Collected Works* (1975) present her views. Jones's papers, "The Early Development of Female Sexuality" (1927), "The Phallic Phase" (1932), and "Early Female Sexuality" (1935) are in his *Papers on Psychoanalysis* (1948). A more recent, very independent survey is Phyllis Greenacre's, "Special Problems of Early Female Sexual Development," *Psychoanalytic Study of the Child* 5 (1950)); and see also her "Penis Awe and Its relation to Penis Envy" in *Emotional Growth* (1971). The cultural-psychoanalysis or Neo-Freudian tradition, which has its antecedents in the opponents of Freud's female psychology, acknowledges the importance of Clara Thompson's essays: "The Role of Women in Culture" is in Strouse, ed., *Women and Psychoanalysis* (1974), and two papers are in Jean B. Miller, ed., *Psychoanalysis and Women* (1973).

I will indicate the recent psychoanalytic literature on female psychology by citing books and anthologies, in chronological order. Books: R. Stoller, *Sex and Gender* (1968); J. Money and A. Ehrhardt, *Man and Woman, Boy and Girl* (1972); E. Maccoby and C. Jacklin, *The Psychology of Sex Differences* (1974); H. Roiphe and E. Galenson, *Infantile Origin of Sexual Identity* (1981); A. Bernstein and G. Warner, *Women Treating Women* (1984); Fast, *Gender Identity: A Differentiation Model* (1984); Bernay and Cantor, *The Psychology of Today's Woman* (1986). Anthologies: Jean B. Miller, ed., *Psychoanalysis and Women* (1973); Jean Strouse, ed., *Women and Analysis* (1974), which contains R. Stoller, "Facts and Fancies: an Examination of Freud's Concept of Bisexuality," a review quite in contrast to my Introduction to this volume; H. Blum, *Female Psychology* (1977); T. Karasu and C. Socarides, eds., *On Sexuality, Psychoanalytic Observations* (1979); C. Stimpson and E. Person, eds., *Sex and Sexuality* (1980); D. Mendel, ed., *Early Female Development* (1982); Judith Alpert, ed., *Psychoanalysis and Women: Contemporary Reappraisals* (1986). A good general anthology has been prepared by Mary Roth Walsh: *The Psychology of Women: Ongoing Debates* (1987).

Recent feminist approaches to psychoanalysis usually take into account or orient themselves from earlier work: Viola Klein, *The Feminine Character* (1946); Simone de Beauvoir, *The Second Sex* (1949, trans. 1952); Betty Friedan, *The Feminine Mystique* (1963); Kate Millet, *Sexual Politics* (1969); Germaine Greer, *The Female Eunuch* (1970); Phyllis Chesler, *Women and Madness* (1972), Shulamith Firestone, *The Dialectic of Sex* (1970). The writings of sex researchers were crucial to these early works:

see Alfred Kinsey's *The Sexual Behavior of the Human Female* (1953) and Wendell Pomeroy's, *Dr. Kinsey and the Institute for Sex Research* (1972); Masters and Johnson's *Human Sexual Response* (1966); and Mary Jane Sherfy's, *The Nature and Evolution of Female Sexuality* (1973). The late-1970s reconsideration in America and England of Freud's work was launched by Juliet Mitchell in *Psychoanalysis and Feminism* (1975) and Jean Baker Miller in *Toward a New Psychology of Women* (1976). Soon after came Dorothy Dinnerstein, *The Mermaid and the Minotaur* (1976); Nancy Chodorow, *The Reproduction of Mothering* (1978); Carol Gilligan, *In A Different Voice* (1982); Jane Gallop, *The Daughter's Seduction: Feminism and Psychoanalysis* (1982); and Juliet Mitchell and Jacqueline Rose, eds., *Feminine Sexuality: Jacques Lacan and the École Freudienne* (1982), with introductions by both editors. Jacqueline Rose's "Femininity and Its Discontents," in her *Sexuality and the Field of Vision* (1986), offers a brief critical history of feminist responses to Freud.

The current psychoanalytic frontiers obvious in child psychoanalytic work have been defined by the work of Anna Freud, especially *Normality and Pathology in Childhood* (1965) and the last volume of *The Writings of Anna Freud*; Margaret Mahler's many works, including *The Psychological Birth of the Human Infant* (1975); Rene Spitz's *The First Year of Life* (1965) and Selma Fraiberg's research; and the work of theorists concerned with early childhood and the psychoses, especially Melanie Klein's followers, D. W. Winnicott and Masud Khan (in England), and André Green (in France).

Index